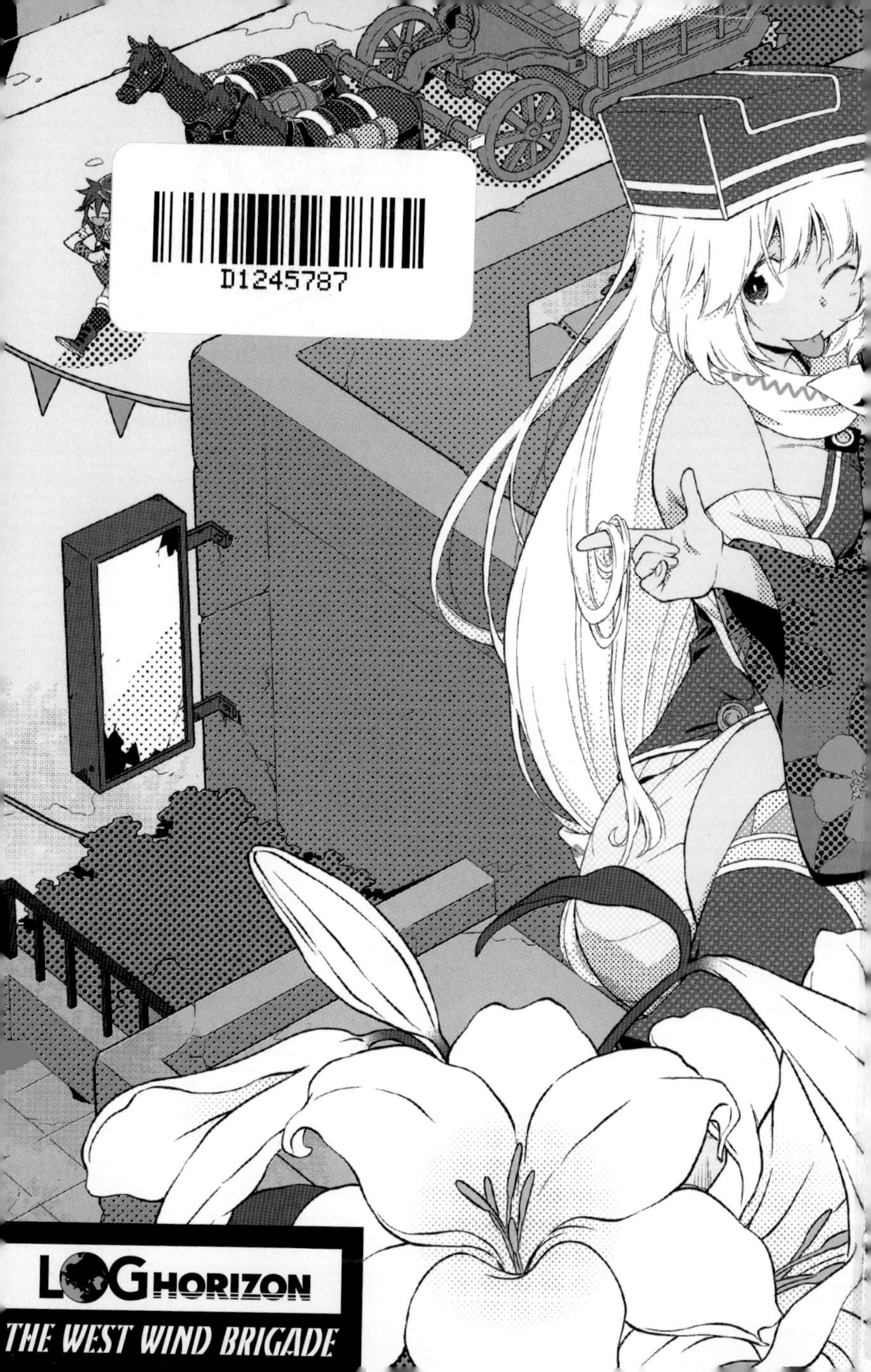
LOG HORIZON
THE WEST WIND BRIGADE

[CONTENTS]

CHAPTER:30 EVERYBODY, DO YOUR BEST...5

CHAPTER:31 KURINON PLOTS...27

CHAPTER:32 THE SLACKER PRINCESS...57

CHAPTER:33 CAPTURE KURINON! PART 1...71

CHAPTER:34 CAPTURE KURINON! PART 2...93

CHAPTER:35 CAPTURE KURINON! PART 3...119

CHAPTER:36 RISK...139

LOG HORIZON **THE WEST WIND BRIGADE**

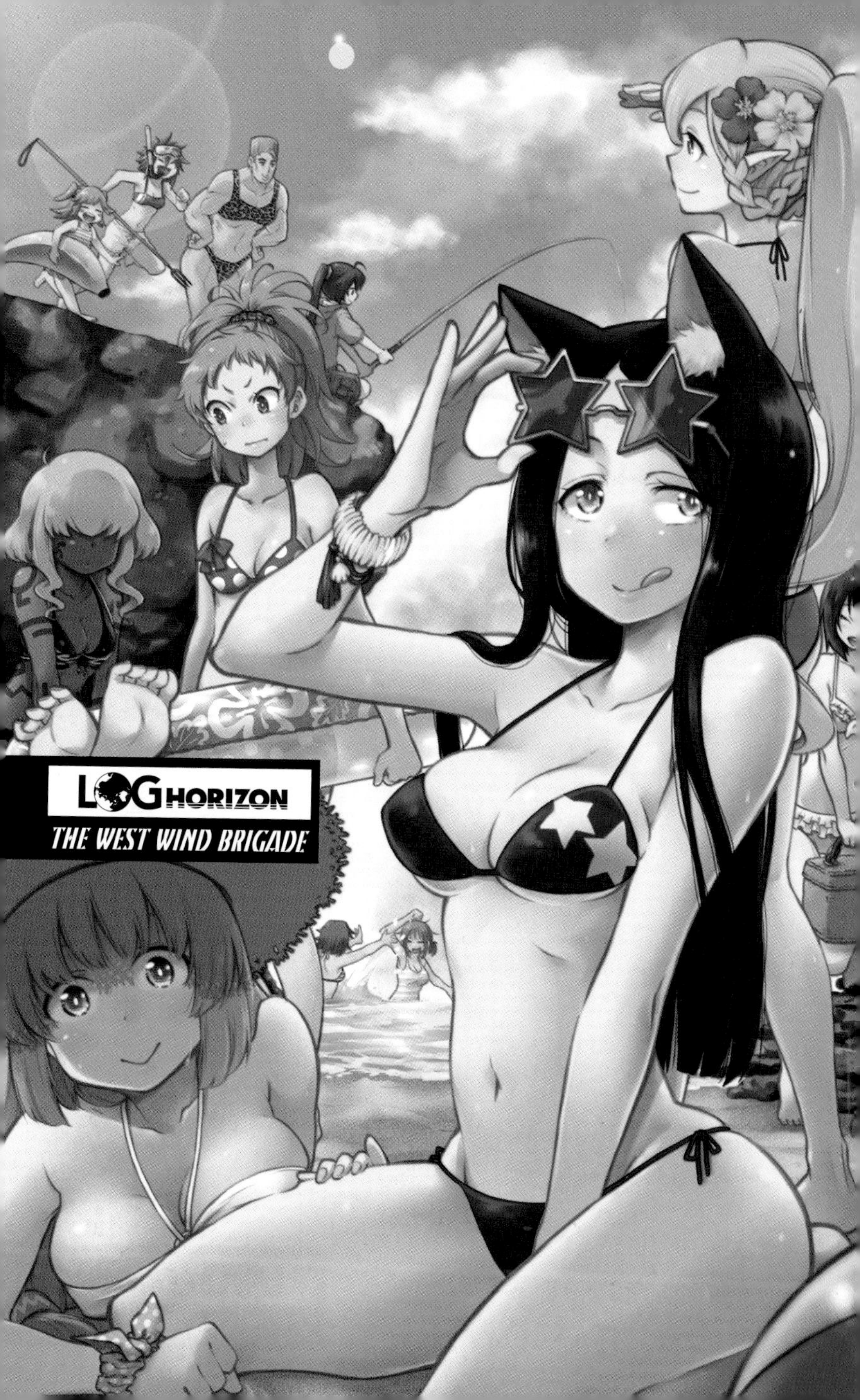
LOG HORIZON
THE WEST WIND BRIGADE

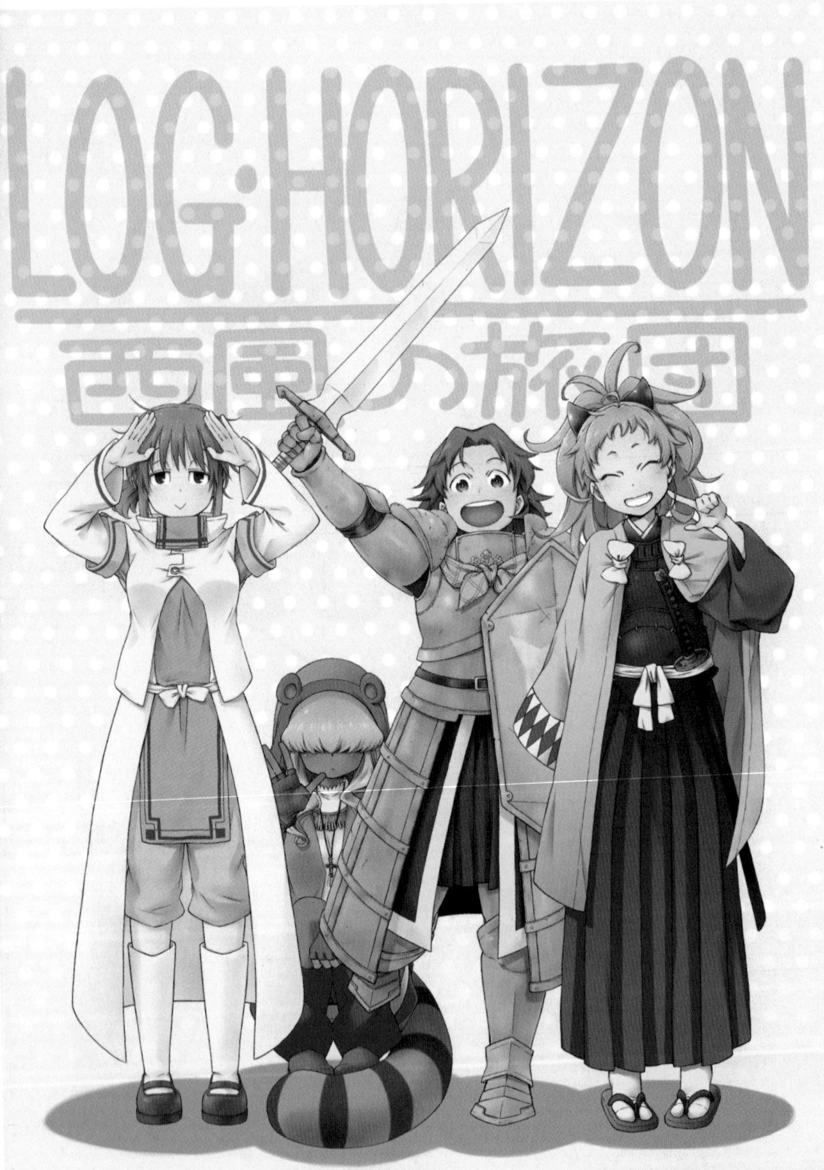
LOG·HORIZON
西風の旅団

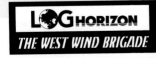

LOG HORIZON
THE WEST WIND BRIGADE

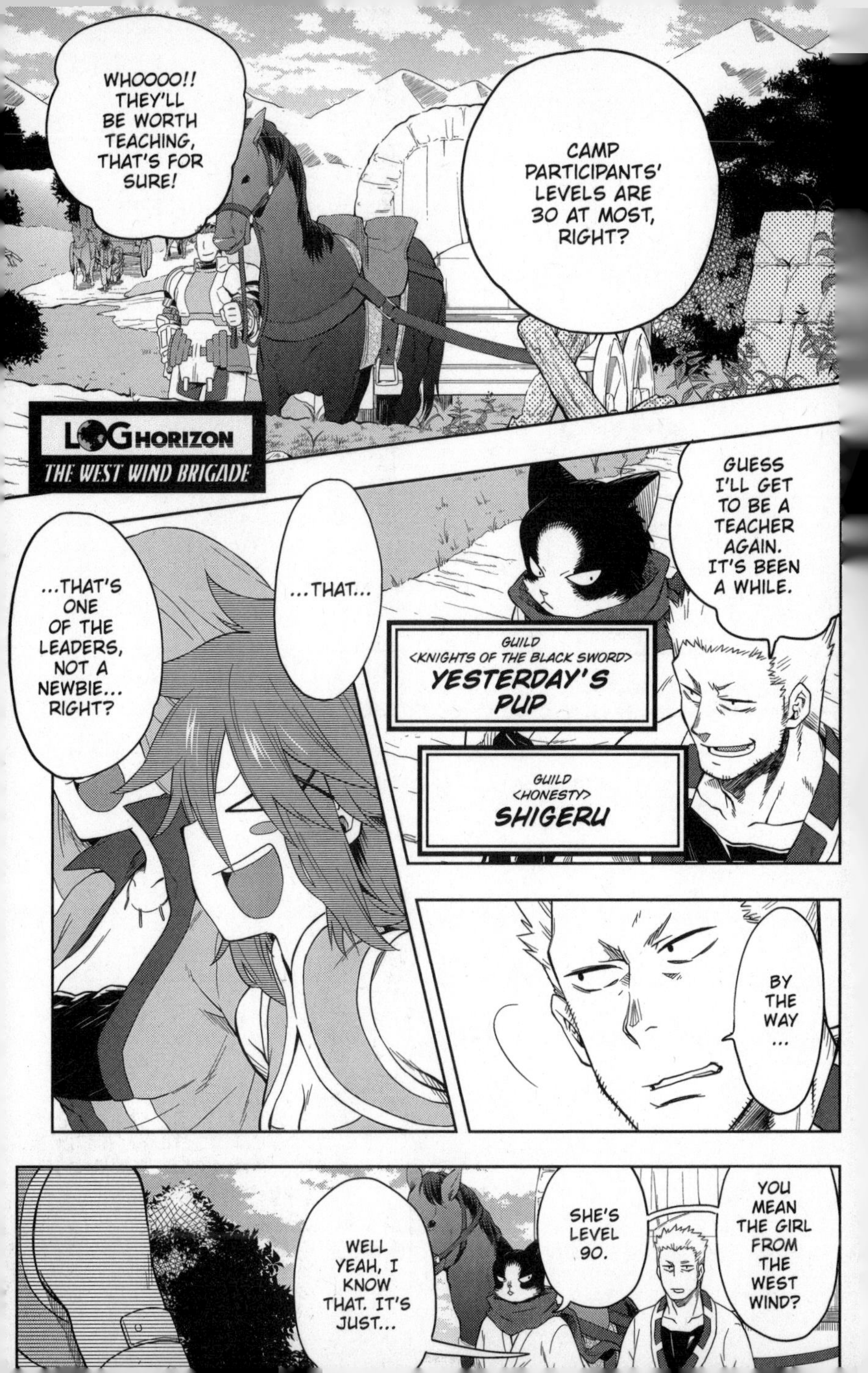
CAMP PARTICIPANTS' LEVELS ARE 30 AT MOST, RIGHT?
WHOOOO!! THEY'LL BE WORTH TEACHING, THAT'S FOR SURE!
LOG HORIZON
THE WEST WIND BRIGADE
GUESS I'LL GET TO BE A TEACHER AGAIN. IT'S BEEN A WHILE.
GUILD <KNIGHTS OF THE BLACK SWORD> YESTERDAY'S PUP
GUILD <HONESTY> SHIGERU
BY THE WAY...
...THAT...
...THAT'S ONE OF THE LEADERS, NOT A NEWBIE... RIGHT?
YOU MEAN THE GIRL FROM THE WEST WIND?
SHE'S LEVEL 90.
WELL YEAH, I KNOW THAT. IT'S JUST...

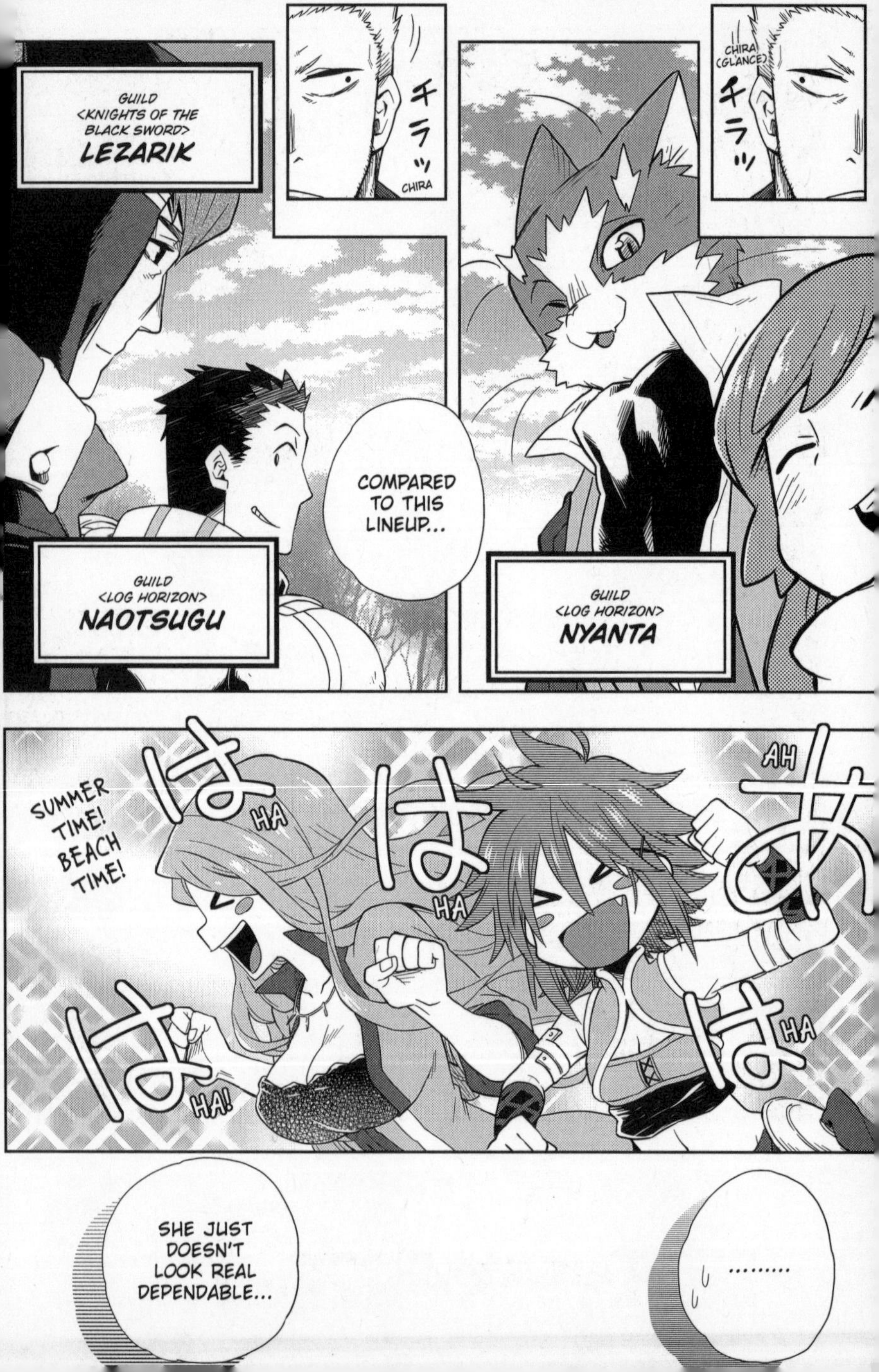
チラッ
CHIRA (GLANCE)
GUILD <LOG HORIZON> NYANTA
チラッ
CHIRA
GUILD <KNIGHTS OF THE BLACK SWORD> LEZARIK
COMPARED TO THIS LINEUP...
GUILD <LOG HORIZON> NAOTSUGU
あ
AH
は
HA
は
HA
は
HA
は
HA!
SUMMER TIME! BEACH TIME!
....
SHE JUST DOESN'T LOOK REAL DEPENDABLE...

[CHAPTER : 30   EVERYBODY, DO YOUR BEST]

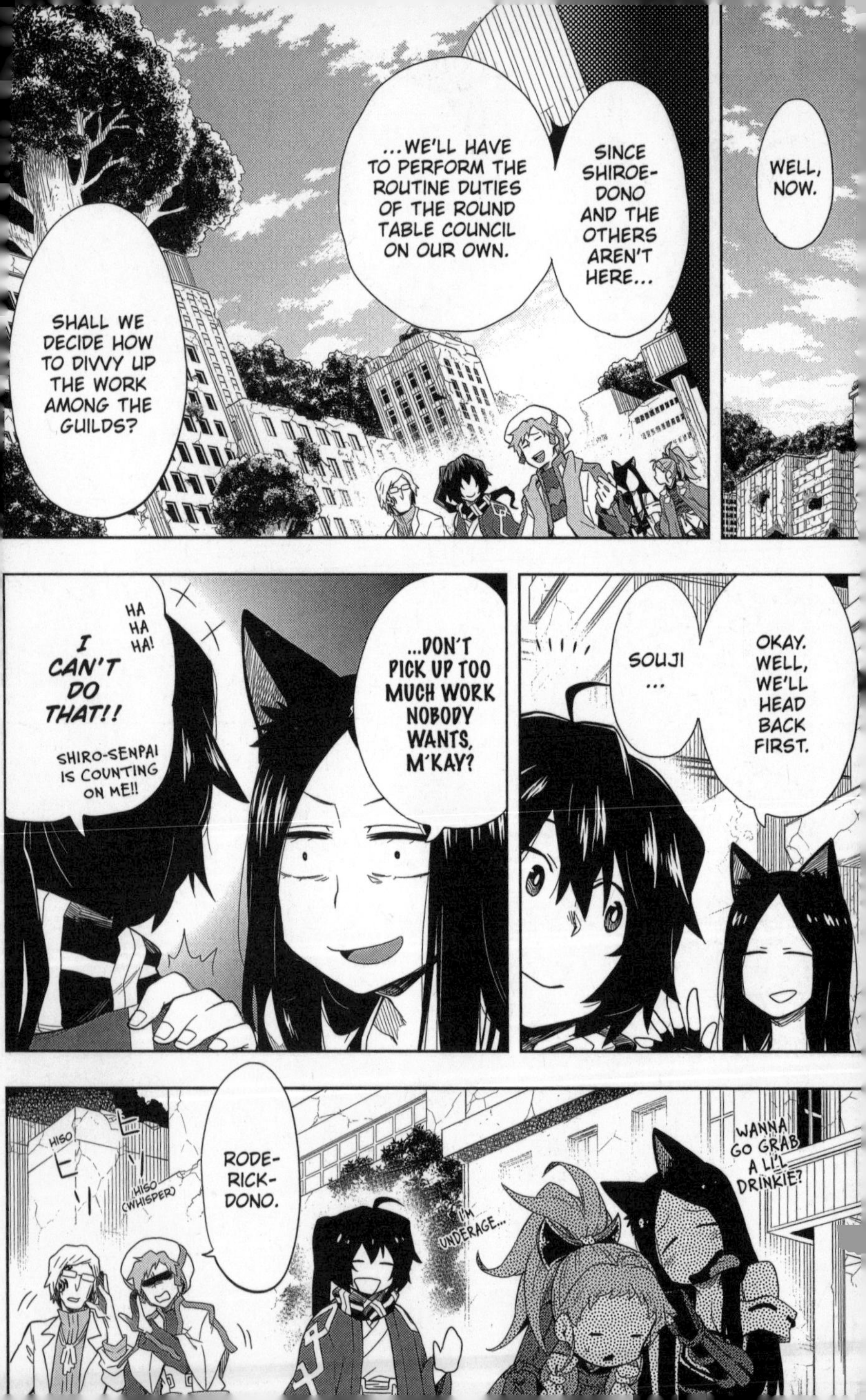
WELL, NOW.
SINCE SHIROE-DONO AND THE OTHERS AREN'T HERE...
...WE'LL HAVE TO PERFORM THE ROUTINE DUTIES OF THE ROUND TABLE COUNCIL ON OUR OWN.
SHALL WE DECIDE HOW TO DIVVY UP THE WORK AMONG THE GUILDS?
OKAY. WELL, WE'LL HEAD BACK FIRST.
SOUJI ...
...DON'T PICK UP TOO MUCH WORK NOBODY WANTS, M'KAY?
HA HA HA!
I CAN'T DO THAT!!
SHIRO-SENPAI IS COUNTING ON ME!!
WANNA GO GRAB A LI'L DRINKIE?
I'M UNDERAGE...
RODE-RICK-DONO.
HISO
HISO (WHISPER)

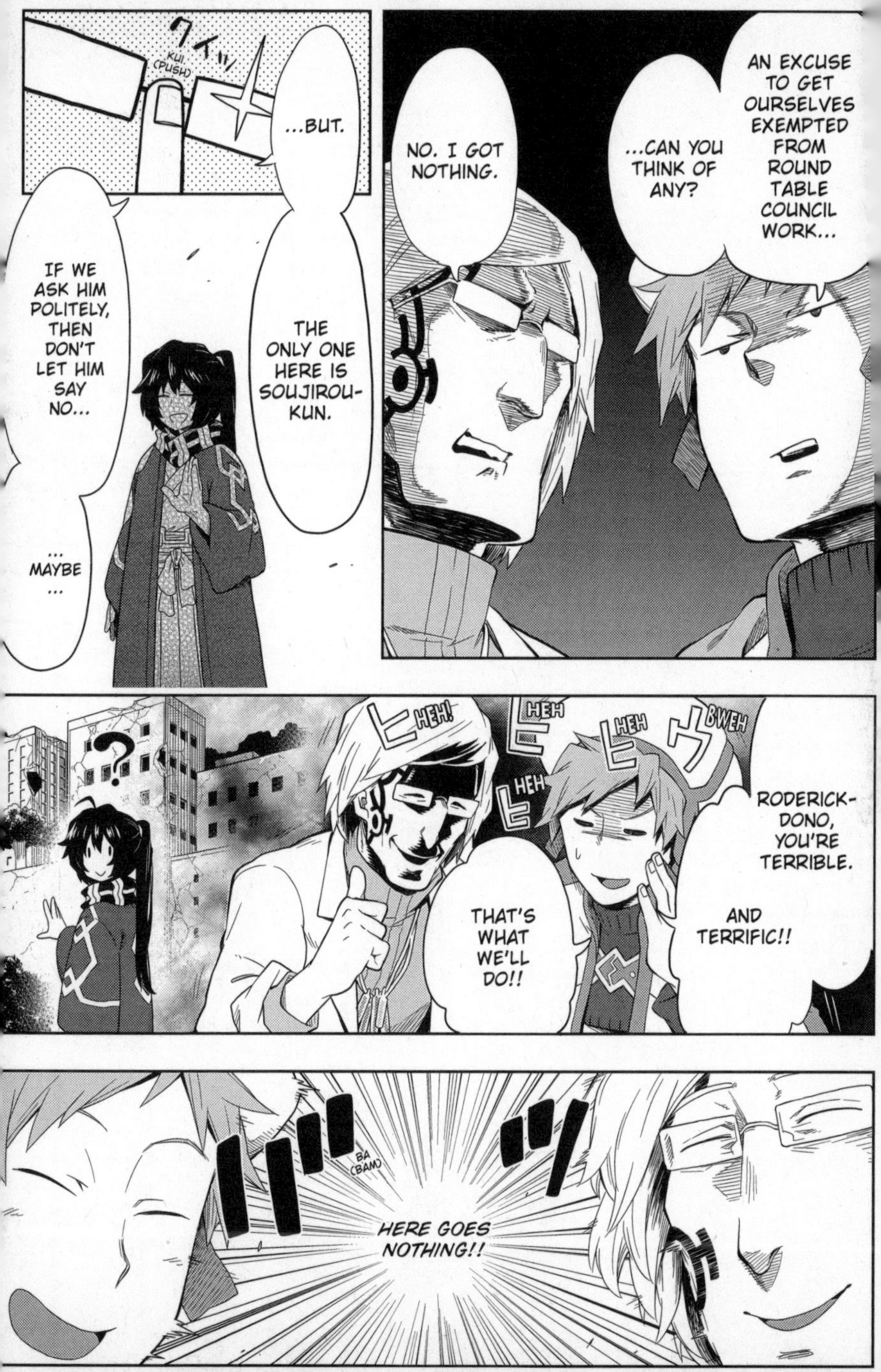
AN EXCUSE TO GET OURSELVES EXEMPTED FROM ROUND TABLE COUNCIL WORK...
...CAN YOU THINK OF ANY?
NO. I GOT NOTHING.
KUI (PUSH)
...BUT.
THE ONLY ONE HERE IS SOUJIROU-KUN.
IF WE ASK HIM POLITELY, THEN DON'T LET HIM SAY NO...
... MAYBE ...
BWEH
HEH
HEH
HEH!
HEH
RODERICK-DONO, YOU'RE TERRIBLE.
AND TERRIFIC!!
THAT'S WHAT WE'LL DO!!
?
BA (BAM)
HERE GOES NOTHING!!

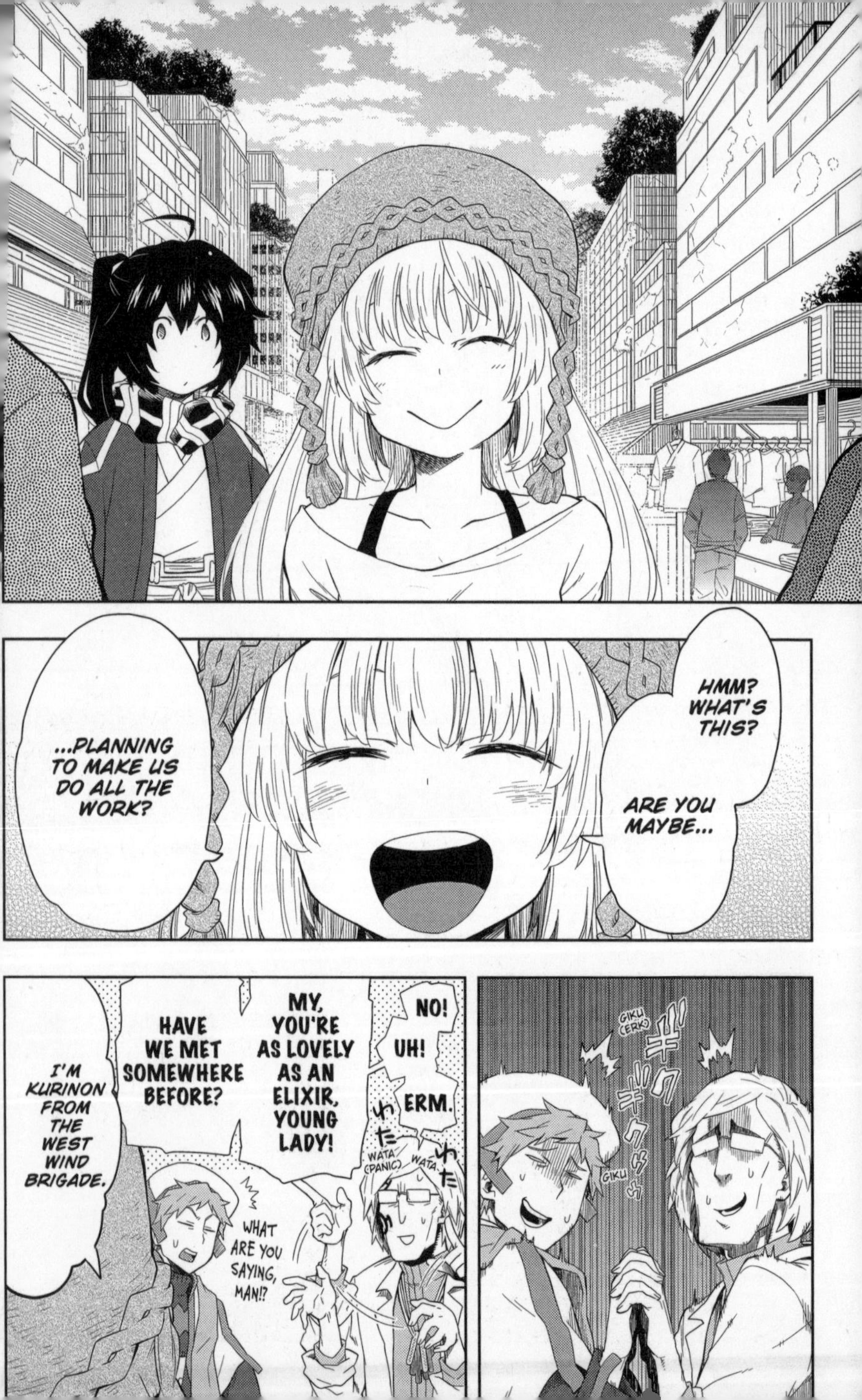
HMM? WHAT'S THIS?
ARE YOU MAYBE...
...PLANNING TO MAKE US DO ALL THE WORK?
GIKU (ERK)
GIKU
NO!
UH!
ERM.
WATA WATA (PANIC)
MY, YOU'RE AS LOVELY AS AN ELIXIR, YOUNG LADY!
WHAT ARE YOU SAYING, MAN!?
HAVE WE MET SOMEWHERE BEFORE?
I'M KURINON FROM THE WEST WIND BRIGADE.

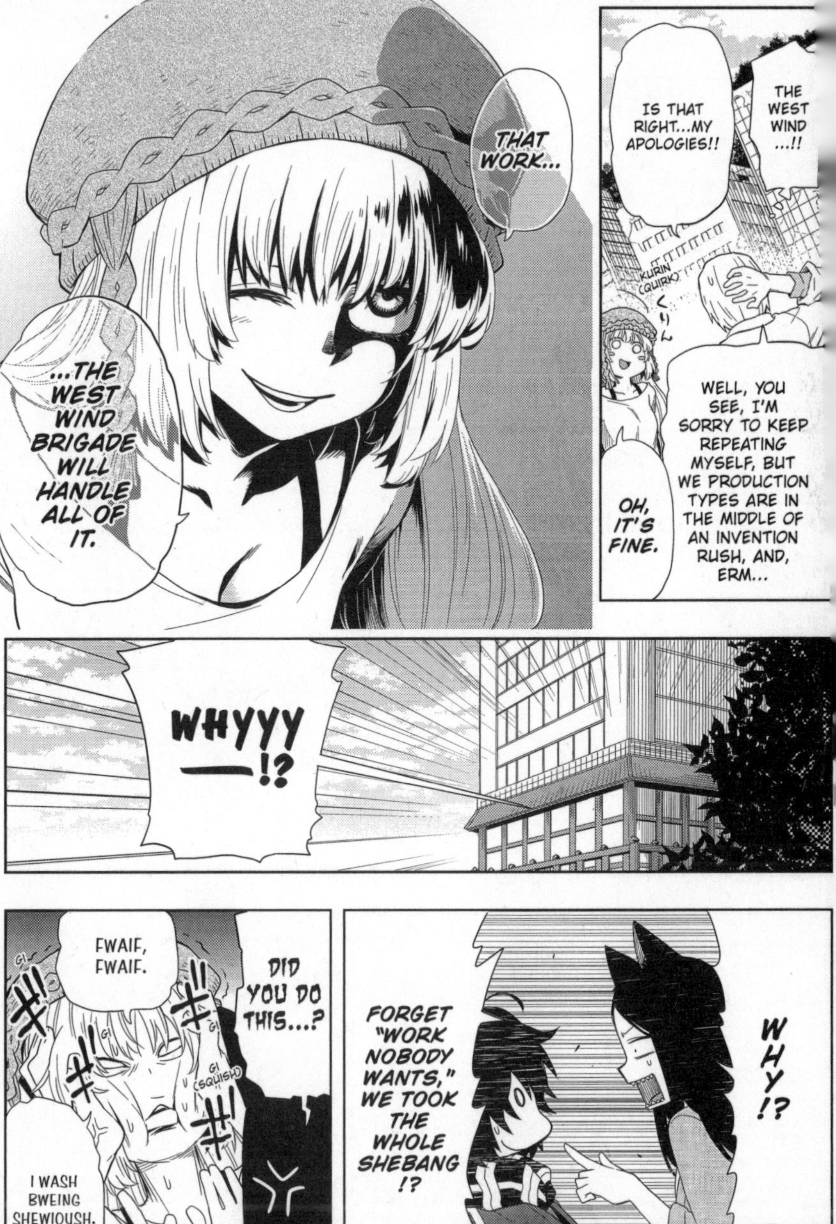
THE WEST WIND ...!!
IS THAT RIGHT...MY APOLOGIES!!
KURIN (QUIRK)
くりん
WELL, YOU SEE, I'M SORRY TO KEEP REPEATING MYSELF, BUT WE PRODUCTION TYPES ARE IN THE MIDDLE OF AN INVENTION RUSH, AND, ERM...
OH, IT'S FINE.
THAT WORK...
...THE WEST WIND BRIGADE WILL HANDLE ALL OF IT.
WHYYY—!?
WHY!?
FORGET "WORK NOBODY WANTS," WE TOOK THE WHOLE SHEBANG!?
DID YOU DO THIS...?
FWAIF, FWAIF.
GI
GI
GI (SQUISH)
I WASH BWEING SHEWIOUSH.

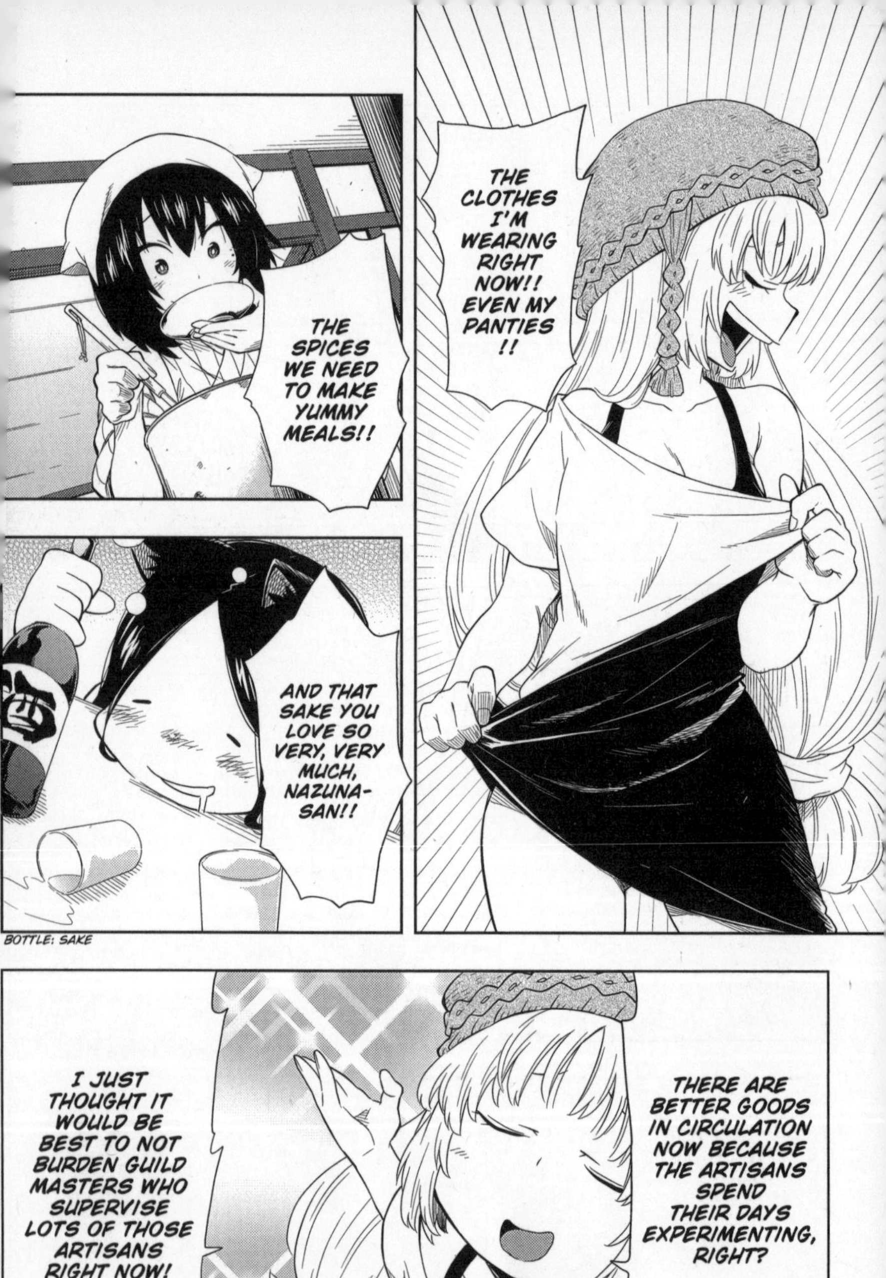
THE CLOTHES I'M WEARING RIGHT NOW!! EVEN MY PANTIES !!
THE SPICES WE NEED TO MAKE YUMMY MEALS!!
AND THAT SAKE YOU LOVE SO VERY, VERY MUCH, NAZUNA-SAN!!
THERE ARE BETTER GOODS IN CIRCULATION NOW BECAUSE THE ARTISANS SPEND THEIR DAYS EXPERIMENTING, RIGHT?
I JUST THOUGHT IT WOULD BE BEST TO NOT BURDEN GUILD MASTERS WHO SUPERVISE LOTS OF THOSE ARTISANS RIGHT NOW!
BOTTLE: SAKE

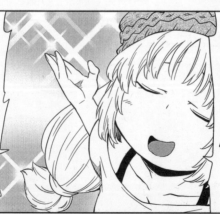

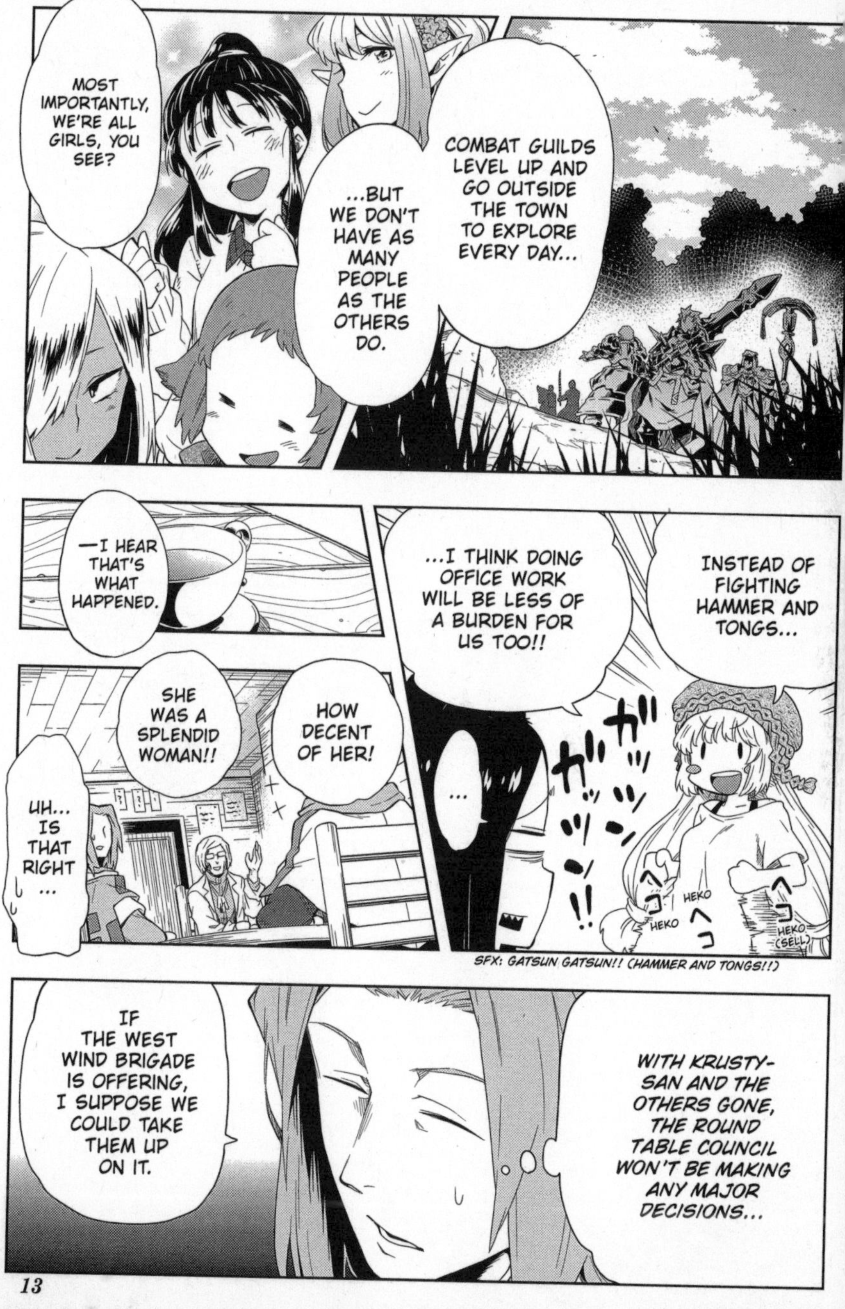
COMBAT GUILDS LEVEL UP AND GO OUTSIDE THE TOWN TO EXPLORE EVERY DAY...
...BUT WE DON'T HAVE AS MANY PEOPLE AS THE OTHERS DO.
MOST IMPORTANTLY, WE'RE ALL GIRLS, YOU SEE?
INSTEAD OF FIGHTING HAMMER AND TONGS...
...I THINK DOING OFFICE WORK WILL BE LESS OF A BURDEN FOR US TOO!!
...
HEKO
HEKO
HEKO (SELL)
SFX: GATSUN GATSUN!! (HAMMER AND TONGS!!)
—I HEAR THAT'S WHAT HAPPENED.
HOW DECENT OF HER!
SHE WAS A SPLENDID WOMAN!!
UH... IS THAT RIGHT...
WITH KRUSTY-SAN AND THE OTHERS GONE, THE ROUND TABLE COUNCIL WON'T BE MAKING ANY MAJOR DECISIONS...
IF THE WEST WIND BRIGADE IS OFFERING, I SUPPOSE WE COULD TAKE THEM UP ON IT.

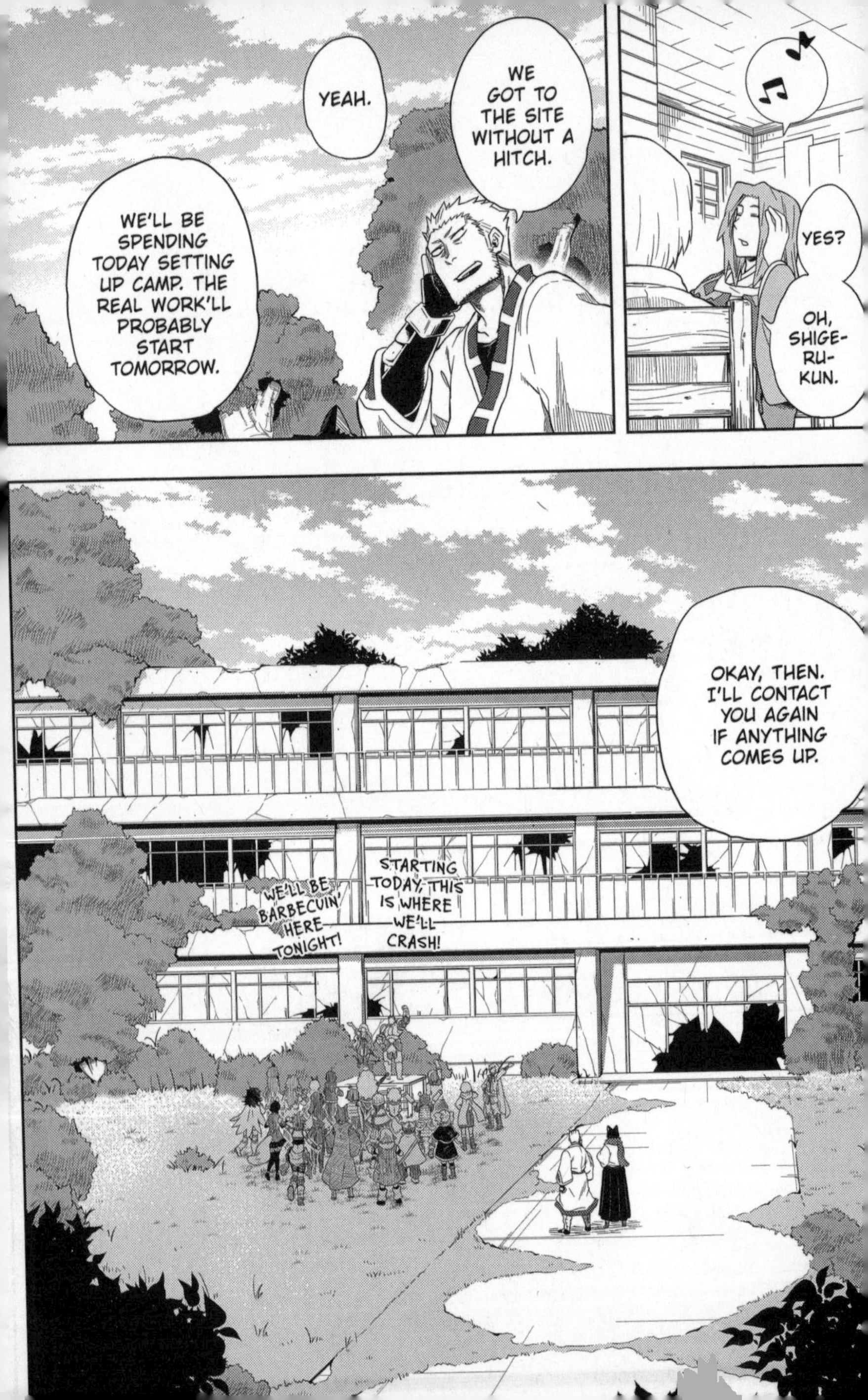
YES?
OH, SHIGERU-KUN.
WE GOT TO THE SITE WITHOUT A HITCH.
YEAH.
WE'LL BE SPENDING TODAY SETTING UP CAMP. THE REAL WORK'LL PROBABLY START TOMORROW.
OKAY, THEN. I'LL CONTACT YOU AGAIN IF ANYTHING COMES UP.
STARTING TODAY, THIS IS WHERE WE'LL CRASH!
WE'LL BE BARBECUIN' HERE TONIGHT!

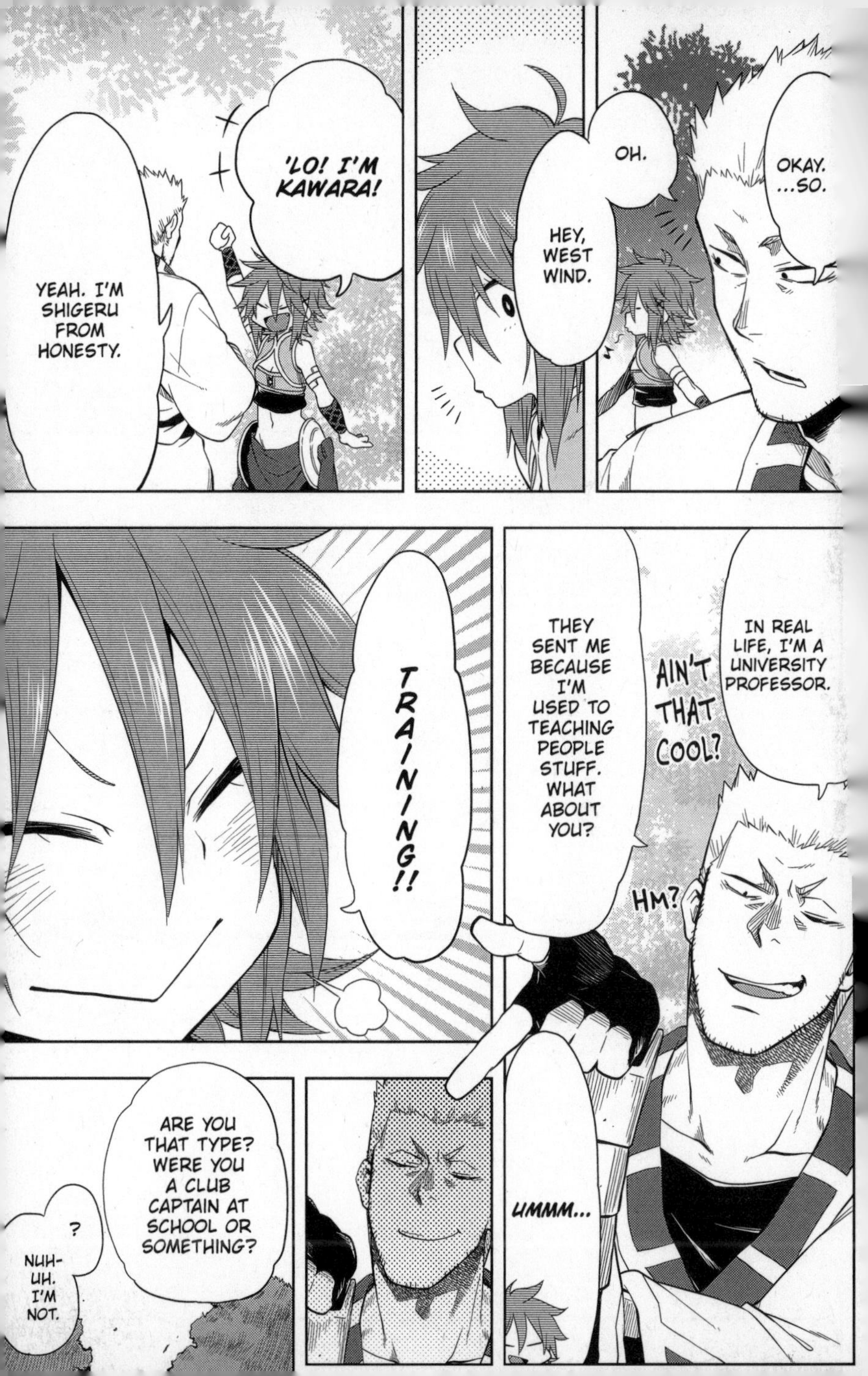
OKAY. ...SO.
OH.
HEY, WEST WIND.
'LO! I'M KAWARA!
YEAH. I'M SHIGERU FROM HONESTY.
IN REAL LIFE, I'M A UNIVERSITY PROFESSOR.
AIN'T THAT COOL?
THEY SENT ME BECAUSE I'M USED TO TEACHING PEOPLE STUFF. WHAT ABOUT YOU?
HM?
UMMM...
TRAINING!!
ARE YOU THAT TYPE? WERE YOU A CLUB CAPTAIN AT SCHOOL OR SOMETHING?
?
NUH-UH. I'M NOT.

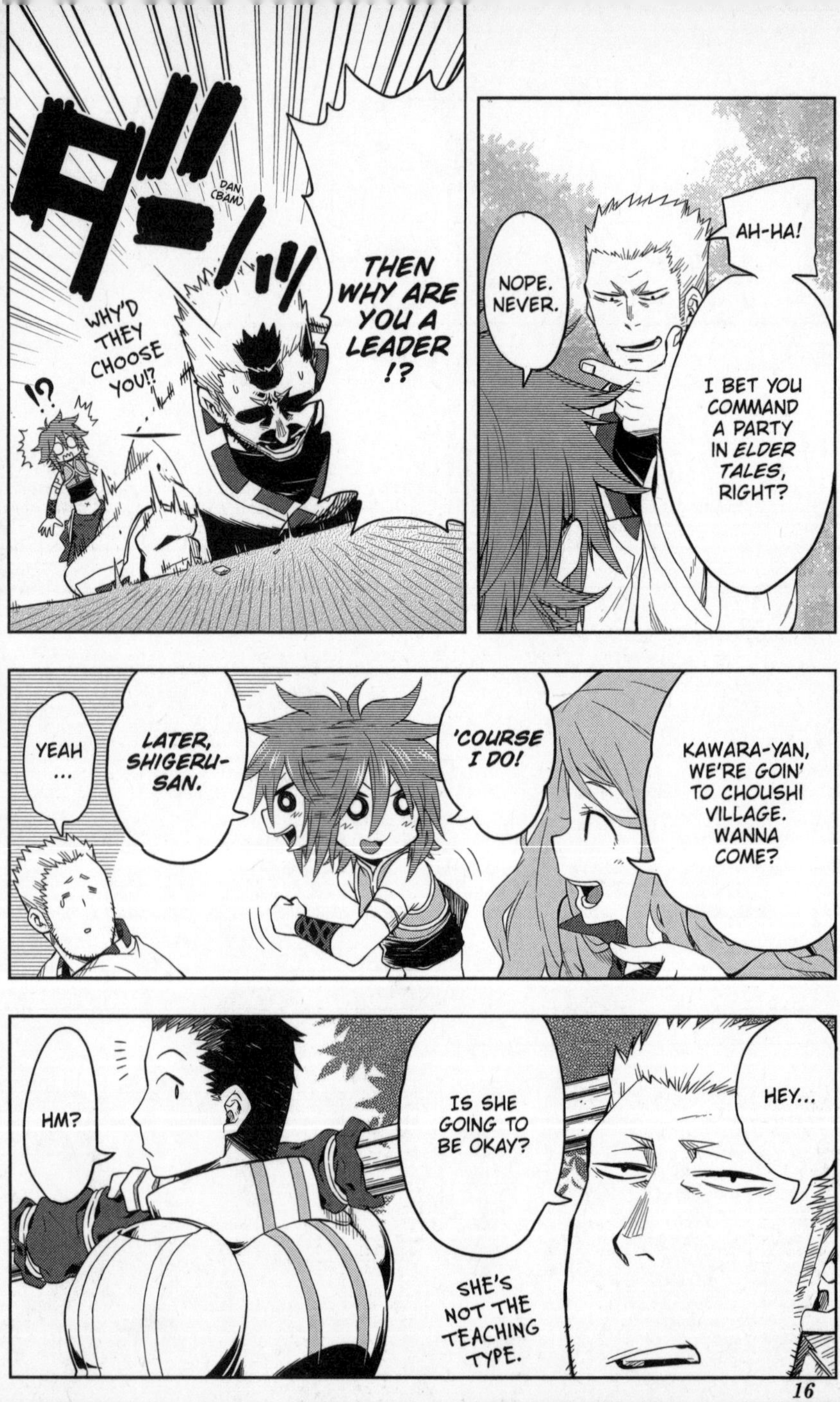
AH-HA!
I BET YOU COMMAND A PARTY IN *ELDER TALES*, RIGHT?
NOPE. NEVER.
THEN WHY ARE YOU A LEADER !?
DAN (BAM)
WHY'D THEY CHOOSE YOU!?
!?
KAWARA-YAN, WE'RE GOIN' TO CHOUSHI VILLAGE. WANNA COME?
'COURSE I DO!
LATER, SHIGERU-SAN.
YEAH ...
HEY...
IS SHE GOING TO BE OKAY?
SHE'S NOT THE TEACHING TYPE.
HM?

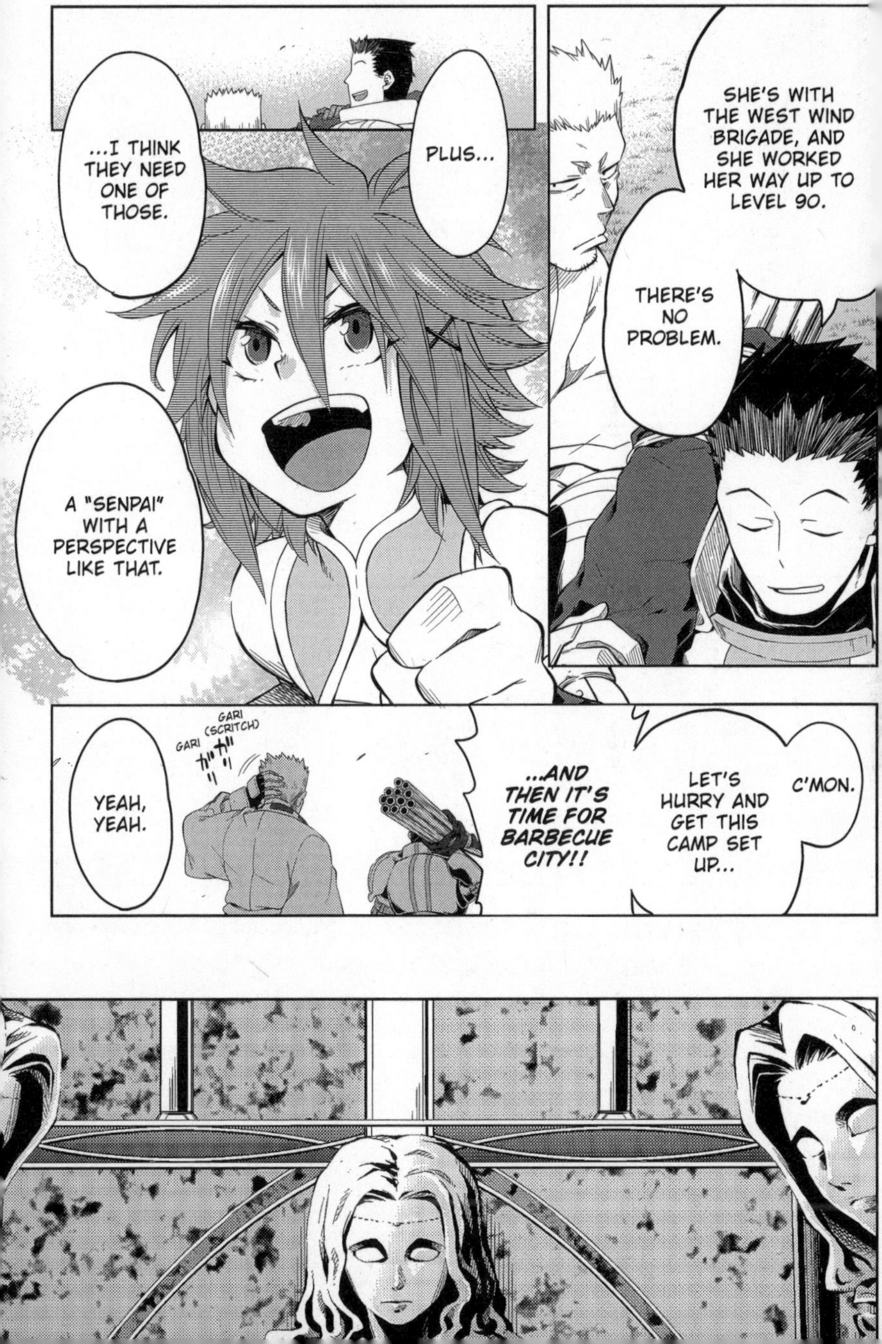
SHE'S WITH THE WEST WIND BRIGADE, AND SHE WORKED HER WAY UP TO LEVEL 90.
THERE'S NO PROBLEM.
PLUS...
...I THINK THEY NEED ONE OF THOSE.
A "SENPAI" WITH A PERSPECTIVE LIKE THAT.
C'MON.
LET'S HURRY AND GET THIS CAMP SET UP...
...AND THEN IT'S TIME FOR BARBECUE CITY!!
GARI (SCRITCH)
GARI
YEAH, YEAH.

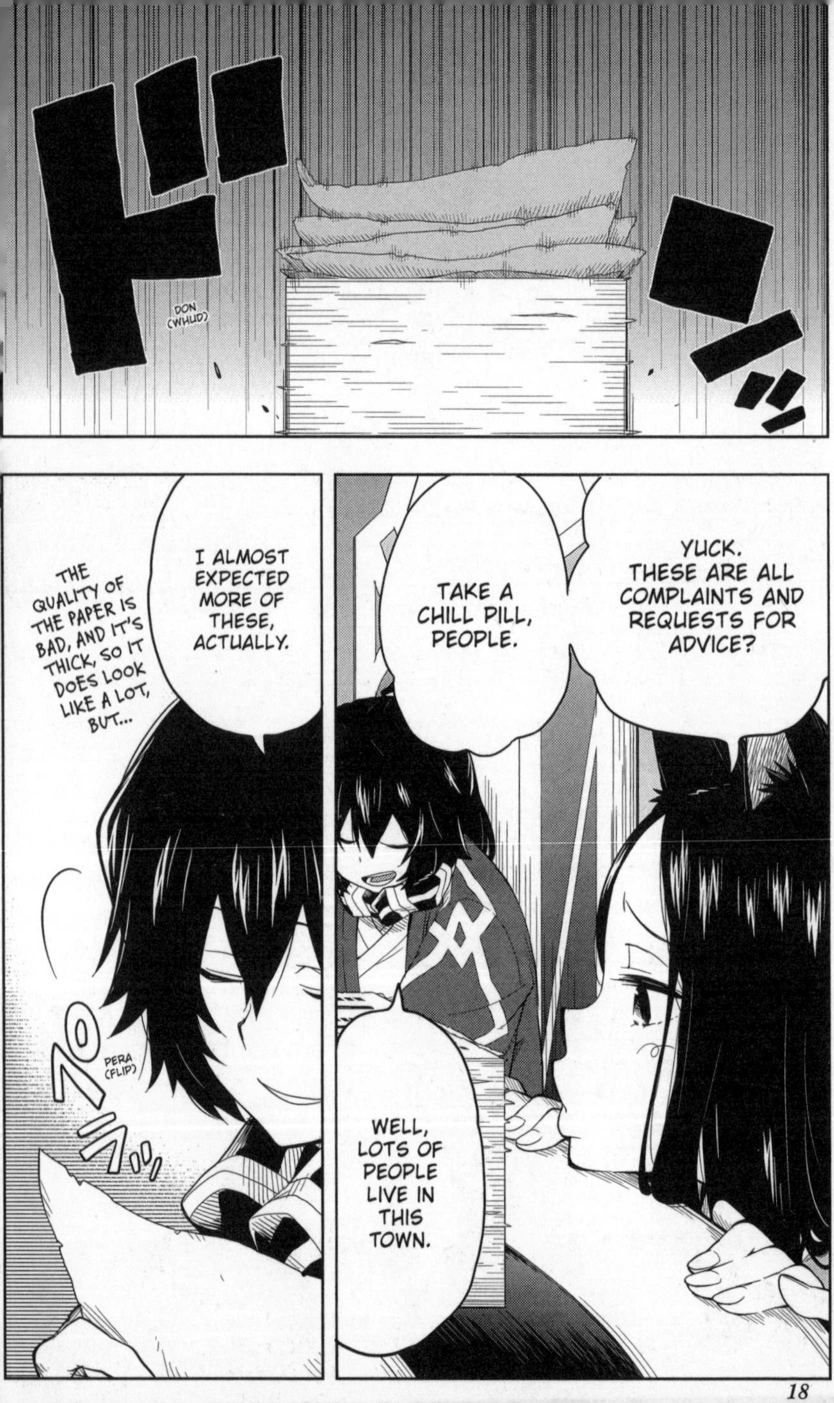
DON (WHUD)
YUCK. THESE ARE ALL COMPLAINTS AND REQUESTS FOR ADVICE?
TAKE A CHILL PILL, PEOPLE.
WELL, LOTS OF PEOPLE LIVE IN THIS TOWN.
I ALMOST EXPECTED MORE OF THESE, ACTUALLY.
THE QUALITY OF THE PAPER IS BAD, AND IT'S THICK, SO IT DOES LOOK LIKE A LOT, BUT...
PERA (FLIP)

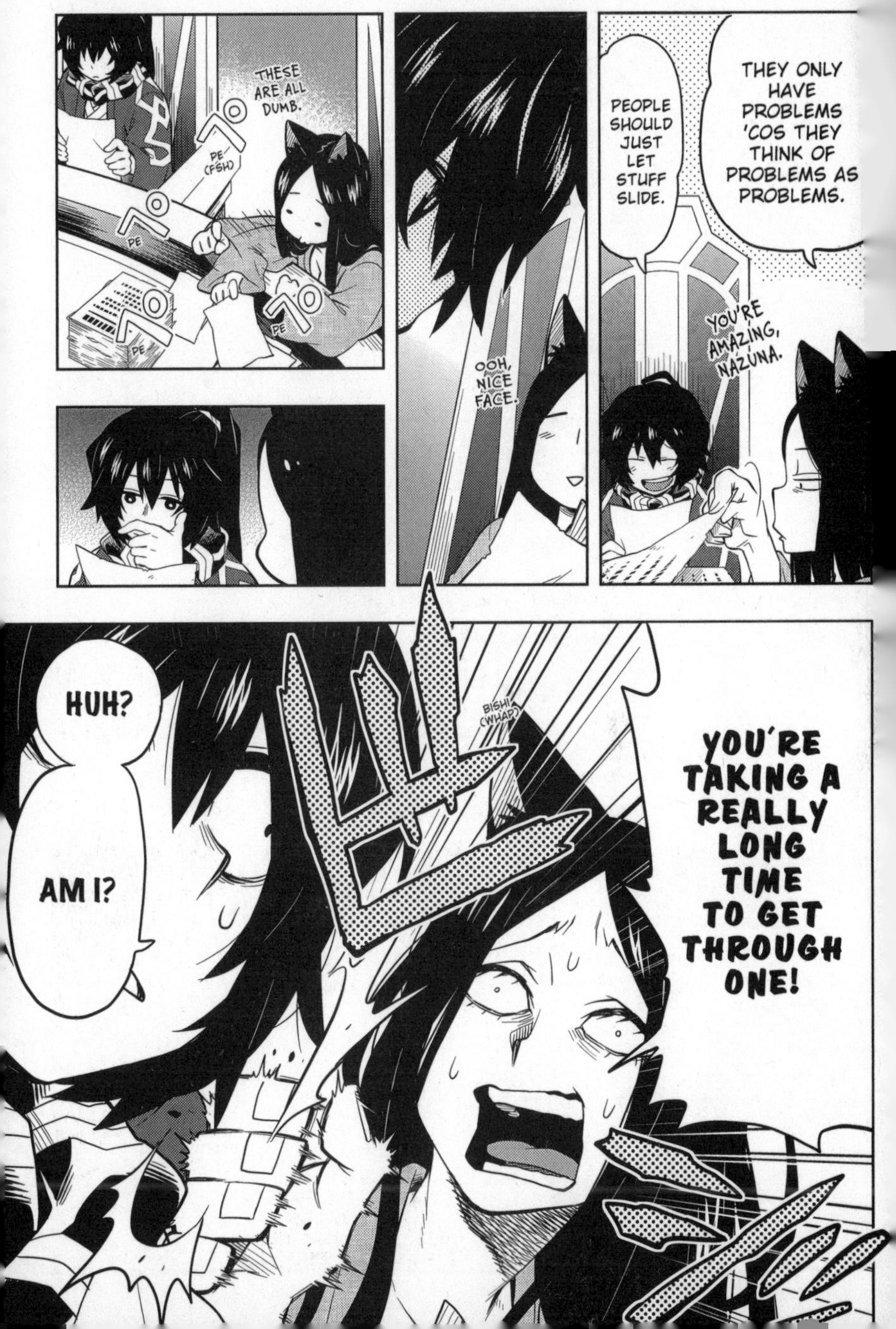
THEY ONLY HAVE PROBLEMS 'COS THEY THINK OF PROBLEMS AS PROBLEMS.
PEOPLE SHOULD JUST LET STUFF SLIDE.
YOU'RE AMAZING, NAZUNA.
OOH, NICE FACE.
THESE ARE ALL DUMB.
PE (FSH)
PE
PE
PE
YOU'RE TAKING A REALLY LONG TIME TO GET THROUGH ONE!
BISHI (WHAP)
HUH?
AM I?

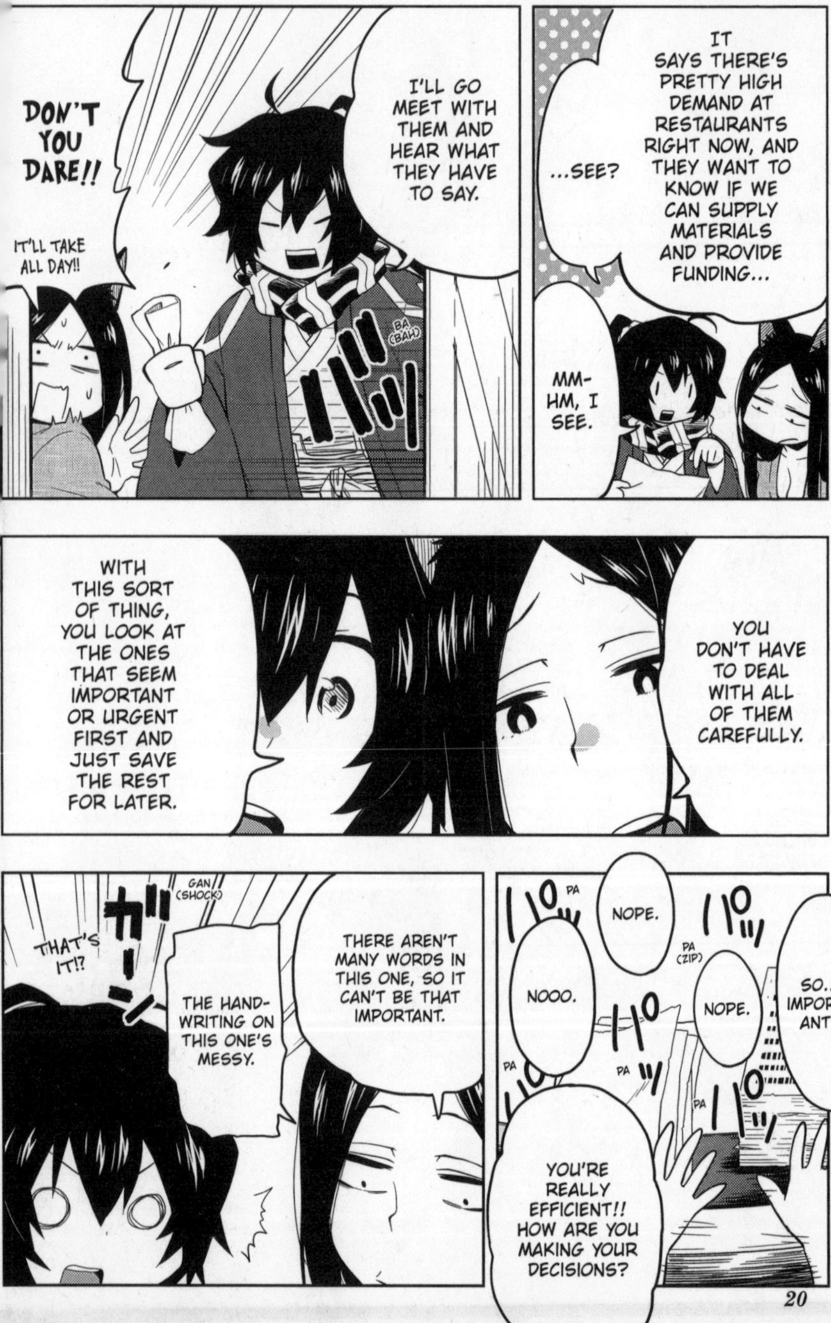
IT SAYS THERE'S PRETTY HIGH DEMAND AT RESTAURANTS RIGHT NOW, AND THEY WANT TO KNOW IF WE CAN SUPPLY MATERIALS AND PROVIDE FUNDING...
...SEE?
MM-HM, I SEE.
I'LL GO MEET WITH THEM AND HEAR WHAT THEY HAVE TO SAY.
BA (BAH)
DON'T YOU DARE!!
IT'LL TAKE ALL DAY!!
YOU DON'T HAVE TO DEAL WITH ALL OF THEM CAREFULLY.
WITH THIS SORT OF THING, YOU LOOK AT THE ONES THAT SEEM IMPORTANT OR URGENT FIRST AND JUST SAVE THE REST FOR LATER.
SO... IMPORT-ANT?
PA
NOPE.
PA (ZIP)
NOPE.
PA
NOOO.
PA
PA
PA
YOU'RE REALLY EFFICIENT!! HOW ARE YOU MAKING YOUR DECISIONS?
THERE AREN'T MANY WORDS IN THIS ONE, SO IT CAN'T BE THAT IMPORTANT.
THE HAND-WRITING ON THIS ONE'S MESSY.
GAN (SHOCK)
THAT'S IT!?

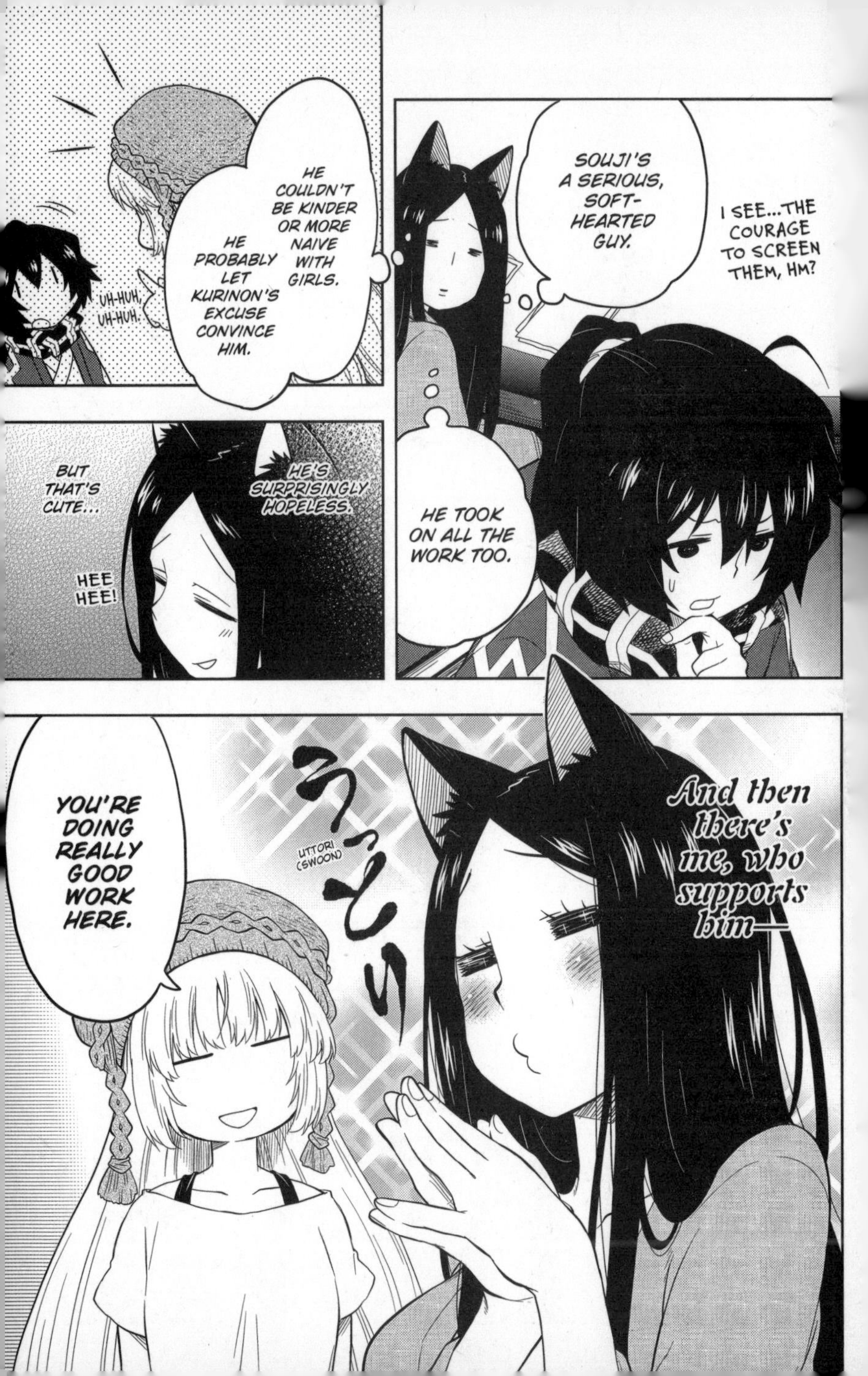
I SEE...THE COURAGE TO SCREEN THEM, HM?
SOUJI'S A SERIOUS, SOFT-HEARTED GUY.
HE TOOK ON ALL THE WORK TOO.
HE COULDN'T BE KINDER OR MORE NAIVE WITH GIRLS.
HE PROBABLY LET KURINON'S EXCUSE CONVINCE HIM.
UH-HUH, UH-HUH.
HE'S SURPRISINGLY HOPELESS.
BUT THAT'S CUTE...
HEE HEE!
And then there's me, who supports him—
うっとり
UTTORI (SWOON)
YOU'RE DOING REALLY GOOD WORK HERE.

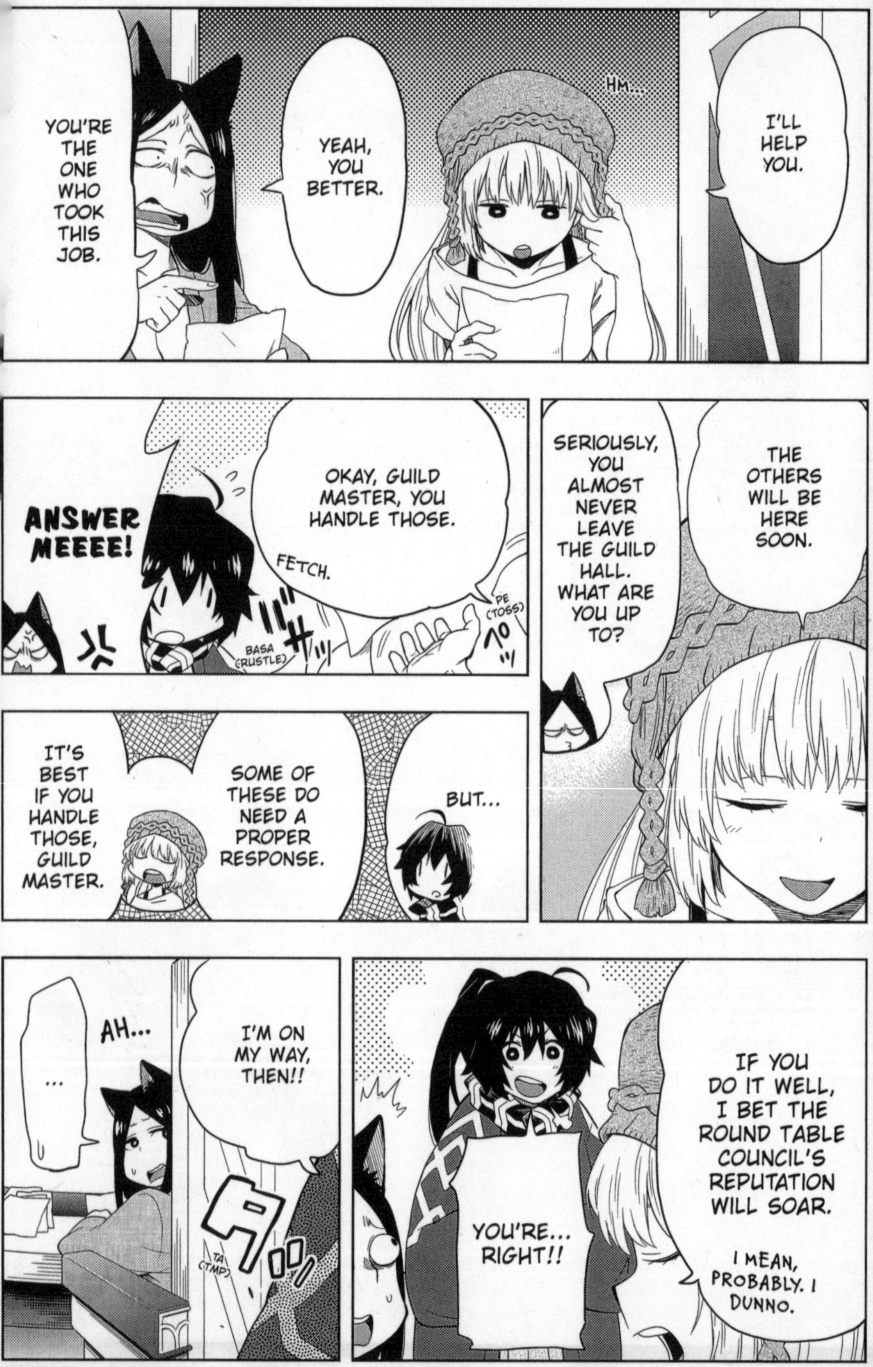
I'LL HELP YOU.
HM...
YEAH, YOU BETTER.
YOU'RE THE ONE WHO TOOK THIS JOB.
THE OTHERS WILL BE HERE SOON.
SERIOUSLY, YOU ALMOST NEVER LEAVE THE GUILD HALL. WHAT ARE YOU UP TO?
OKAY, GUILD MASTER, YOU HANDLE THOSE.
PE (TOSS)
FETCH.
BASA (RUSTLE)
ANSWER MEEEE!
BUT...
SOME OF THESE DO NEED A PROPER RESPONSE.
IT'S BEST IF YOU HANDLE THOSE, GUILD MASTER.
IF YOU DO IT WELL, I BET THE ROUND TABLE COUNCIL'S REPUTATION WILL SOAR.
I MEAN, PROBABLY. I DUNNO.
YOU'RE... RIGHT!!
I'M ON MY WAY, THEN!!
TA (TMP)
AH...
...

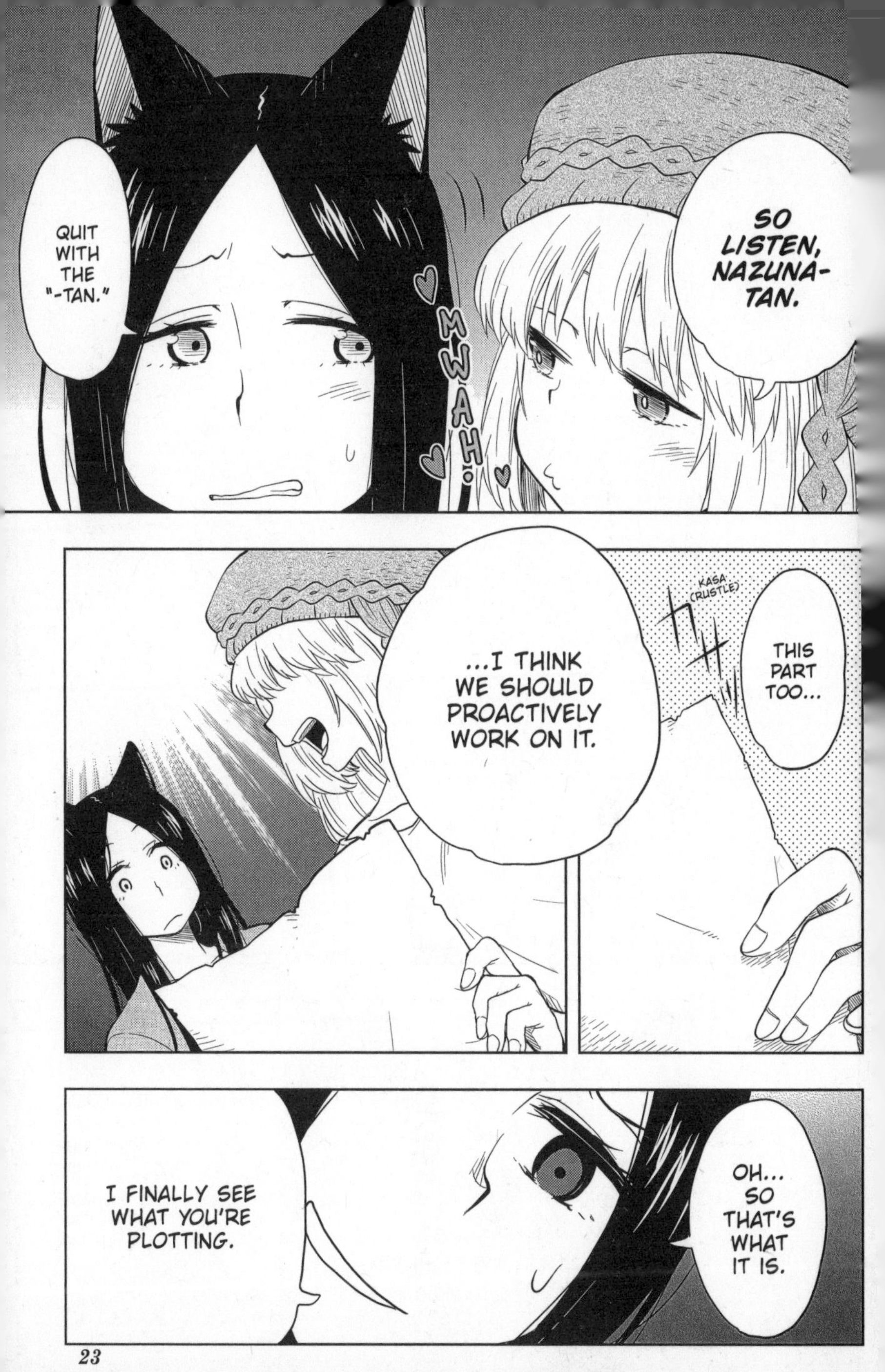
SO LISTEN, NAZUNA-TAN.
MWAH!
QUIT WITH THE "-TAN."
KASA (RUSTLE)
THIS PART TOO...
...I THINK WE SHOULD PROACTIVELY WORK ON IT.
OH... SO THAT'S WHAT IT IS.
I FINALLY SEE WHAT YOU'RE PLOTTING.

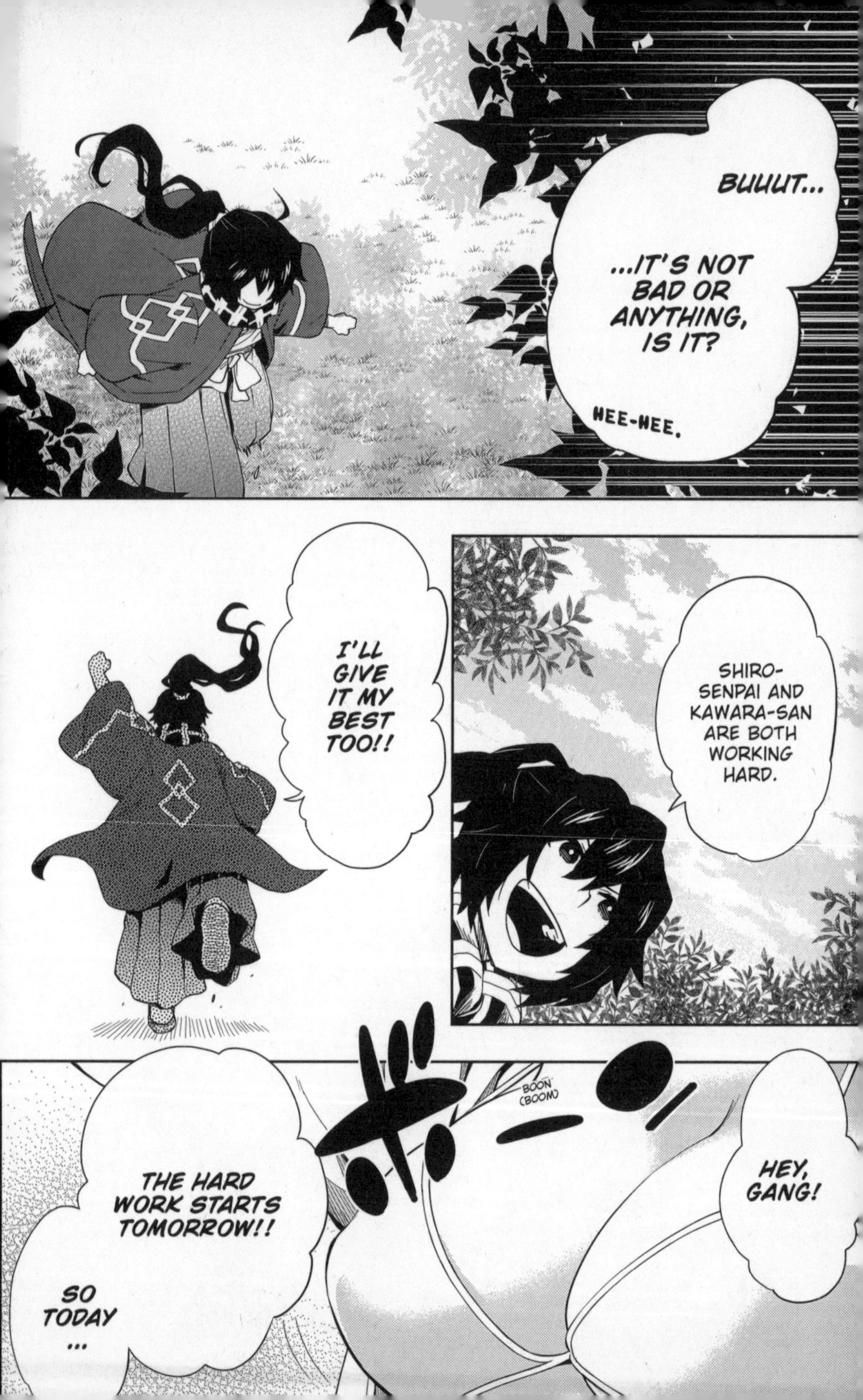
BUUUT...
...IT'S NOT BAD OR ANYTHING, IS IT?
HEE-HEE.
SHIRO-SENPAI AND KAWARA-SAN ARE BOTH WORKING HARD.
I'LL GIVE IT MY BEST TOO!!
HEY, GANG!
BOON (BOOM)
THE HARD WORK STARTS TOMORROW!!
SO TODAY ...

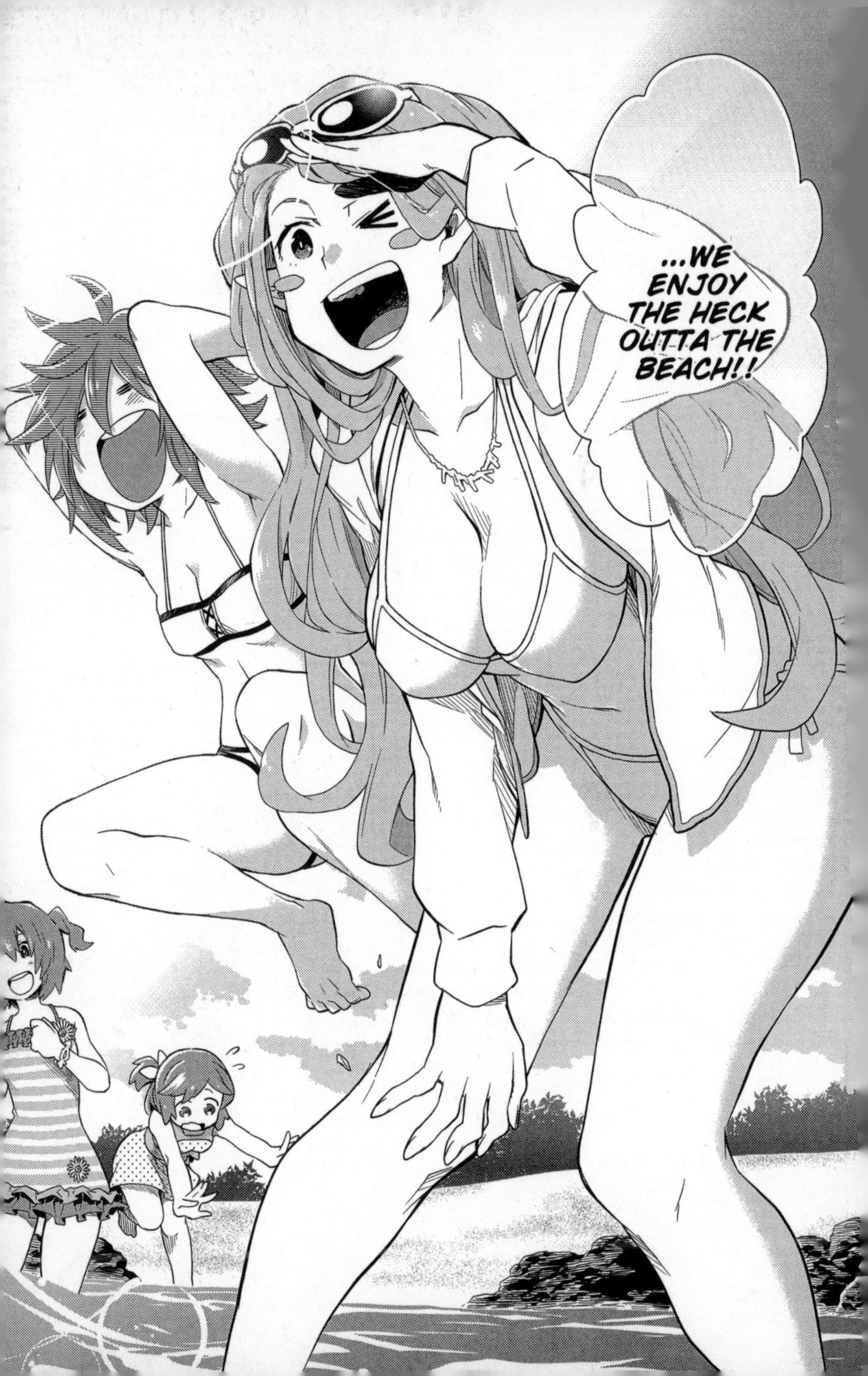
...WE ENJOY THE HECK OUTTA THE BEACH!!

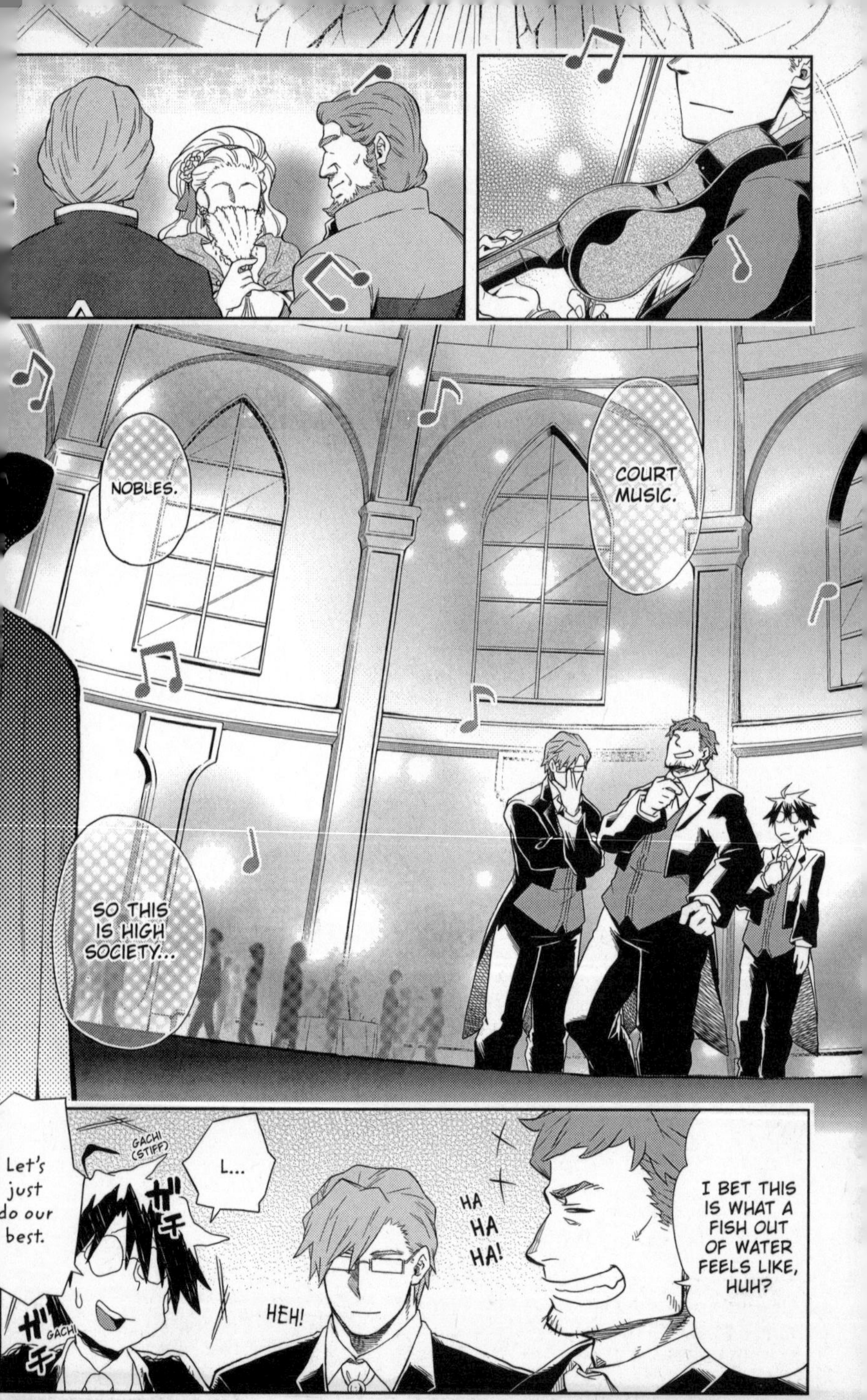
COURT MUSIC.
NOBLES.
SO THIS IS HIGH SOCIETY...
I BET THIS IS WHAT A FISH OUT OF WATER FEELS LIKE, HUH?
HA HA HA!
HEH!
L...
ガチ
GACHI (STIFF)
ガチ
GACHI
Let's just do our best.

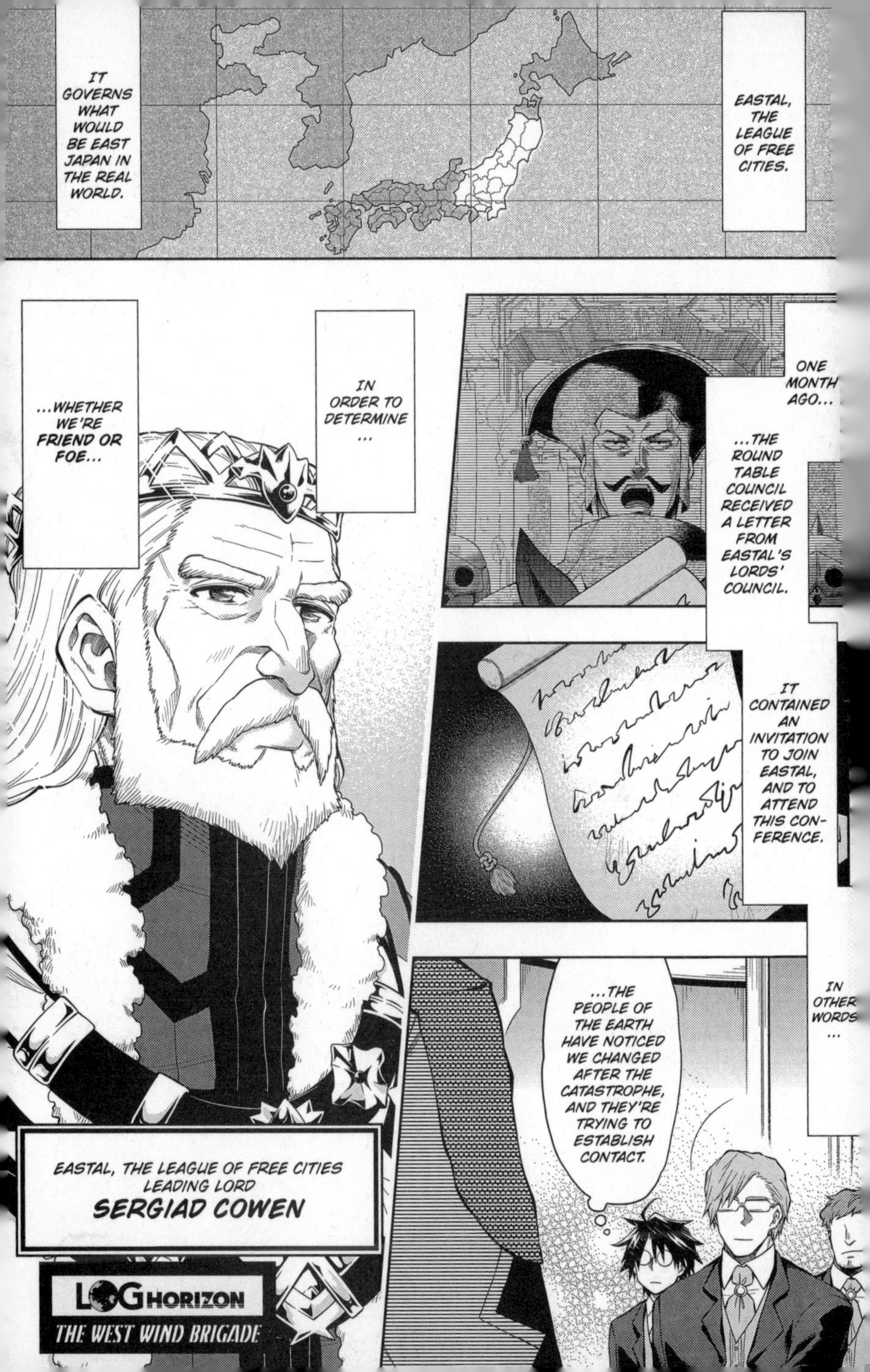
EASTAL, THE LEAGUE OF FREE CITIES.
IT GOVERNS WHAT WOULD BE EAST JAPAN IN THE REAL WORLD.
ONE MONTH AGO...
...THE ROUND TABLE COUNCIL RECEIVED A LETTER FROM EASTAL'S LORDS' COUNCIL.
IT CONTAINED AN INVITATION TO JOIN EASTAL, AND TO ATTEND THIS CONFERENCE.
IN OTHER WORDS...
...THE PEOPLE OF THE EARTH HAVE NOTICED WE CHANGED AFTER THE CATASTROPHE, AND THEY'RE TRYING TO ESTABLISH CONTACT.
IN ORDER TO DETERMINE...
...WHETHER WE'RE FRIEND OR FOE...
EASTAL, THE LEAGUE OF FREE CITIES LEADING LORD
SERGIAD COWEN
LOG HORIZON
THE WEST WIND BRIGADE

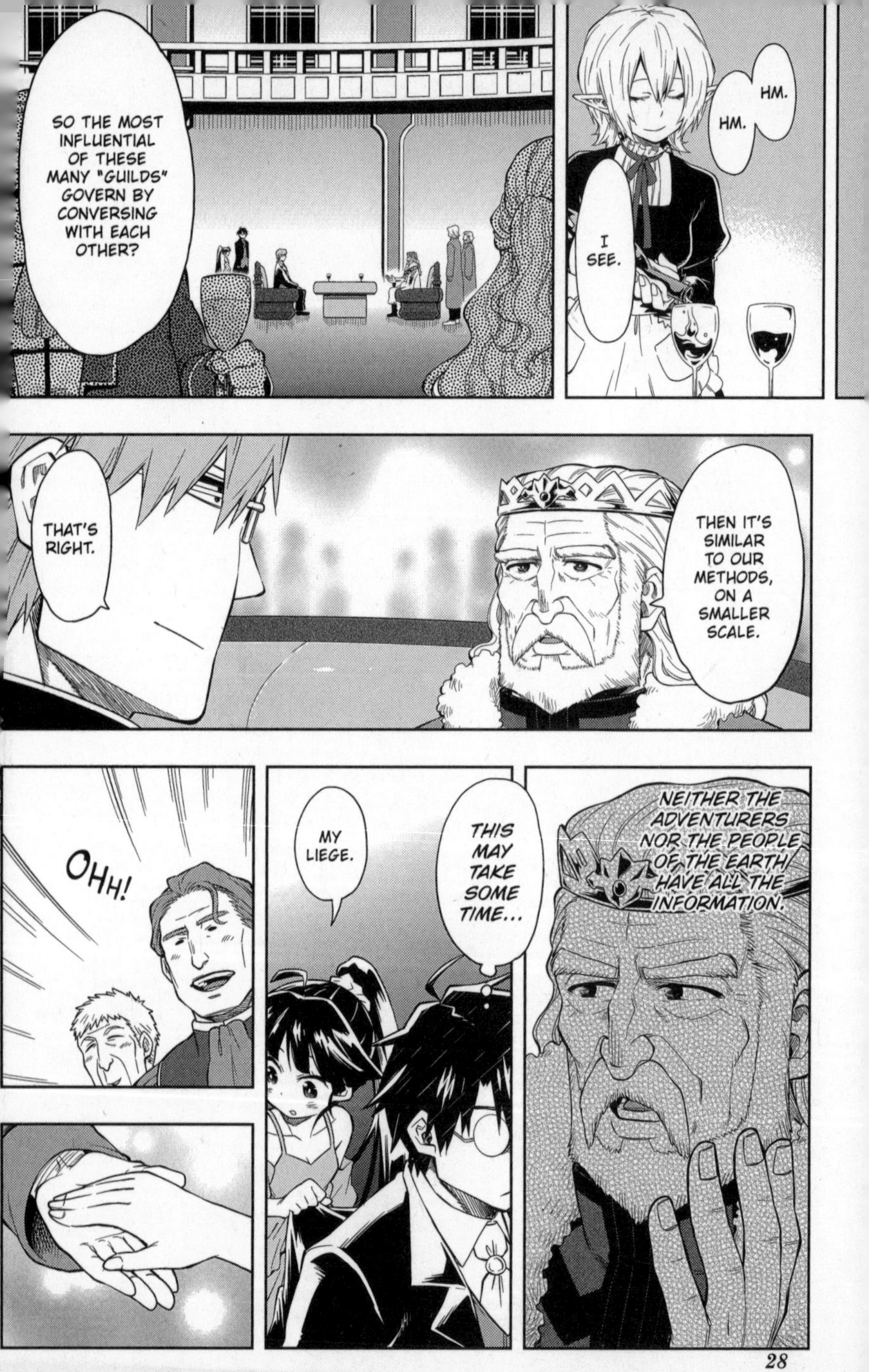
HM.
HM.
I SEE.
SO THE MOST INFLUENTIAL OF THESE MANY "GUILDS" GOVERN BY CONVERSING WITH EACH OTHER?
THEN IT'S SIMILAR TO OUR METHODS, ON A SMALLER SCALE.
THAT'S RIGHT.
NEITHER THE ADVENTURERS NOR THE PEOPLE OF THE EARTH HAVE ALL THE INFORMATION.
THIS MAY TAKE SOME TIME...
MY LIEGE.
OHH!

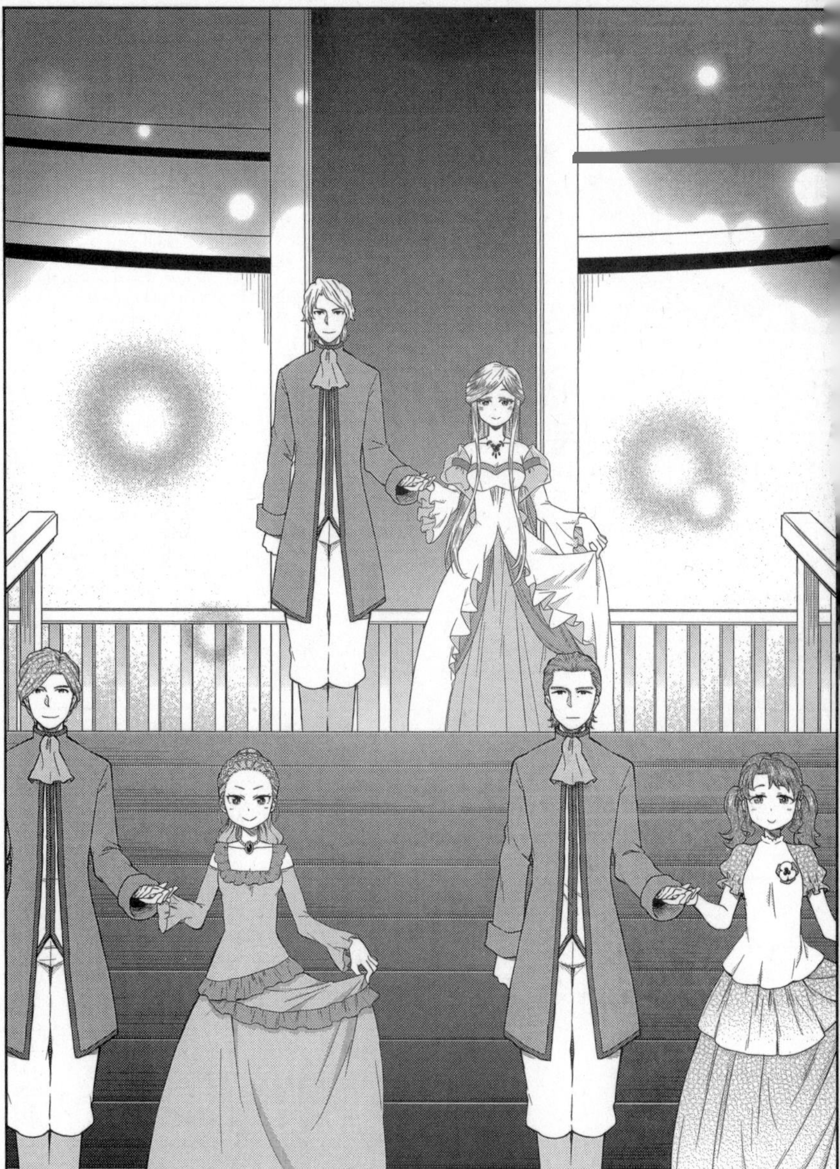

CHAPTER : 31 KURINON PLOTS

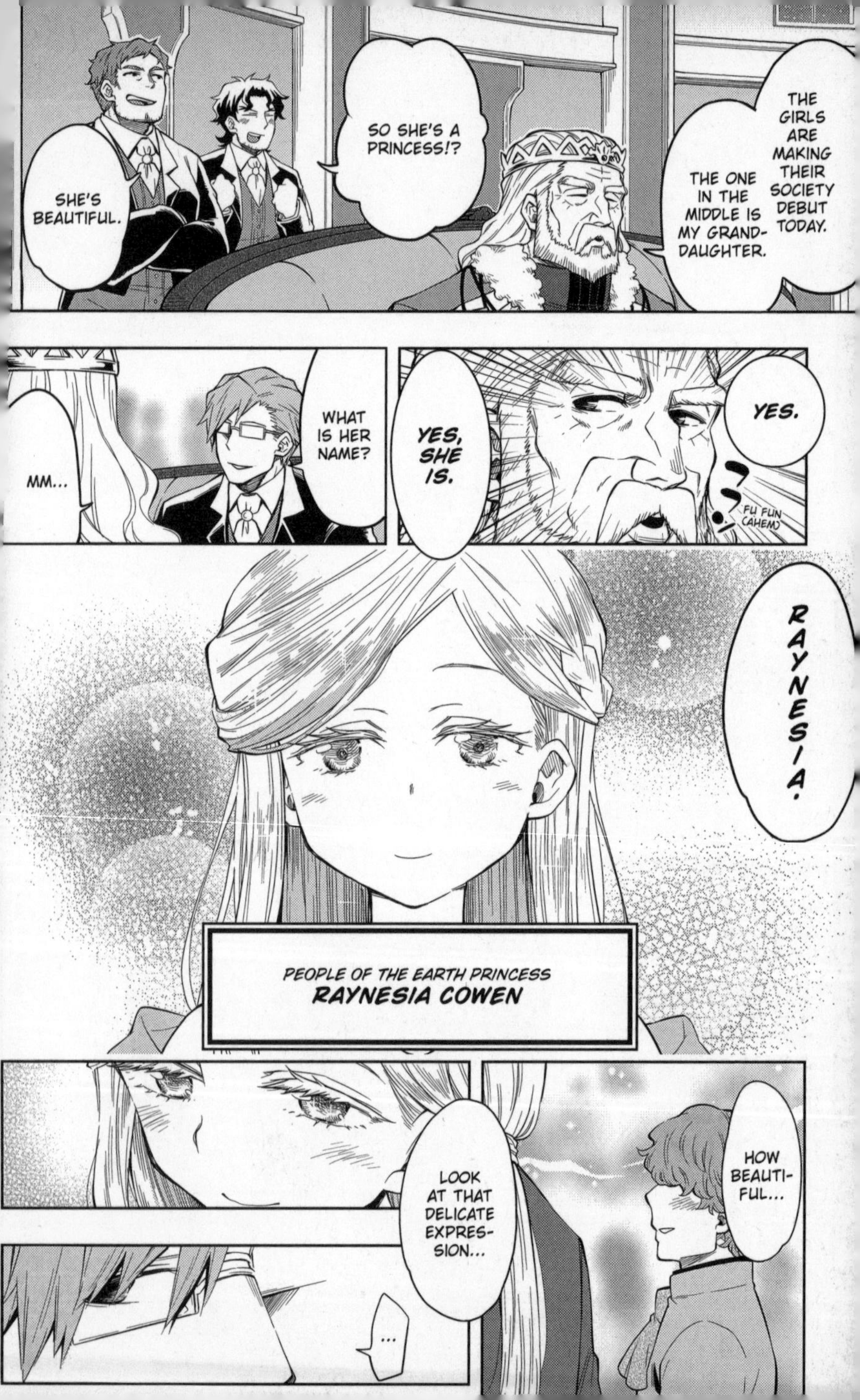
THE GIRLS ARE MAKING THEIR SOCIETY DEBUT TODAY.
THE ONE IN THE MIDDLE IS MY GRAND-DAUGHTER.
SO SHE'S A PRINCESS!?
SHE'S BEAUTIFUL.
YES.
FU FUN (AHEM)
YES, SHE IS.
WHAT IS HER NAME?
MM...
RAYNESIA.
PEOPLE OF THE EARTH PRINCESS
RAYNESIA COWEN
HOW BEAUTIFUL...
LOOK AT THAT DELICATE EXPRESSION...
...

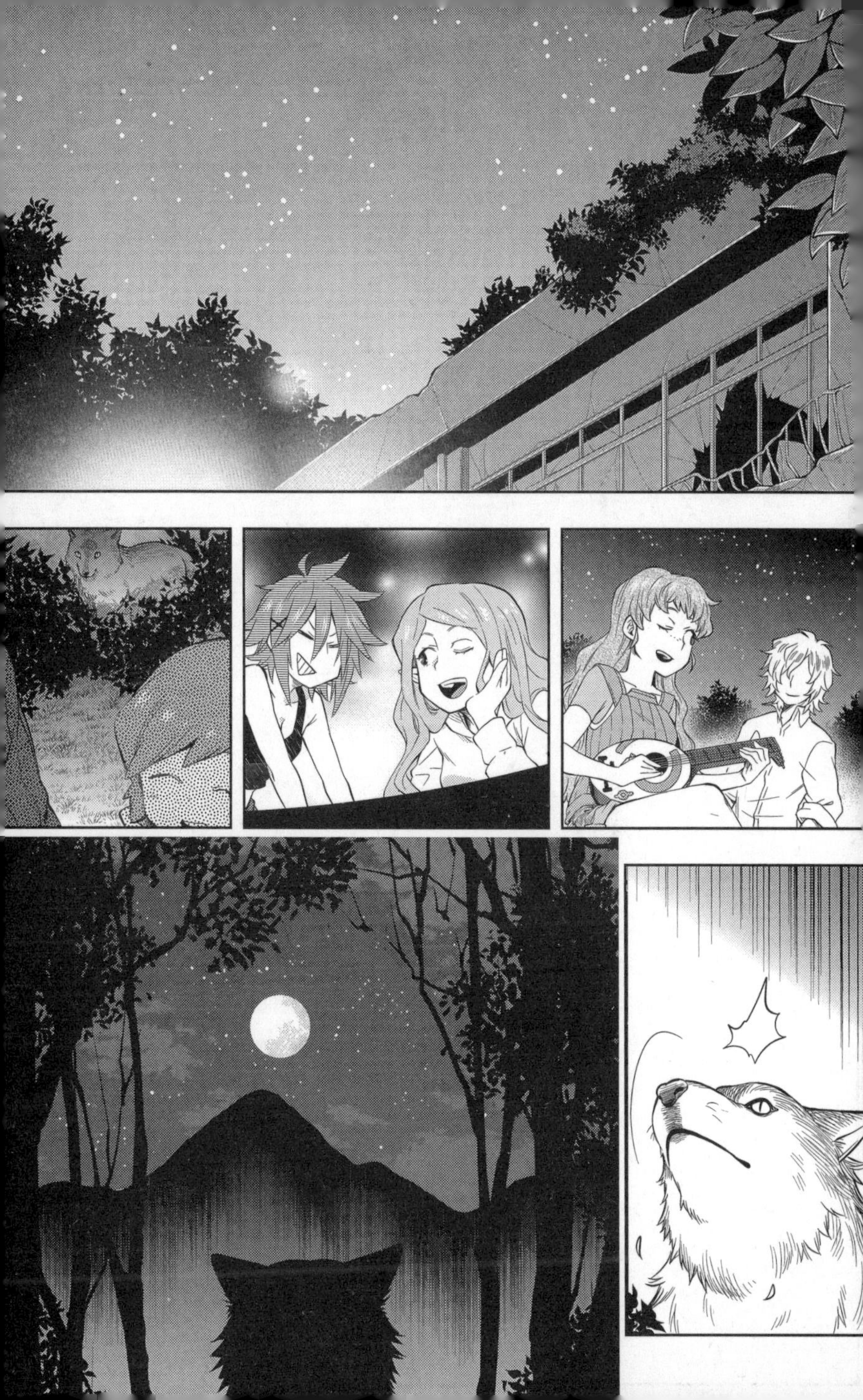

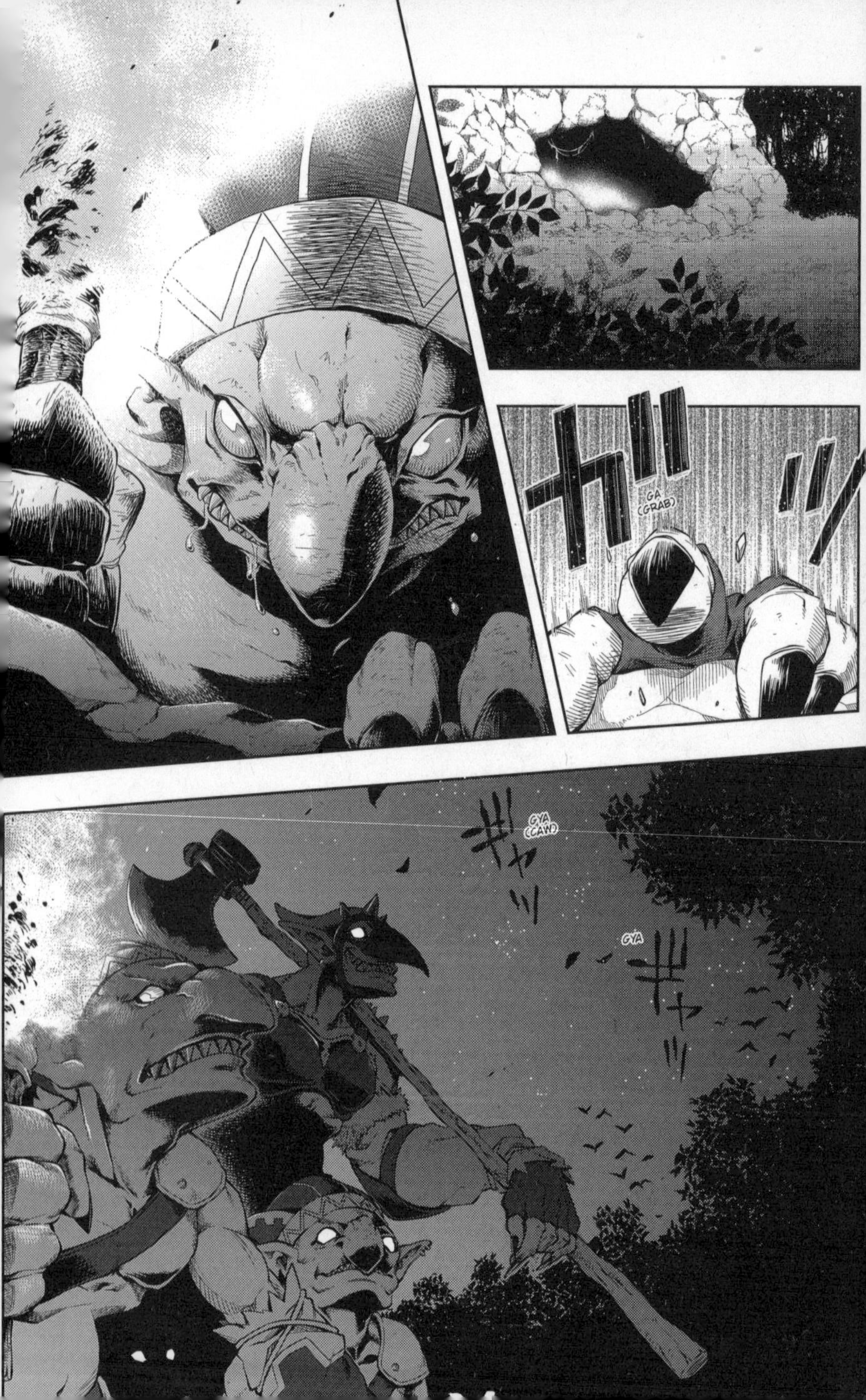
GA
(GRAB)
GYA
(CAW)
GYA

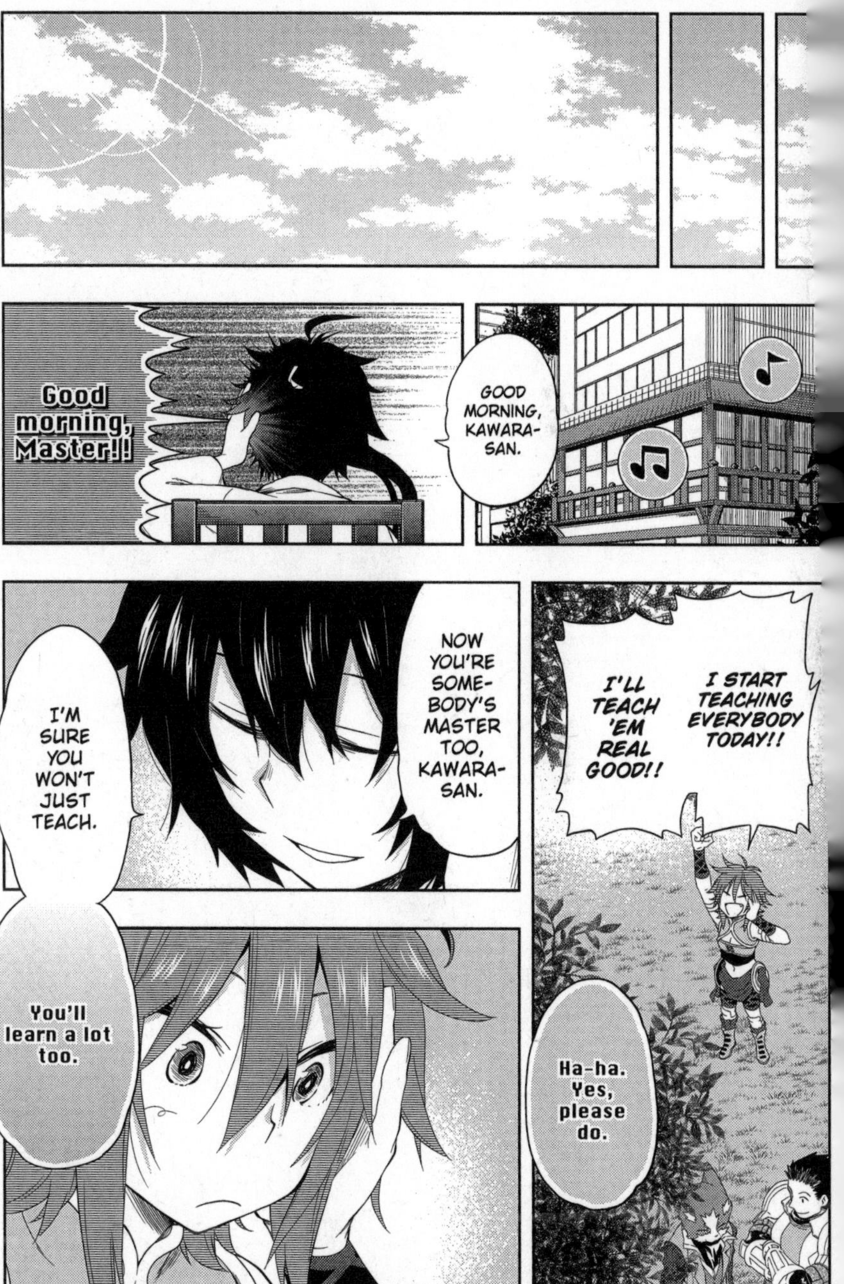
GOOD MORNING, KAWARA-SAN.
Good morning, Master!!
I START TEACHING EVERYBODY TODAY!!
I'LL TEACH 'EM REAL GOOD!!
Ha-ha. Yes, please do.
NOW YOU'RE SOMEBODY'S MASTER TOO, KAWARA-SAN.
I'M SURE YOU WON'T JUST TEACH.
You'll learn a lot too.

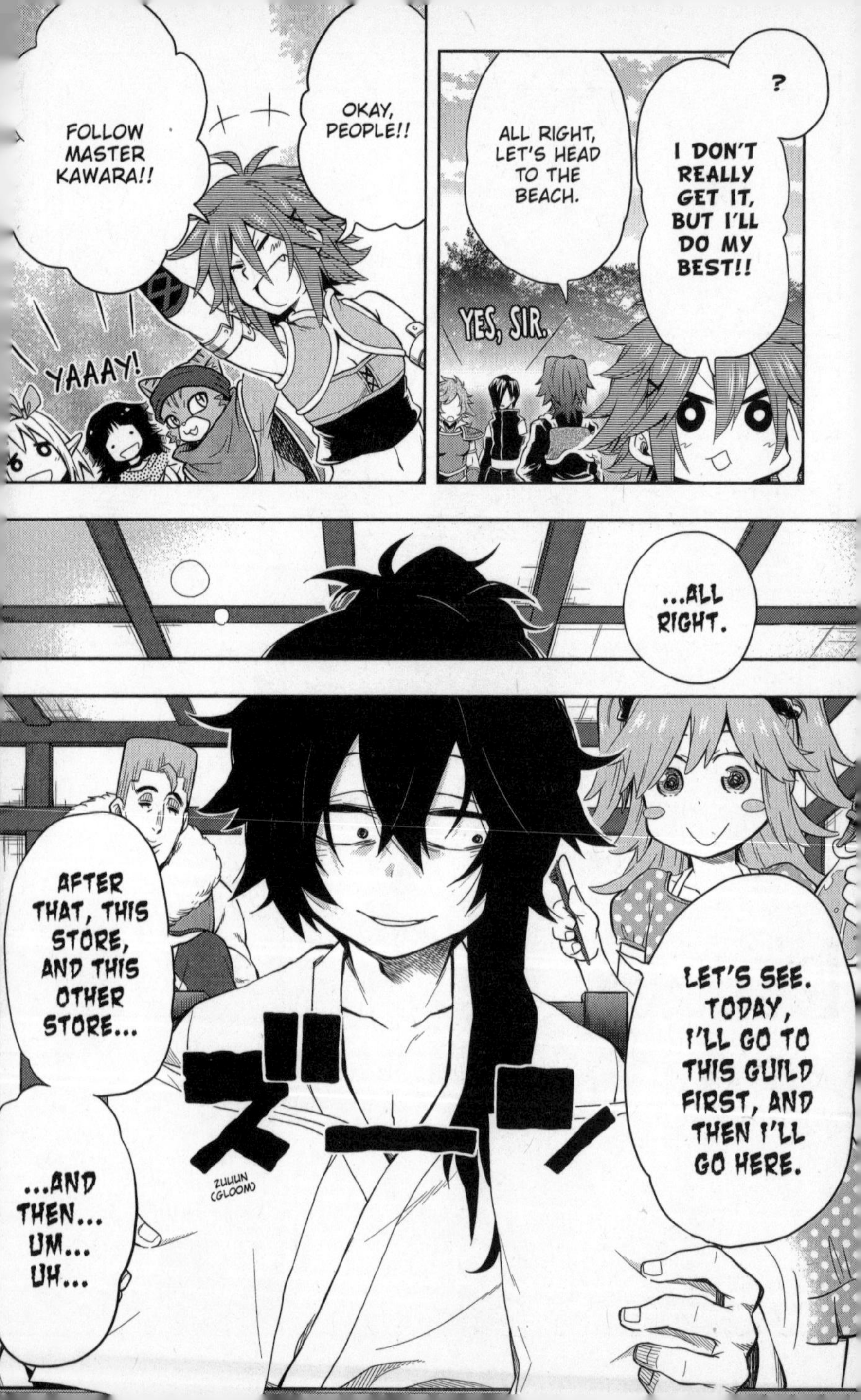
?
I DON'T REALLY GET IT, BUT I'LL DO MY BEST!!
ALL RIGHT, LET'S HEAD TO THE BEACH.
YES, SIR.
OKAY, PEOPLE!!
FOLLOW MASTER KAWARA!!
YAAAY!
...ALL RIGHT.
LET'S SEE. TODAY, I'LL GO TO THIS GUILD FIRST, AND THEN I'LL GO HERE.
AFTER THAT, THIS STORE, AND THIS OTHER STORE...
ZUUUN (GLOOM)
...AND THEN... UM... UH...

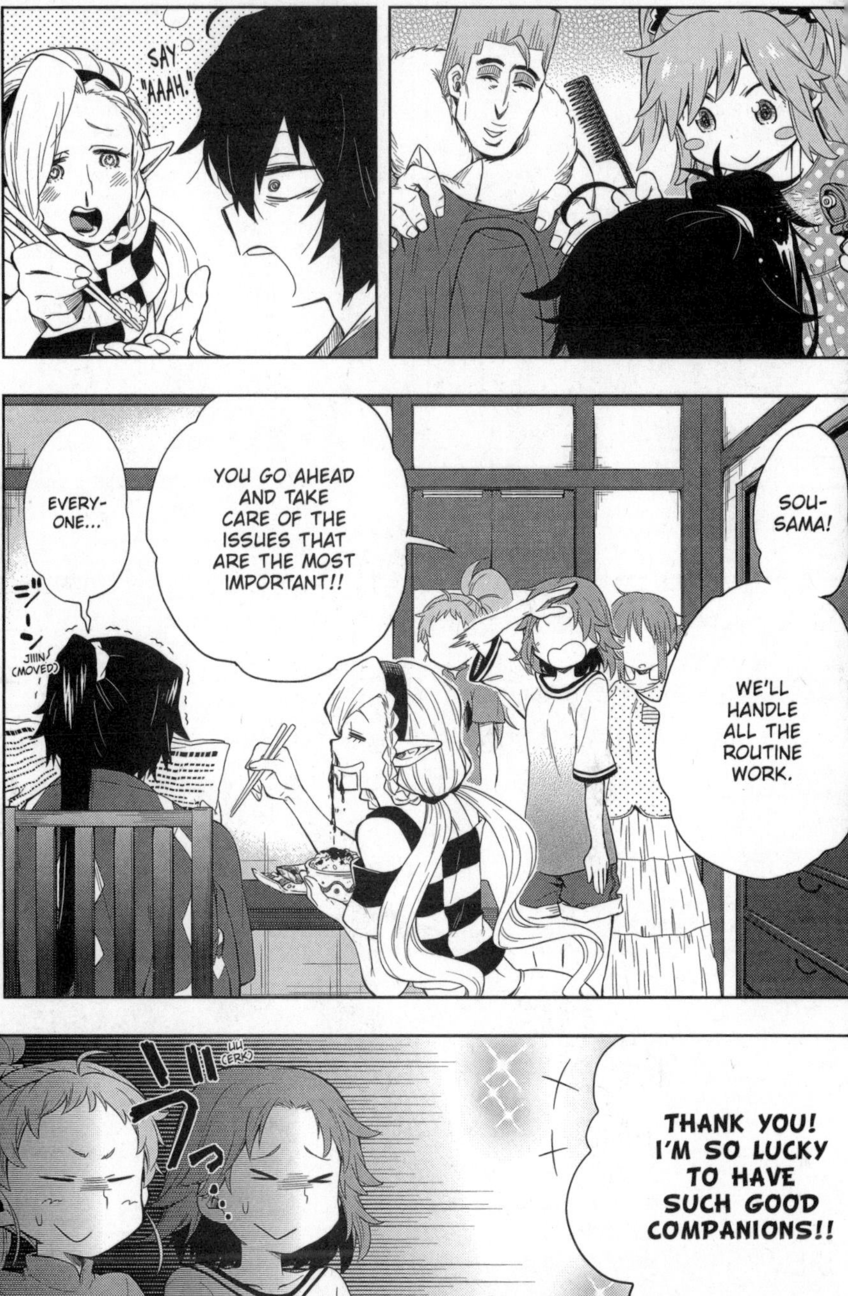
SAY "AAAH."
SOU-SAMA!
WE'LL HANDLE ALL THE ROUTINE WORK.
YOU GO AHEAD AND TAKE CARE OF THE ISSUES THAT ARE THE MOST IMPORTANT!!
EVERYONE...
JIIIN (MOVED)
THANK YOU! I'M SO LUCKY TO HAVE SUCH GOOD COMPANIONS!!
(ERK)

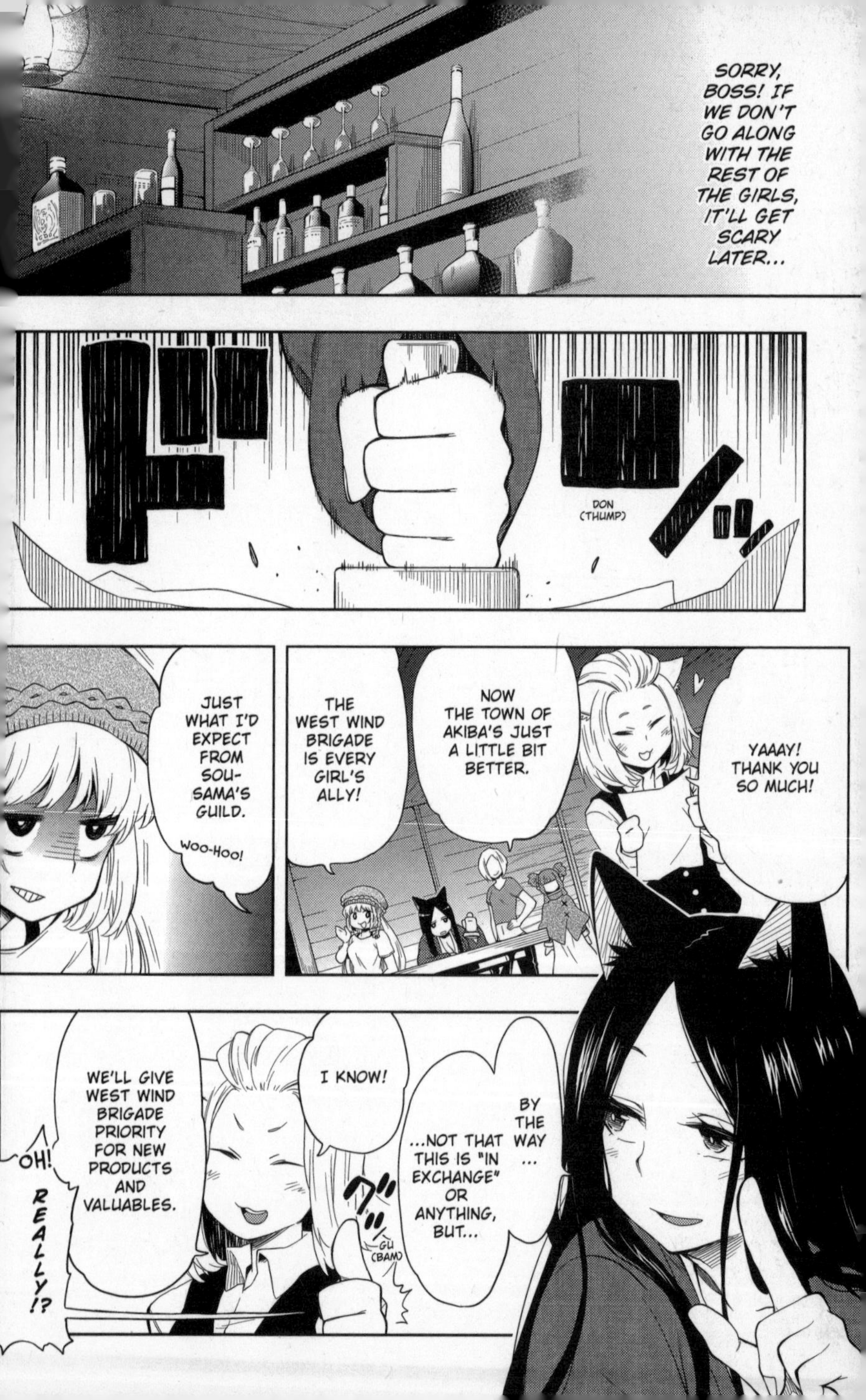
SORRY, BOSS! IF WE DON'T GO ALONG WITH THE REST OF THE GIRLS, IT'LL GET SCARY LATER...
DON (THUMP)
YAAAY! THANK YOU SO MUCH!
NOW THE TOWN OF AKIBA'S JUST A LITTLE BIT BETTER.
THE WEST WIND BRIGADE IS EVERY GIRL'S ALLY!
JUST WHAT I'D EXPECT FROM SOU-SAMA'S GUILD.
WOO-HOO!
BY THE WAY...
...NOT THAT THIS IS "IN EXCHANGE" OR ANYTHING, BUT...
I KNOW!
GU (BAM)
WE'LL GIVE WEST WIND BRIGADE PRIORITY FOR NEW PRODUCTS AND VALUABLES.
OH! REALLY!?

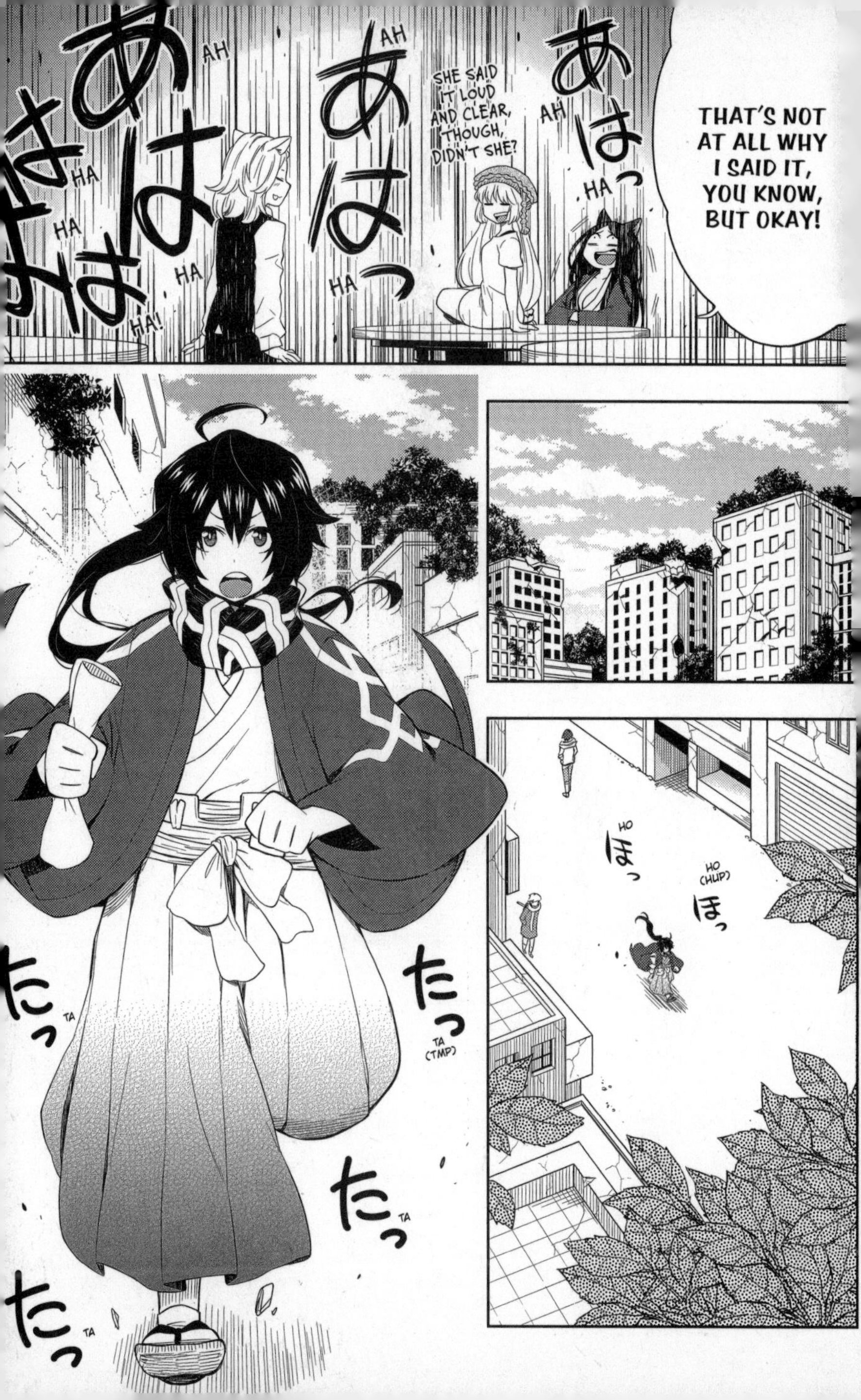
THAT'S NOT AT ALL WHY I SAID IT, YOU KNOW, BUT OKAY!
あはっ
AH HA
SHE SAID IT LOUD AND CLEAR, THOUGH, DIDN'T SHE?
あはっ
AH HA
あははは
AH HA HA HA HA!
ほっ
HO
ほっ
HO (HUP)
たっ
TA (TMP)
たっ
TA
たっ
TA
たっ
TA

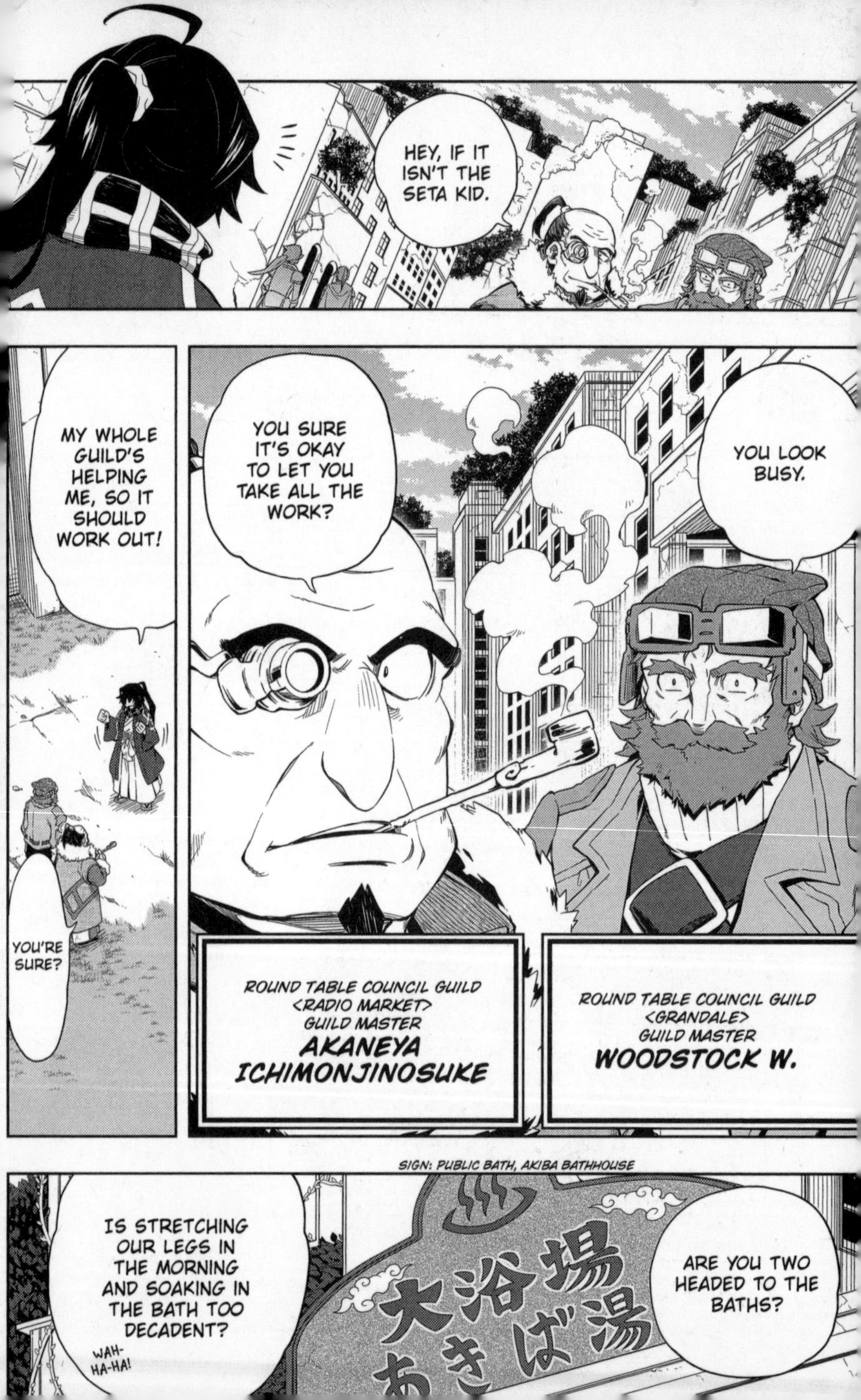
HEY, IF IT ISN'T THE SETA KID.
YOU LOOK BUSY.
YOU SURE IT'S OKAY TO LET YOU TAKE ALL THE WORK?
ROUND TABLE COUNCIL GUILD <GRANDALE> GUILD MASTER WOODSTOCK W.
ROUND TABLE COUNCIL GUILD <RADIO MARKET> GUILD MASTER AKANEYA ICHIMONJINOSUKE
MY WHOLE GUILD'S HELPING ME, SO IT SHOULD WORK OUT!
YOU'RE SURE?
SIGN: PUBLIC BATH, AKIBA BATHHOUSE
ARE YOU TWO HEADED TO THE BATHS?
大浴場
あきば湯
IS STRETCHING OUR LEGS IN THE MORNING AND SOAKING IN THE BATH TOO DECADENT?
WAH-HA-HA!

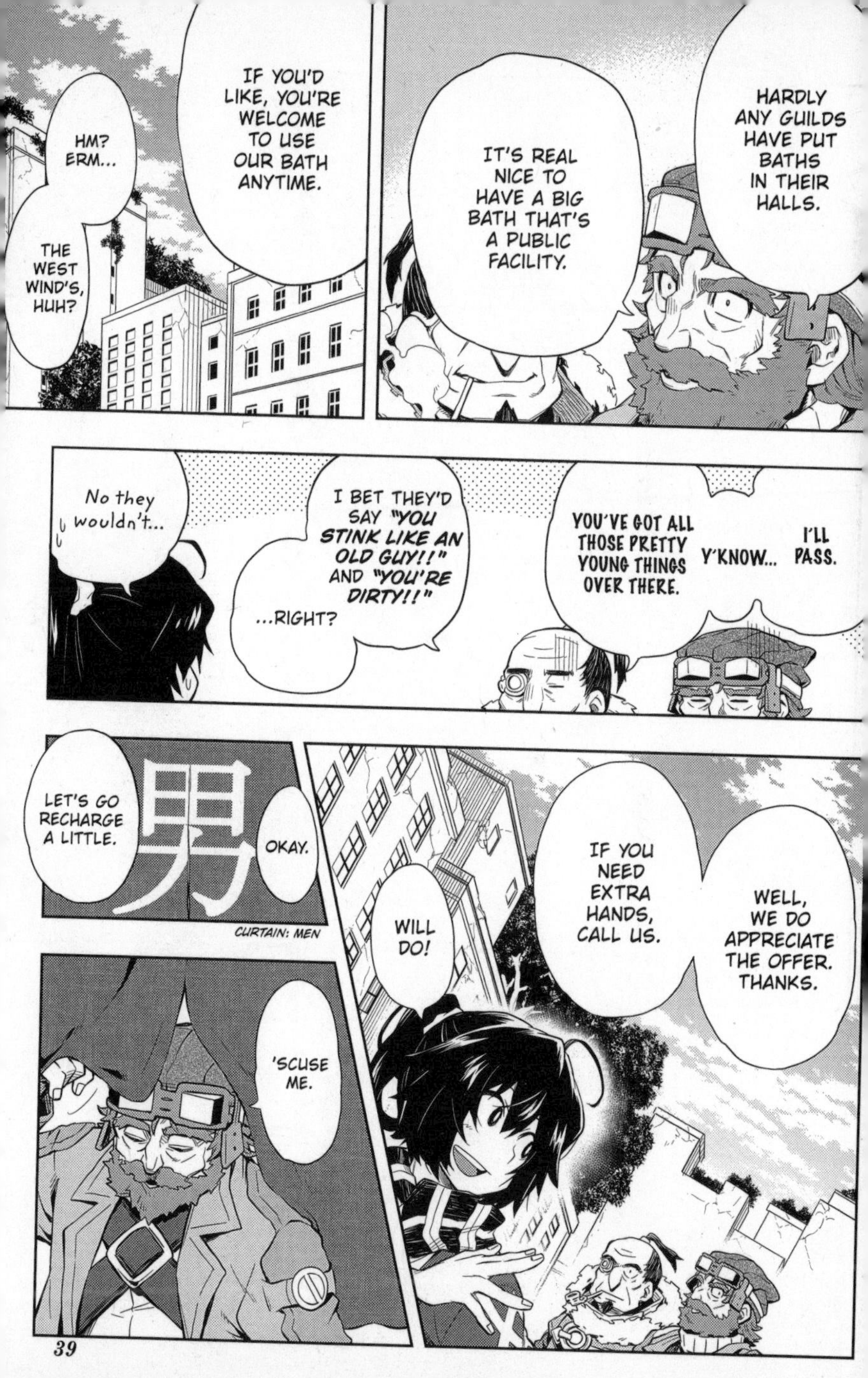
HARDLY ANY GUILDS HAVE PUT BATHS IN THEIR HALLS.
IT'S REAL NICE TO HAVE A BIG BATH THAT'S A PUBLIC FACILITY.
IF YOU'D LIKE, YOU'RE WELCOME TO USE OUR BATH ANYTIME.
HM? ERM...
THE WEST WIND'S, HUH?
I'LL PASS.
Y'KNOW...
YOU'VE GOT ALL THOSE PRETTY YOUNG THINGS OVER THERE.
I BET THEY'D SAY "YOU STINK LIKE AN OLD GUY!!" AND "YOU'RE DIRTY!!"
...RIGHT?
No they wouldn't...
WELL, WE DO APPRECIATE THE OFFER. THANKS.
IF YOU NEED EXTRA HANDS, CALL US.
WILL DO!
OKAY.
LET'S GO RECHARGE A LITTLE.
男
CURTAIN: MEN
'SCUSE ME.

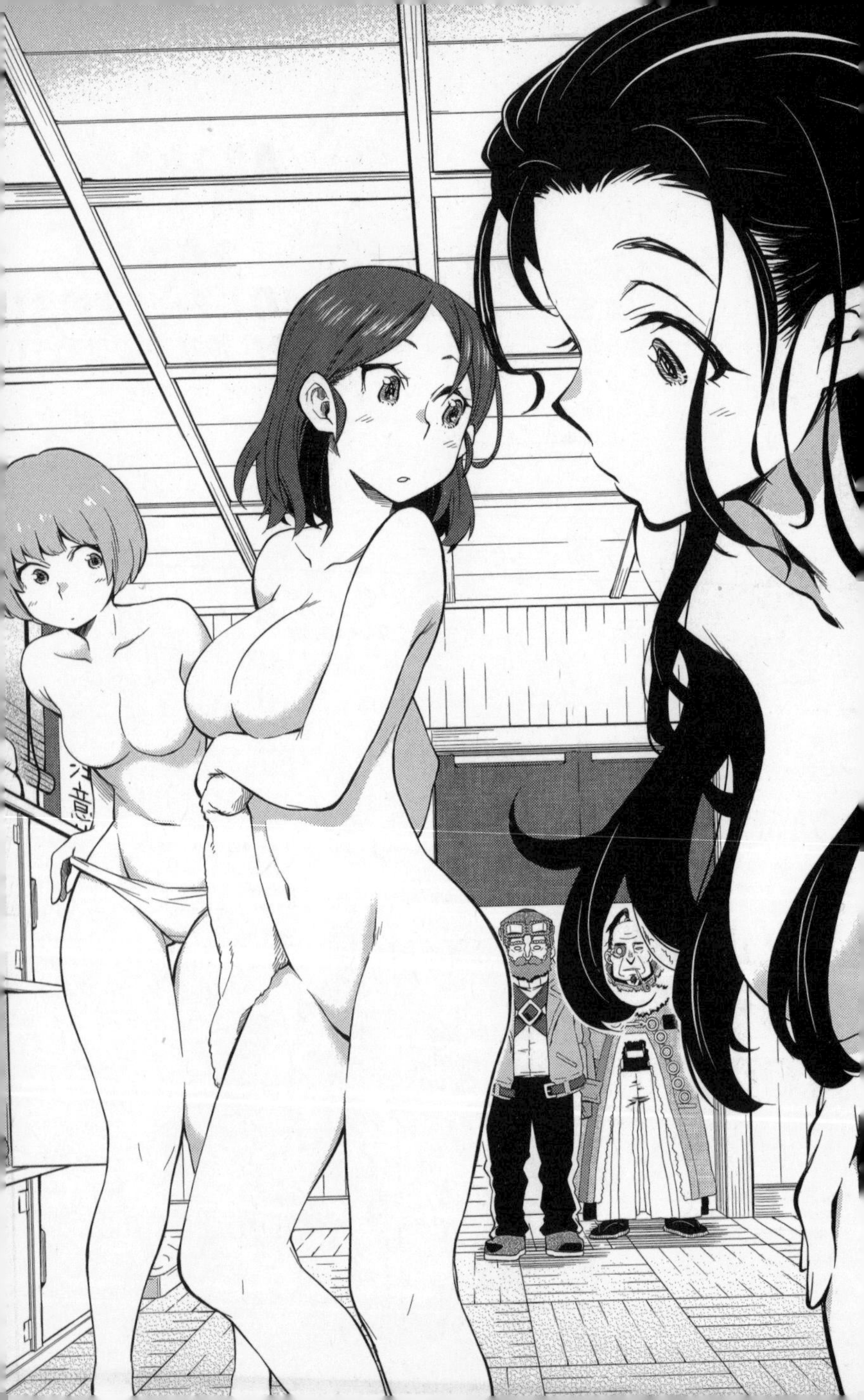

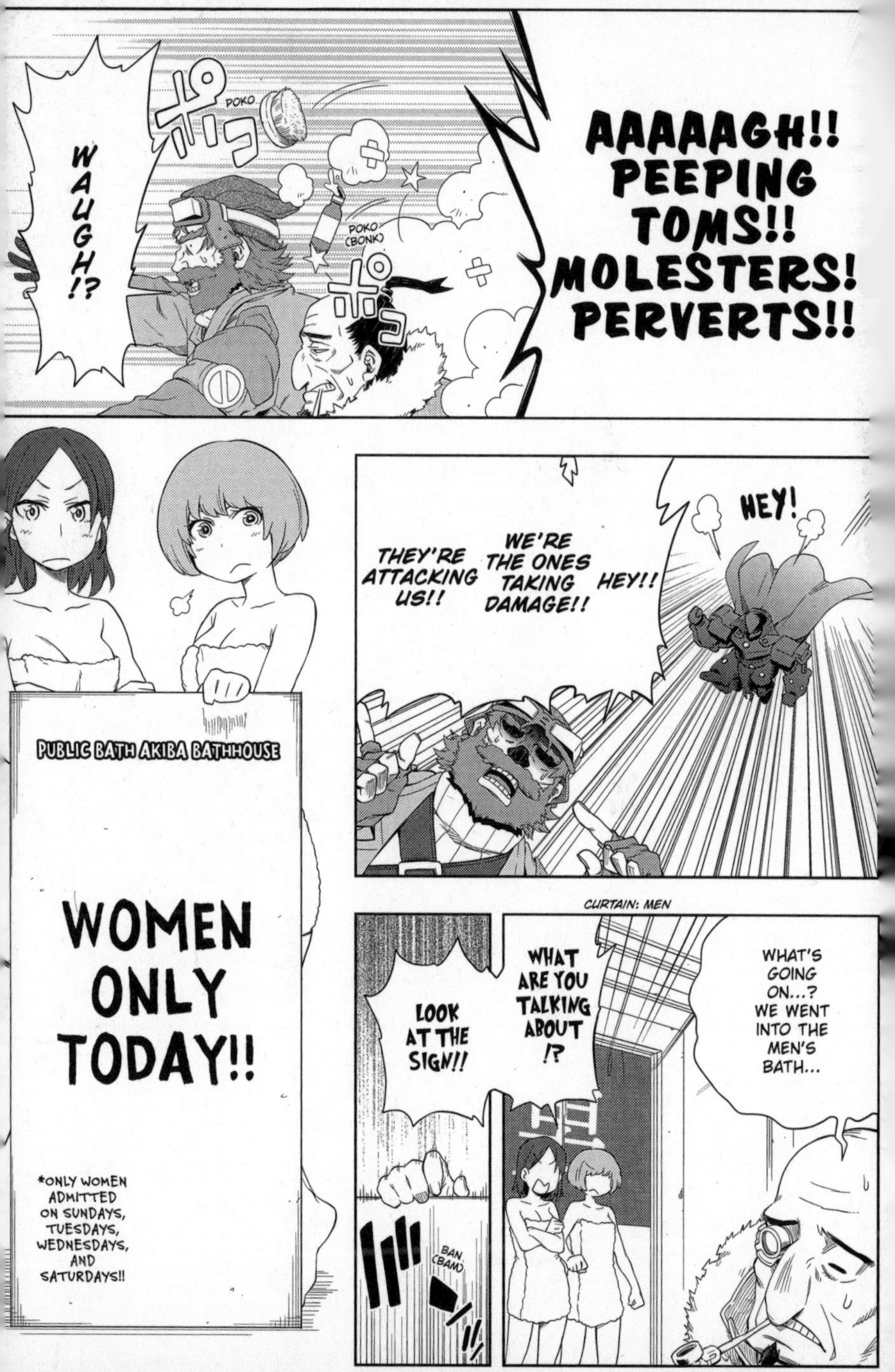
AAAAAGH!! PEEPING TOMS!! MOLESTERS! PERVERTS!!
ポコ
POKO (BONK)
ポコ
POKO
WAUGH!?
HEY!
HEY!!
WE'RE THE ONES TAKING DAMAGE!!
THEY'RE ATTACKING US!!
CURTAIN: MEN
WHAT'S GOING ON...? WE WENT INTO THE MEN'S BATH...
WHAT ARE YOU TALKING ABOUT!?
LOOK AT THE SIGN!!
BAN (BAM)
PUBLIC BATH AKIBA BATHHOUSE
WOMEN ONLY TODAY!!
*ONLY WOMEN ADMITTED ON SUNDAYS, TUESDAYS, WEDNESDAYS, AND SATURDAYS!!

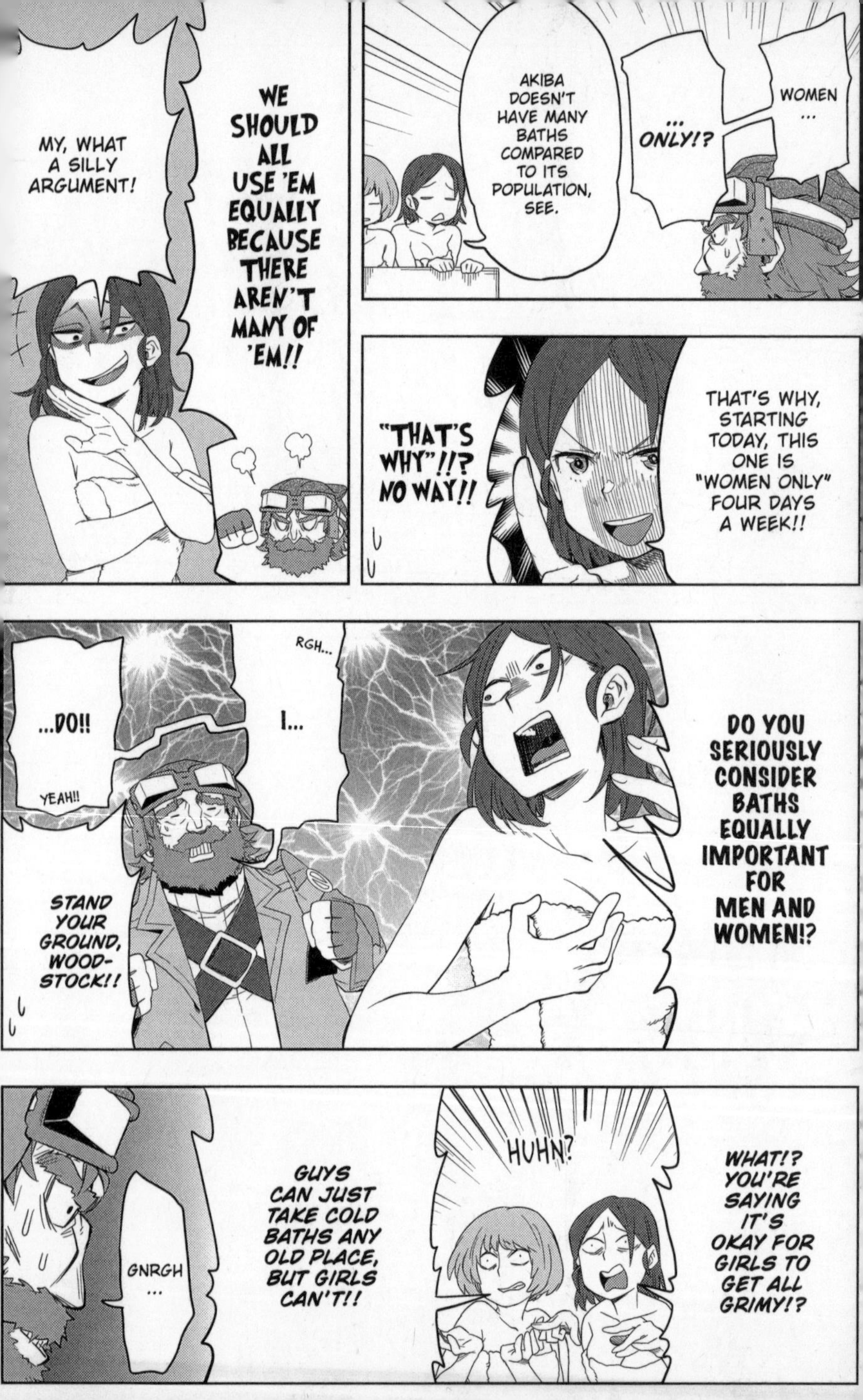
WOMEN ...
... ONLY!?
AKIBA DOESN'T HAVE MANY BATHS COMPARED TO ITS POPULATION, SEE.
THAT'S WHY, STARTING TODAY, THIS ONE IS "WOMEN ONLY" FOUR DAYS A WEEK!!
"THAT'S WHY"!!? NO WAY!!
WE SHOULD ALL USE 'EM EQUALLY BECAUSE THERE AREN'T MANY OF 'EM!!
MY, WHAT A SILLY ARGUMENT!
DO YOU SERIOUSLY CONSIDER BATHS EQUALLY IMPORTANT FOR MEN AND WOMEN!?
RGH...
I...
...DO!!
YEAH!!
STAND YOUR GROUND, WOODSTOCK!!
WHAT!? YOU'RE SAYING IT'S OKAY FOR GIRLS TO GET ALL GRIMY!?
HUHN?
GUYS CAN JUST TAKE COLD BATHS ANY OLD PLACE, BUT GIRLS CAN'T!!
GNRGH ...

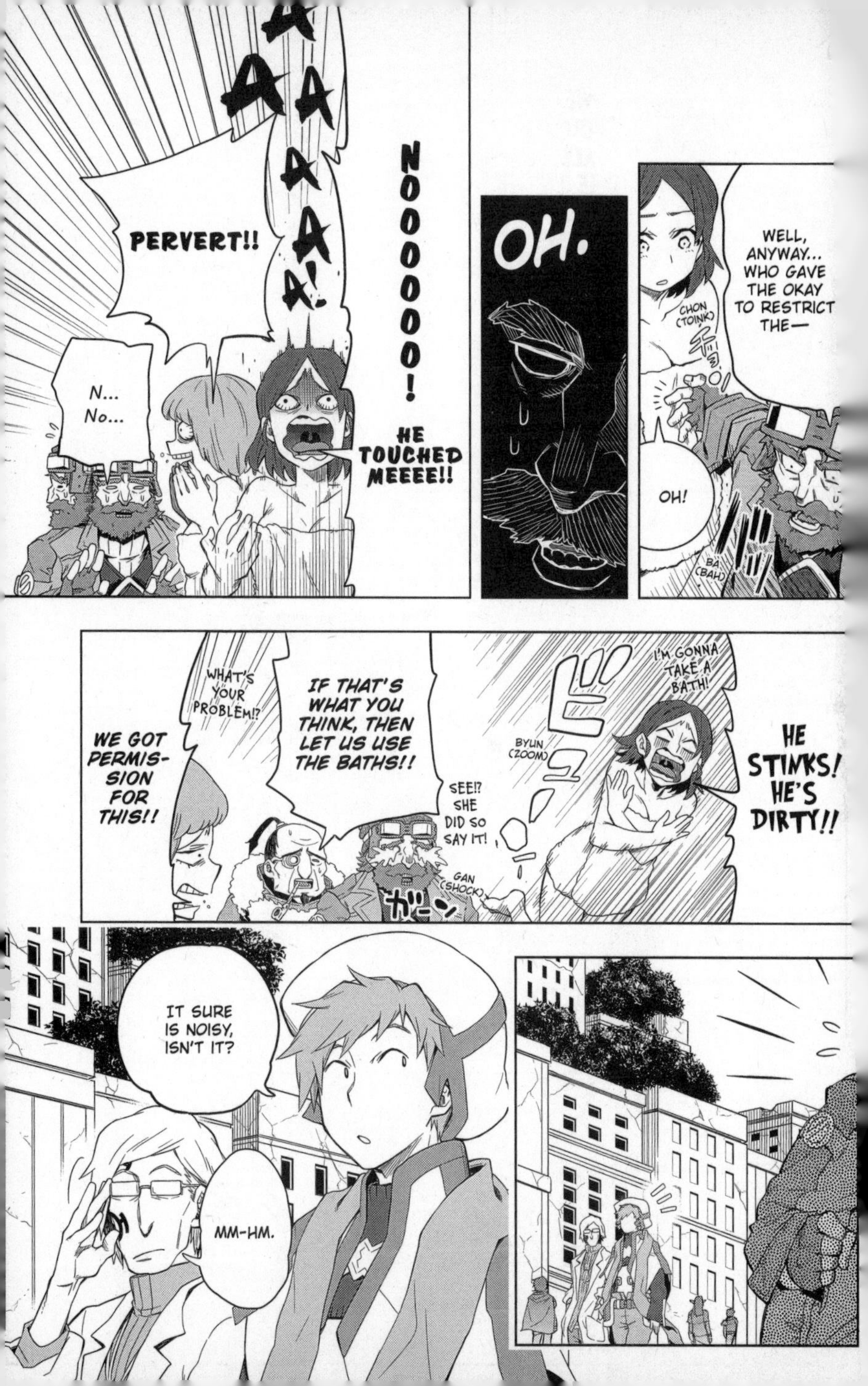

WELL, ANYWAY... WHO GAVE THE OKAY TO RESTRICT THE—
CHON (TOINK)
OH!
BA (BAH)
OH.
NOOOOOOO!
AAAAAA!
PERVERT!!
HE TOUCHED MEEEE!!
N... No...
HE STINKS! HE'S DIRTY!!
I'M GONNA TAKE A BATH!
BYUN (ZOOM)
SEE!? SHE DID SO SAY IT!
GAN (SHOCK)
IF THAT'S WHAT YOU THINK, THEN LET US USE THE BATHS!!
WHAT'S YOUR PROBLEM!?
WE GOT PERMIS-SION FOR THIS!!
IT SURE IS NOISY, ISN'T IT?
MM-HM.

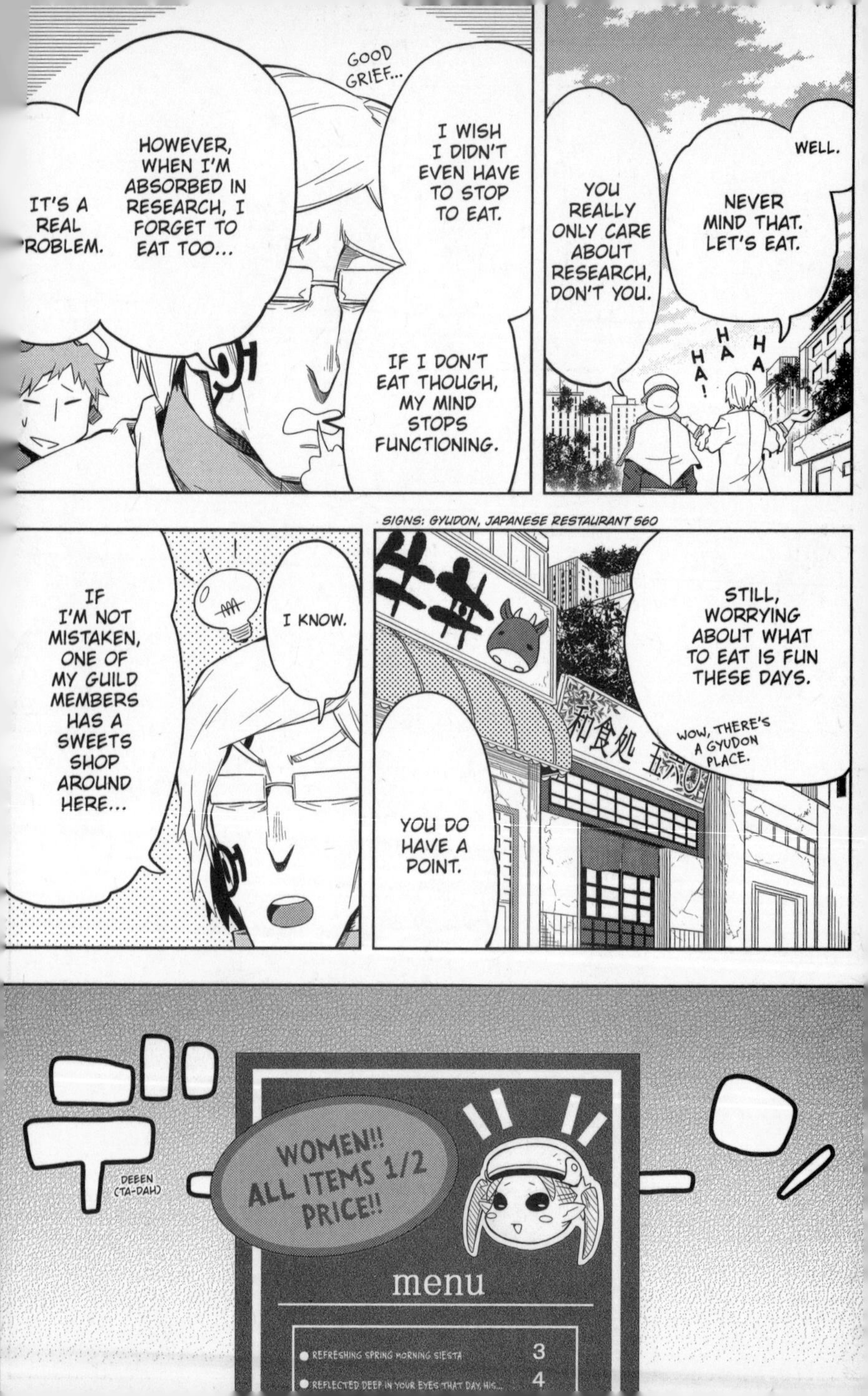
WELL.
NEVER MIND THAT. LET'S EAT.
YOU REALLY ONLY CARE ABOUT RESEARCH, DON'T YOU.
HA HA HA HA!
GOOD GRIEF...
I WISH I DIDN'T EVEN HAVE TO STOP TO EAT.
IF I DON'T EAT THOUGH, MY MIND STOPS FUNCTIONING.
HOWEVER, WHEN I'M ABSORBED IN RESEARCH, I FORGET TO EAT TOO...
IT'S A REAL PROBLEM.
SIGNS: GYUDON, JAPANESE RESTAURANT 560
STILL, WORRYING ABOUT WHAT TO EAT IS FUN THESE DAYS.
WOW, THERE'S A GYUDON PLACE.
牛丼
和食処
YOU DO HAVE A POINT.
I KNOW.
IF I'M NOT MISTAKEN, ONE OF MY GUILD MEMBERS HAS A SWEETS SHOP AROUND HERE...
DEEEN (TA-DAH)
WOMEN!! ALL ITEMS 1/2 PRICE!!
menu
REFRESHING SPRING MORNING SIESTA 3
REFLECTED DEEP IN YOUR EYES THAT DAY, HIS... 4

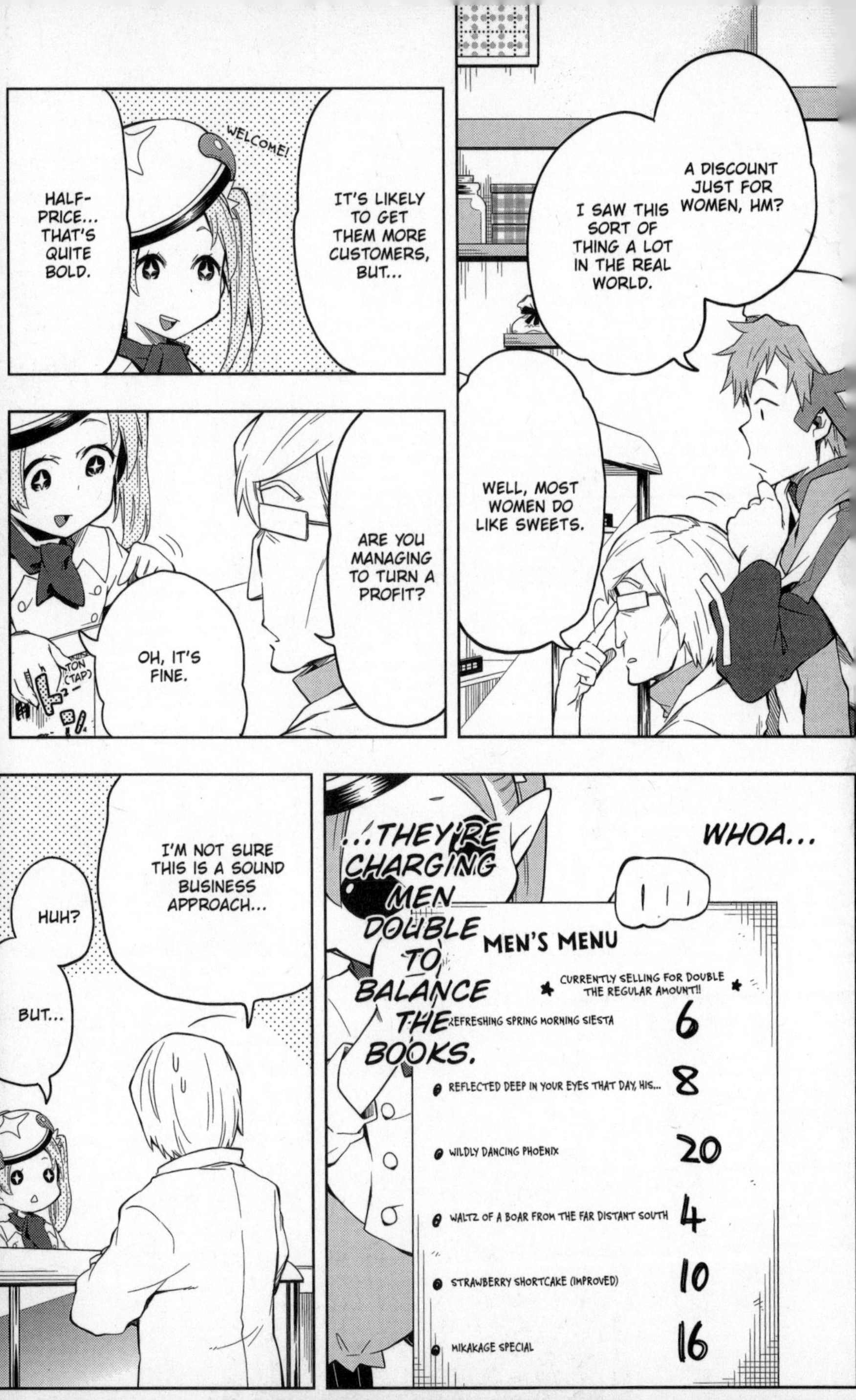
A DISCOUNT JUST FOR WOMEN, HM?
I SAW THIS SORT OF THING A LOT IN THE REAL WORLD.
WELL, MOST WOMEN DO LIKE SWEETS.
WELCOME!
IT'S LIKELY TO GET THEM MORE CUSTOMERS, BUT...
HALF-PRICE... THAT'S QUITE BOLD.
ARE YOU MANAGING TO TURN A PROFIT?
TON (TAP)
OH, IT'S FINE.
WHOA...
...THEY'RE CHARGING MEN DOUBLE TO BALANCE THE BOOKS.
MEN'S MENU
CURRENTLY SELLING FOR DOUBLE THE REGULAR AMOUNT!!
REFRESHING SPRING MORNING SIESTA 6
REFLECTED DEEP IN YOUR EYES THAT DAY, HIS... 8
WILDLY DANCING PHOENIX 20
WALTZ OF A BOAR FROM THE FAR DISTANT SOUTH 4
STRAWBERRY SHORTCAKE (IMPROVED) 10
MIKAKAGE SPECIAL 16
I'M NOT SURE THIS IS A SOUND BUSINESS APPROACH...
HUH?
BUT...

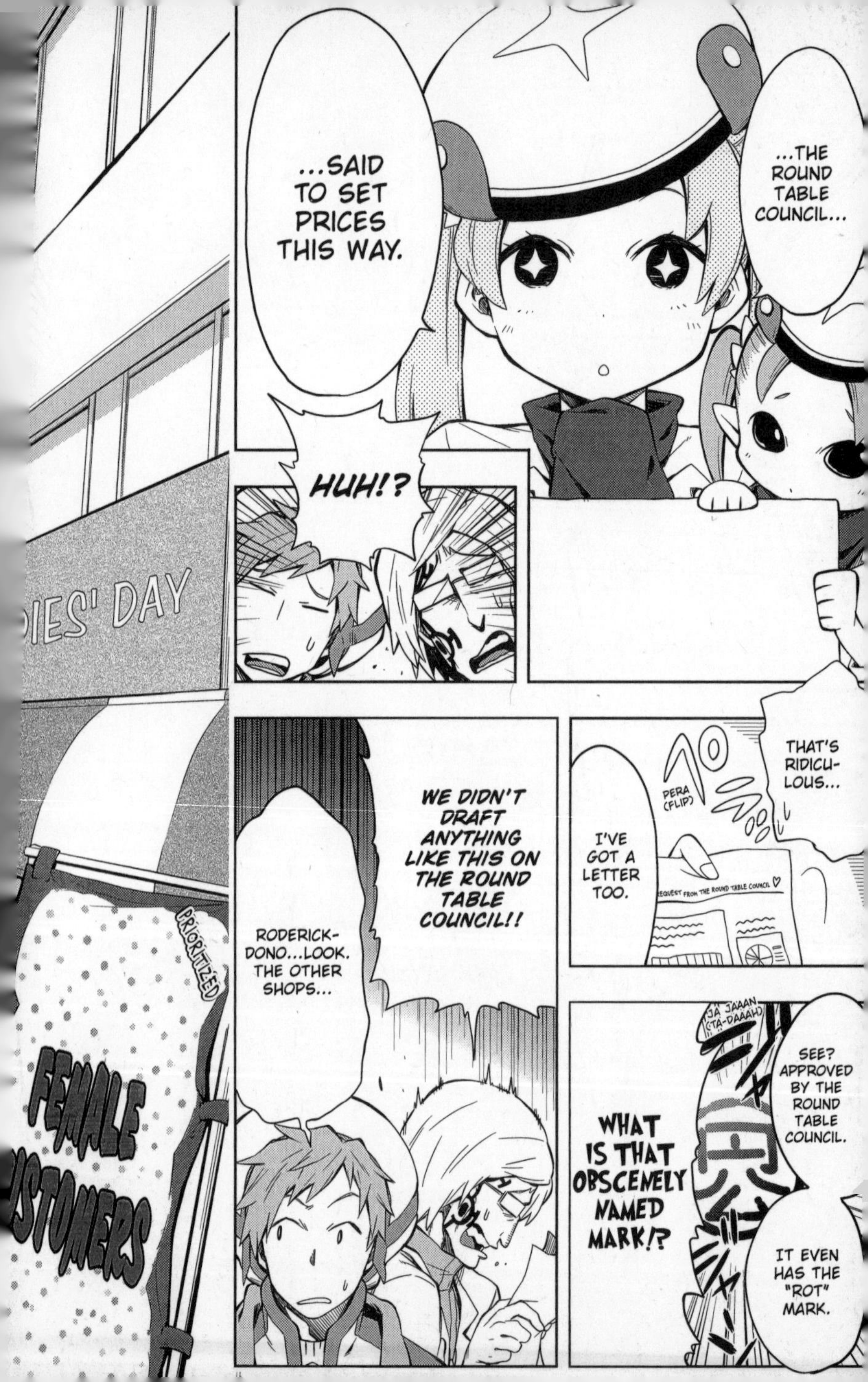
...THE ROUND TABLE COUNCIL...
...SAID TO SET PRICES THIS WAY.
HUH!?
THAT'S RIDICULOUS...
PERA (FLIP)
I'VE GOT A LETTER TOO.
REQUEST FROM THE ROUND TABLE COUNCIL ♡
JA JAAAN (STA-DAAAH)
SEE? APPROVED BY THE ROUND TABLE COUNCIL.
IT EVEN HAS THE "ROT" MARK.
WHAT IS THAT OBSCENELY NAMED MARK!?
WE DIDN'T DRAFT ANYTHING LIKE THIS ON THE ROUND TABLE COUNCIL!!
RODERICK-DONO...LOOK. THE OTHER SHOPS...
DIES' DAY
PRIORITIZED
FEMALE
ISTOMERS

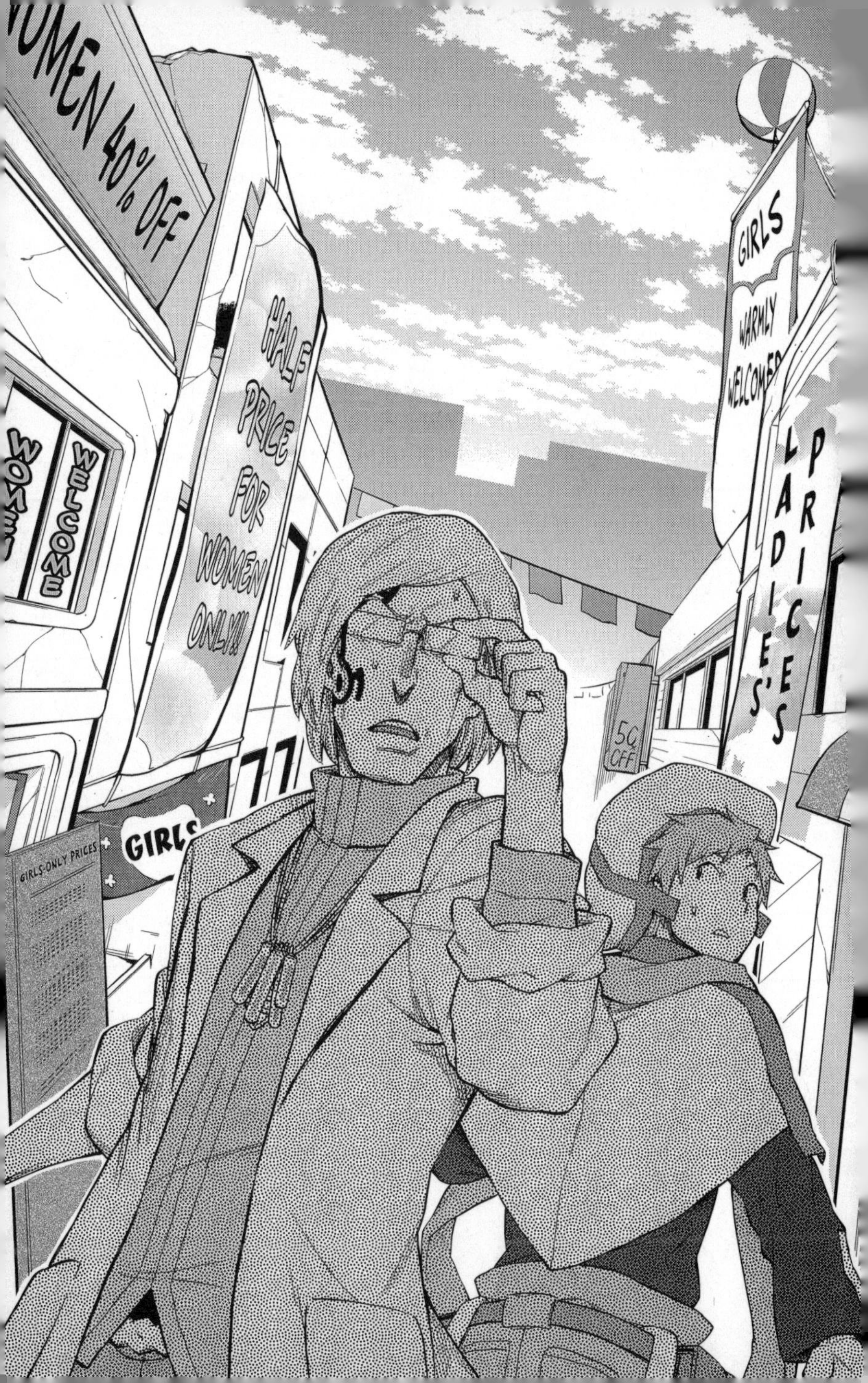

GIRLS WARMLY WELCOMED
LADIES' PRICES
50 OFF
HALF PRICE FOR WOMEN ONLY!!
WOMEN 40% OFF
WELCOME
GIRLS
GIRLS-ONLY PRICES

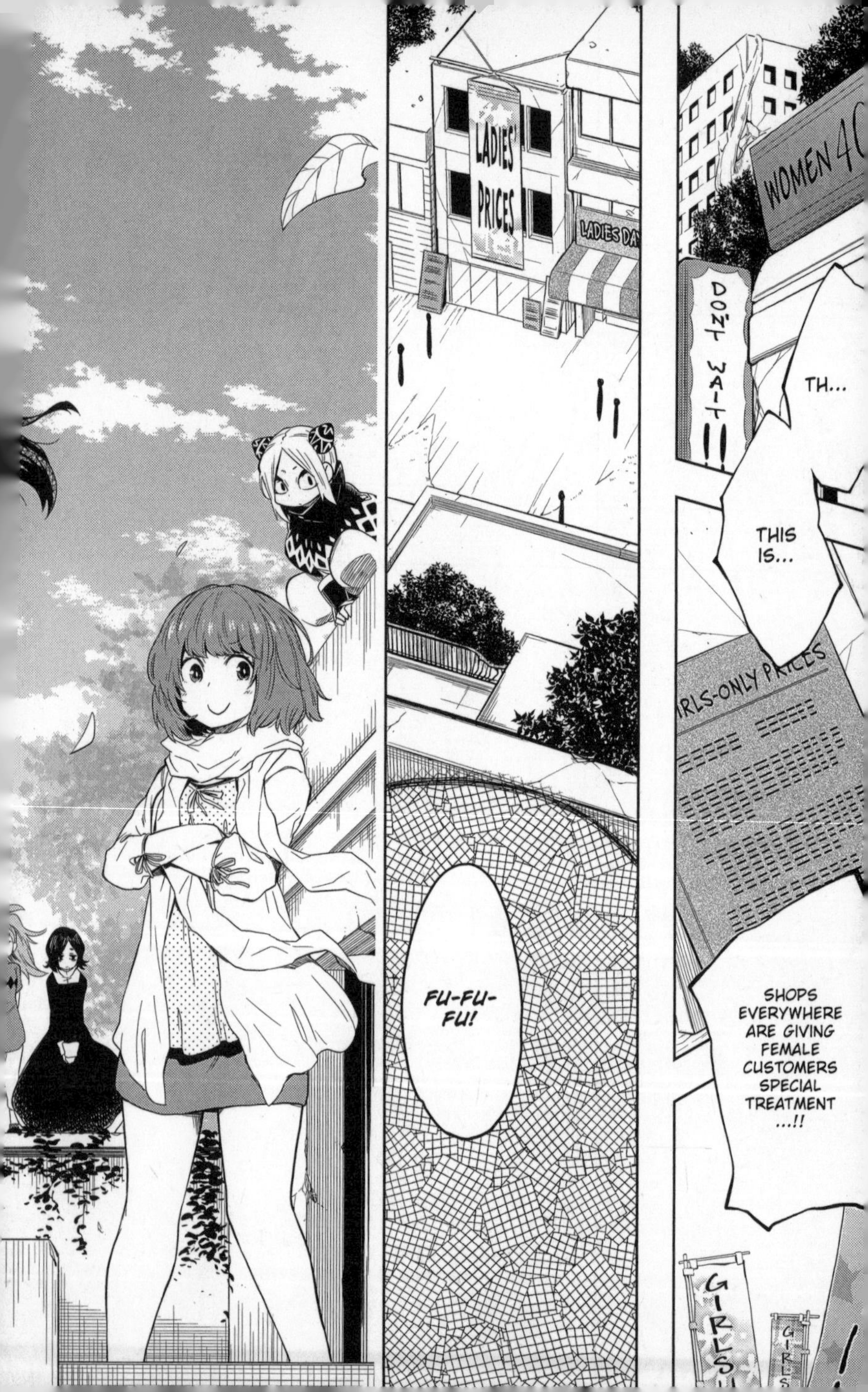
WOMEN 4
DON'T WAIT!!
TH...
THIS IS...
IRLS-ONLY PRICES
SHOPS EVERYWHERE ARE GIVING FEMALE CUSTOMERS SPECIAL TREATMENT ...!!
GIRLS
LADIES' PRICES
LADIES DA
FU-FU-FU!

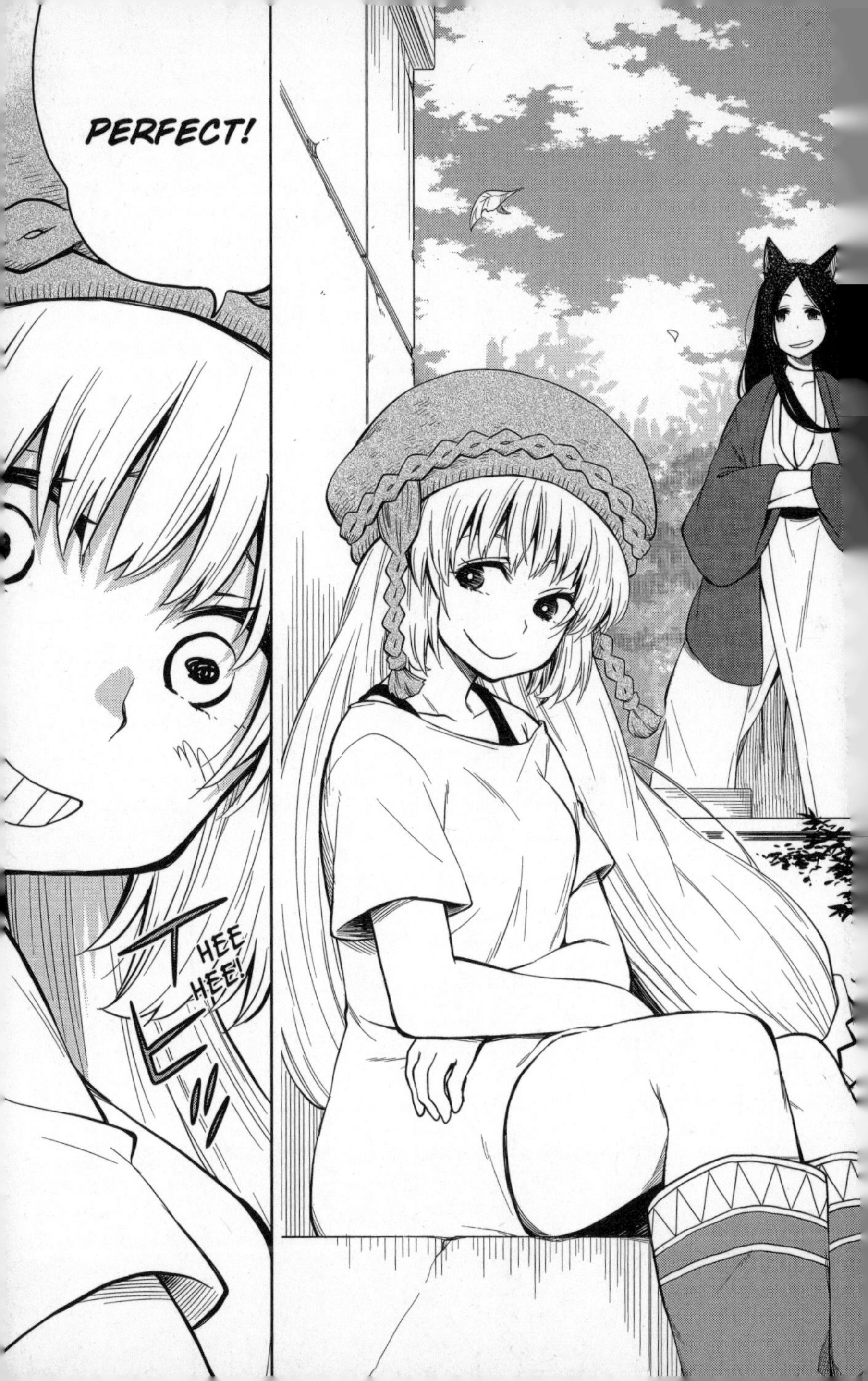
PERFECT!
HEE HEE!

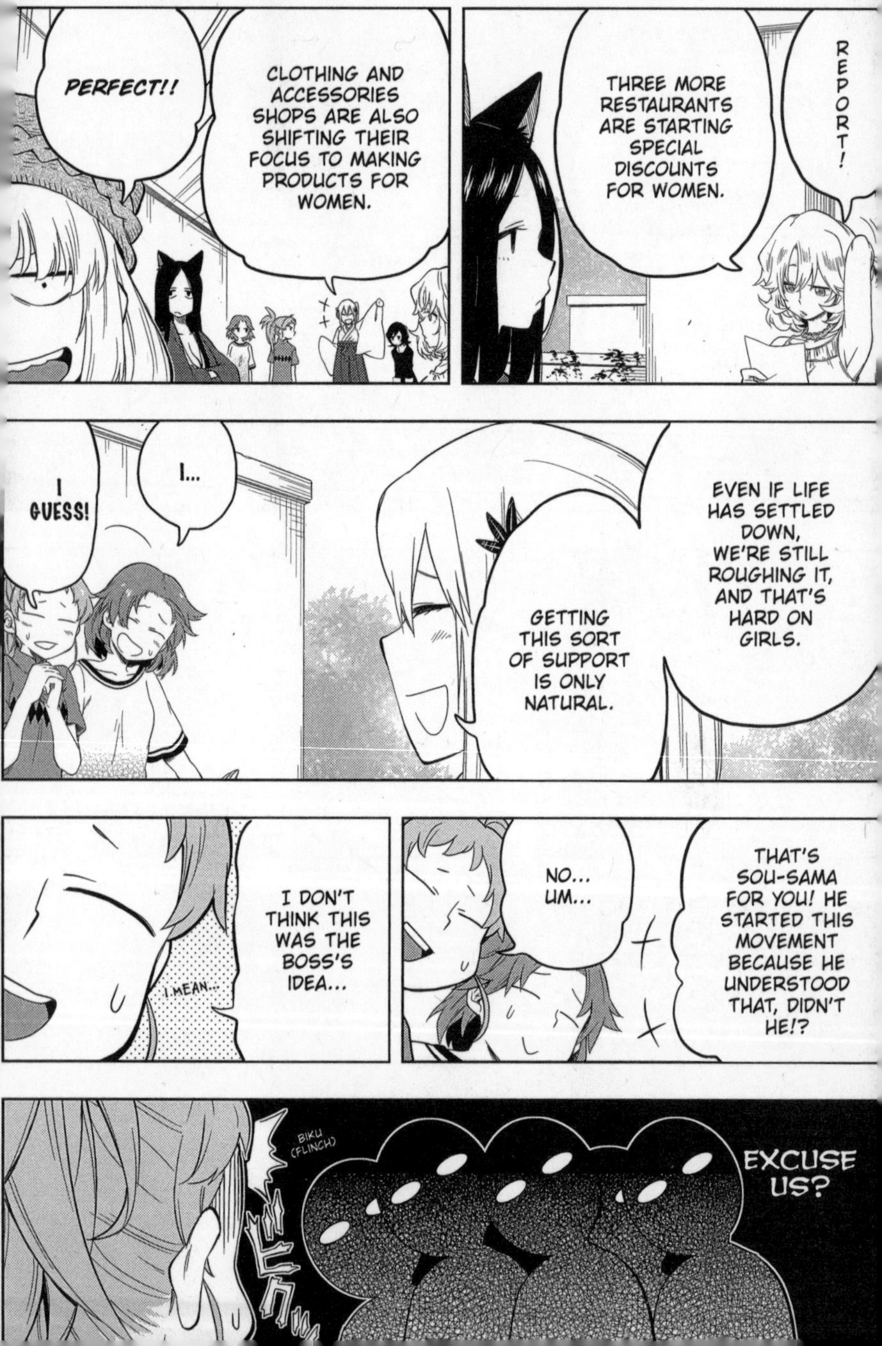
REPORT!
THREE MORE RESTAURANTS ARE STARTING SPECIAL DISCOUNTS FOR WOMEN.
CLOTHING AND ACCESSORIES SHOPS ARE ALSO SHIFTING THEIR FOCUS TO MAKING PRODUCTS FOR WOMEN.
PERFECT!!
EVEN IF LIFE HAS SETTLED DOWN, WE'RE STILL ROUGHING IT, AND THAT'S HARD ON GIRLS.
GETTING THIS SORT OF SUPPORT IS ONLY NATURAL.
I...
I GUESS!
THAT'S SOU-SAMA FOR YOU! HE STARTED THIS MOVEMENT BECAUSE HE UNDERSTOOD THAT, DIDN'T HE!?
NO... UM...
I DON'T THINK THIS WAS THE BOSS'S IDEA...
I MEAN...
EXCUSE US?
BIKU (FLINCH)

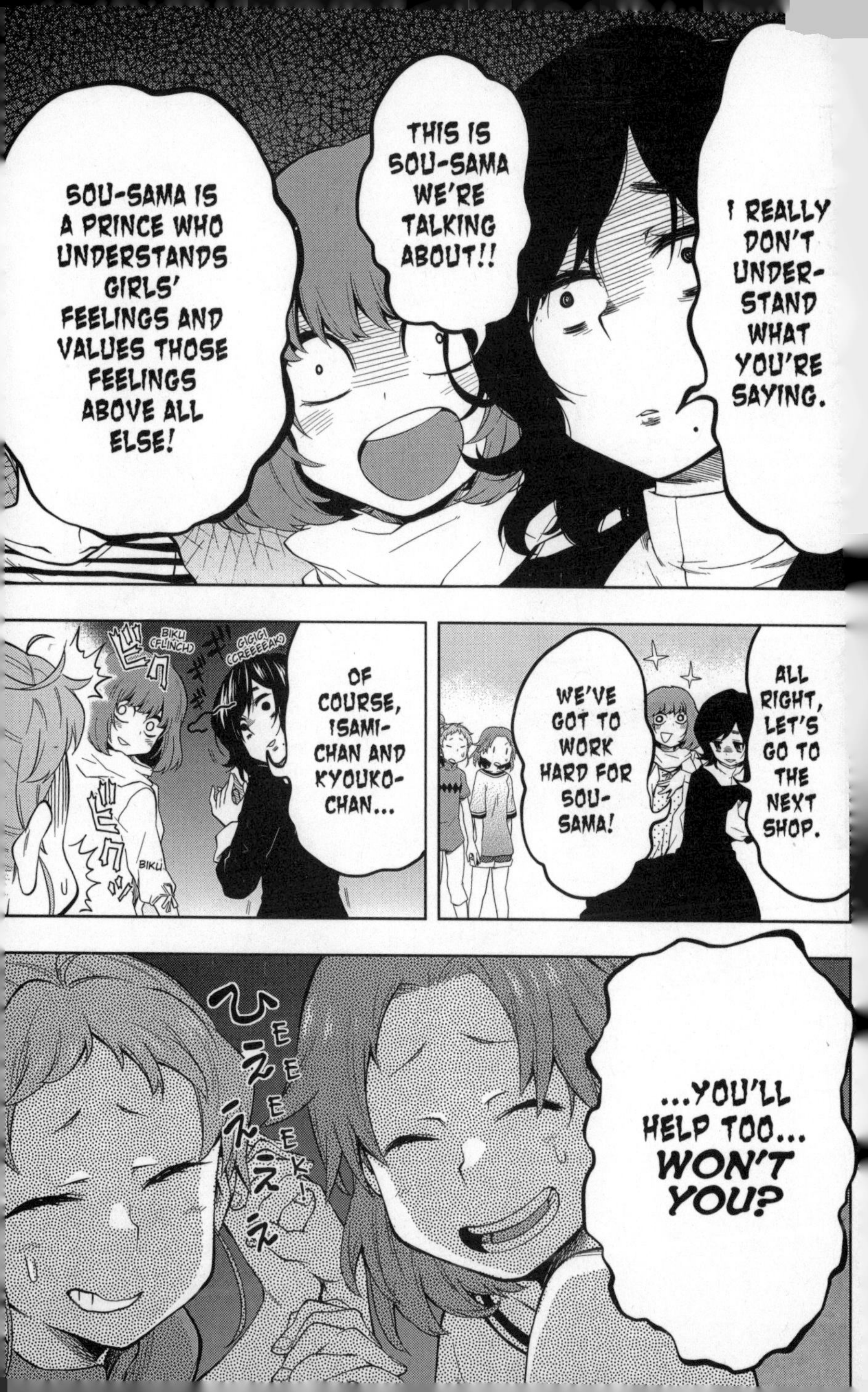
I REALLY DON'T UNDER-STAND WHAT YOU'RE SAYING.
THIS IS SOU-SAMA WE'RE TALKING ABOUT!!
SOU-SAMA IS A PRINCE WHO UNDERSTANDS GIRLS' FEELINGS AND VALUES THOSE FEELINGS ABOVE ALL ELSE!
ALL RIGHT, LET'S GO TO THE NEXT SHOP.
WE'VE GOT TO WORK HARD FOR SOU-SAMA!
OF COURSE, ISAMI-CHAN AND KYOUKO-CHAN...
GIGIGI (CREEEEAK)
BIKU (FLINCH)
BIKU
...YOU'LL HELP TOO... WON'T YOU?
EEEEK!

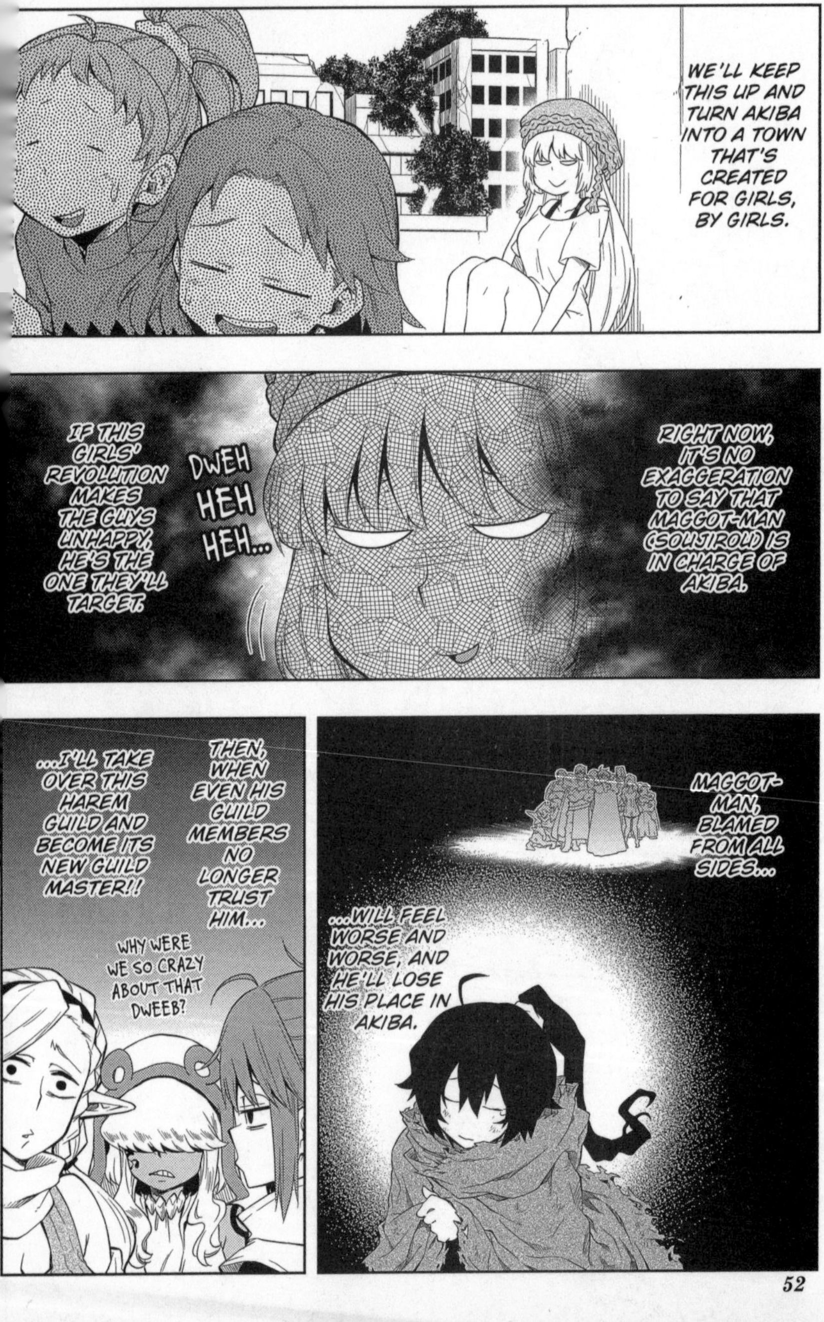

WE'LL KEEP THIS UP AND TURN AKIBA INTO A TOWN THAT'S CREATED FOR GIRLS, BY GIRLS.
RIGHT NOW, IT'S NO EXAGGERATION TO SAY THAT MAGGOT-MAN (SOUJIROU) IS IN CHARGE OF AKIBA.
DWEH HEH HEH...
IF THIS GIRLS' REVOLUTION MAKES THE GUYS UNHAPPY, HE'S THE ONE THEY'LL TARGET.
MAGGOT-MAN, BLAMED FROM ALL SIDES...
...WILL FEEL WORSE AND WORSE, AND HE'LL LOSE HIS PLACE IN AKIBA.
THEN, WHEN EVEN HIS GUILD MEMBERS NO LONGER TRUST HIM...
...I'LL TAKE OVER THIS HAREM GUILD AND BECOME ITS NEW GUILD MASTER!!
WHY WERE WE SO CRAZY ABOUT THAT DWEEB?

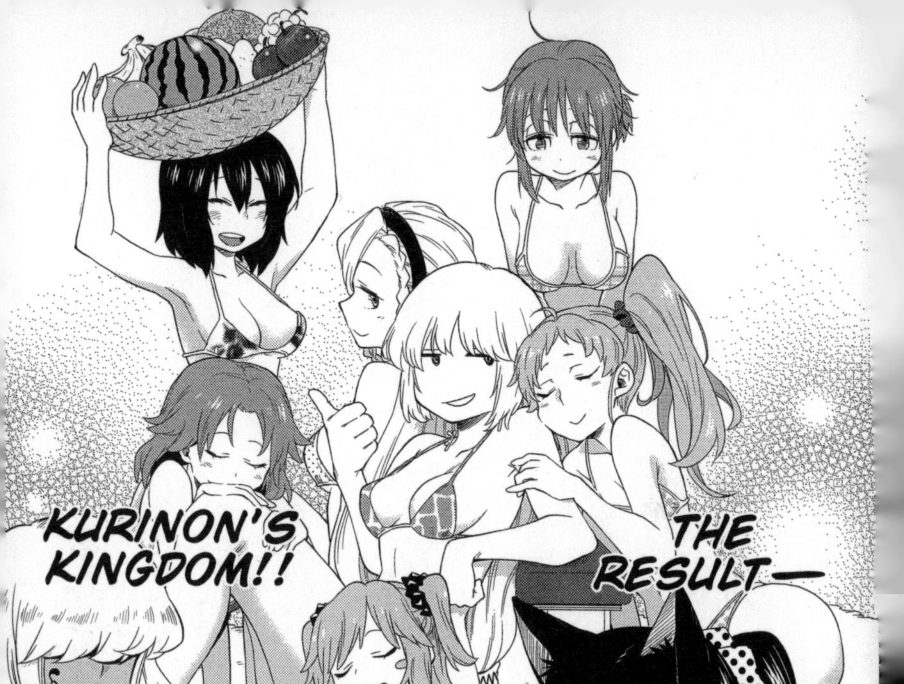
THE RESULT—
KURINON'S KINGDOM!!
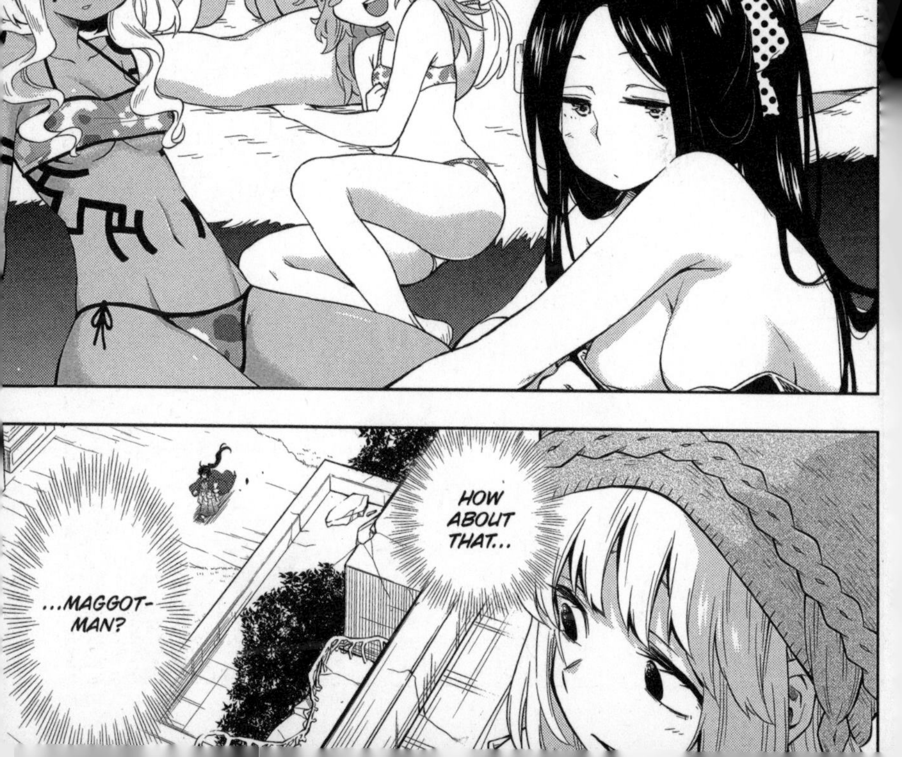
HOW ABOUT THAT...
...MAGGOT-MAN?

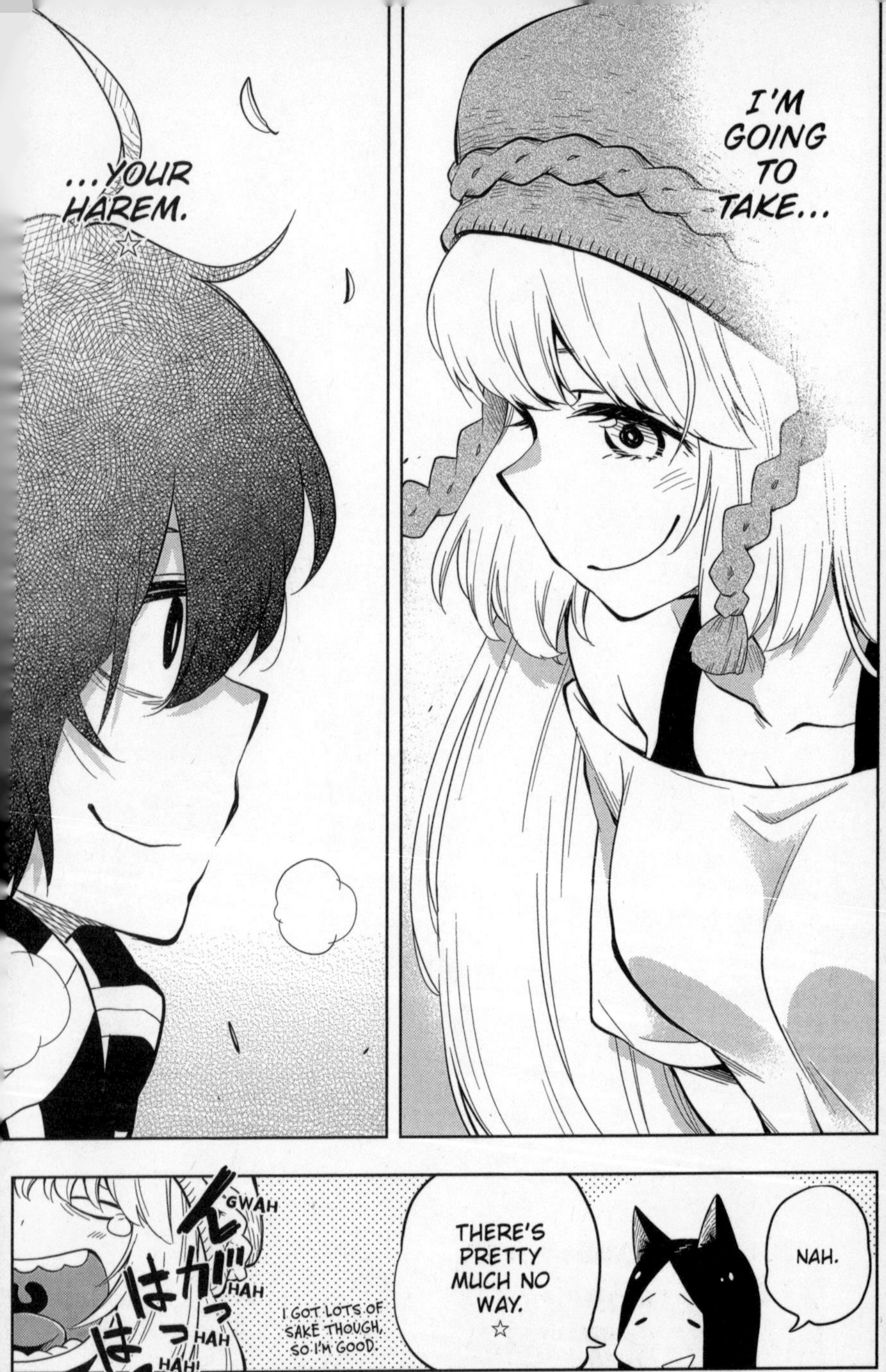
I'M GOING TO TAKE...
...YOUR HAREM.
NAH.
THERE'S PRETTY MUCH NO WAY. ☆
I GOT LOTS OF SAKE THOUGH, SO I'M GOOD.
GWAH HAH HAH HAH!

LOG HORIZON

THE WEST WIND BRIGADE

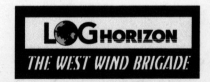

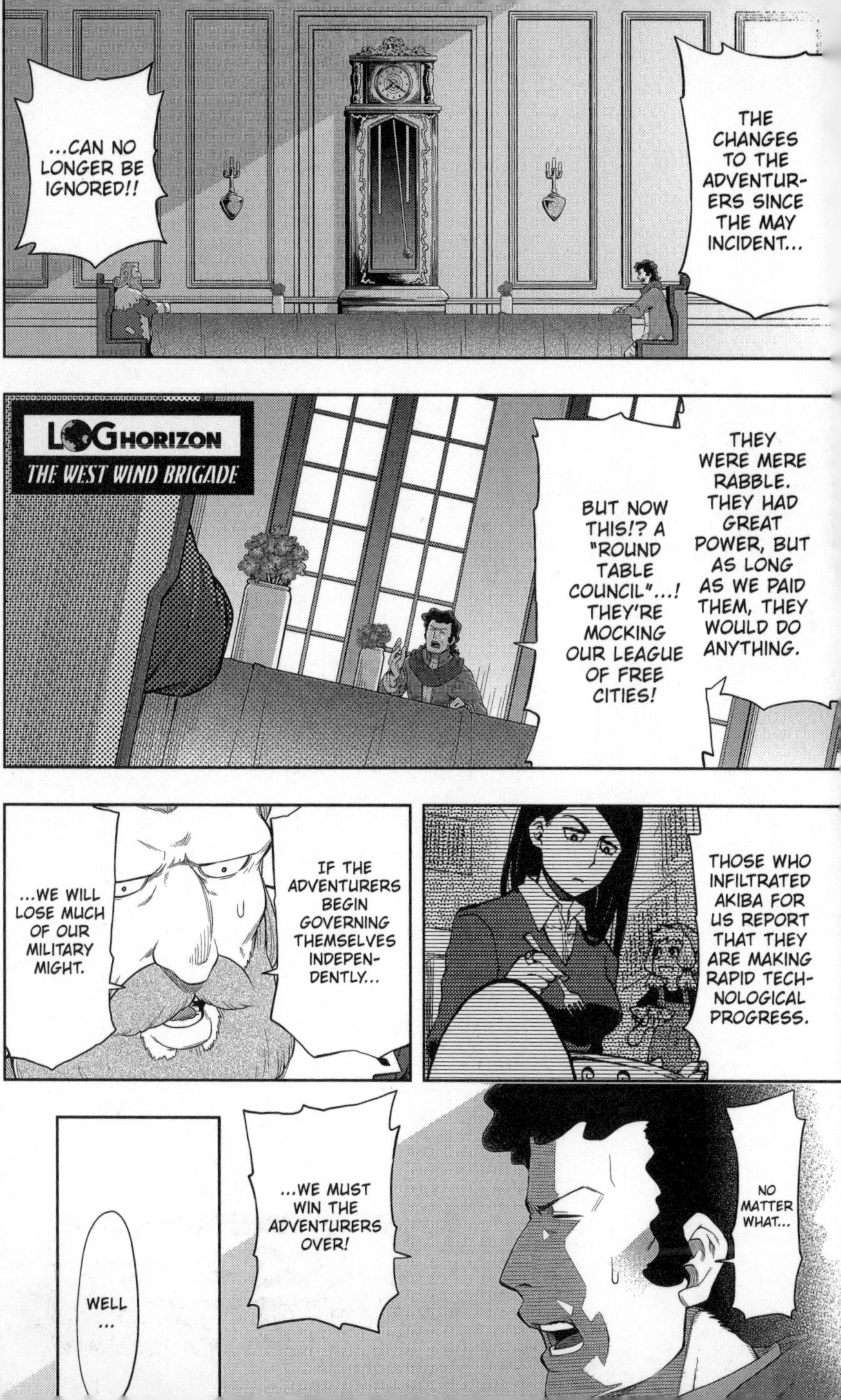
THE CHANGES TO THE ADVENTURERS SINCE THE MAY INCIDENT...
...CAN NO LONGER BE IGNORED!!
LOG HORIZON
THE WEST WIND BRIGADE
THEY WERE MERE RABBLE. THEY HAD GREAT POWER, BUT AS LONG AS WE PAID THEM, THEY WOULD DO ANYTHING.
BUT NOW THIS!? A "ROUND TABLE COUNCIL"...! THEY'RE MOCKING OUR LEAGUE OF FREE CITIES!
THOSE WHO INFILTRATED AKIBA FOR US REPORT THAT THEY ARE MAKING RAPID TECHNOLOGICAL PROGRESS.
IF THE ADVENTURERS BEGIN GOVERNING THEMSELVES INDEPENDENTLY...
...WE WILL LOSE MUCH OF OUR MILITARY MIGHT.
NO MATTER WHAT...
...WE MUST WIN THE ADVENTURERS OVER!
WELL ...

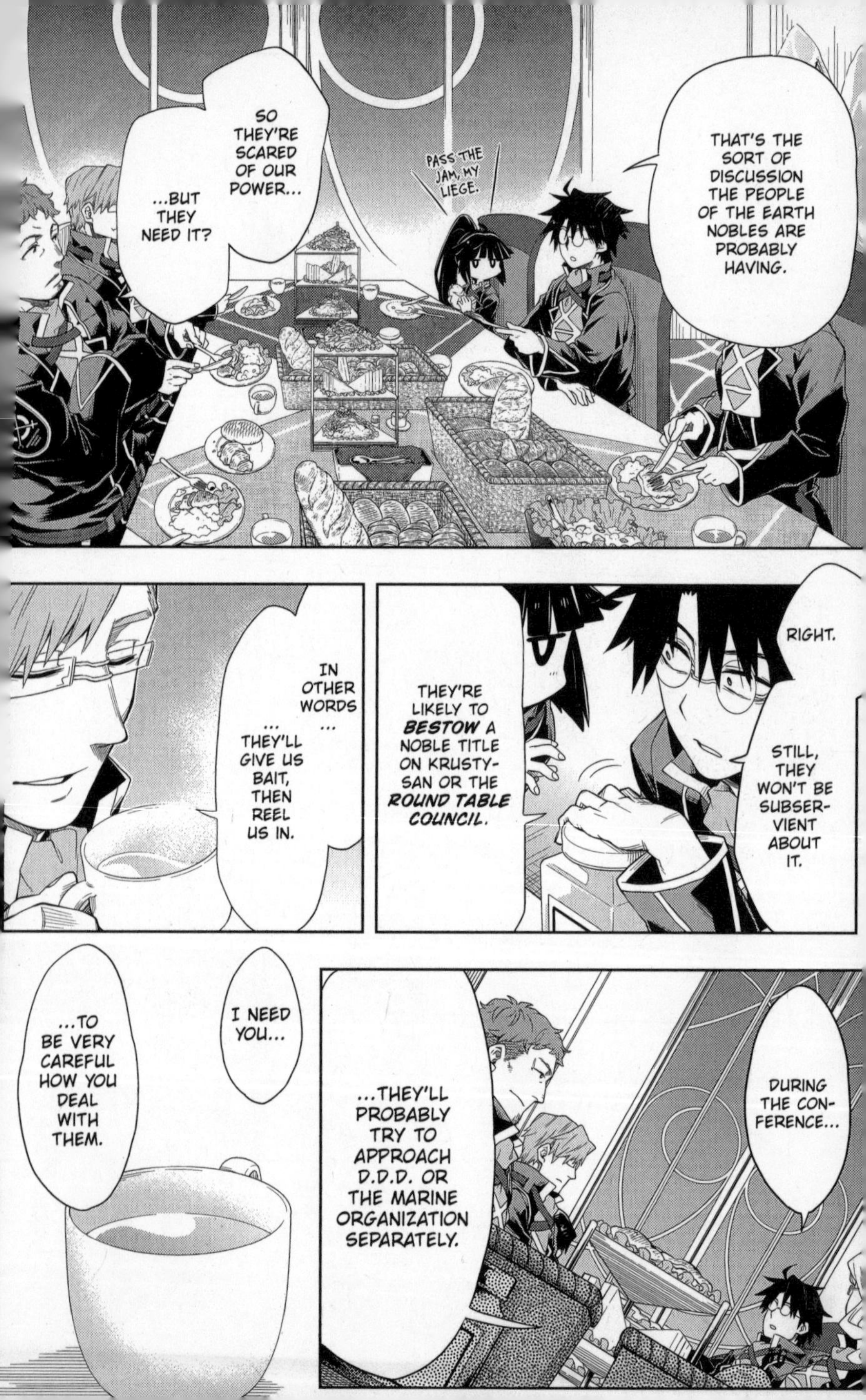
THAT'S THE SORT OF DISCUSSION THE PEOPLE OF THE EARTH NOBLES ARE PROBABLY HAVING.
PASS THE JAM, MY LIEGE.
SO THEY'RE SCARED OF OUR POWER...
...BUT THEY NEED IT?
RIGHT.
STILL, THEY WON'T BE SUBSER-VIENT ABOUT IT.
THEY'RE LIKELY TO **BESTOW** A NOBLE TITLE ON KRUSTY-SAN OR THE ***ROUND TABLE COUNCIL***.
...
IN OTHER WORDS...
...THEY'LL GIVE US BAIT, THEN REEL US IN.
DURING THE CON-FERENCE...
...THEY'LL PROBABLY TRY TO APPROACH D.D.D. OR THE MARINE ORGANIZATION SEPARATELY.
I NEED YOU...
...TO BE VERY CAREFUL HOW YOU DEAL WITH THEM.

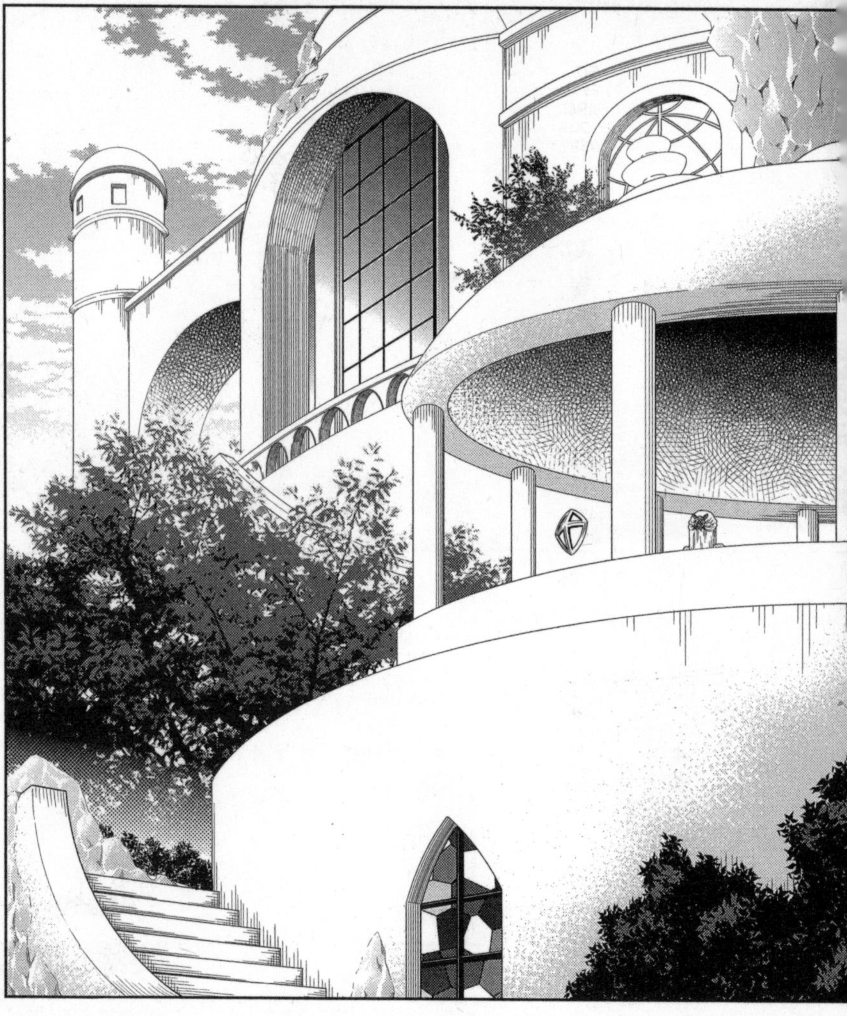

CHAPTER : 32 THE SLACKER PRINCESS

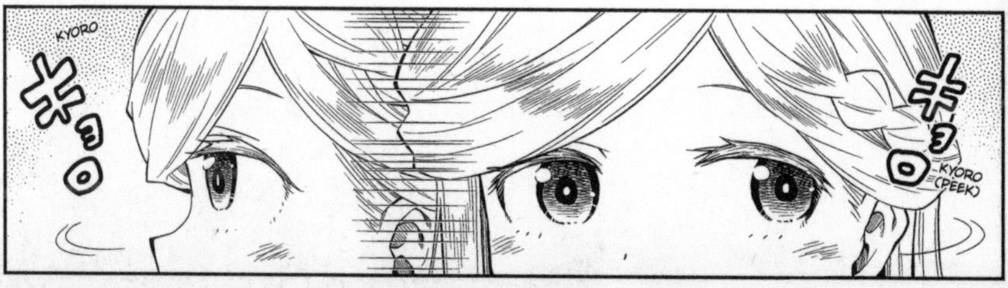
KYORO (PEEK)
KYORO

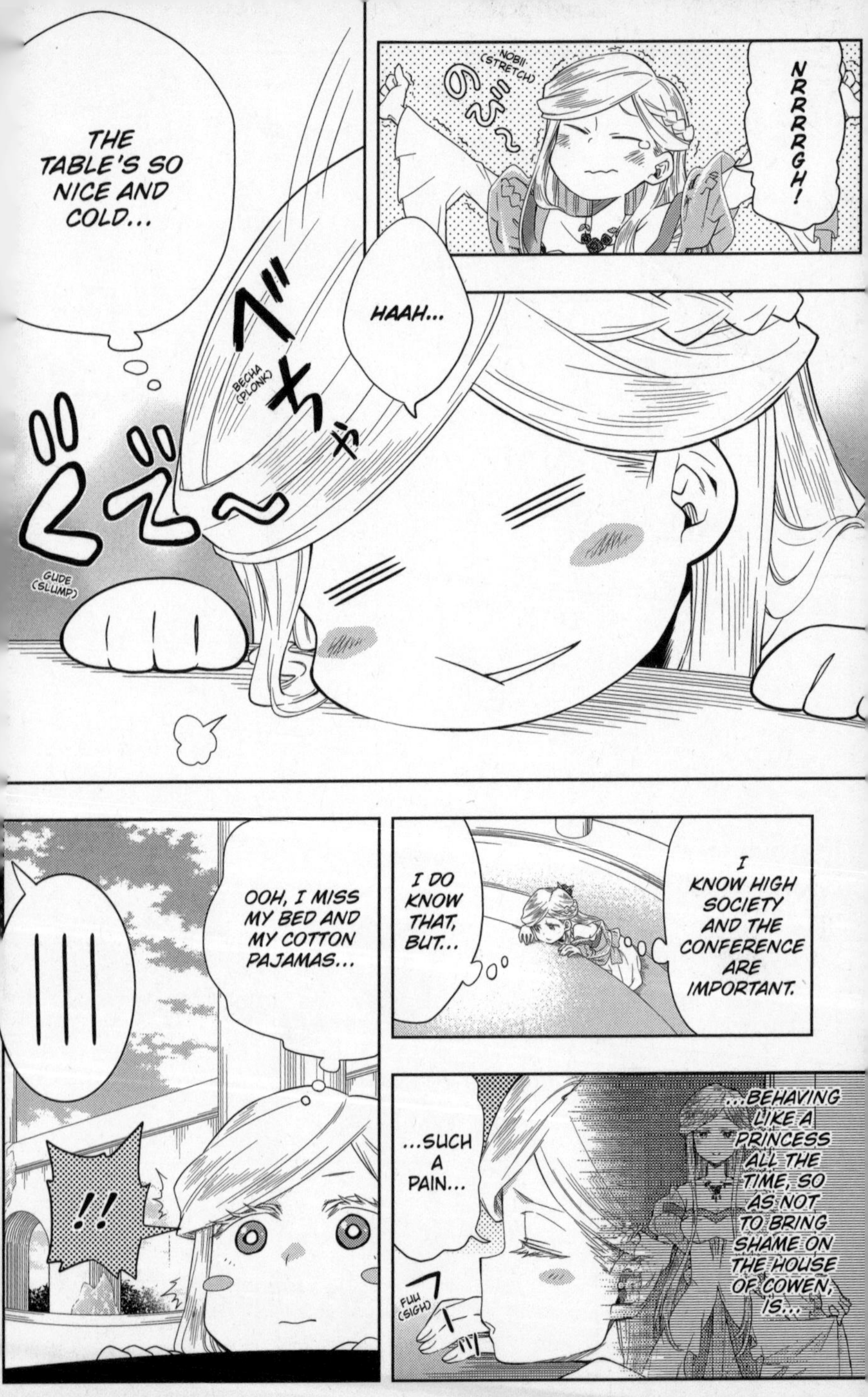
NRRRRGH!
NOBII (STRETCH)
HAAH...
BECHA (PLONK)
THE TABLE'S SO NICE AND COLD...
GUDE (SLUMP)
I KNOW HIGH SOCIETY AND THE CONFERENCE ARE IMPORTANT.
I DO KNOW THAT, BUT...
...BEHAVING LIKE A PRINCESS ALL THE TIME, SO AS NOT TO BRING SHAME ON THE HOUSE OF COWEN, IS...
...SUCH A PAIN...
FUU (SIGH)
OOH, I MISS MY BED AND MY COTTON PAJAMAS...
!!

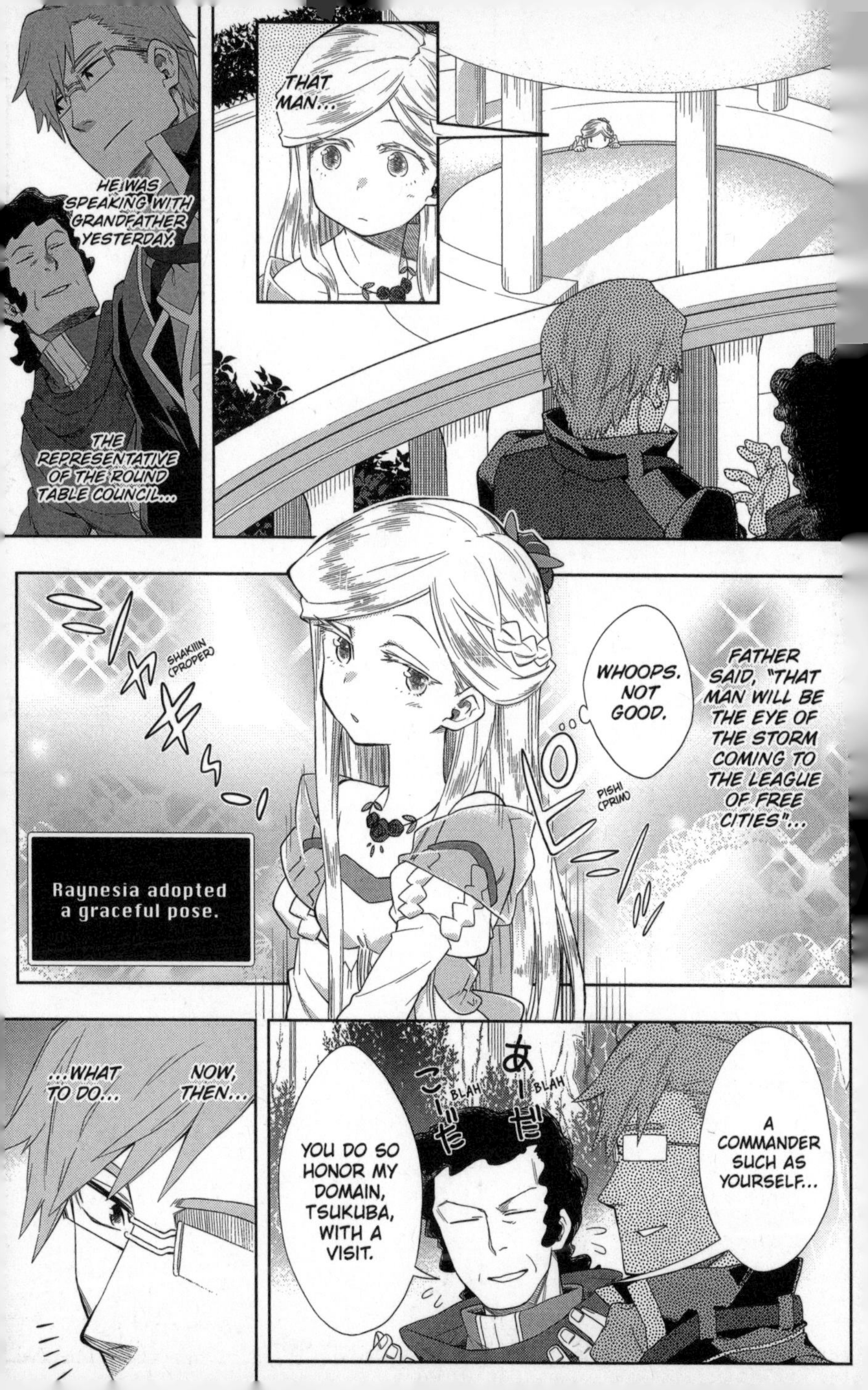
THAT MAN...
HE WAS SPEAKING WITH GRANDFATHER YESTERDAY.
THE REPRESENTATIVE OF THE ROUND TABLE COUNCIL...
FATHER SAID, "THAT MAN WILL BE THE EYE OF THE STORM COMING TO THE LEAGUE OF FREE CITIES"...
WHOOPS. NOT GOOD.
PISHI (PRIM)
SHAKIIN (PROPER)
Raynesia adopted a graceful pose.
A COMMANDER SUCH AS YOURSELF...
あーだ BLAH
こーだ BLAH
YOU DO SO HONOR MY DOMAIN, TSUKUBA, WITH A VISIT.
NOW, THEN...
...WHAT TO DO...

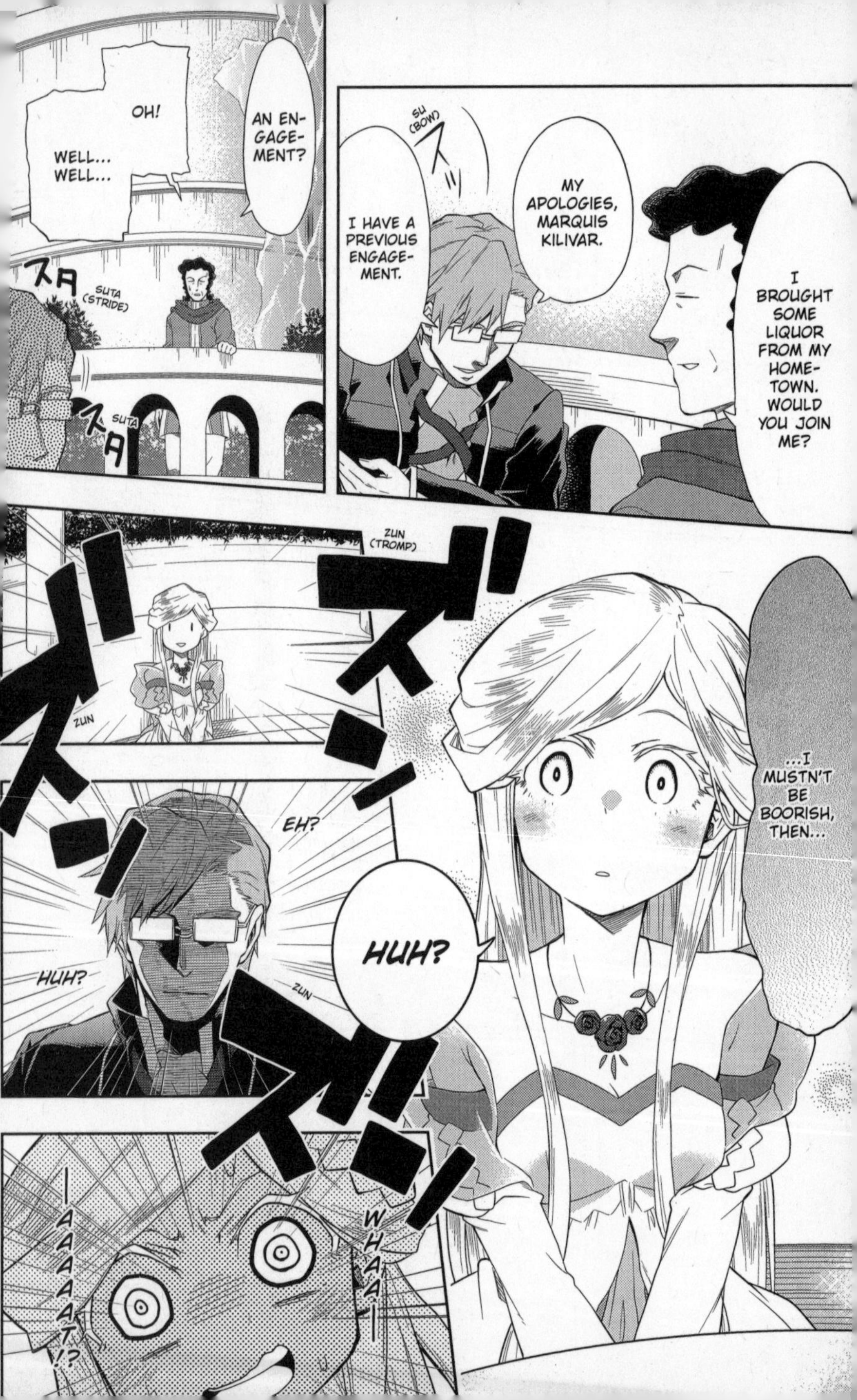
I BROUGHT SOME LIQUOR FROM MY HOMETOWN. WOULD YOU JOIN ME?
MY APOLOGIES, MARQUIS KILIVAR.
スッ
SU (BOW)
I HAVE A PREVIOUS ENGAGEMENT.
AN ENGAGEMENT?
OH!
WELL... WELL...
スタ
SUTA (STRIDE)
SUTA
スタ
...I MUSTN'T BE BOORISH, THEN...
ズーン
ZUN (TROMP)
HUH?
ZUN
EH?
HUH?
ズーン
ZUN
WHAA—
—AAAAAT!?

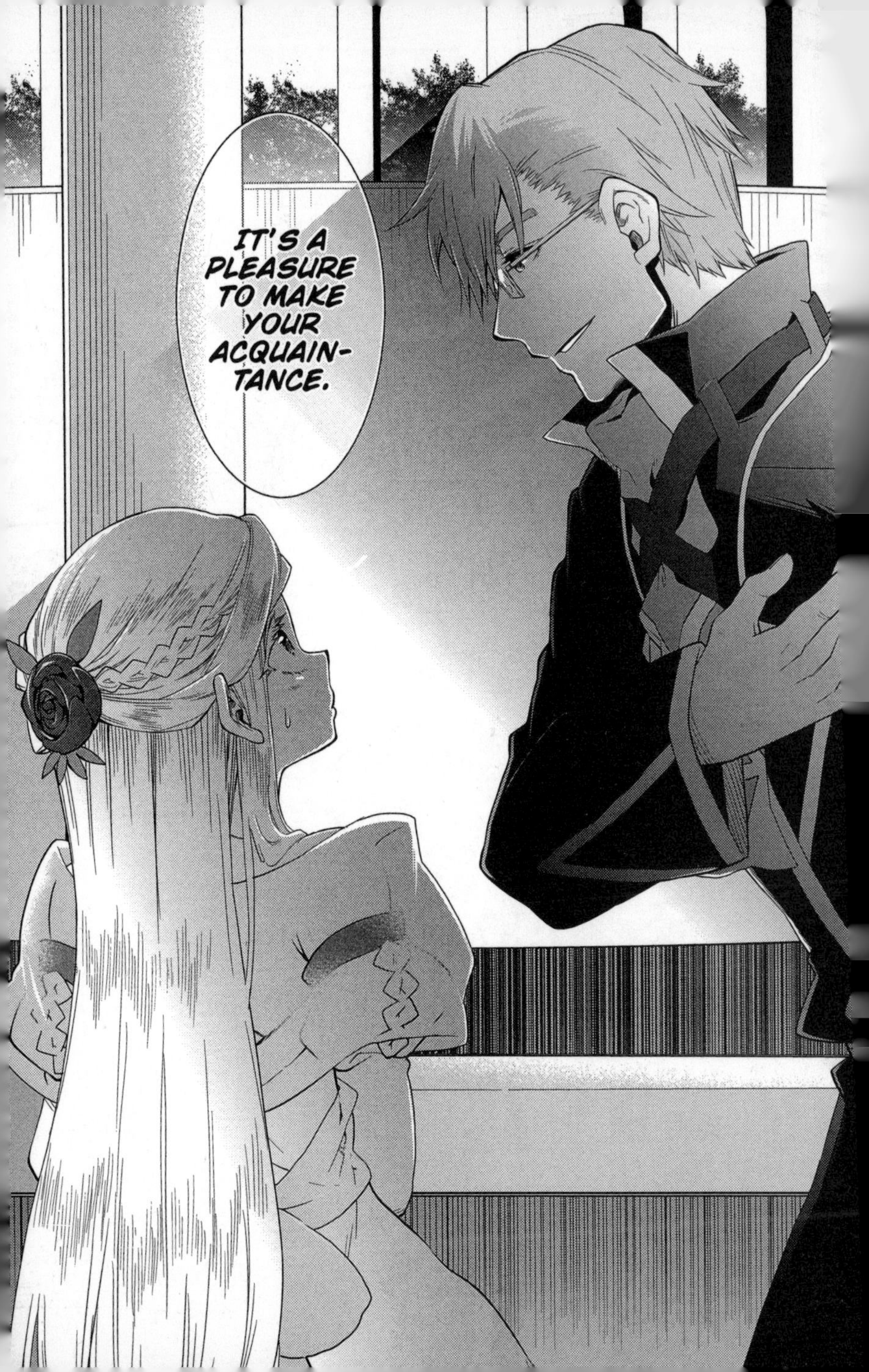
IT'S A PLEASURE TO MAKE YOUR ACQUAIN-TANCE.

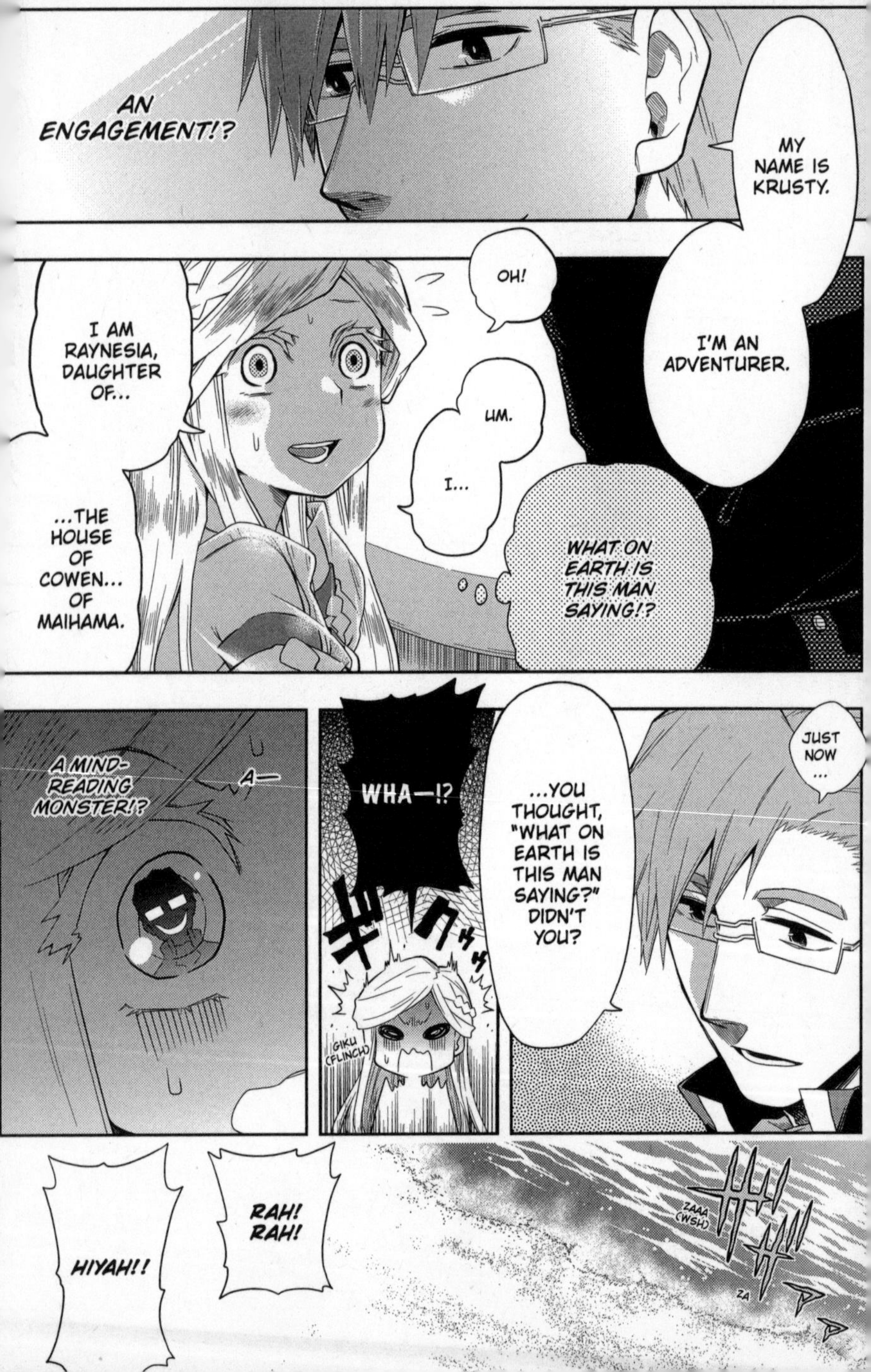
MY NAME IS KRUSTY.
AN ENGAGEMENT!?
I'M AN ADVENTURER.
OH!
UM.
I...
I AM RAYNESIA, DAUGHTER OF...
...THE HOUSE OF COWEN... OF MAIHAMA.
WHAT ON EARTH IS THIS MAN SAYING!?
JUST NOW ...
...YOU THOUGHT, "WHAT ON EARTH IS THIS MAN SAYING?" DIDN'T YOU?
WHA—!?
GIKU (FLINCH)
A—
A MIND-READING MONSTER!?
ZAAA (WSH)
ZA
RAH! RAH!
HIYAH!!

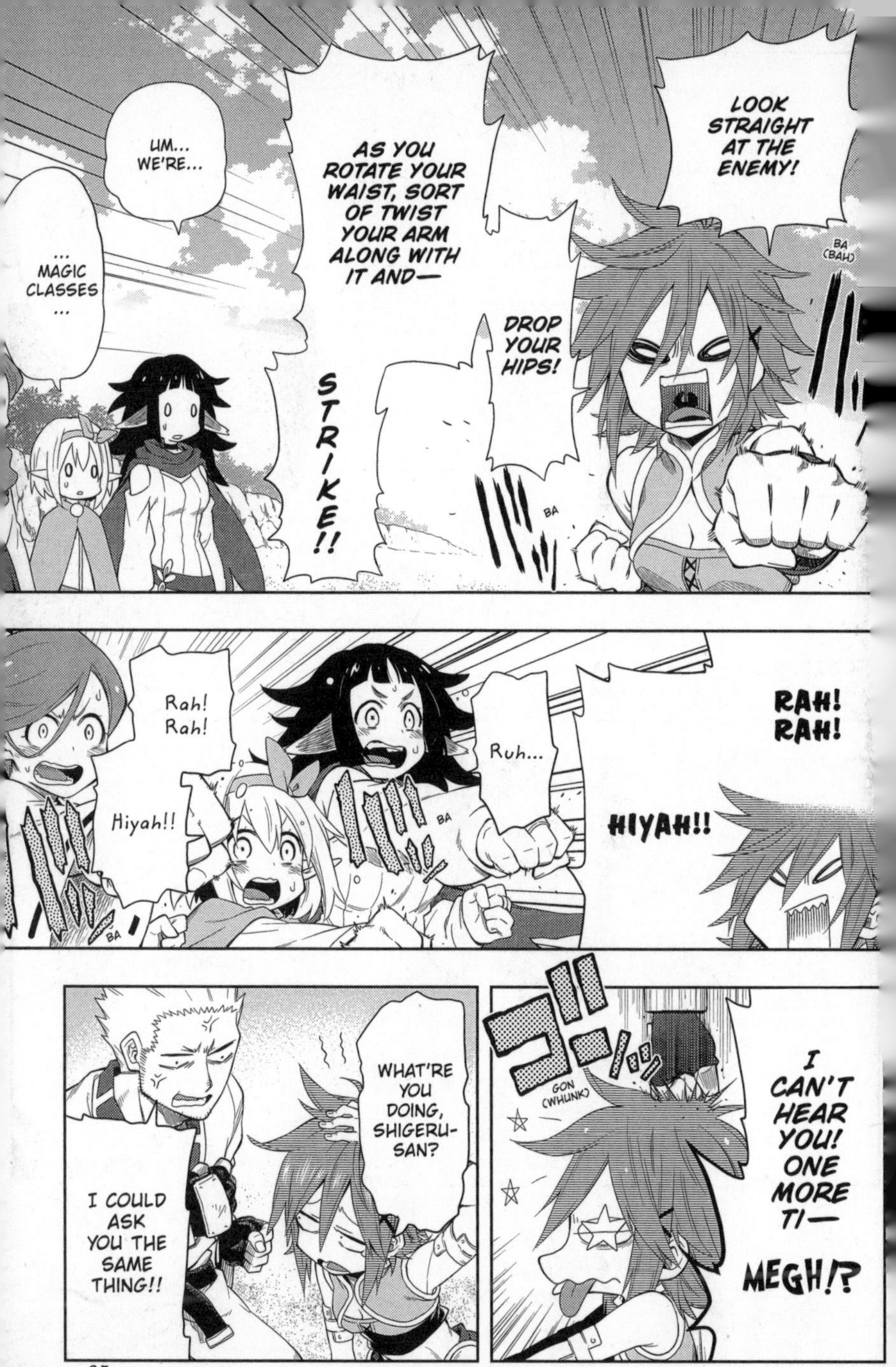
LOOK STRAIGHT AT THE ENEMY!
BA (BAH)
DROP YOUR HIPS!
BA
AS YOU ROTATE YOUR WAIST, SORT OF TWIST YOUR ARM ALONG WITH IT AND—
STRIKE!!
UM... WE'RE...
... MAGIC CLASSES ...
RAH! RAH!
HIYAH!!
Ruh...
BA
Rah! Rah!
Hiyah!!
BA
I CAN'T HEAR YOU! ONE MORE TI—
GON (WHUNK)
MEGH!?
WHAT'RE YOU DOING, SHIGERU-SAN?
I COULD ASK YOU THE SAME THING!!

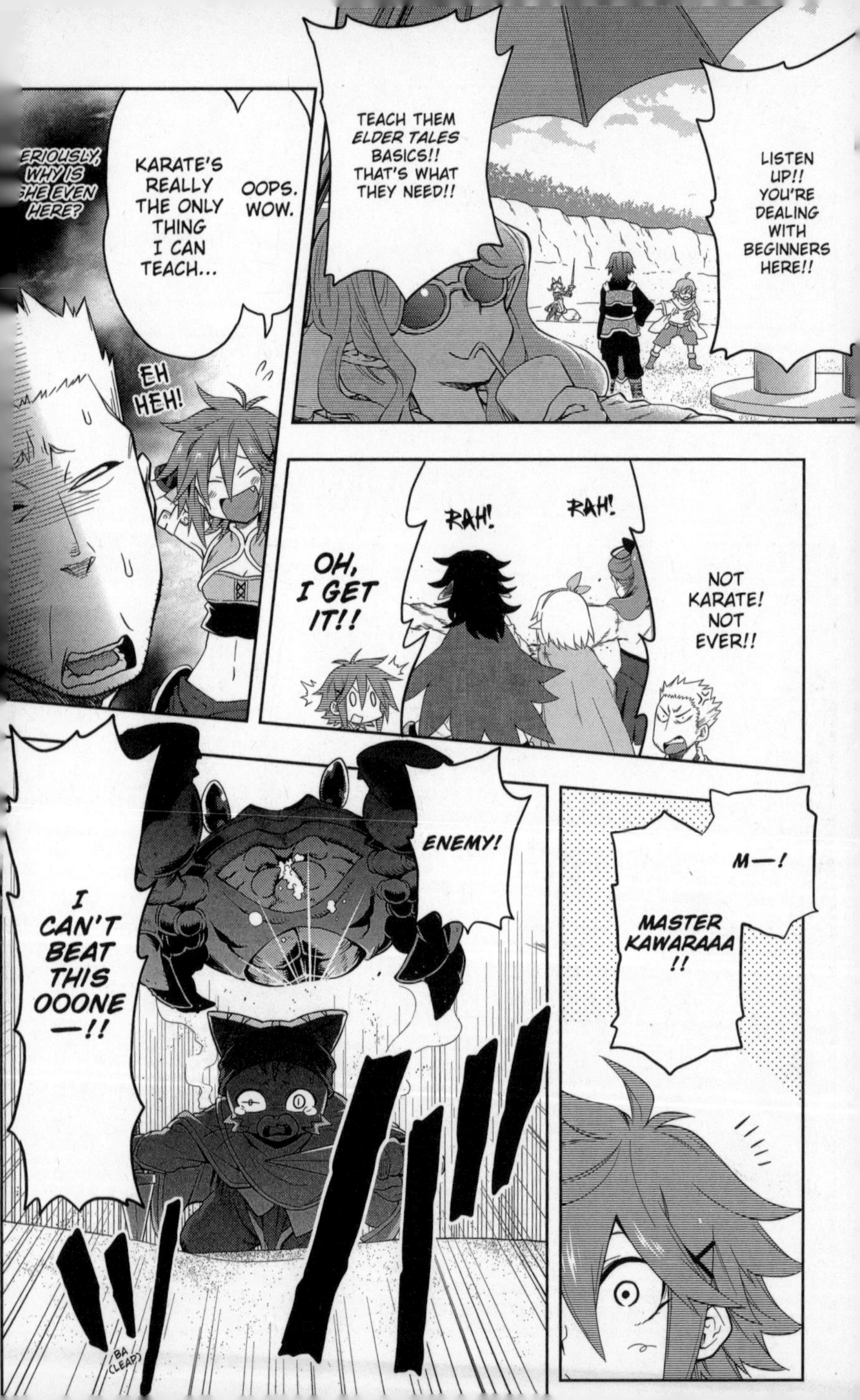
LISTEN UP!! YOU'RE DEALING WITH BEGINNERS HERE!!
TEACH THEM ELDER TALES BASICS!! THAT'S WHAT THEY NEED!!
RAH!
RAH!
NOT KARATE! NOT EVER!!
OH, I GET IT!!
KARATE'S REALLY THE ONLY THING I CAN TEACH...
OOPS. WOW.
ERIOUSLY, WHY IS SHE EVEN HERE?
EH HEH!
M—!
MASTER KAWARAAA!!
ENEMY!
I CAN'T BEAT THIS OOONE—!!
BA (LEAP)

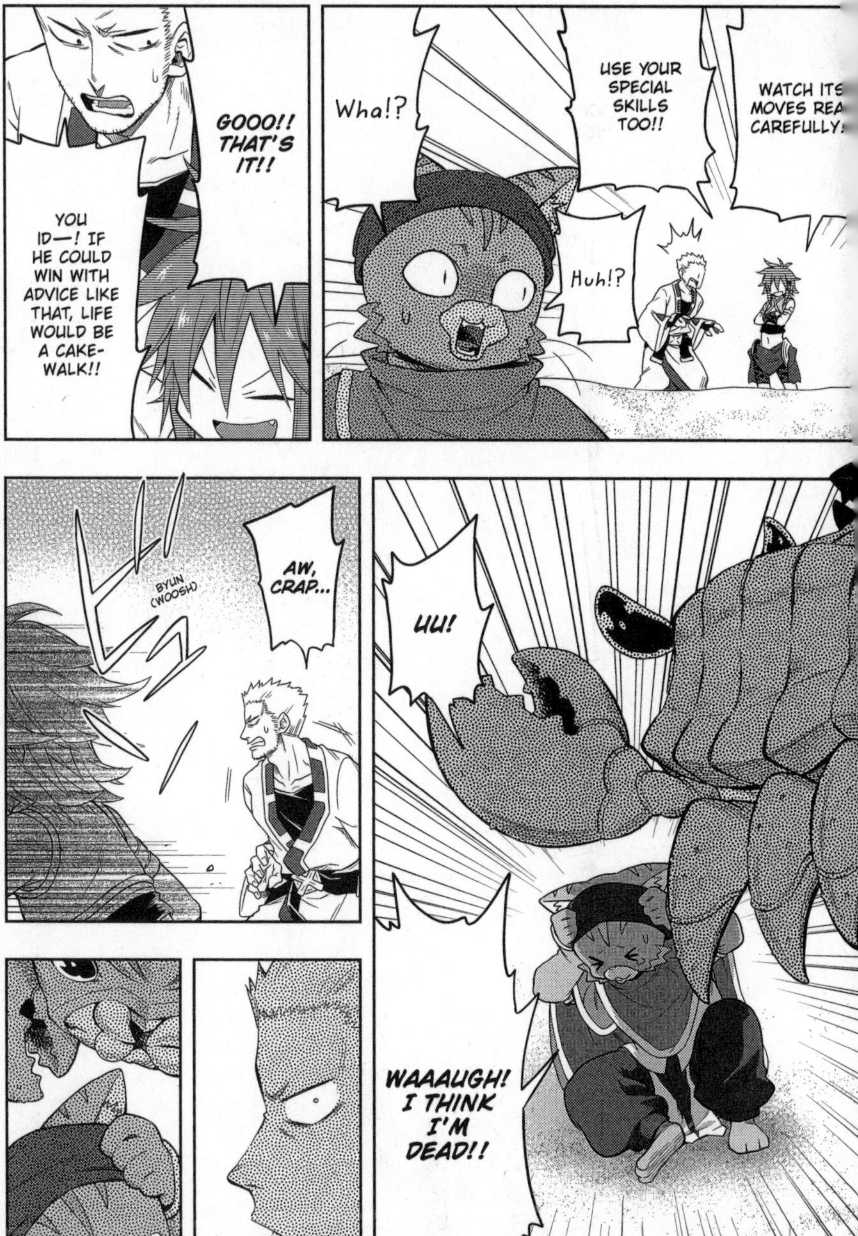
WATCH ITS MOVES REA CAREFULLY!
USE YOUR SPECIAL SKILLS TOO!!
Huh!?
Wha!?
GOOO!! THAT'S IT!!
YOU ID—! IF HE COULD WIN WITH ADVICE LIKE THAT, LIFE WOULD BE A CAKE-WALK!!
UU!
WAAAUGH! I THINK I'M DEAD!!
AW, CRAP...
BYUN (WOOSH)

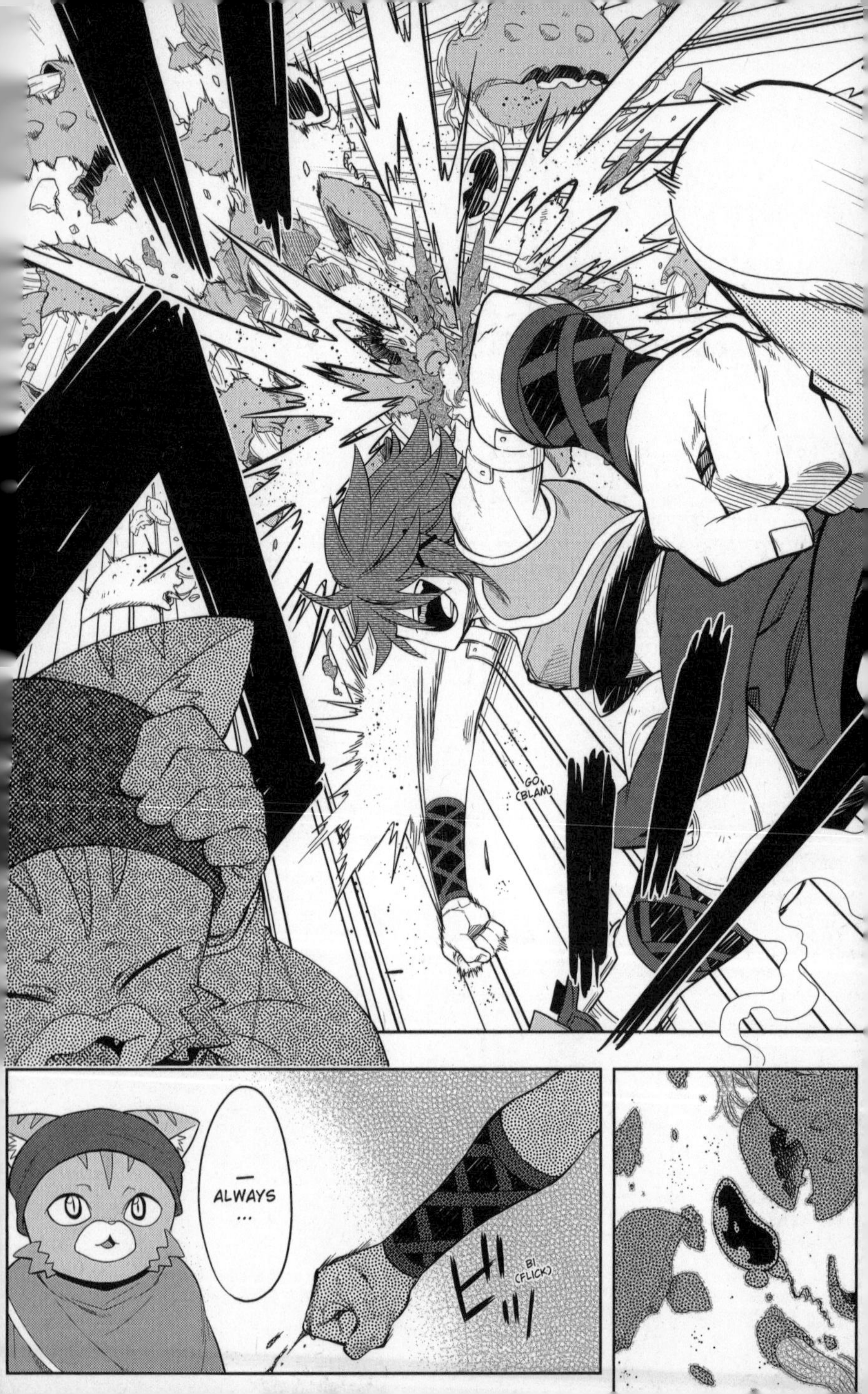
GO (BLAM)
— ALWAYS ...
BI (FLICK)

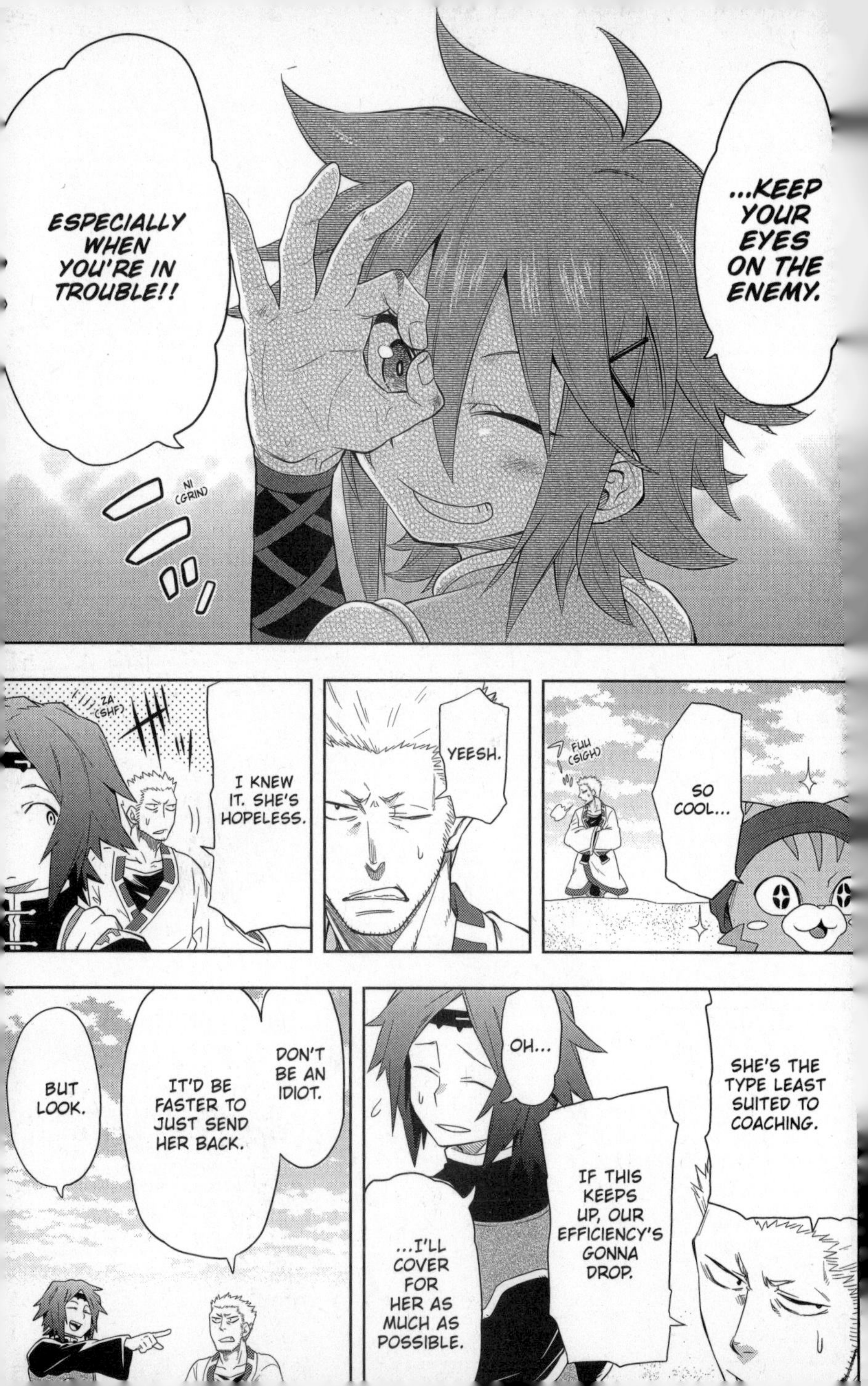
...KEEP YOUR EYES ON THE ENEMY.
ESPECIALLY WHEN YOU'RE IN TROUBLE!!
NI (GRIN)
SO COOL...
FUU (SIGH)
YEESH.
ZA (SHF)
I KNEW IT. SHE'S HOPELESS.
SHE'S THE TYPE LEAST SUITED TO COACHING.
OH...
IF THIS KEEPS UP, OUR EFFICIENCY'S GONNA DROP.
...I'LL COVER FOR HER AS MUCH AS POSSIBLE.
DON'T BE AN IDIOT.
IT'D BE FASTER TO JUST SEND HER BACK.
BUT LOOK.

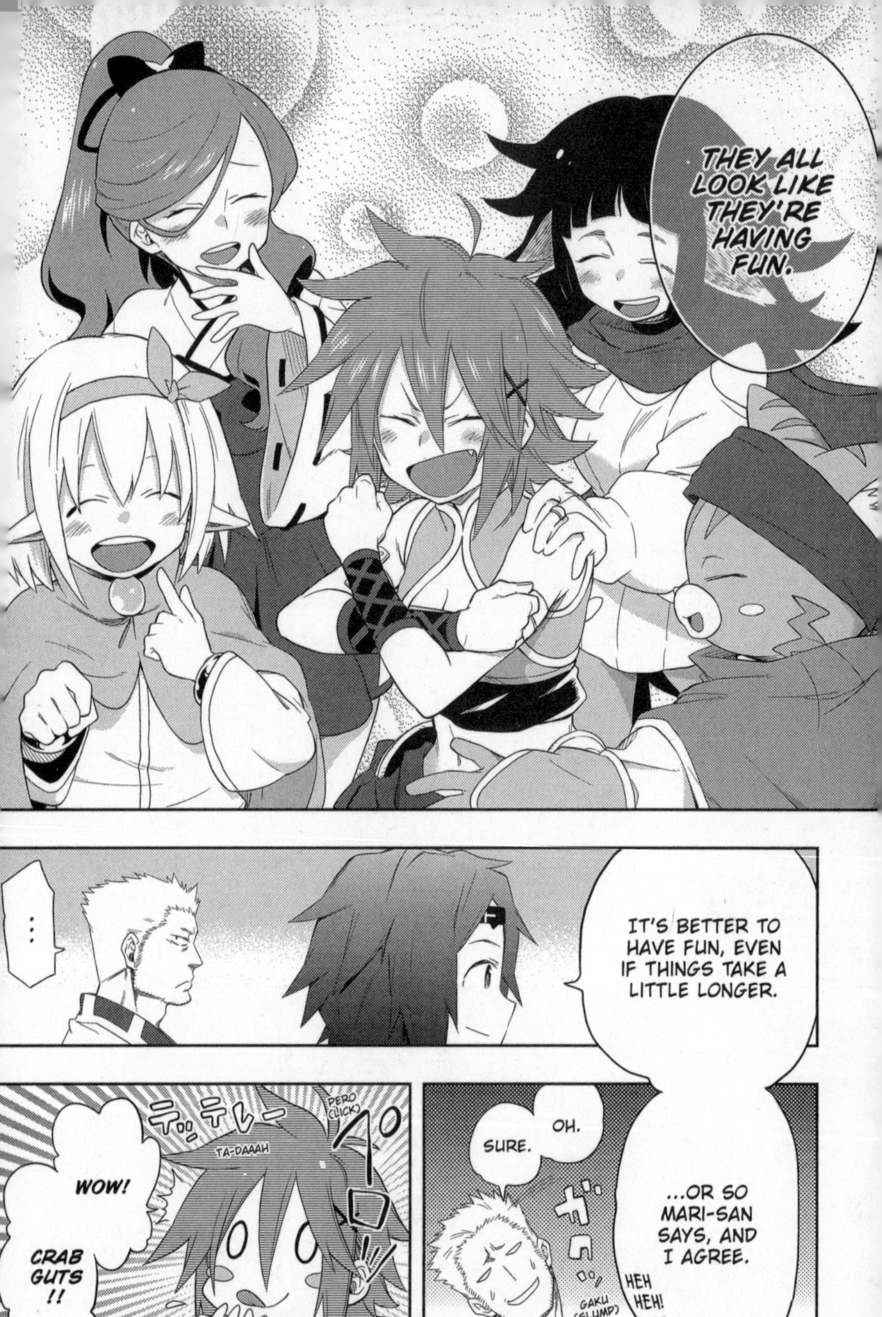
THEY ALL LOOK LIKE THEY'RE HAVING FUN.
IT'S BETTER TO HAVE FUN, EVEN IF THINGS TAKE A LITTLE LONGER.
...
...OR SO MARI-SAN SAYS, AND I AGREE.
OH.
SURE.
GAKU (SLUMP)
HEH HEH!
PERO (LICK)
TA-DAAAH
WOW!
CRAB GUTS !!

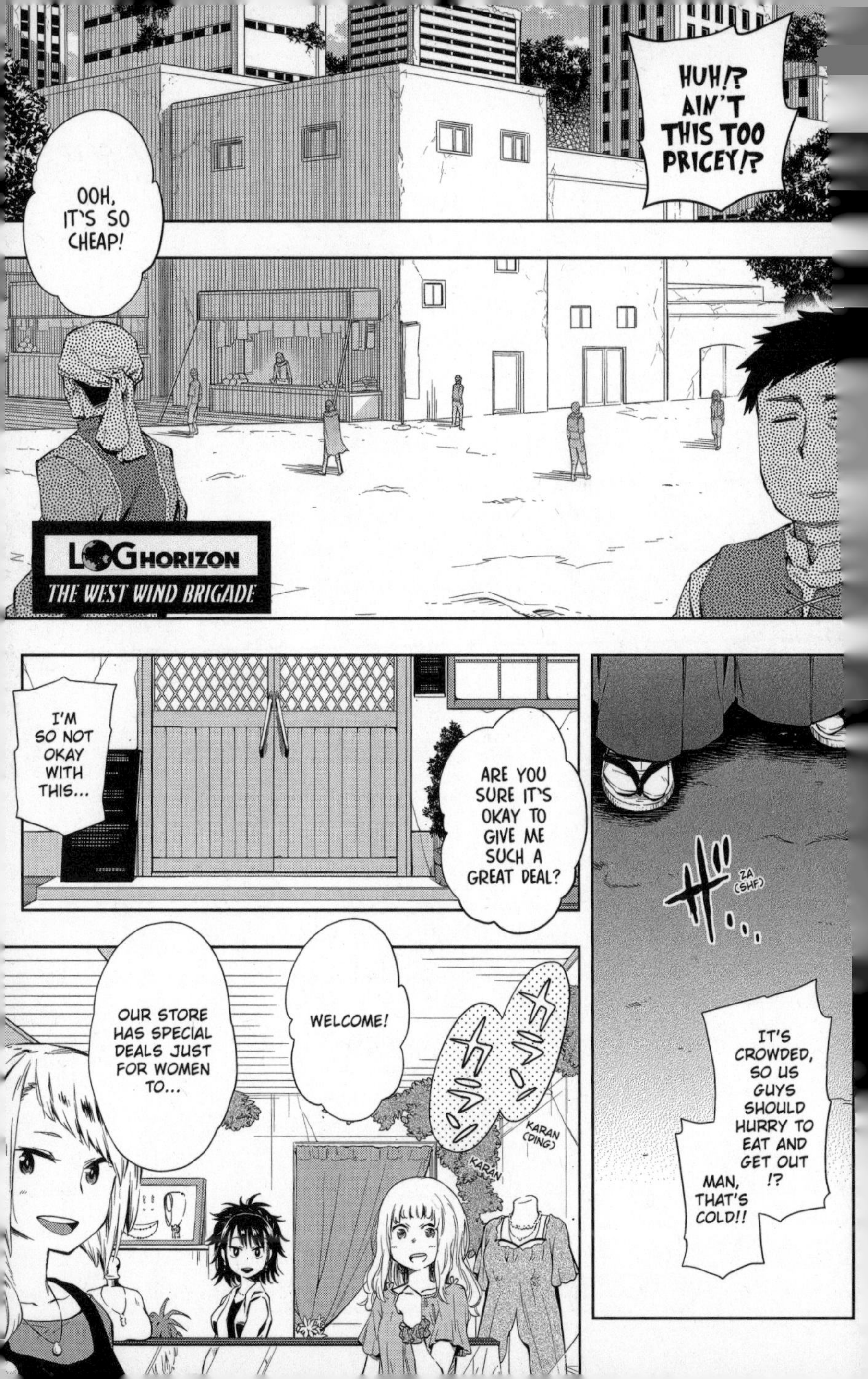
HUH!? AIN'T THIS TOO PRICEY!?
OOH, IT'S SO CHEAP!
LOG HORIZON
THE WEST WIND BRIGADE
ZA (SHF)
IT'S CROWDED, SO US GUYS SHOULD HURRY TO EAT AND GET OUT!?
MAN, THAT'S COLD!!
ARE YOU SURE IT'S OKAY TO GIVE ME SUCH A GREAT DEAL?
I'M SO NOT OKAY WITH THIS...
KARAN (DING)
KARAN
WELCOME!
OUR STORE HAS SPECIAL DEALS JUST FOR WOMEN TO...

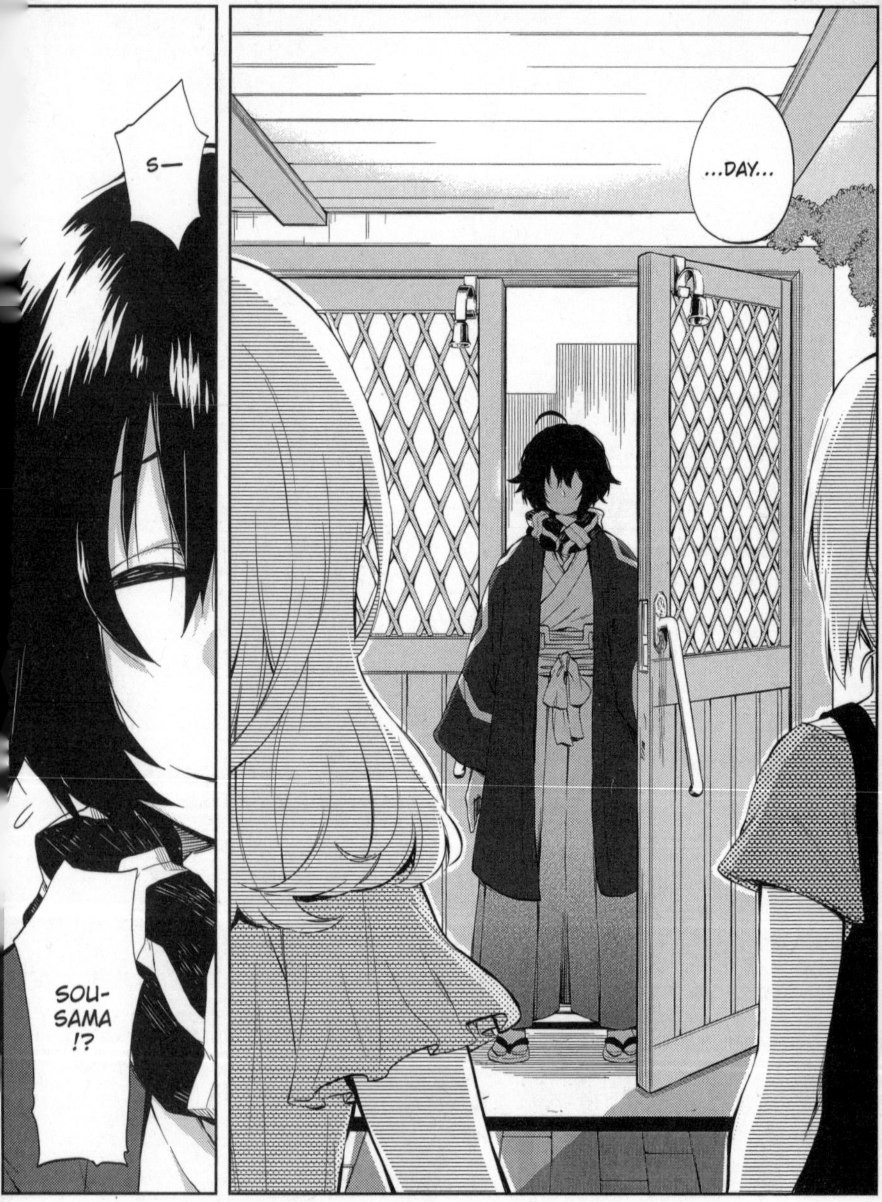
...DAY...
S—
SOU-SAMA!?

CHAPTER: 33 CAPTURE KURINON! (PART 1)

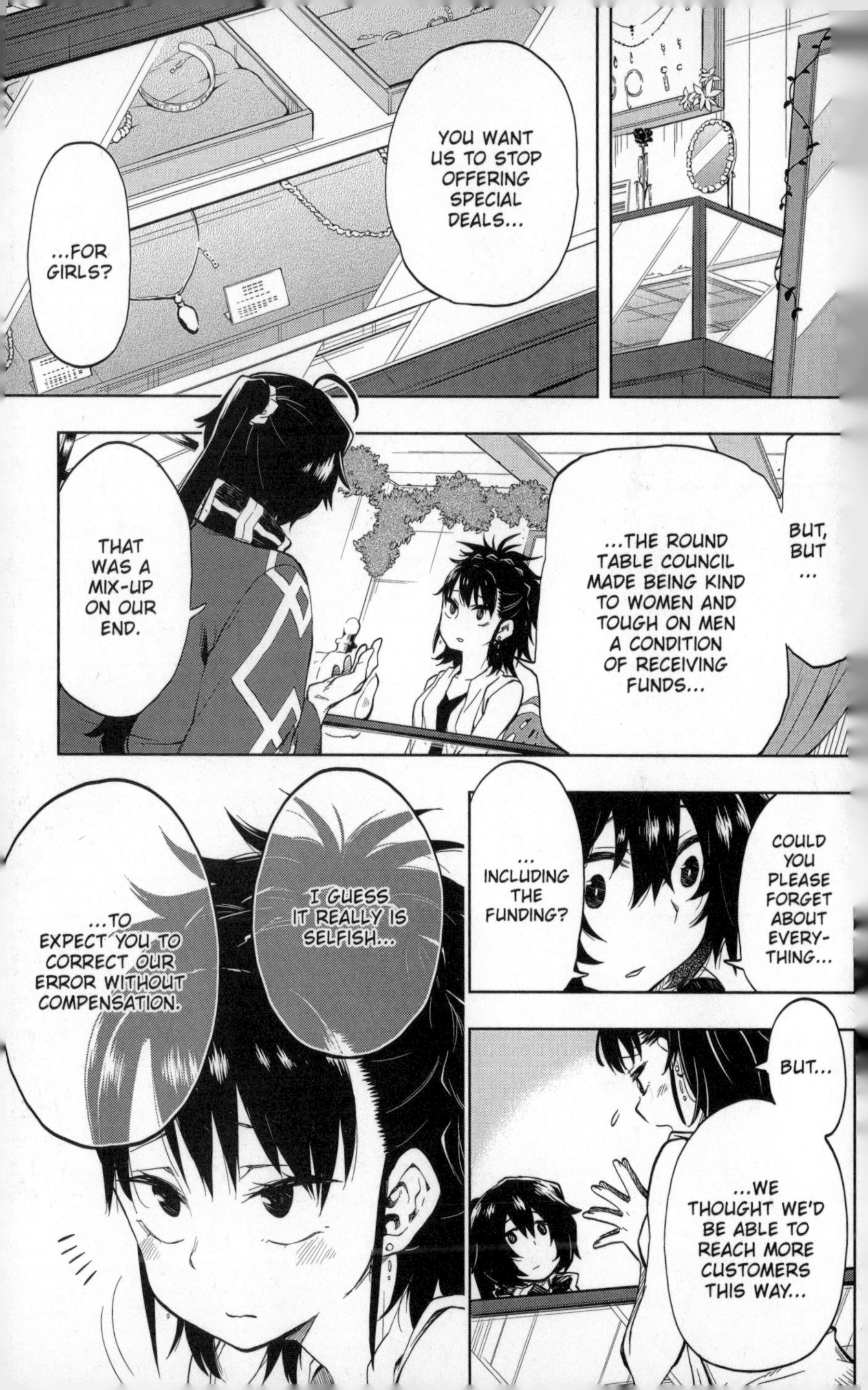
YOU WANT US TO STOP OFFERING SPECIAL DEALS...
...FOR GIRLS?
BUT, BUT ...
...THE ROUND TABLE COUNCIL MADE BEING KIND TO WOMEN AND TOUGH ON MEN A CONDITION OF RECEIVING FUNDS...
THAT WAS A MIX-UP ON OUR END.
COULD YOU PLEASE FORGET ABOUT EVERY-THING...
...INCLUDING THE FUNDING?
BUT...
...WE THOUGHT WE'D BE ABLE TO REACH MORE CUSTOMERS THIS WAY...
I GUESS IT REALLY IS SELFISH...
...TO EXPECT YOU TO CORRECT OUR ERROR WITHOUT COMPENSATION.

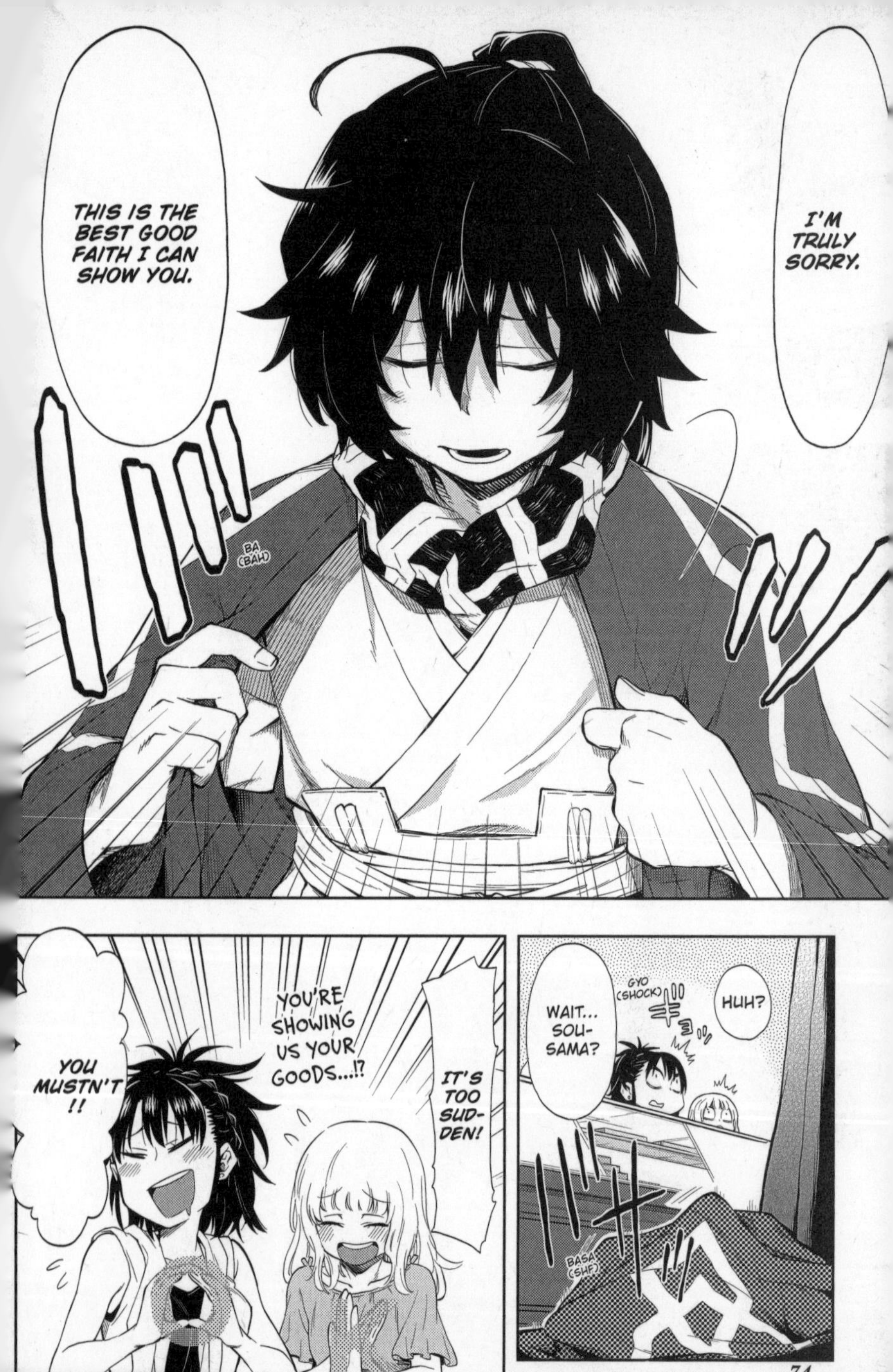

I'M TRULY SORRY.
THIS IS THE BEST GOOD FAITH I CAN SHOW YOU.
BA (BAH)
HUH?
GYO (SHOCK)
WAIT... SOU-SAMA?
BASA (SHF)
IT'S TOO SUDDEN!
YOU'RE SHOWING US YOUR GOODS...!?
YOU MUSTN'T !!

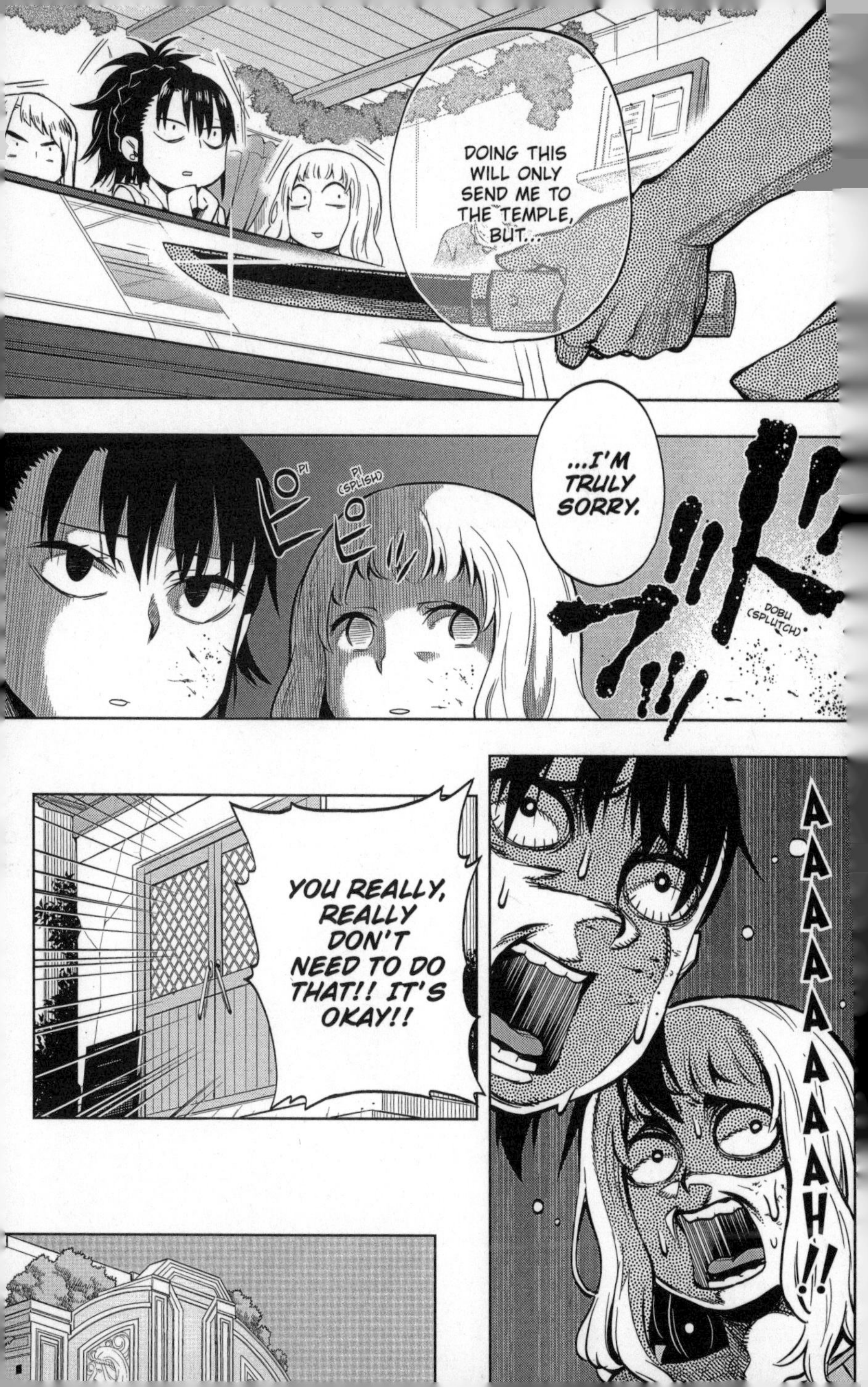
DOING THIS WILL ONLY SEND ME TO THE TEMPLE, BUT...
...I'M TRULY SORRY.
DOBU (SPLUTCH)
PI
PI (SPLISH)
AAAAAAAAAH!!
YOU REALLY, REALLY DON'T NEED TO DO THAT!! IT'S OKAY!!

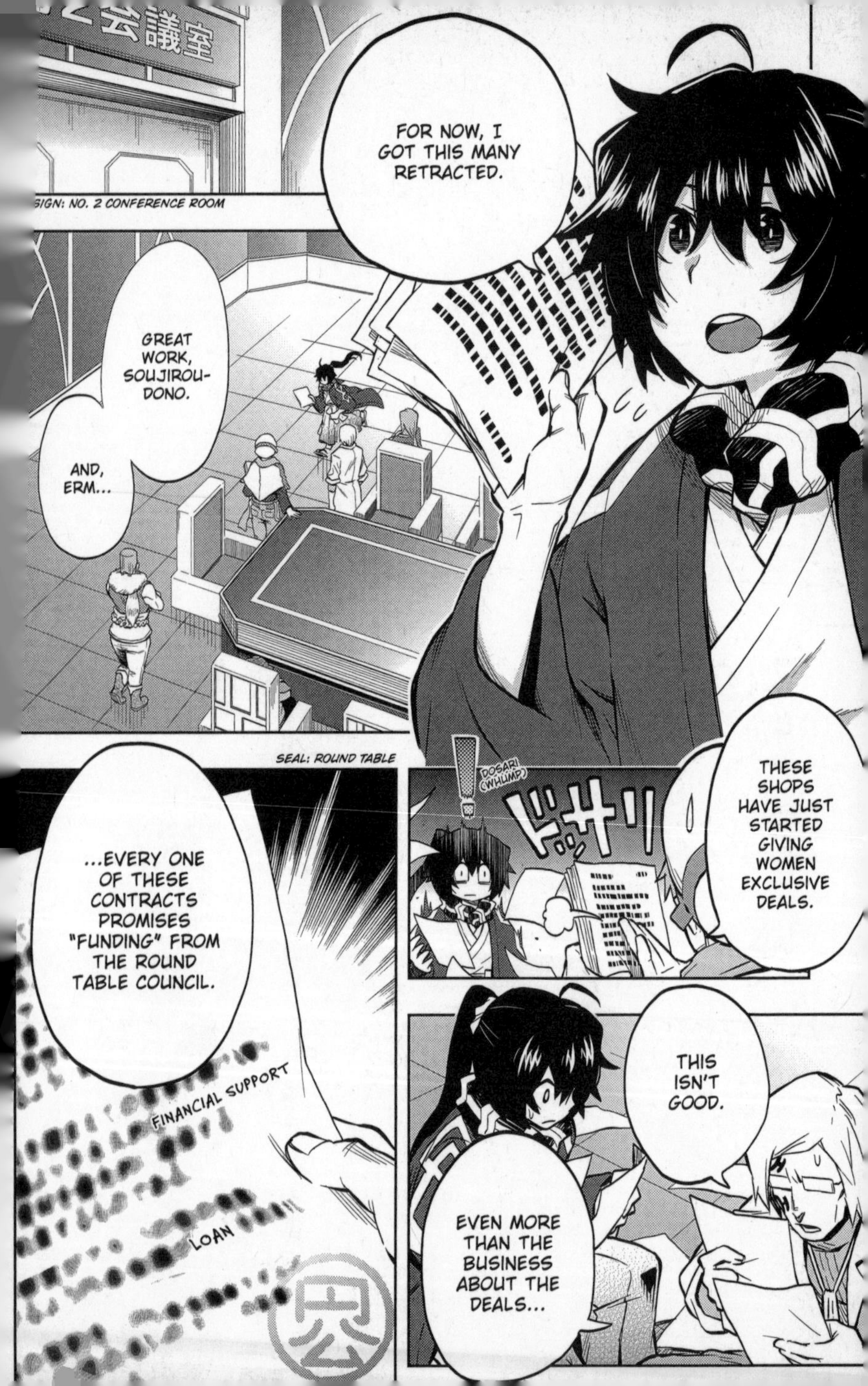
FOR NOW, I GOT THIS MANY RETRACTED.
SIGN: NO. 2 CONFERENCE ROOM
GREAT WORK, SOUJIROU-DONO.
AND, ERM...
THESE SHOPS HAVE JUST STARTED GIVING WOMEN EXCLUSIVE DEALS.
DOSARI (WHUMP)
THIS ISN'T GOOD.
EVEN MORE THAN THE BUSINESS ABOUT THE DEALS...
...EVERY ONE OF THESE CONTRACTS PROMISES "FUNDING" FROM THE ROUND TABLE COUNCIL.
FINANCIAL SUPPORT
LOAN
SEAL: ROUND TABLE

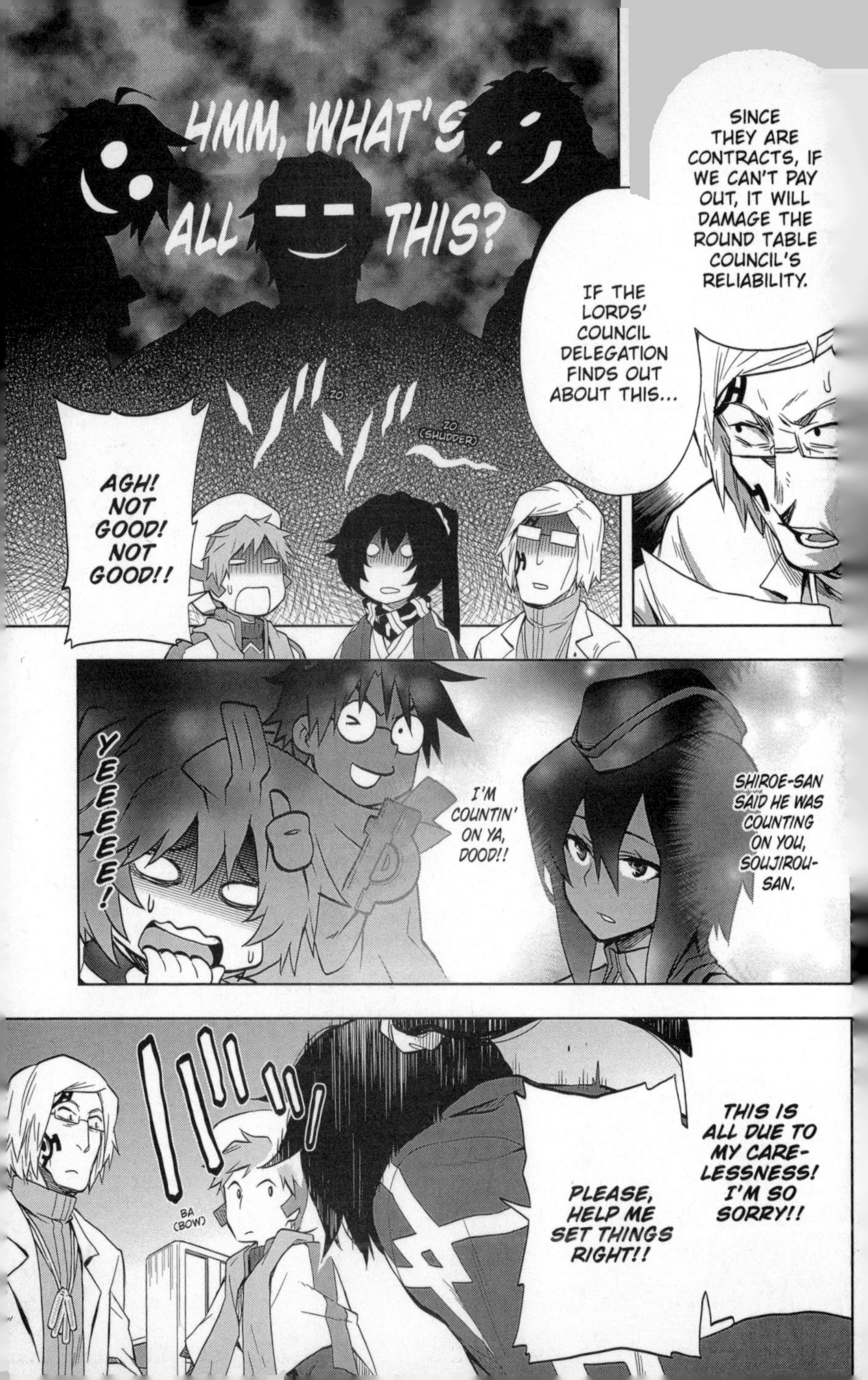
SINCE THEY ARE CONTRACTS, IF WE CAN'T PAY OUT, IT WILL DAMAGE THE ROUND TABLE COUNCIL'S RELIABILITY.
IF THE LORDS' COUNCIL DELEGATION FINDS OUT ABOUT THIS...
HMM, WHAT'S ALL THIS?
ZO
ZO (SHUDDER)
AGH! NOT GOOD! NOT GOOD!!
SHIROE-SAN SAID HE WAS COUNTING ON YOU, SOUJIROU-SAN.
I'M COUNTIN' ON YA, DOOD!!
YEEEEEE!
THIS IS ALL DUE TO MY CARE-LESSNESS! I'M SO SORRY!!
PLEASE, HELP ME SET THINGS RIGHT!!
BA (BOW)

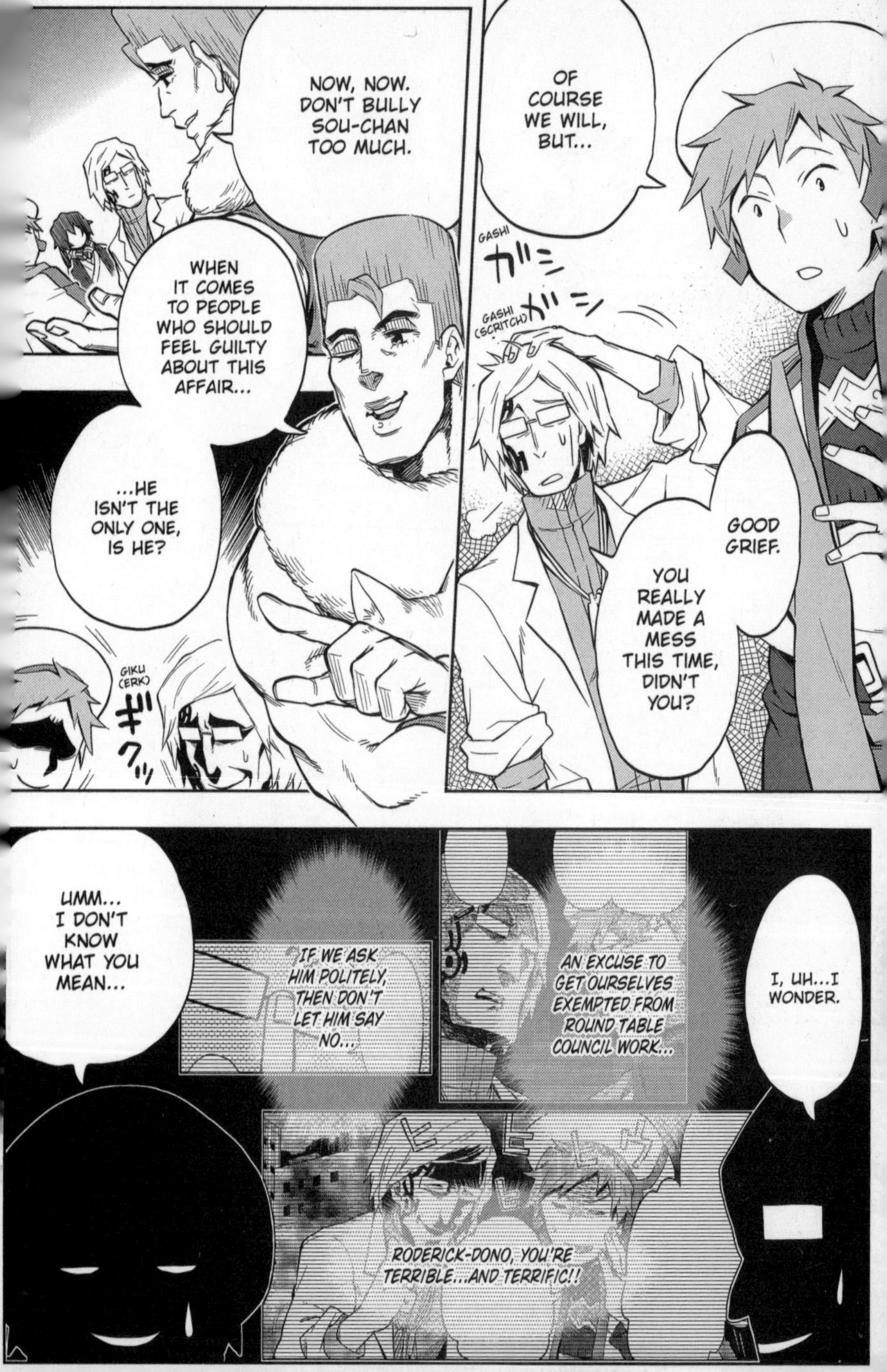
OF COURSE WE WILL, BUT...
GASHI
GASHI (SCRITCH)
GOOD GRIEF.
YOU REALLY MADE A MESS THIS TIME, DIDN'T YOU?
NOW, NOW. DON'T BULLY SOU-CHAN TOO MUCH.
WHEN IT COMES TO PEOPLE WHO SHOULD FEEL GUILTY ABOUT THIS AFFAIR...
...HE ISN'T THE ONLY ONE, IS HE?
GIKU (ERK)
I, UH...I WONDER.
AN EXCUSE TO GET OURSELVES EXEMPTED FROM ROUND TABLE COUNCIL WORK...
IF WE ASK HIM POLITELY, THEN DON'T LET HIM SAY NO...
UMM... I DON'T KNOW WHAT YOU MEAN...
RODERICK-DONO, YOU'RE TERRIBLE...AND TERRIFIC!!

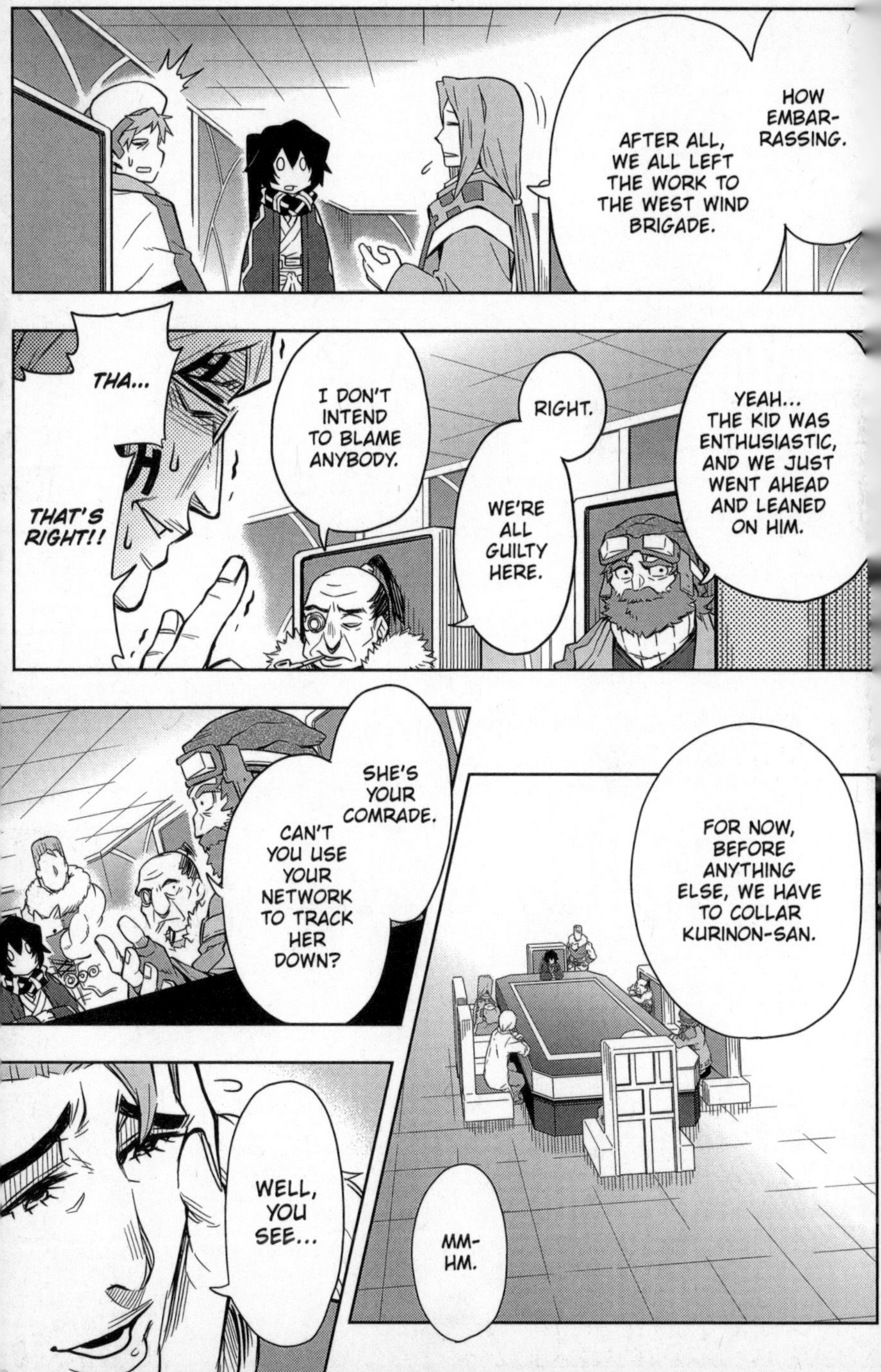
HOW EMBAR-RASSING.
AFTER ALL, WE ALL LEFT THE WORK TO THE WEST WIND BRIGADE.
YEAH... THE KID WAS ENTHUSIASTIC, AND WE JUST WENT AHEAD AND LEANED ON HIM.
RIGHT.
WE'RE ALL GUILTY HERE.
I DON'T INTEND TO BLAME ANYBODY.
THA...
THAT'S RIGHT!!
FOR NOW, BEFORE ANYTHING ELSE, WE HAVE TO COLLAR KURINON-SAN.
MM-HM.
SHE'S YOUR COMRADE.
CAN'T YOU USE YOUR NETWORK TO TRACK HER DOWN?
WELL, YOU SEE...

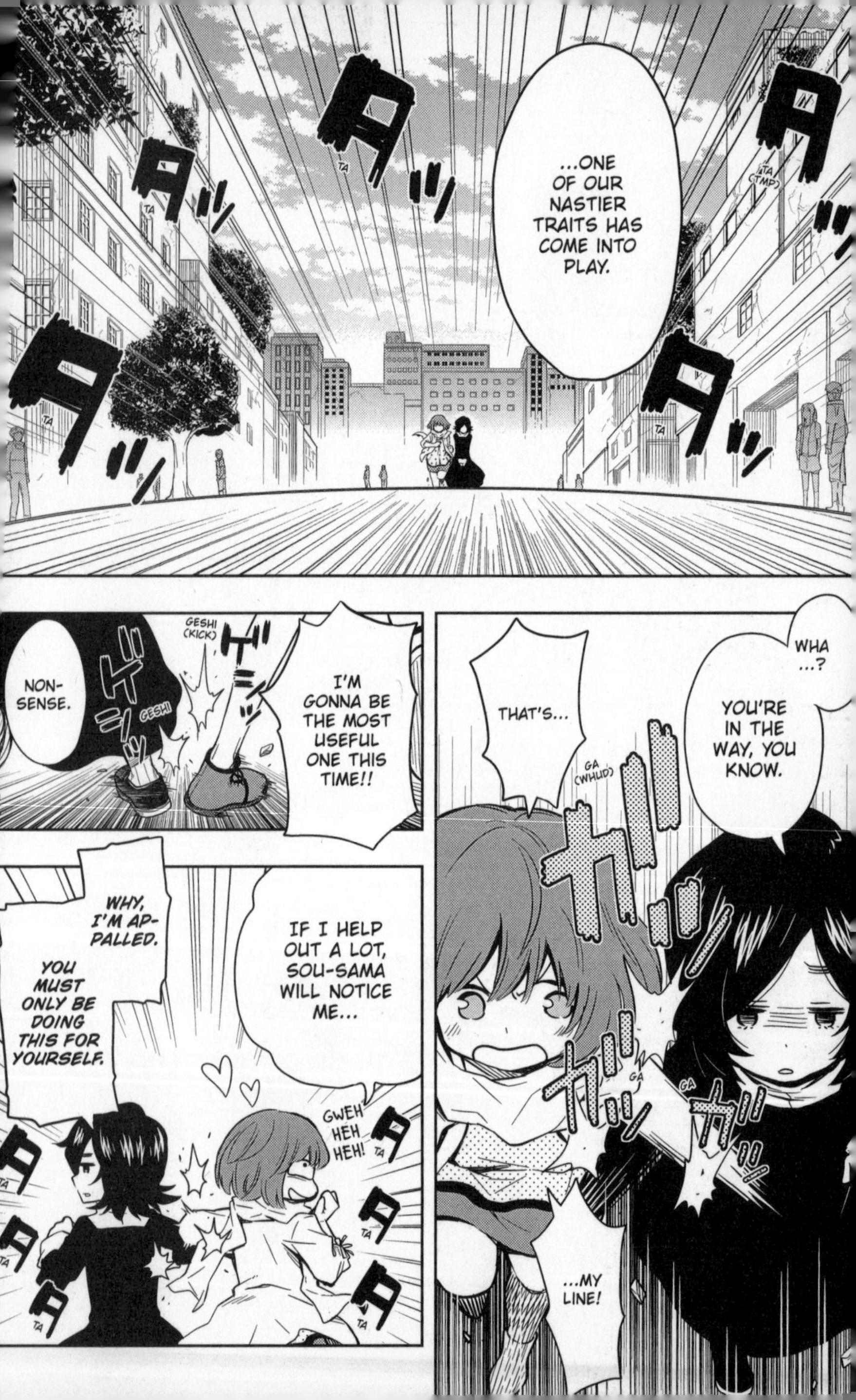
TA (TMP)
...ONE OF OUR NASTIER TRAITS HAS COME INTO PLAY.
TA
TA
TA
TA
WHA ...?
YOU'RE IN THE WAY, YOU KNOW.
THAT'S...
GA (WHUD)
GA
GA
...MY LINE!
I'M GONNA BE THE MOST USEFUL ONE THIS TIME!!
GESHI (KICK)
GESHI
NON-SENSE.
IF I HELP OUT A LOT, SOU-SAMA WILL NOTICE ME...
GWEH HEH HEH!
TA
TA
TA
WHY, I'M AP-PALLED.
YOU MUST ONLY BE DOING THIS FOR YOURSELF.
TA
TA
TA

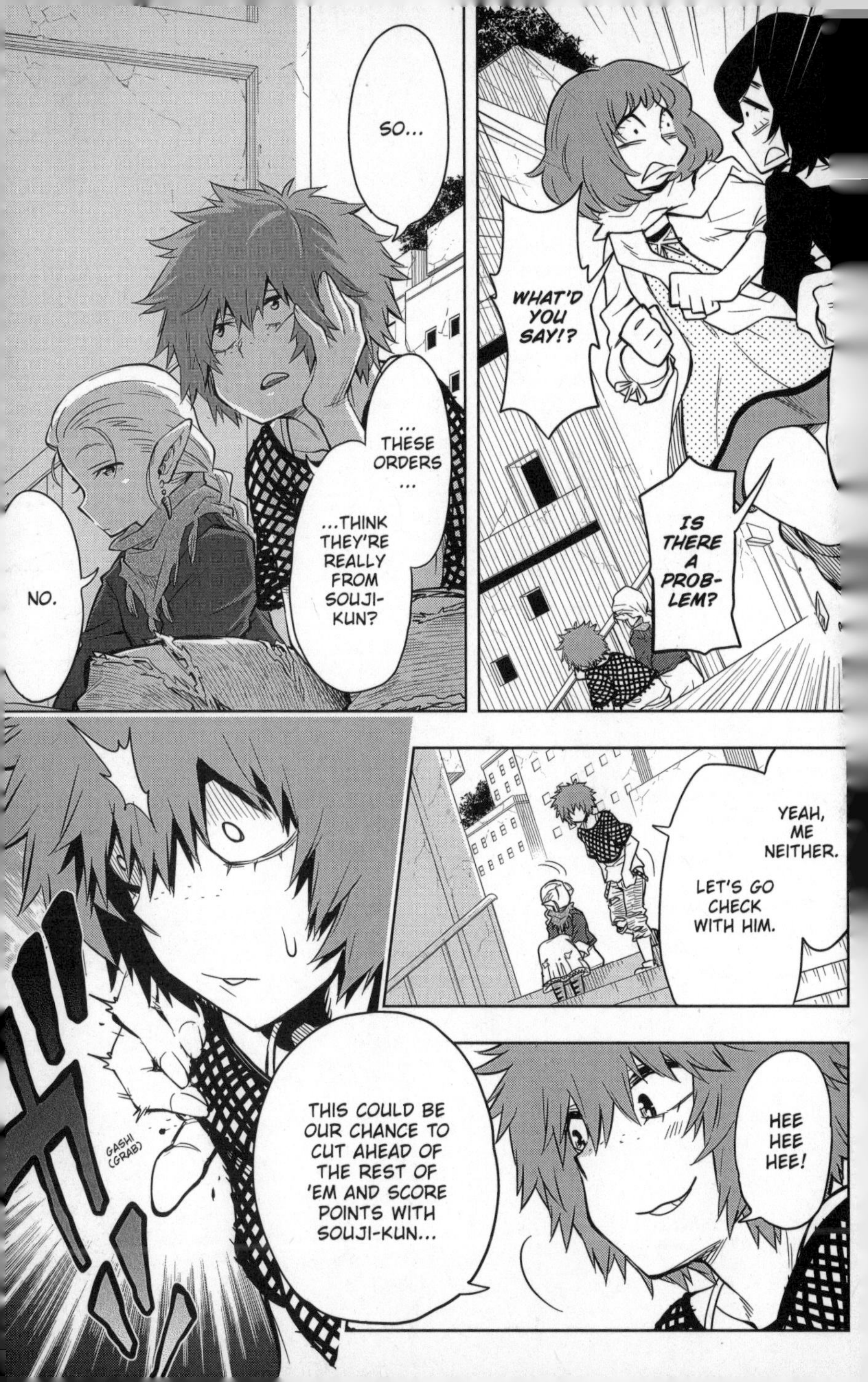
WHAT'D YOU SAY!?
IS THERE A PROB-LEM?
SO...
... THESE ORDERS ...
...THINK THEY'RE REALLY FROM SOUJI-KUN?
NO.
YEAH, ME NEITHER.
LET'S GO CHECK WITH HIM.
HEE HEE HEE!
THIS COULD BE OUR CHANCE TO CUT AHEAD OF THE REST OF 'EM AND SCORE POINTS WITH SOUJI-KUN...
GASHI (GRAB)

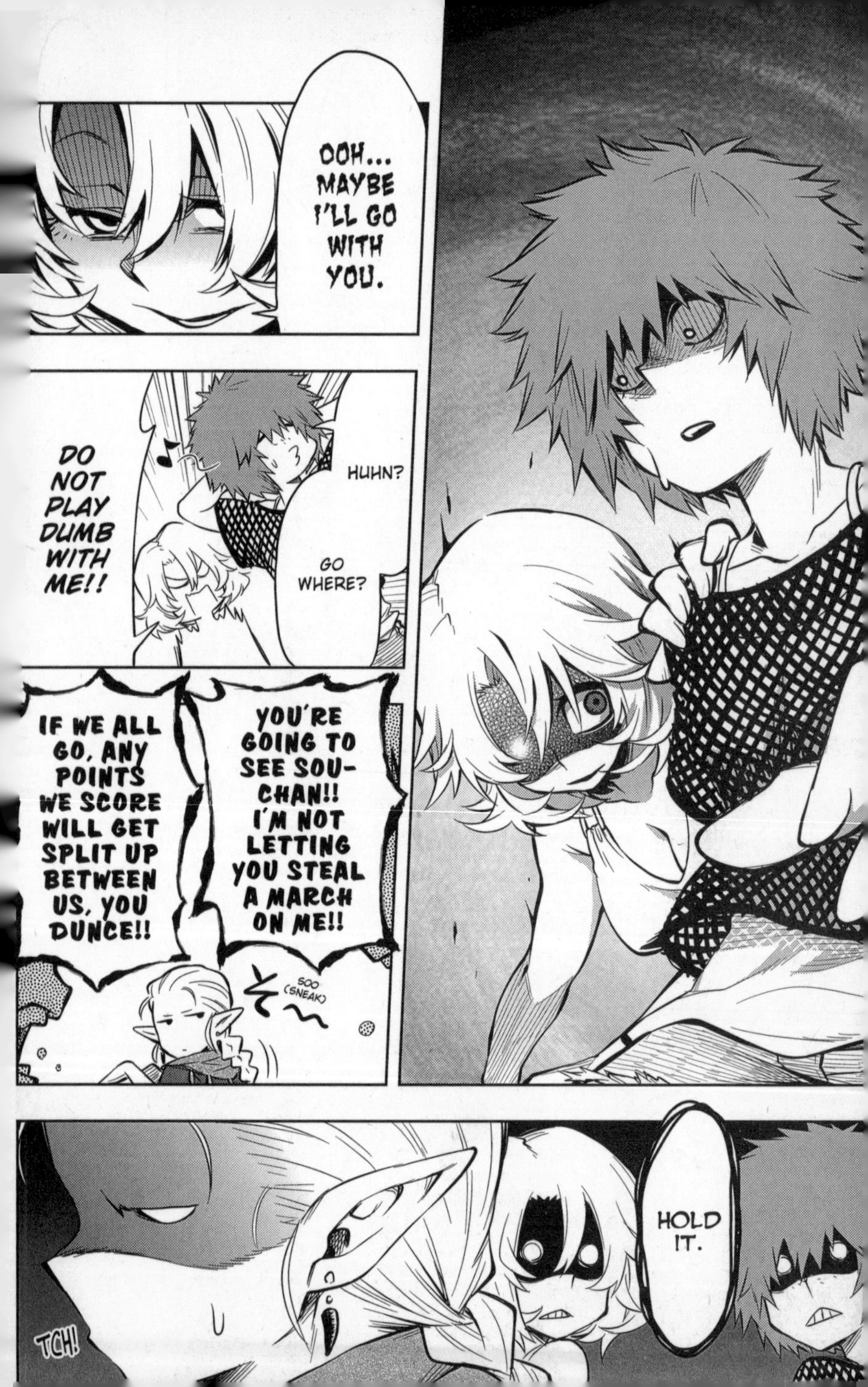
OOH... MAYBE I'LL GO WITH YOU.
HUHN?
GO WHERE?
DO NOT PLAY DUMB WITH ME!!
YOU'RE GOING TO SEE SOU-CHAN!! I'M NOT LETTING YOU STEAL A MARCH ON ME!!
IF WE ALL GO, ANY POINTS WE SCORE WILL GET SPLIT UP BETWEEN US, YOU DUNCE!!
そ〜
SOO (SNEAK)
HOLD IT.
TCH!

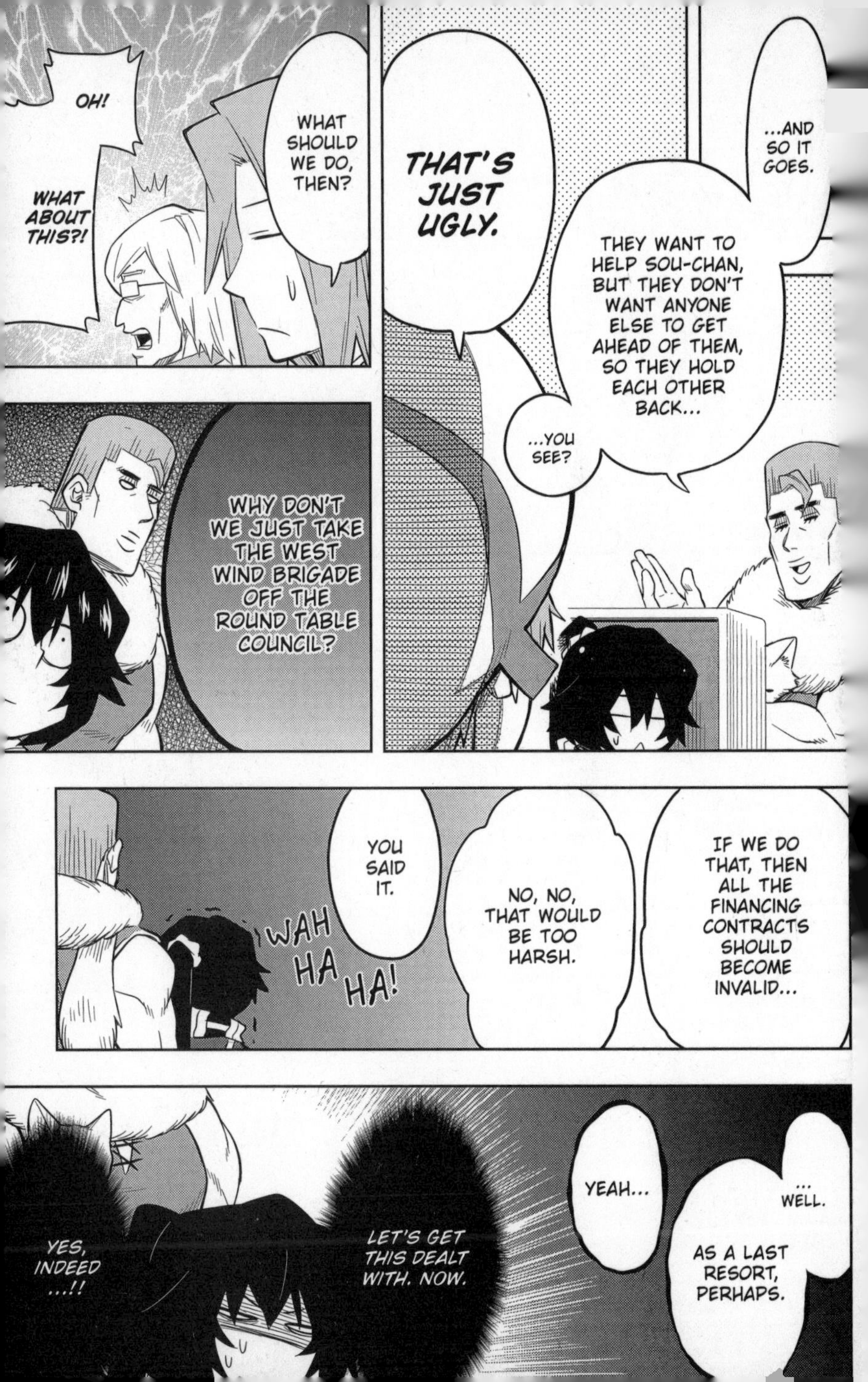
...AND SO IT GOES.
THEY WANT TO HELP SOU-CHAN, BUT THEY DON'T WANT ANYONE ELSE TO GET AHEAD OF THEM, SO THEY HOLD EACH OTHER BACK...
...YOU SEE?
THAT'S JUST UGLY.
WHAT SHOULD WE DO, THEN?
OH!
WHAT ABOUT THIS?!
WHY DON'T WE JUST TAKE THE WEST WIND BRIGADE OFF THE ROUND TABLE COUNCIL?
IF WE DO THAT, THEN ALL THE FINANCING CONTRACTS SHOULD BECOME INVALID...
NO, NO, THAT WOULD BE TOO HARSH.
YOU SAID IT.
WAH HA HA!
... WELL.
AS A LAST RESORT, PERHAPS.
YEAH...
LET'S GET THIS DEALT WITH. NOW.
YES, INDEED ...!!

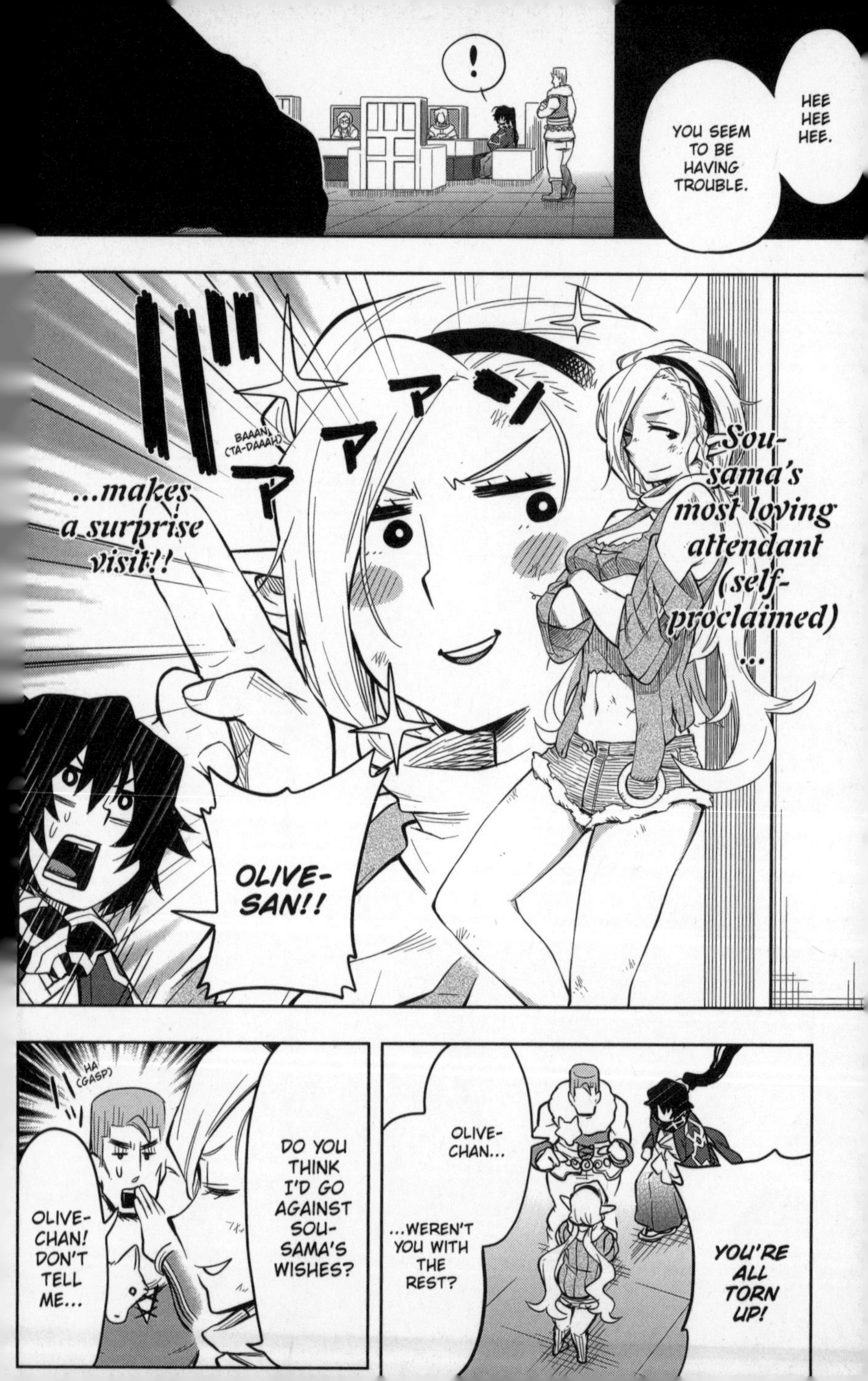
HEE HEE HEE.
YOU SEEM TO BE HAVING TROUBLE.
!
Sou-sama's most loving attendant (self-proclaimed)...
BAAAN (TA-DAAAH)
...makes a surprise visit!!
OLIVE-SAN!!
OLIVE-CHAN...
...WEREN'T YOU WITH THE REST?
YOU'RE ALL TORN UP!
HA (GASP)
OLIVE-CHAN! DON'T TELL ME...
DO YOU THINK I'D GO AGAINST SOU-SAMA'S WISHES?

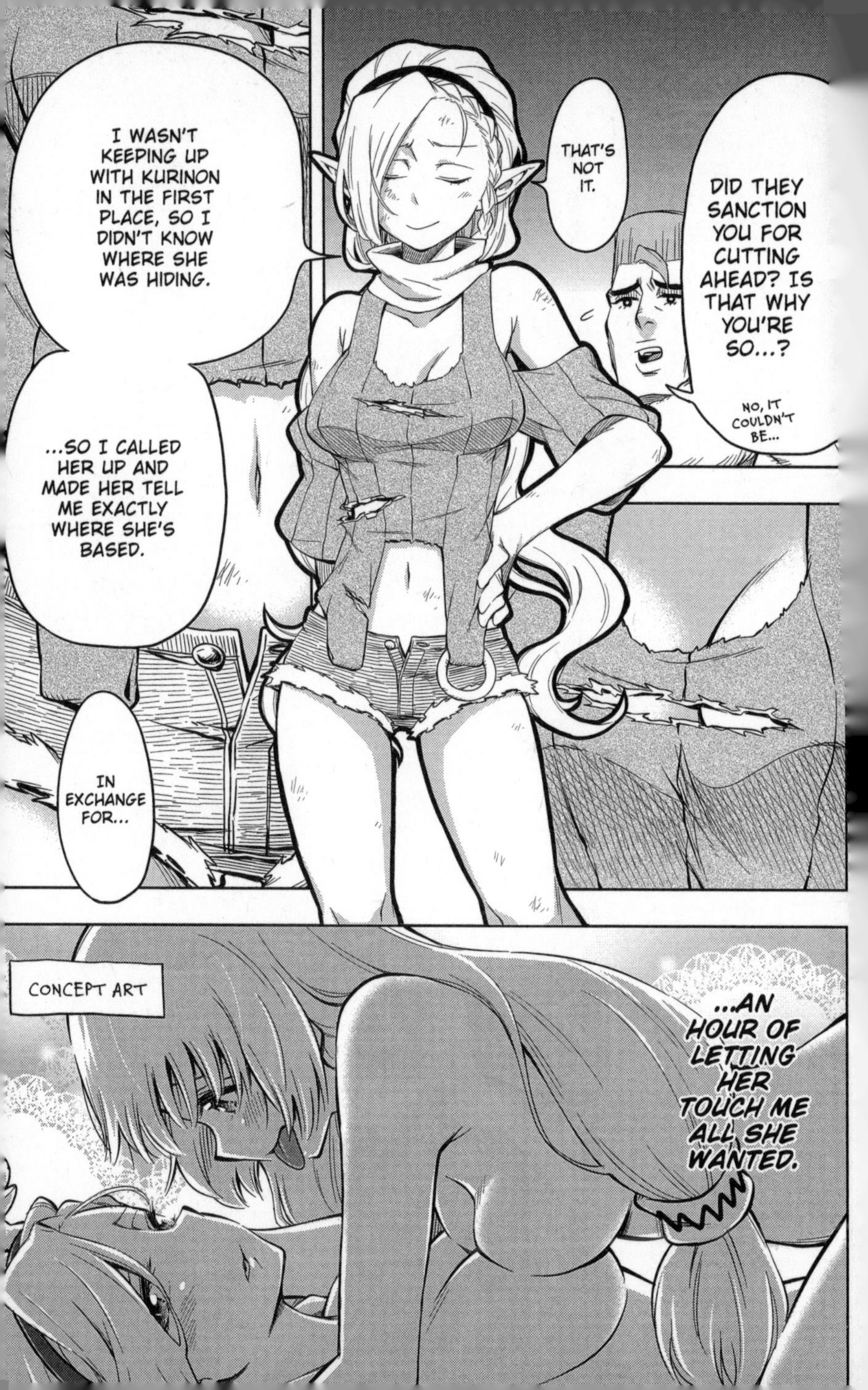
DID THEY SANCTION YOU FOR CUTTING AHEAD? IS THAT WHY YOU'RE SO...?
NO, IT COULDN'T BE...
THAT'S NOT IT.
I WASN'T KEEPING UP WITH KURINON IN THE FIRST PLACE, SO I DIDN'T KNOW WHERE SHE WAS HIDING.
...SO I CALLED HER UP AND MADE HER TELL ME EXACTLY WHERE SHE'S BASED.
IN EXCHANGE FOR...
...AN HOUR OF LETTING HER TOUCH ME ALL SHE WANTED.
CONCEPT ART

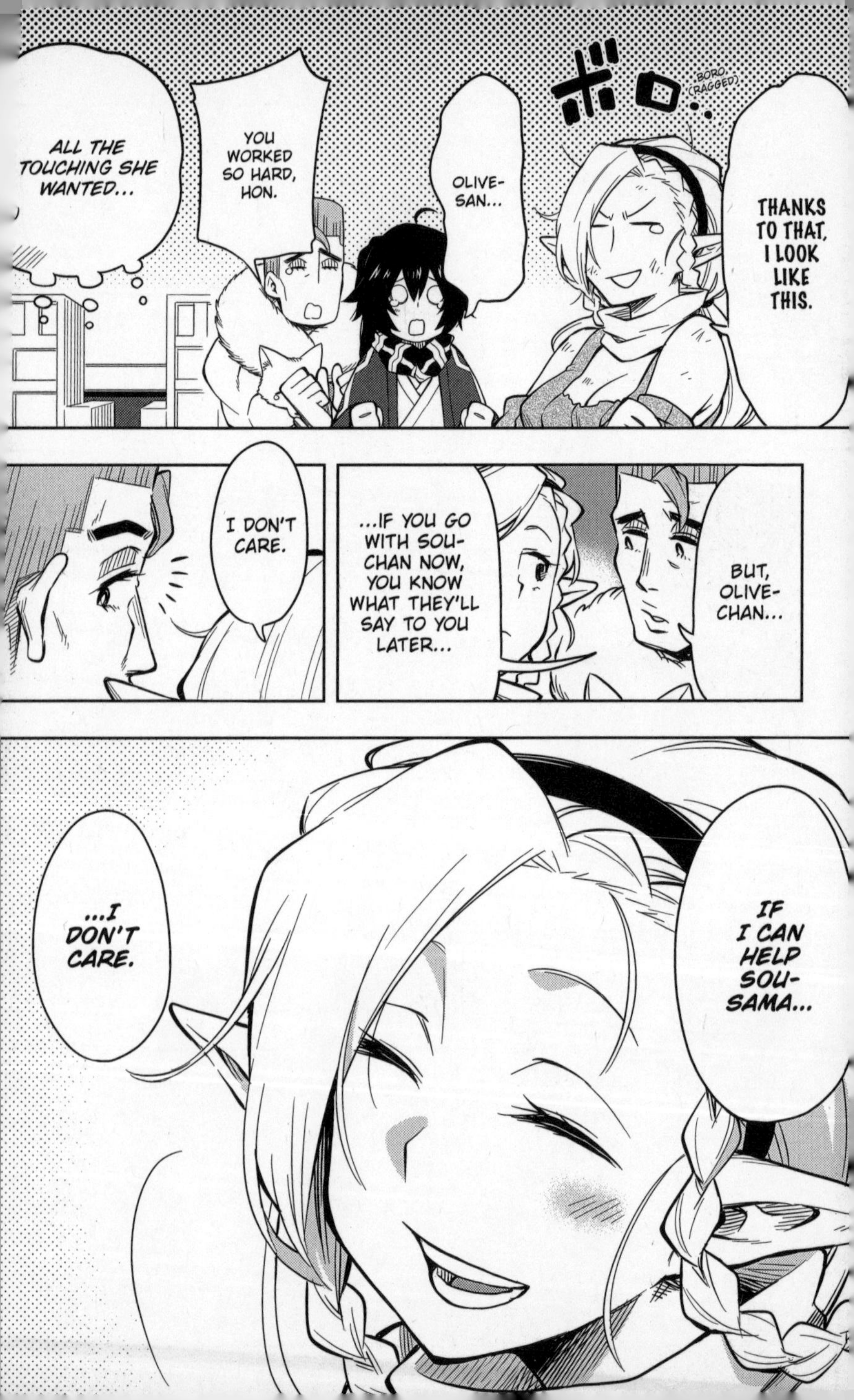
ボロ…
BORO (RAGGED)
THANKS TO THAT, I LOOK LIKE THIS.
OLIVE-SAN...
YOU WORKED SO HARD, HON.
ALL THE TOUCHING SHE WANTED...
BUT, OLIVE-CHAN...
...IF YOU GO WITH SOU-CHAN NOW, YOU KNOW WHAT THEY'LL SAY TO YOU LATER...
I DON'T CARE.
IF I CAN HELP SOU-SAMA...
...I DON'T CARE.

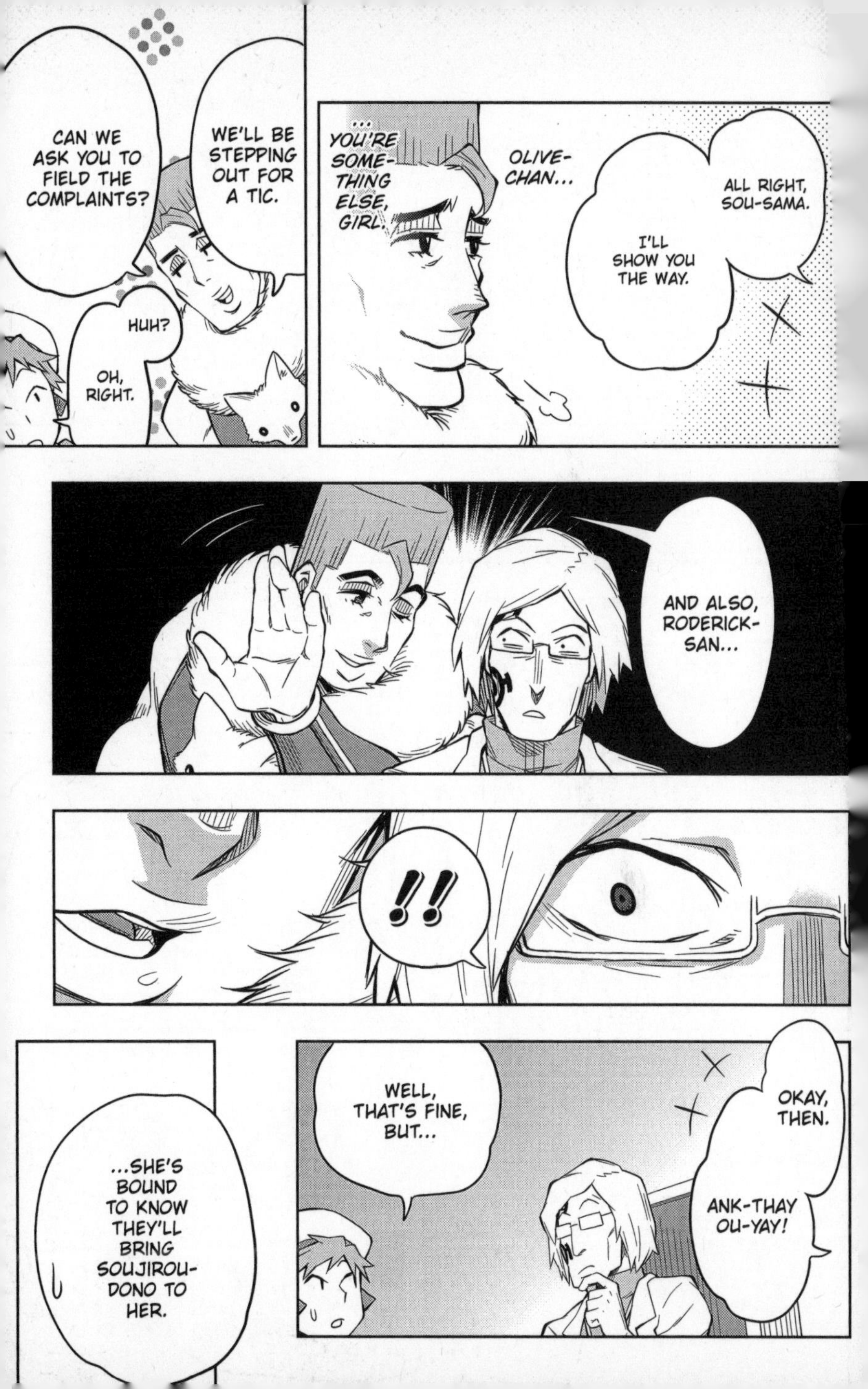
ALL RIGHT, SOU-SAMA.
I'LL SHOW YOU THE WAY.
OLIVE-CHAN...
...YOU'RE SOMETHING ELSE, GIRL.
WE'LL BE STEPPING OUT FOR A TIC.
CAN WE ASK YOU TO FIELD THE COMPLAINTS?
HUH?
OH, RIGHT.
AND ALSO, RODERICK-SAN...
!!
OKAY, THEN.
ANK-THAY OU-YAY!
WELL, THAT'S FINE, BUT...
...SHE'S BOUND TO KNOW THEY'LL BRING SOUJIROU-DONO TO HER.

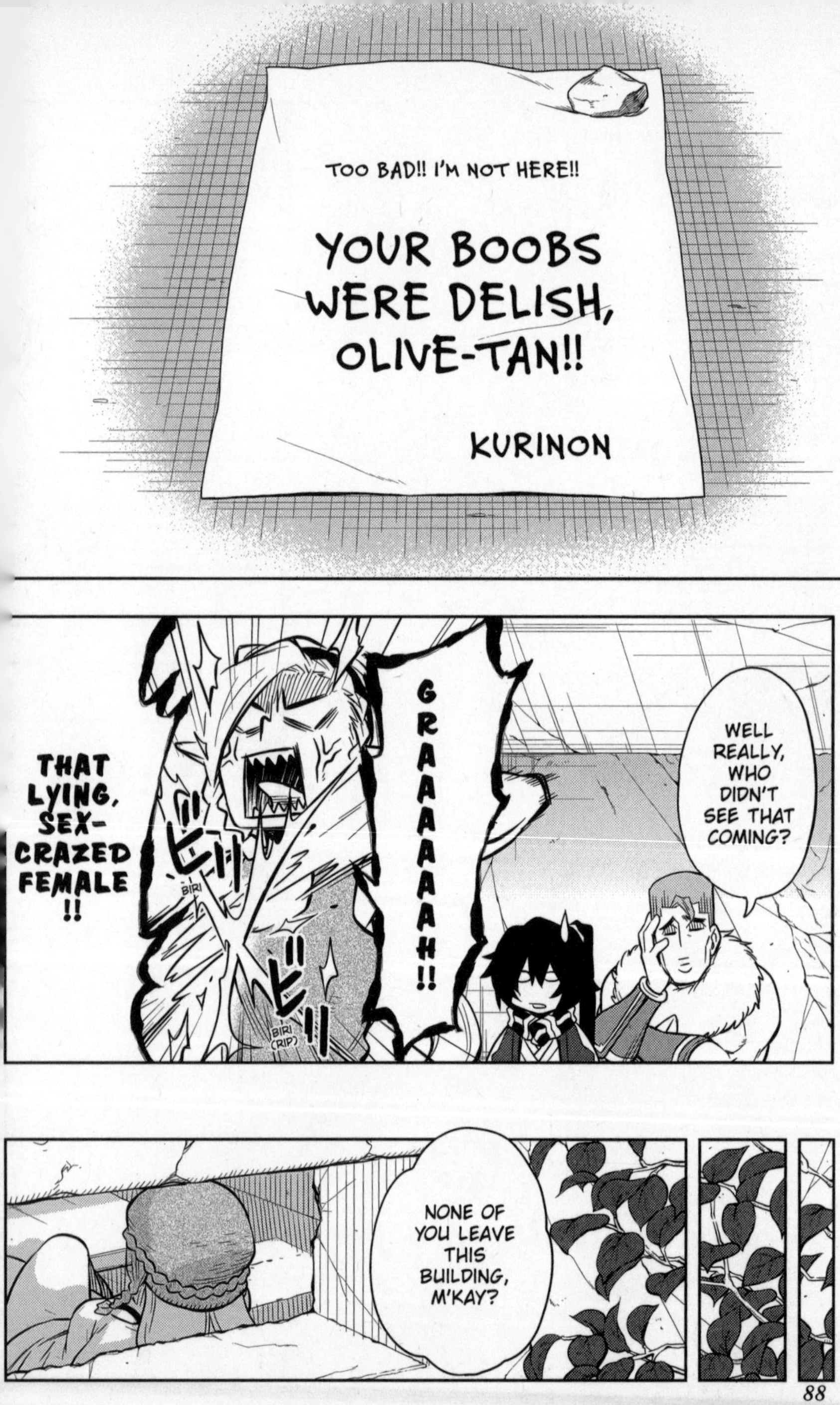
TOO BAD!! I'M NOT HERE!!
YOUR BOOBS WERE DELISH, OLIVE-TAN!!
KURINON
WELL REALLY, WHO DIDN'T SEE THAT COMING?
GRAAAAAAAH!!
BIRI (RIP)
BIRI
THAT LYING, SEX-CRAZED FEMALE!!
NONE OF YOU LEAVE THIS BUILDING, M'KAY?

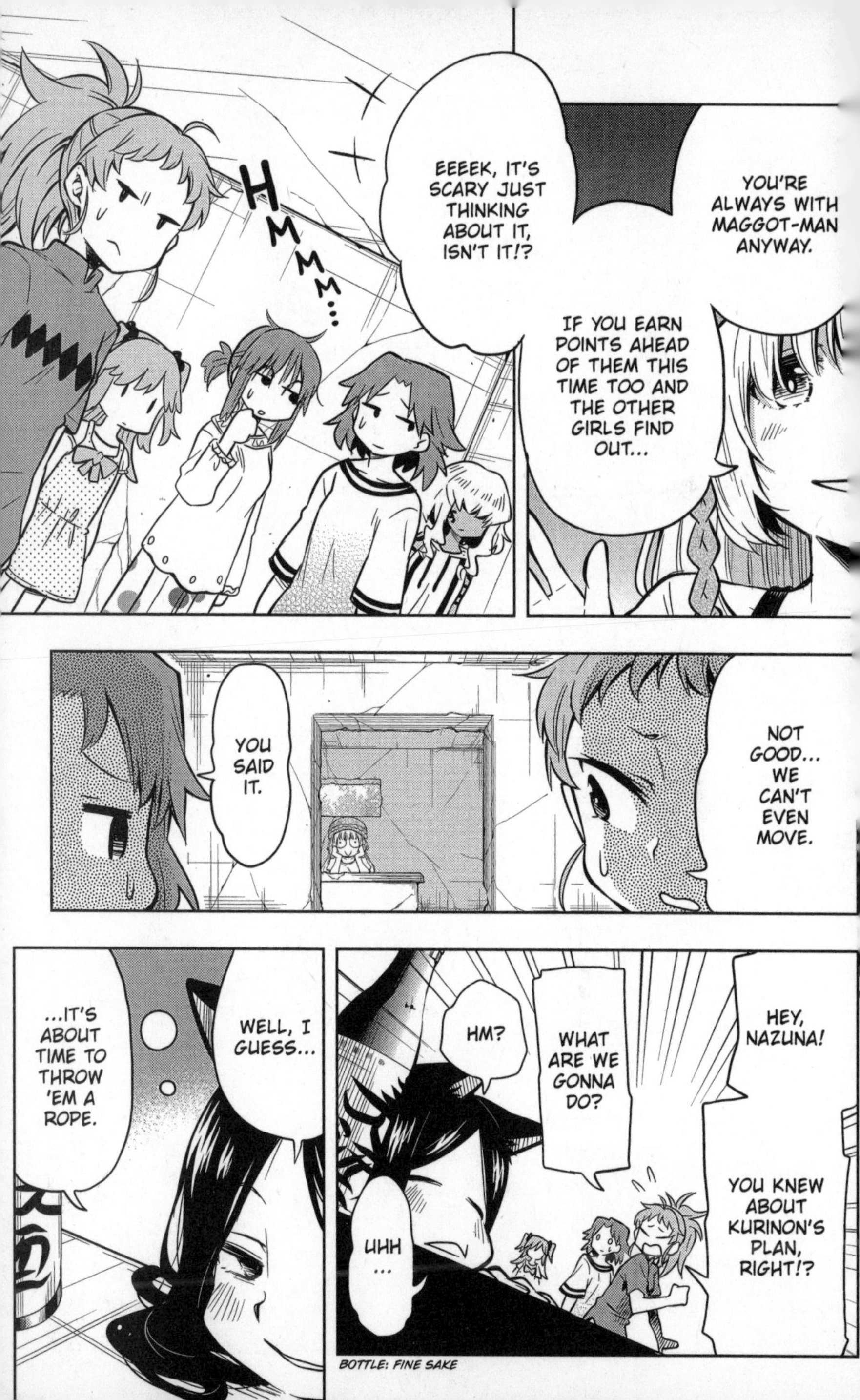
YOU'RE ALWAYS WITH MAGGOT-MAN ANYWAY.
IF YOU EARN POINTS AHEAD OF THEM THIS TIME TOO AND THE OTHER GIRLS FIND OUT...
EEEEK, IT'S SCARY JUST THINKING ABOUT IT, ISN'T IT!?
HMMM...
NOT GOOD... WE CAN'T EVEN MOVE.
YOU SAID IT.
HEY, NAZUNA!
YOU KNEW ABOUT KURINON'S PLAN, RIGHT!?
WHAT ARE WE GONNA DO?
HM?
UHH...
WELL, I GUESS...
...IT'S ABOUT TIME TO THROW 'EM A ROPE.

BOTTLE: FINE SAKE

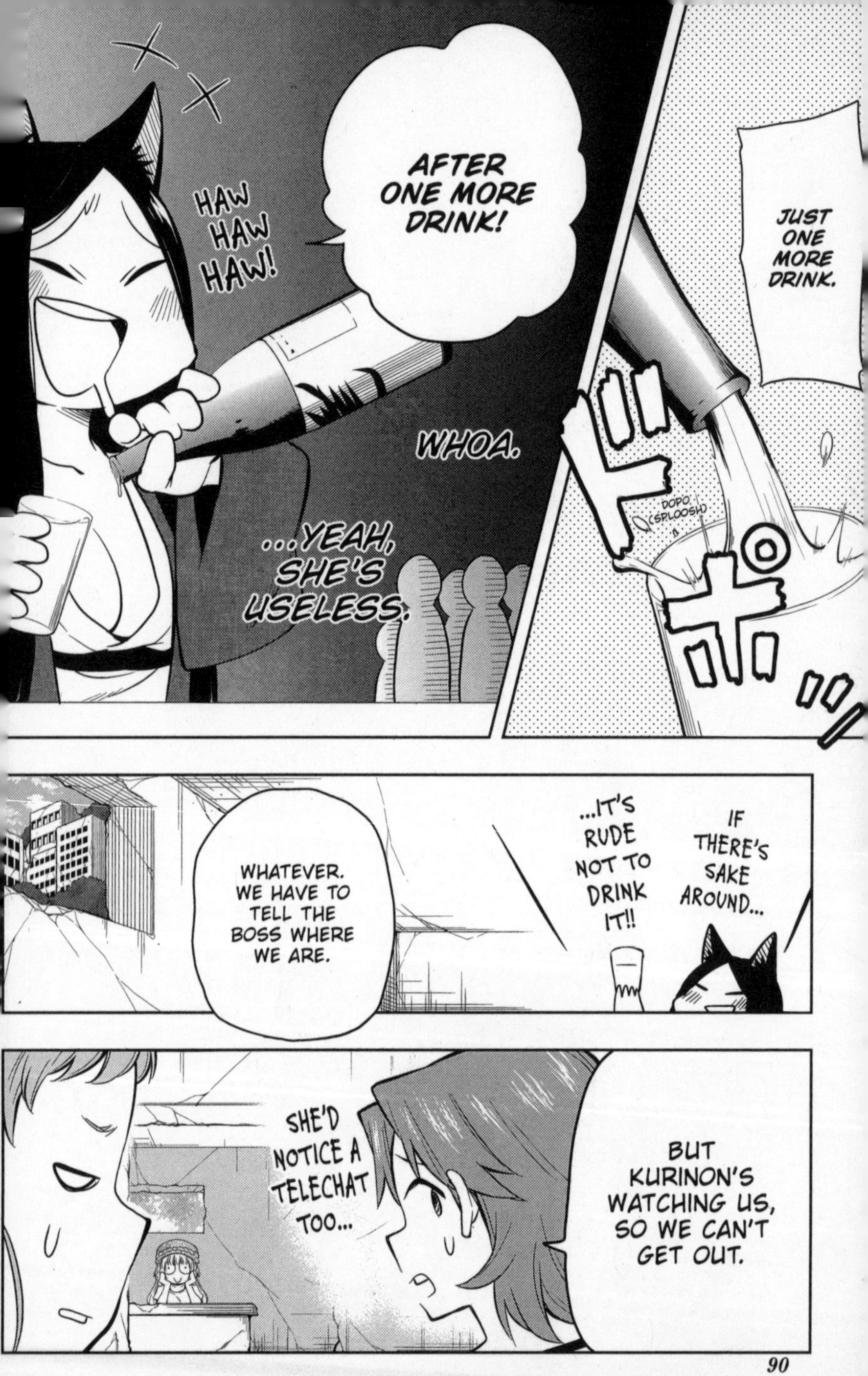
JUST ONE MORE DRINK.
DOPO (SPLOOSH)
AFTER ONE MORE DRINK!
HAW HAW HAW!
WHOA.
...YEAH, SHE'S USELESS.
IF THERE'S SAKE AROUND...
...IT'S RUDE NOT TO DRINK IT!!
WHATEVER. WE HAVE TO TELL THE BOSS WHERE WE ARE.
BUT KURINON'S WATCHING US, SO WE CAN'T GET OUT.
SHE'D NOTICE A TELECHAT TOO...

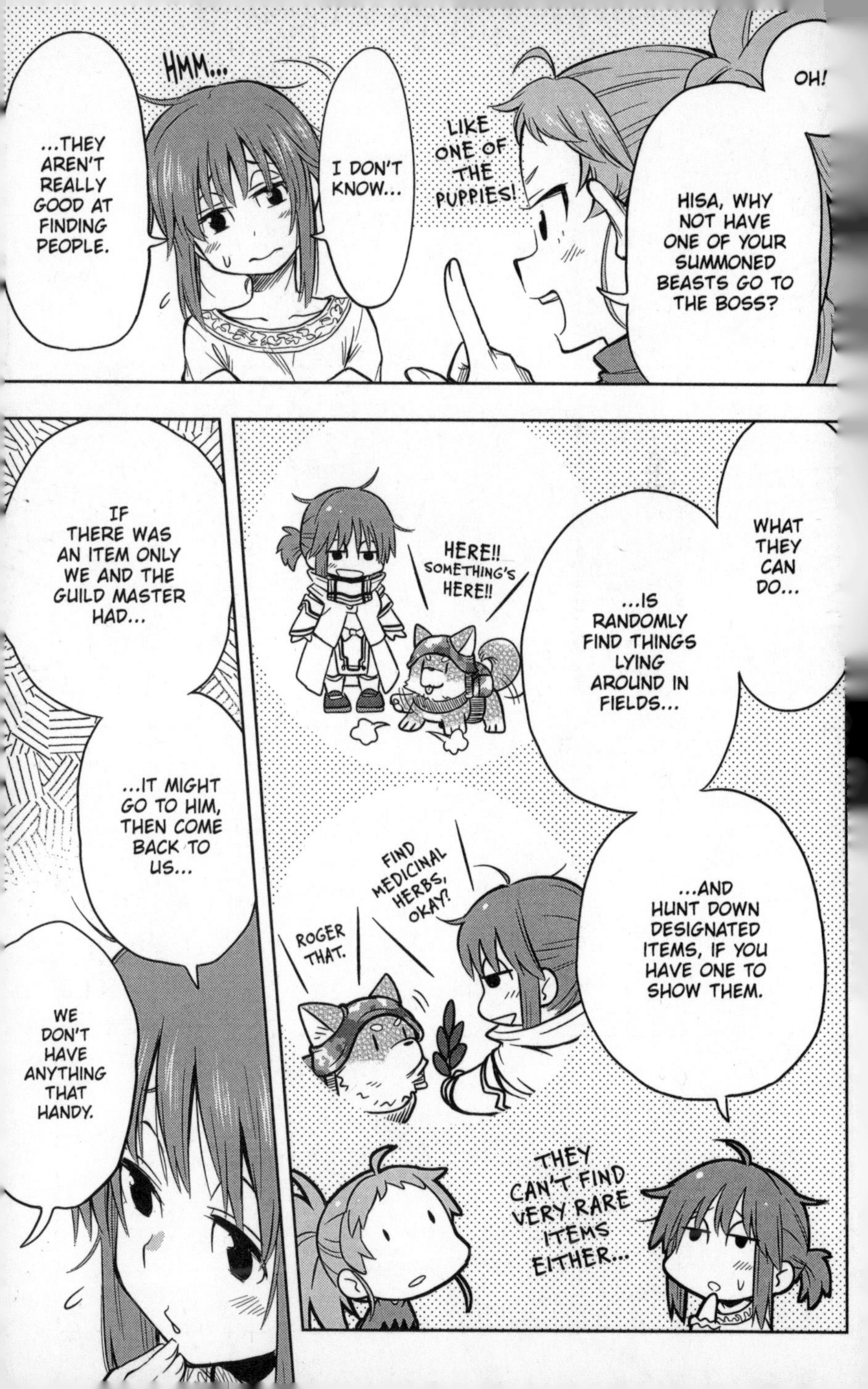
OH!
HISA, WHY NOT HAVE ONE OF YOUR SUMMONED BEASTS GO TO THE BOSS?
LIKE ONE OF THE PUPPIES!
HMM...
I DON'T KNOW...
...THEY AREN'T REALLY GOOD AT FINDING PEOPLE.
WHAT THEY CAN DO...
...IS RANDOMLY FIND THINGS LYING AROUND IN FIELDS...
HERE!! SOMETHING'S HERE!!
...AND HUNT DOWN DESIGNATED ITEMS, IF YOU HAVE ONE TO SHOW THEM.
FIND MEDICINAL HERBS, OKAY?
ROGER THAT.
THEY CAN'T FIND VERY RARE ITEMS EITHER...
IF THERE WAS AN ITEM ONLY WE AND THE GUILD MASTER HAD...
...IT MIGHT GO TO HIM, THEN COME BACK TO US...
WE DON'T HAVE ANYTHING THAT HANDY.

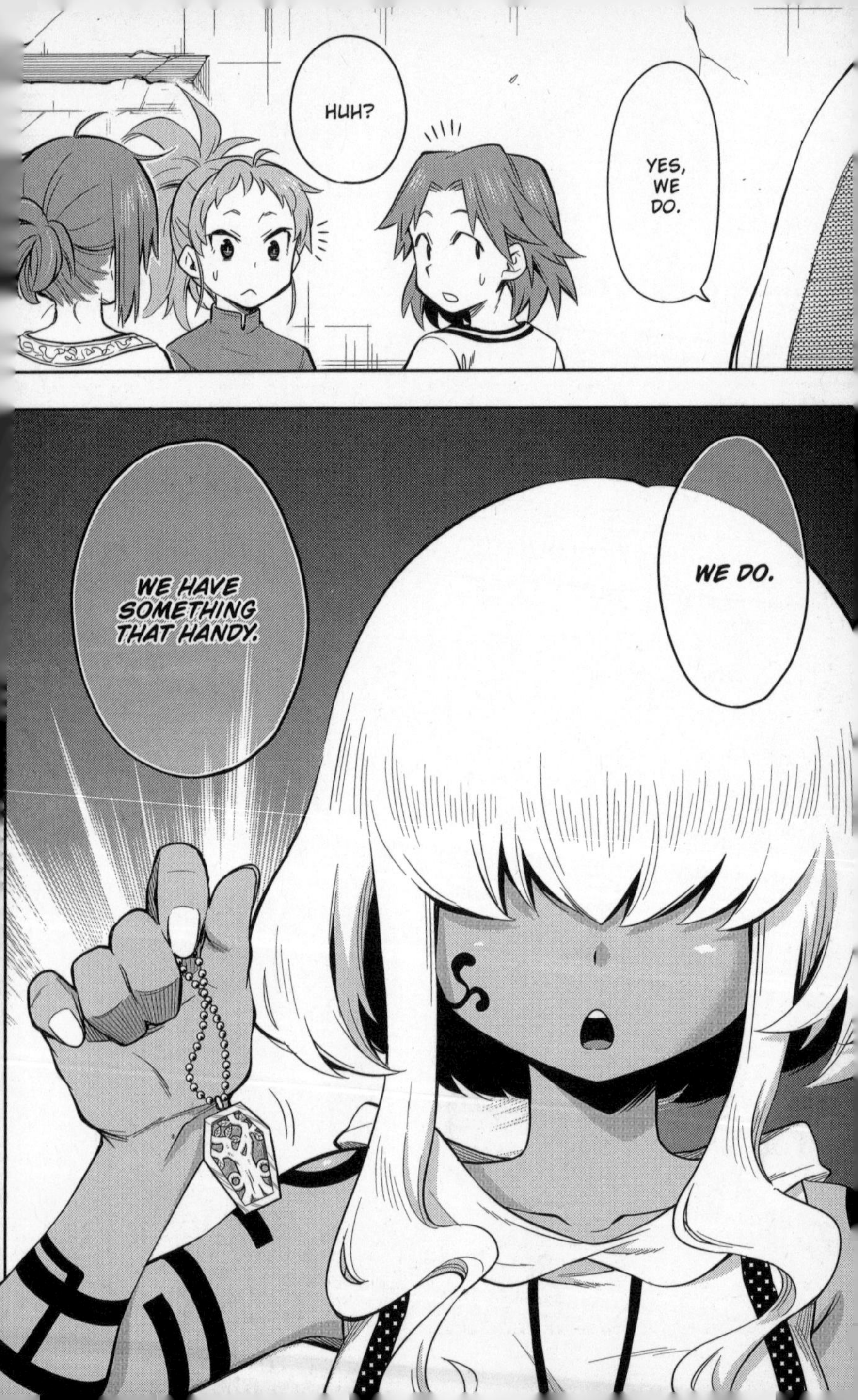
YES, WE DO.
HUH?
WE DO.
WE HAVE SOMETHING THAT HANDY.

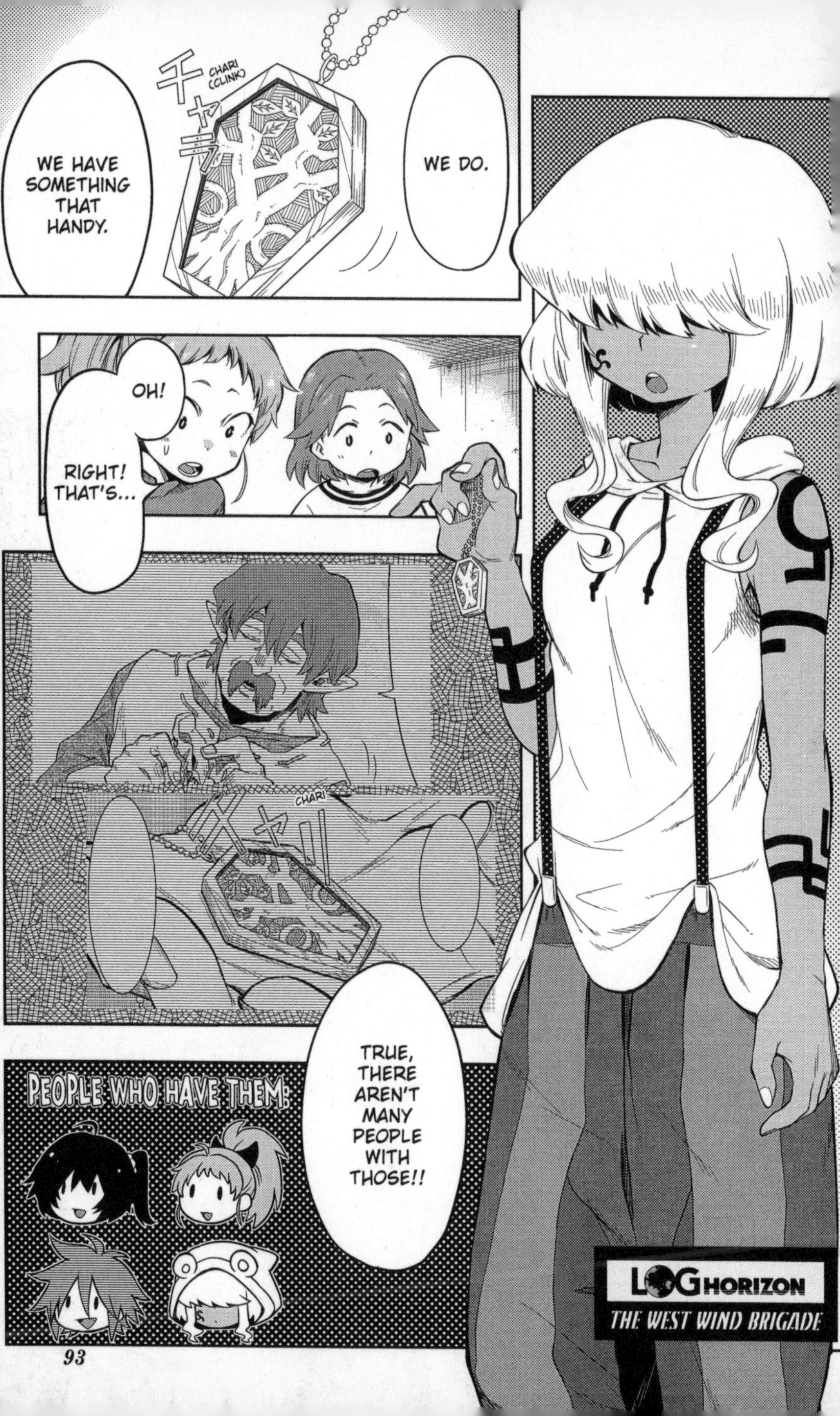
WE DO.
CHARI (CLINK)
WE HAVE SOMETHING THAT HANDY.
LOG HORIZON
THE WEST WIND BRIGADE
OH!
RIGHT! THAT'S...
CHARI
TRUE, THERE AREN'T MANY PEOPLE WITH THOSE!!
PEOPLE WHO HAVE THEM:

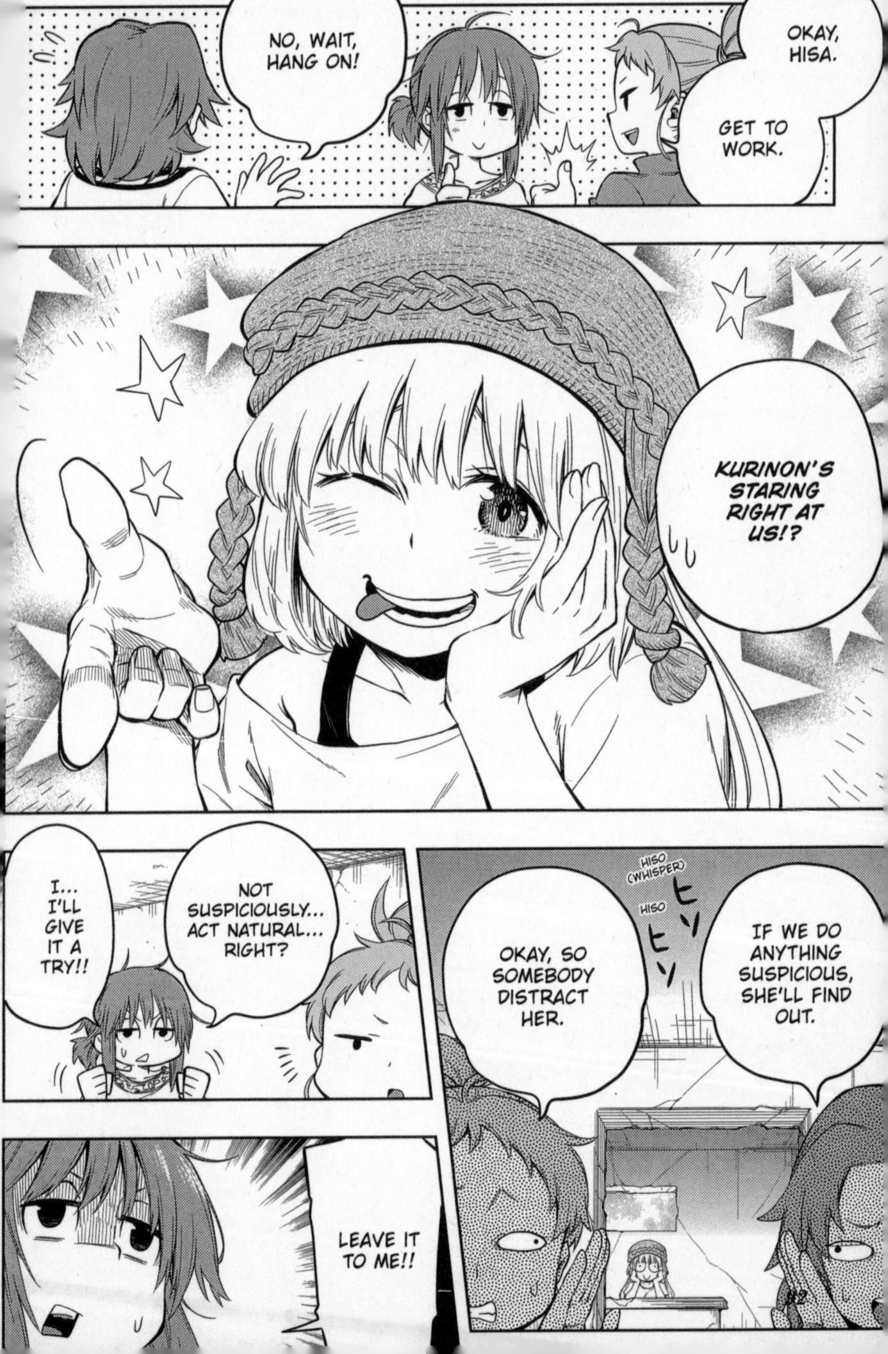
OKAY, HISA.
GET TO WORK.
NO, WAIT, HANG ON!
KURINON'S STARING RIGHT AT US!?
IF WE DO ANYTHING SUSPICIOUS, SHE'LL FIND OUT.
HISO (WHISPER)
HISO
OKAY, SO SOMEBODY DISTRACT HER.
NOT SUSPICIOUSLY... ACT NATURAL... RIGHT?
I... I'LL GIVE IT A TRY!!
LEAVE IT TO ME!!

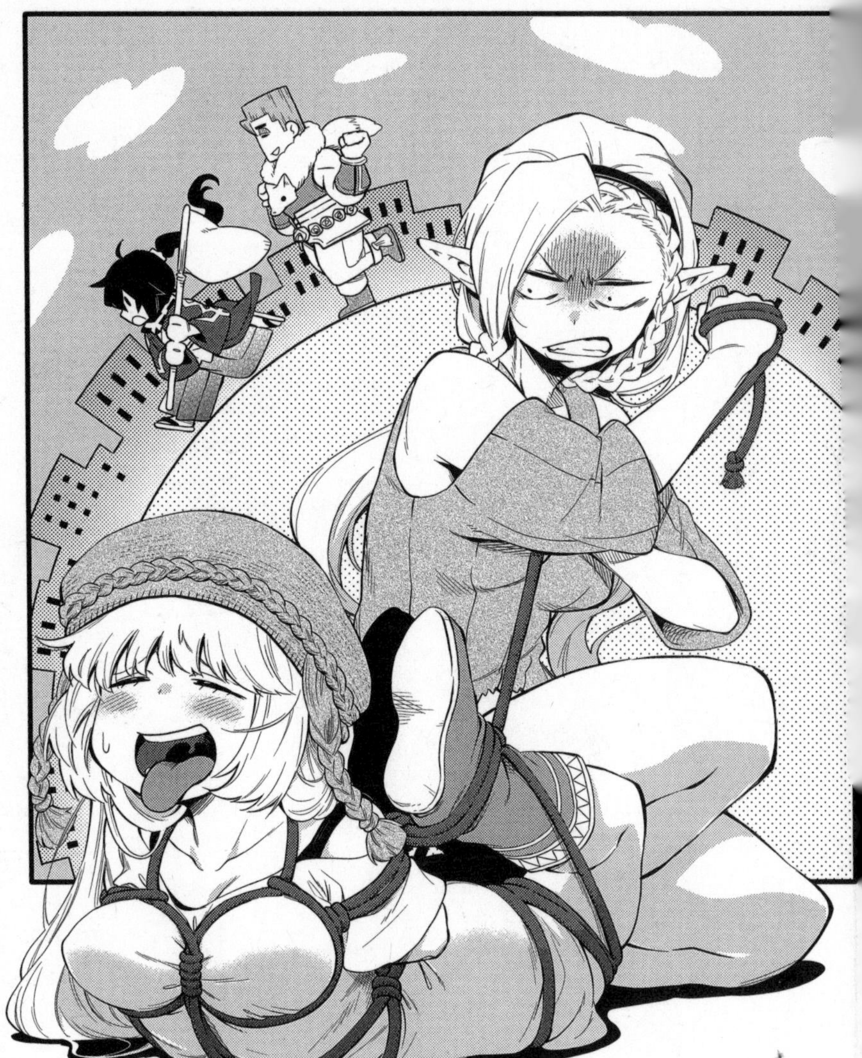

[CHAPTER: 34 CAPTURE KURINON! (PART 2)]

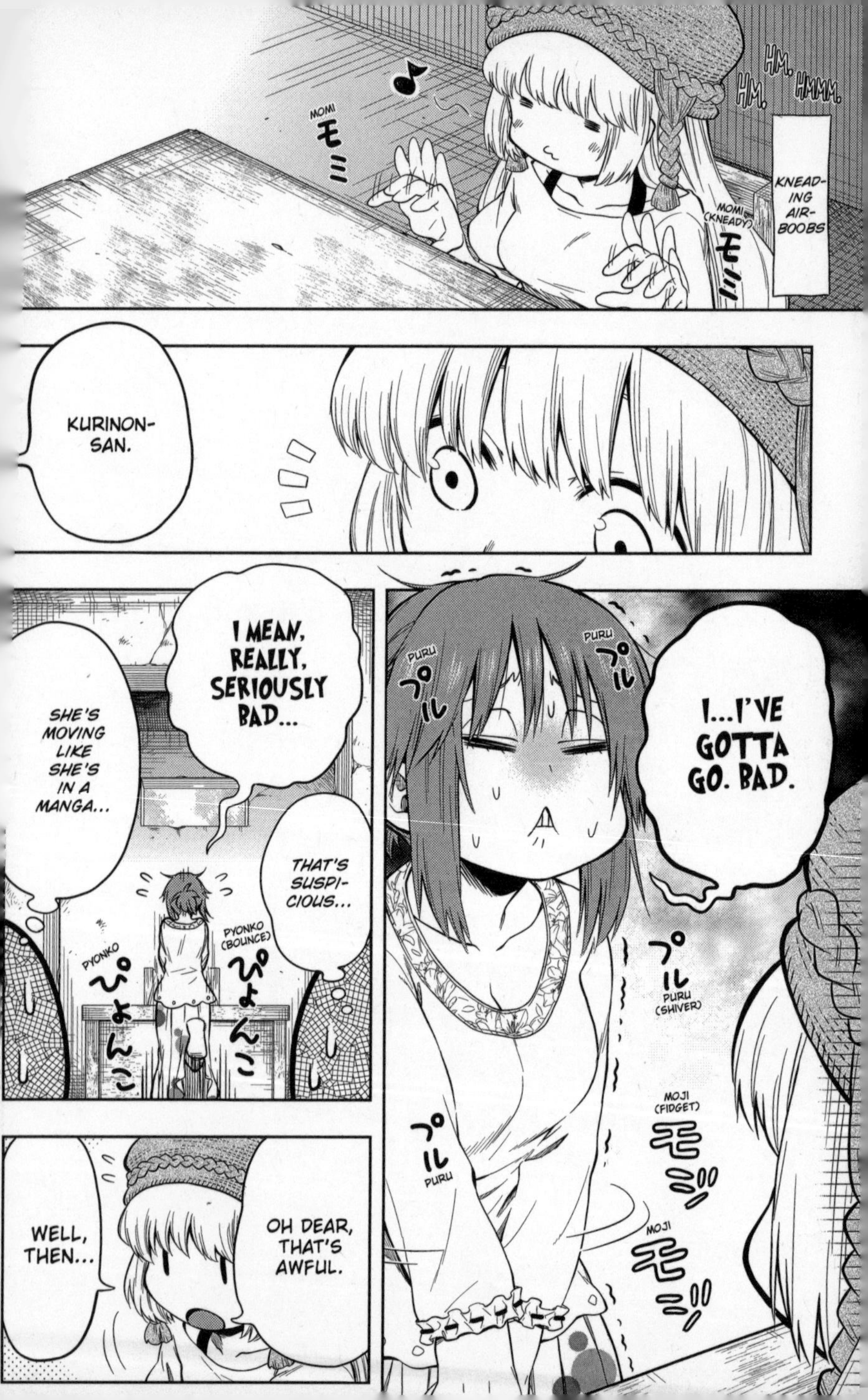
HM. HM. HMMM.
KNEADING AIR-BOOBS
MOMI (KNEADY)
モミ
MOMI
モミ
KURINON-SAN.
PURU
プル
PURU
プル
I...I'VE GOTTA GO. BAD.
プル
PURU (SHIVER)
MOJI (FIDGET)
モジ
プル
PURU
MOJI
モジ
I MEAN, REALLY, SERIOUSLY BAD...
THAT'S SUSPICIOUS...
SHE'S MOVING LIKE SHE'S IN A MANGA...
PYONKO (BOUNCE)
ぴょんこ
PYONKO
ぴょんこ
OH DEAR, THAT'S AWFUL.
WELL, THEN...

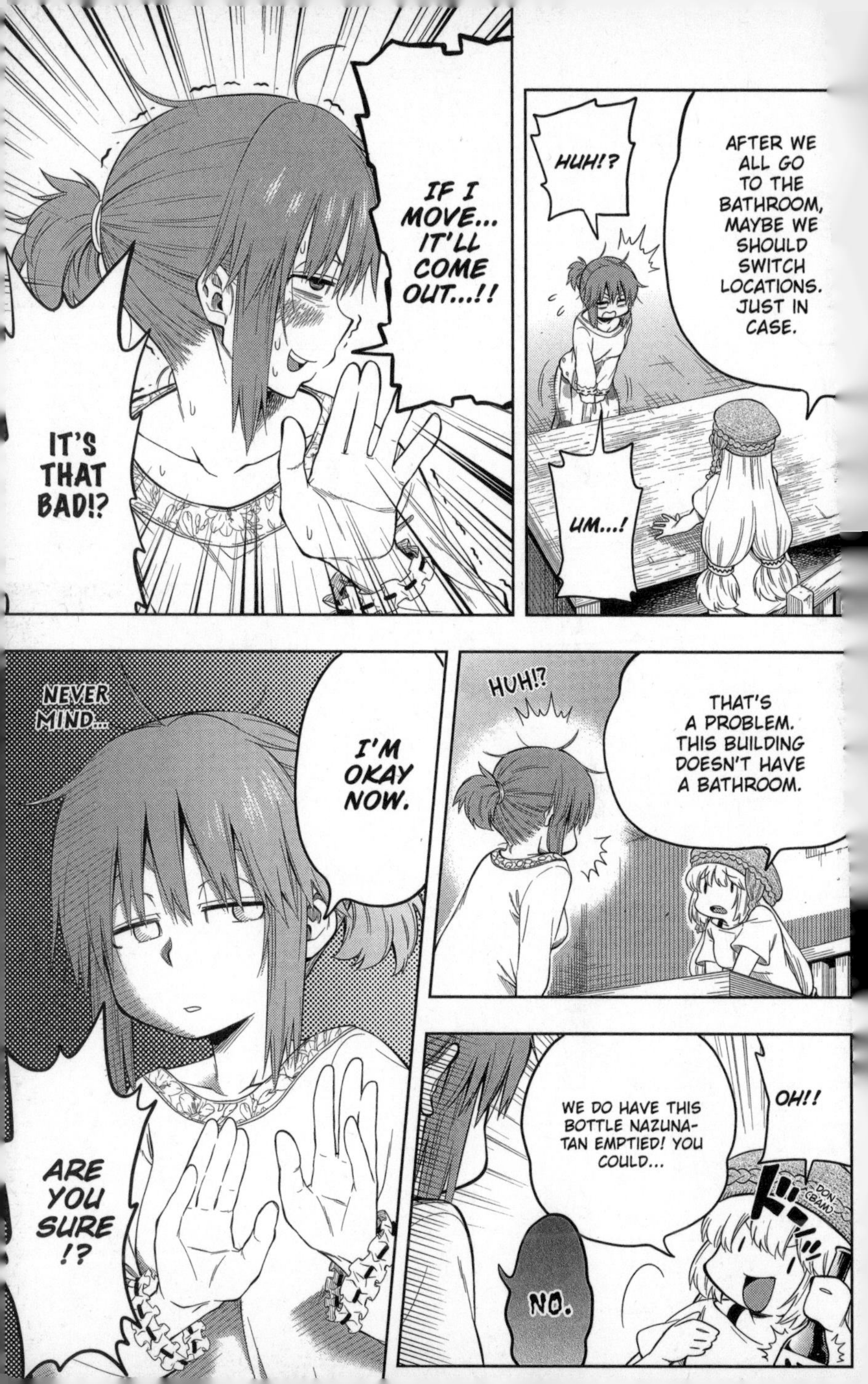

AFTER WE ALL GO TO THE BATHROOM, MAYBE WE SHOULD SWITCH LOCATIONS. JUST IN CASE.
HUH!?
UM...!
IF I MOVE... IT'LL COME OUT...!!
IT'S THAT BAD!?
THAT'S A PROBLEM. THIS BUILDING DOESN'T HAVE A BATHROOM.
HUH!?
OH!!
DON (BAM)
WE DO HAVE THIS BOTTLE NAZUNA-TAN EMPTIED! YOU COULD...
NO.
I'M OKAY NOW.
NEVER MIND...
ARE YOU SURE!?

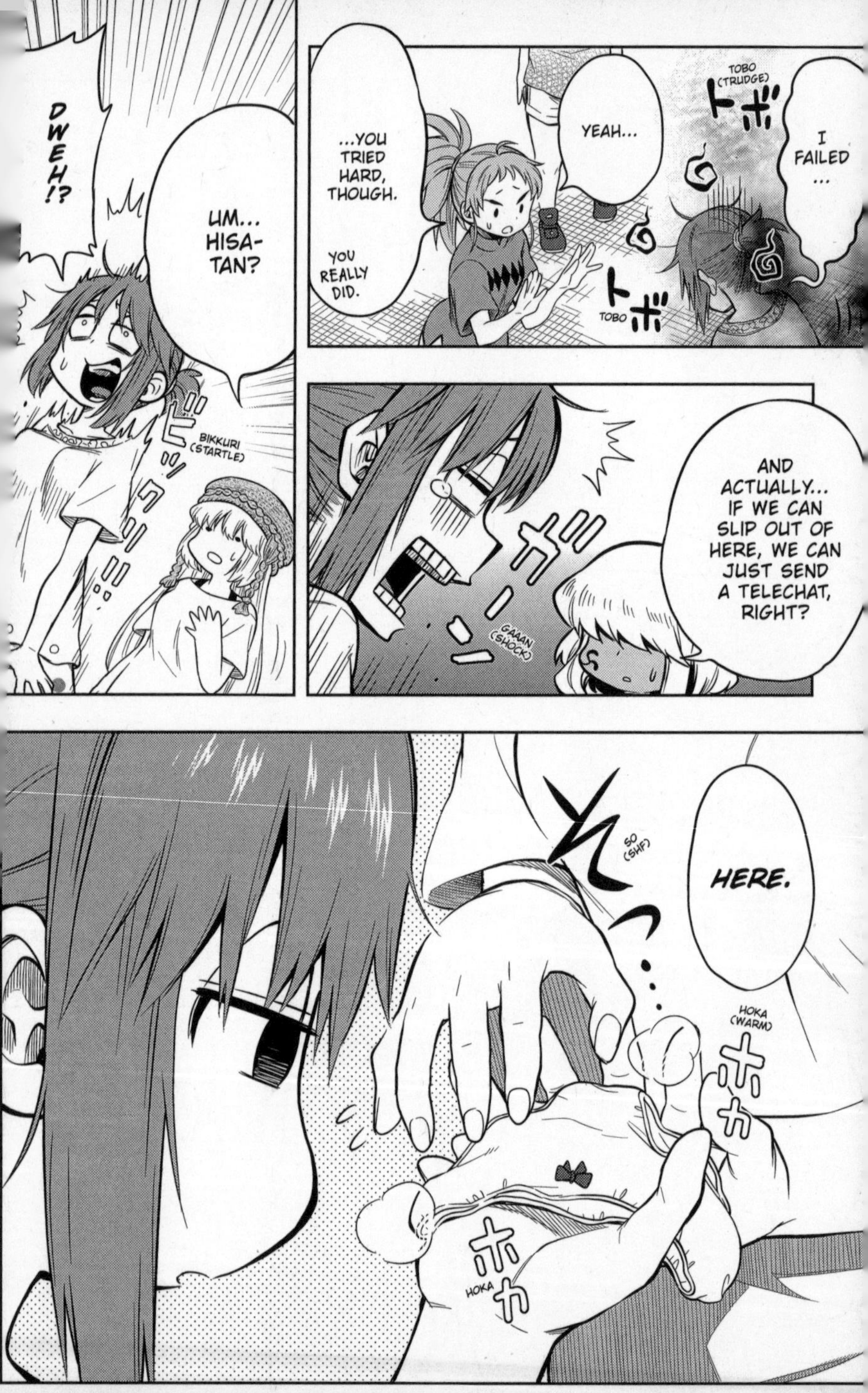
I FAILED...
TOBO (TRUDGE)
トボ
TOBO
トボ
YEAH...
...YOU TRIED HARD, THOUGH.
YOU REALLY DID.
UM... HISA-TAN?
DWEH!?
BIKKURI (STARTLE)
ビクッ!!
AND ACTUALLY... IF WE CAN SLIP OUT OF HERE, WE CAN JUST SEND A TELECHAT, RIGHT?
GAAAN (SHOCK)
ガーン
HERE.
SO (SHF)
そっ
HOKA (WARM)
ホカ
HOKA
ホカ

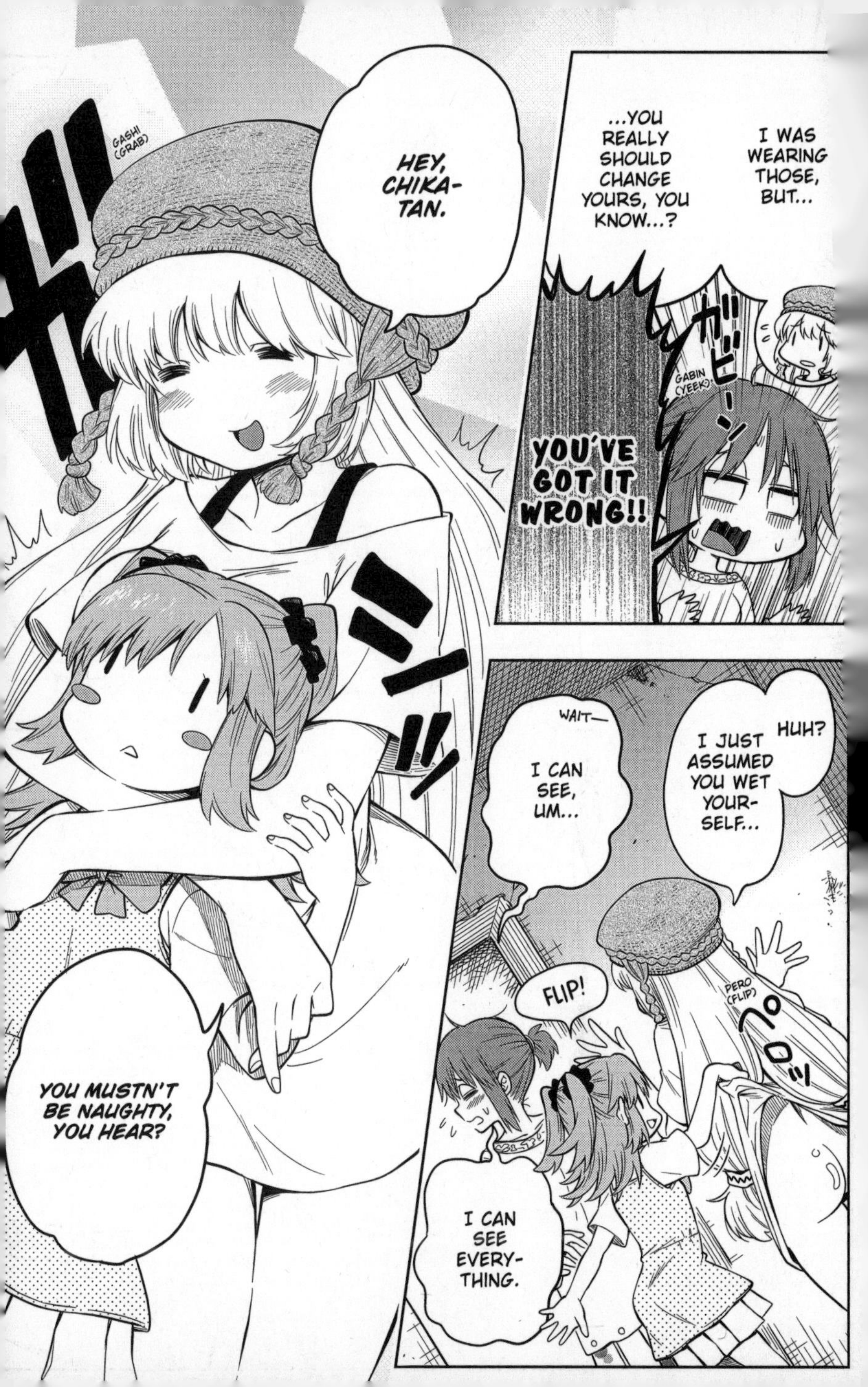
I WAS WEARING THOSE, BUT...
...YOU REALLY SHOULD CHANGE YOURS, YOU KNOW...?
GABIN (YEEK)
YOU'VE GOT IT WRONG!!
HUH?
I JUST ASSUMED YOU WET YOURSELF...
WAIT—
I CAN SEE, UM...
PERO (FLIP)
FLIP!
I CAN SEE EVERYTHING.
GASHI (GRAB)
HEY, CHIKA-TAN.
YOU MUSTN'T BE NAUGHTY, YOU HEAR?

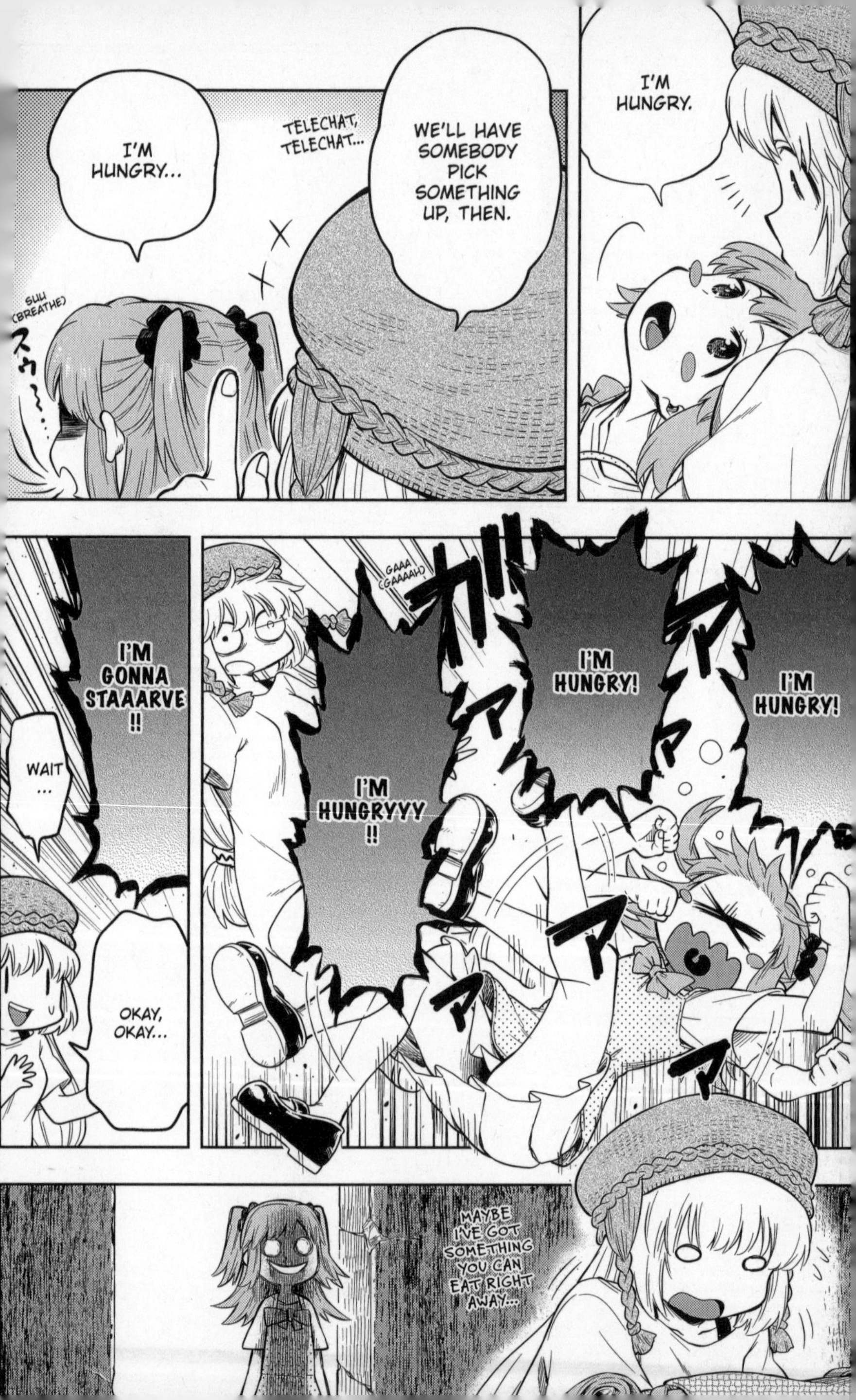
I'M HUNGRY.
WE'LL HAVE SOMEBODY PICK SOMETHING UP, THEN.
TELECHAT, TELECHAT...
I'M HUNGRY...
SUU (BREATHE)
GAAA (GAAAAH)
I'M HUNGRY!
I'M HUNGRY!
I'M HUNGRYYY !!
I'M GONNA STAAARVE !!
WAIT ...
OKAY, OKAY...
MAYBE I'VE GOT SOMETHING YOU CAN EAT RIGHT AWAY...

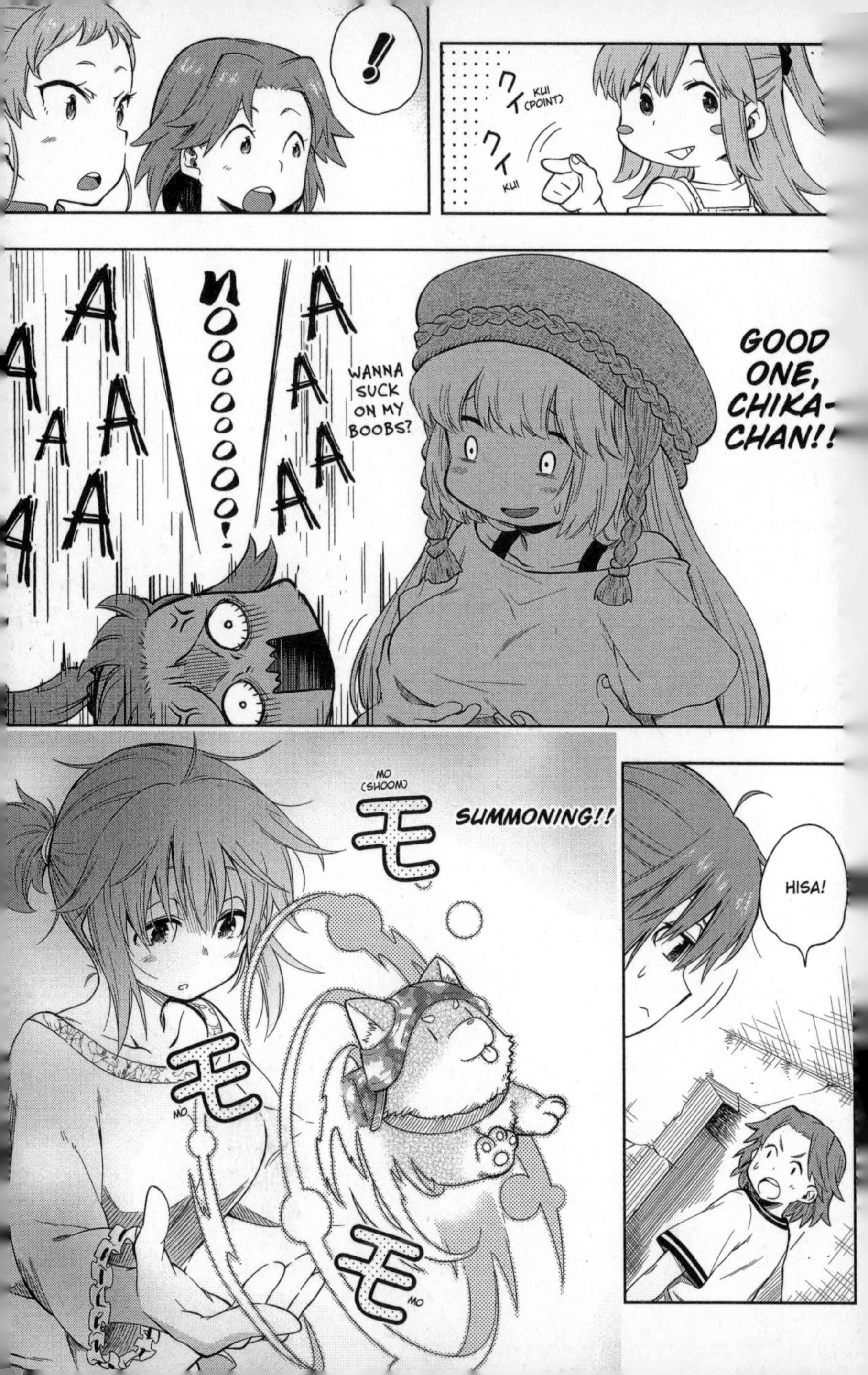

クイ KUI (POINT)
クイ KUI
!
GOOD ONE, CHIKA-CHAN!!
WANNA SUCK ON MY BOOBS?
AAAA
nOOOOOOOOOOO!
AAAAAAAAA
HISA!
SUMMONING!!
モ MO (SHOOM)
モ MO
モ MO

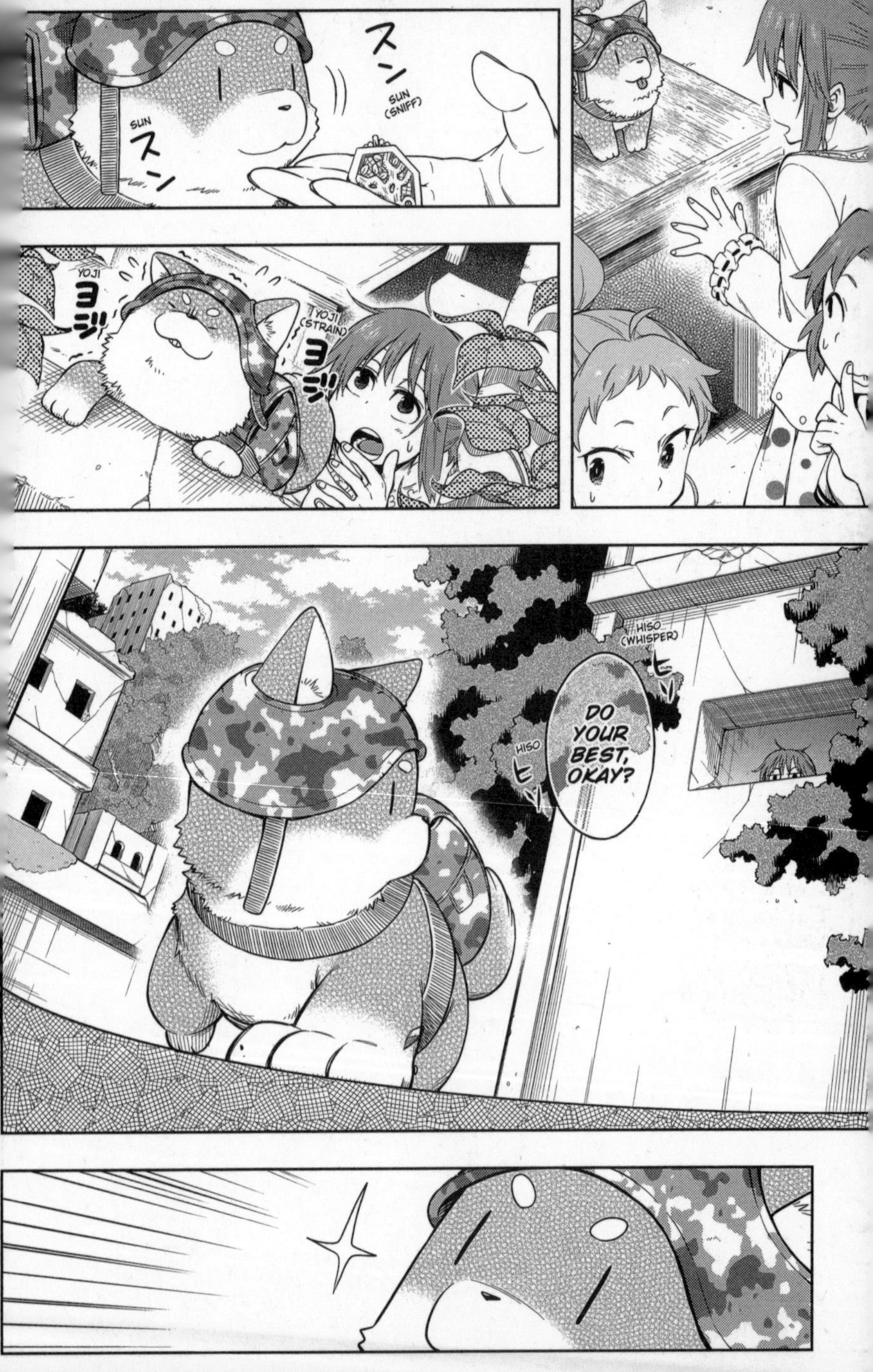
スン
SUN (SNIFF)
SUN
スン
YOJI (STRAIN)
ヨジ
YOJI
ヨジ
HISO (WHISPER)
ヒ
DO YOUR BEST, OKAY?
HISO
ヒ

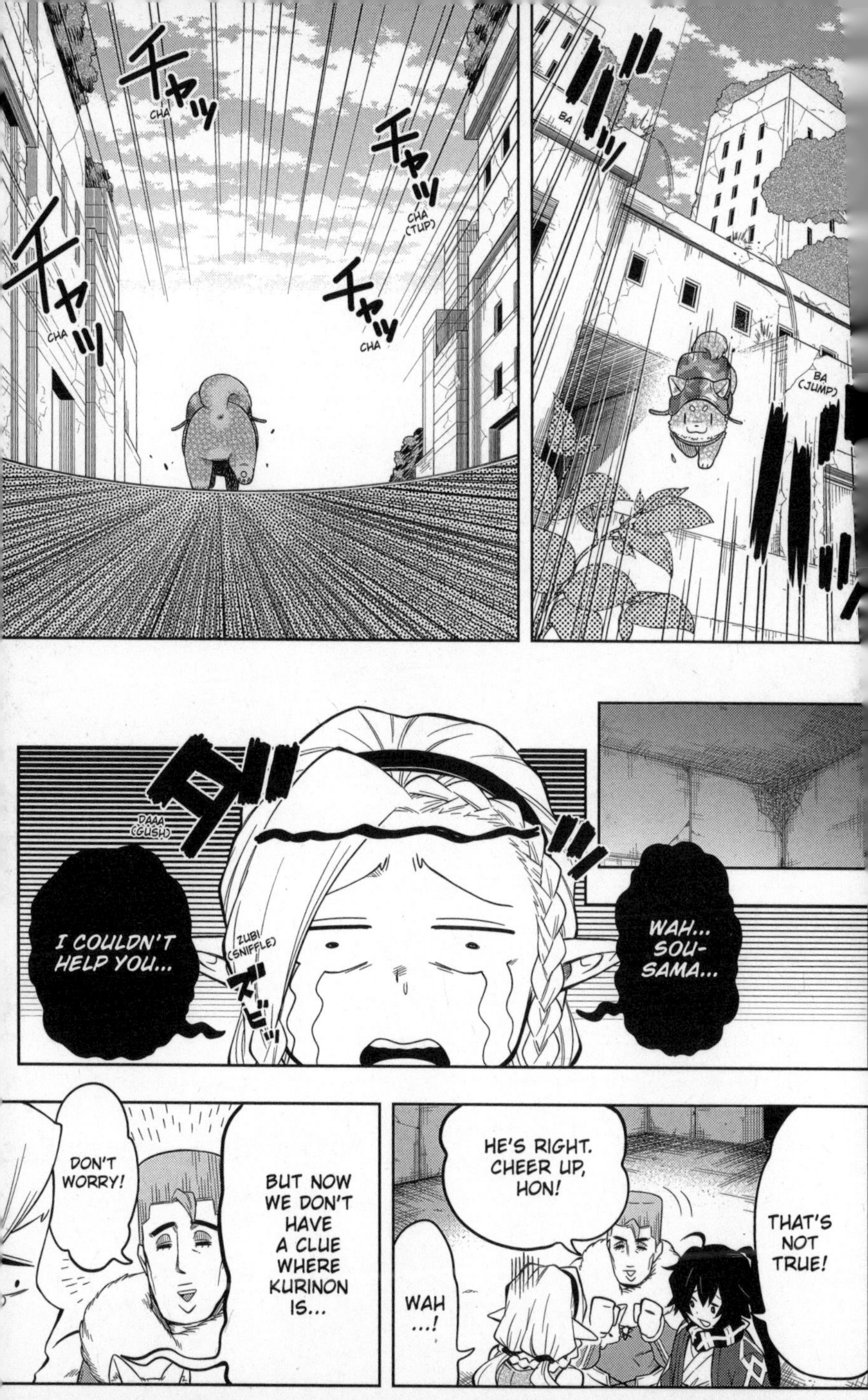
バッ
BA
BA (JUMP)
チャッ
CHA
チャッ
CHA (TUP)
チャッ
CHA
チャッ
CHA
WAH... SOU-SAMA...
ダッ
DAAA (GUSH)
ズビッ
ZUBI (SNIFFLE)
I COULDN'T HELP YOU...
THAT'S NOT TRUE!
HE'S RIGHT. CHEER UP, HON!
WAH ...!
BUT NOW WE DON'T HAVE A CLUE WHERE KURINON IS...
DON'T WORRY!

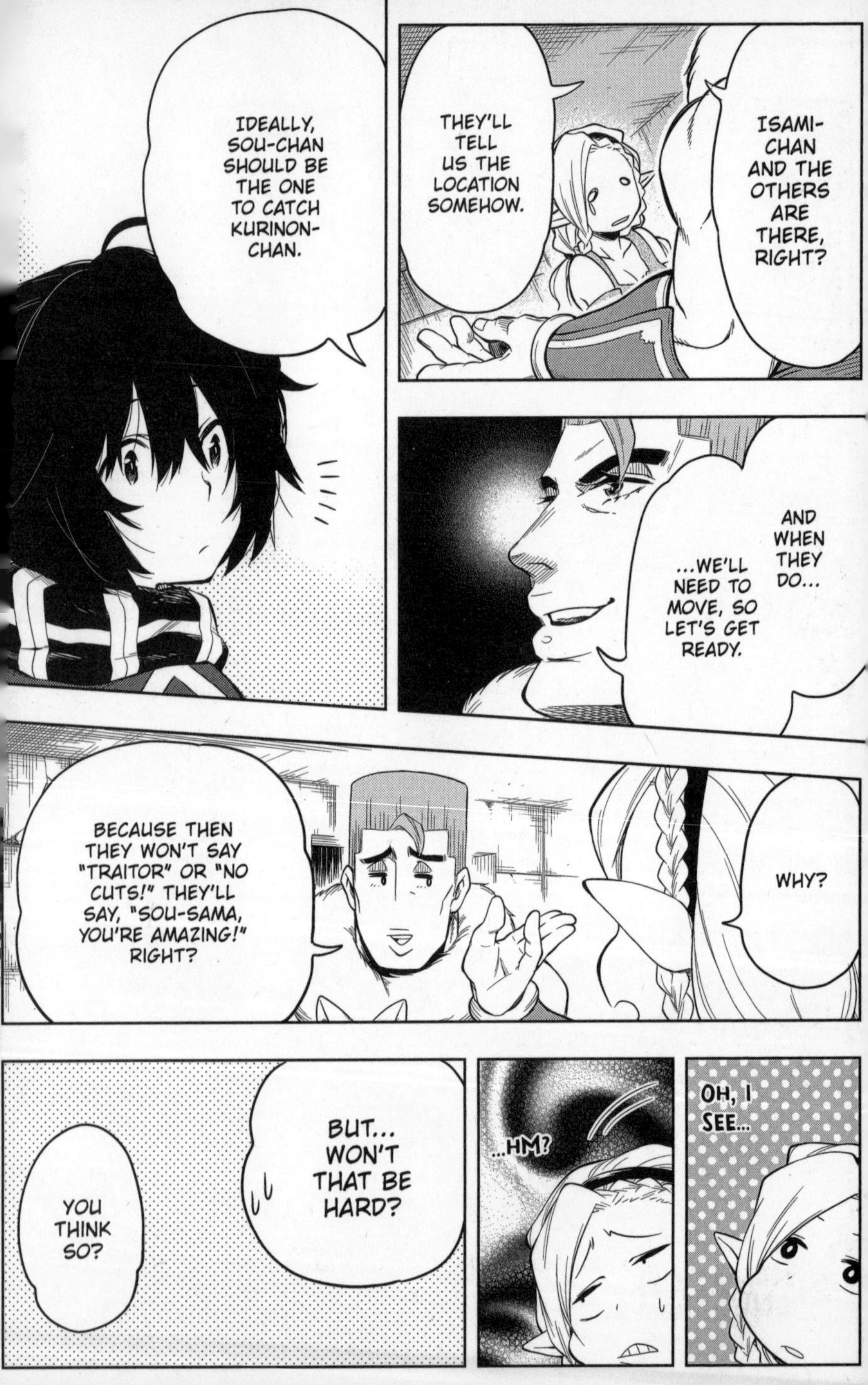
ISAMI-CHAN AND THE OTHERS ARE THERE, RIGHT?
THEY'LL TELL US THE LOCATION SOMEHOW.
AND WHEN THEY DO...
...WE'LL NEED TO MOVE, SO LET'S GET READY.
IDEALLY, SOU-CHAN SHOULD BE THE ONE TO CATCH KURINON-CHAN.
WHY?
BECAUSE THEN THEY WON'T SAY "TRAITOR" OR "NO CUTS!" THEY'LL SAY, "SOU-SAMA, YOU'RE AMAZING!" RIGHT?
OH, I SEE...
...HM?
BUT... WON'T THAT BE HARD?
YOU THINK SO?

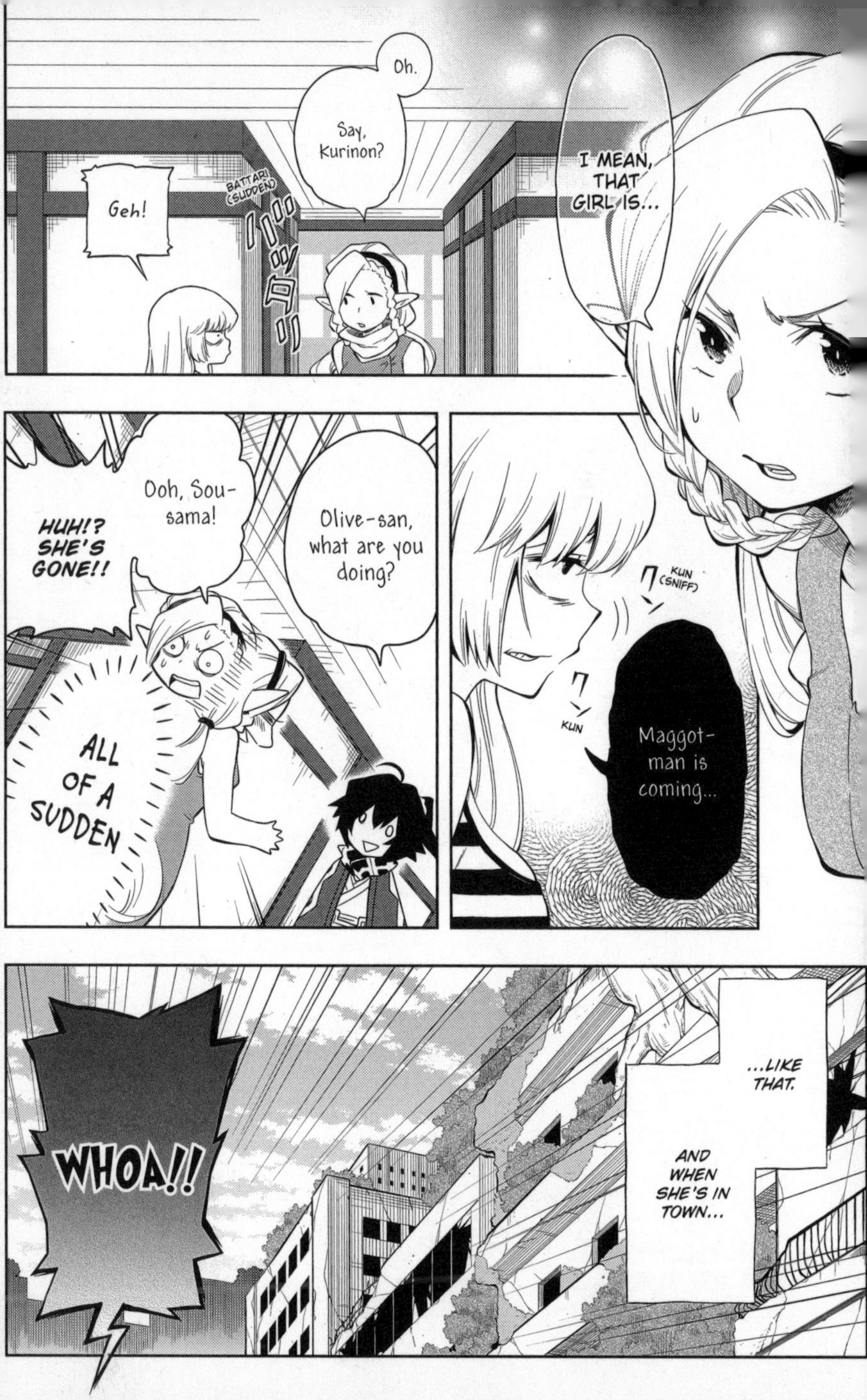
I MEAN, THAT GIRL IS...
Oh.
Say, Kurinon?
BATTARI (SUDDEN)
Geh!
KUN (SNIFF)
KUN
Maggot-man is coming...
Olive-san, what are you doing?
Ooh, Sou-sama!
HUH!? SHE'S GONE!!
ALL OF A SUDDEN
...LIKE THAT.
AND WHEN SHE'S IN TOWN...
WHOA!!

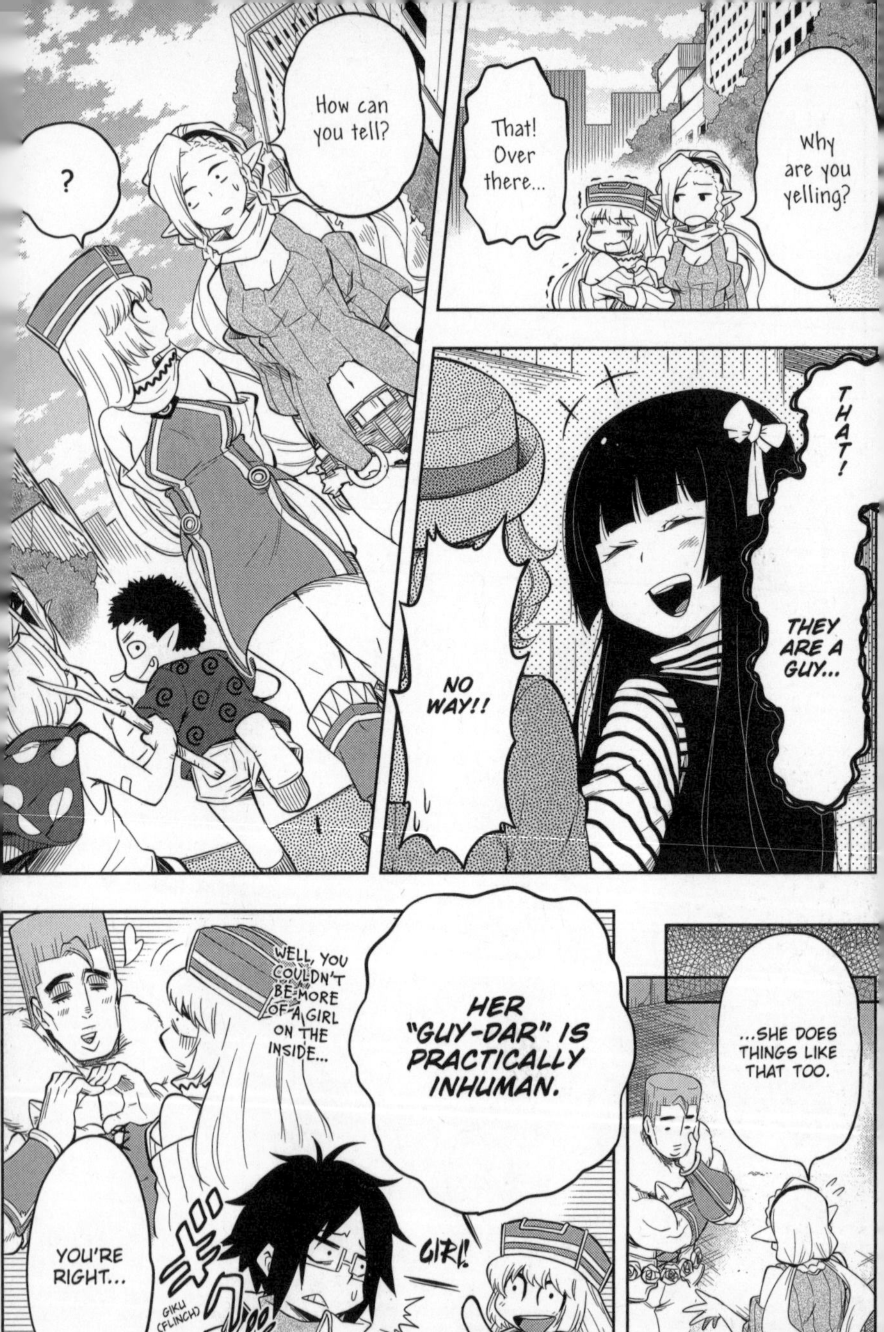
Why are you yelling?
That! Over there...
THAT!
THEY ARE A GUY...
NO WAY!!
How can you tell?
?
...SHE DOES THINGS LIKE THAT TOO.
HER "GUY-DAR" IS PRACTICALLY INHUMAN.
GIRL!
WELL, YOU COULDN'T BE MORE OF A GIRL ON THE INSIDE...
GIKU (FLINCH)
YOU'RE RIGHT...

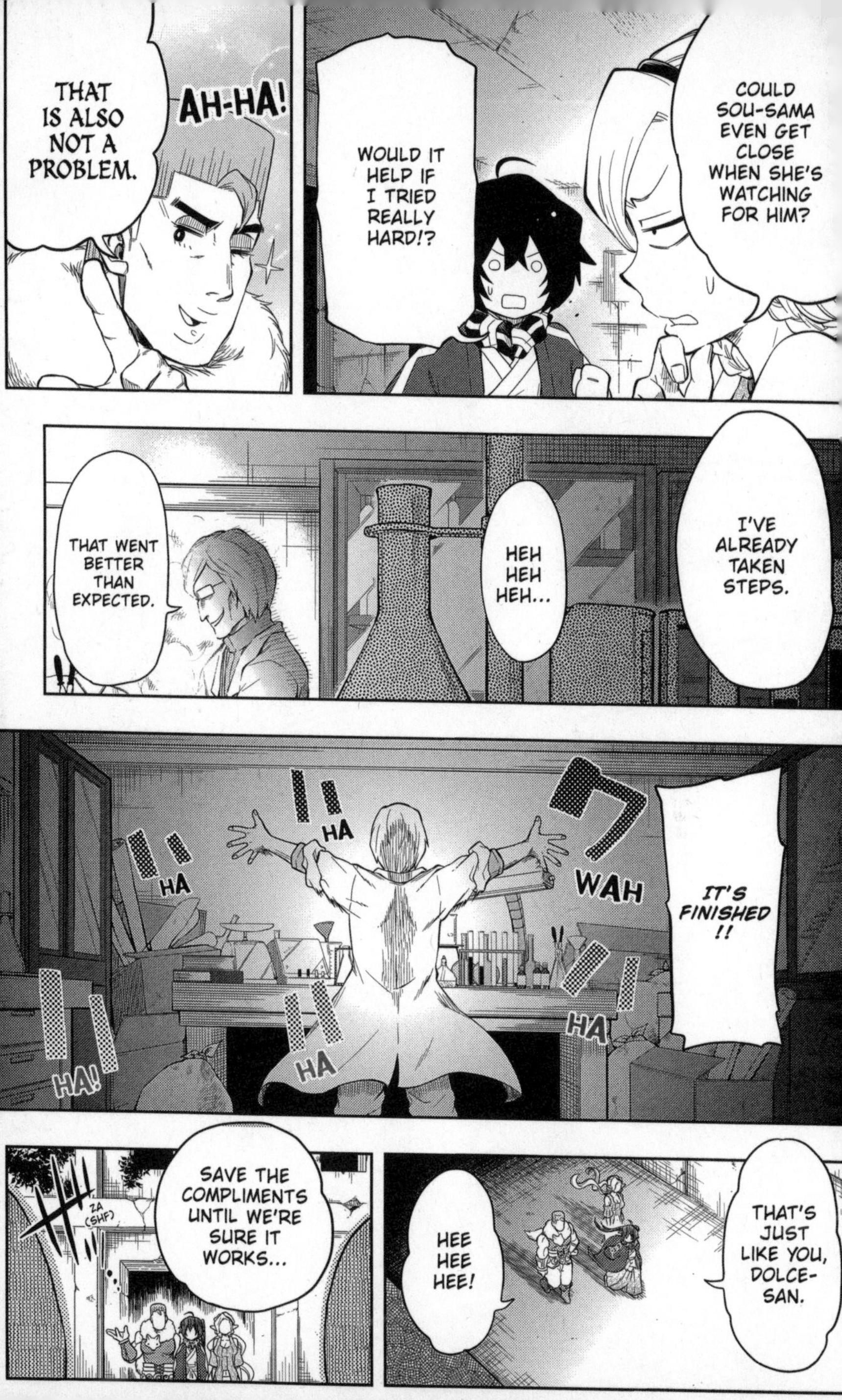
COULD SOU-SAMA EVEN GET CLOSE WHEN SHE'S WATCHING FOR HIM?
WOULD IT HELP IF I TRIED REALLY HARD!?
AH-HA!
THAT IS ALSO NOT A PROBLEM.
I'VE ALREADY TAKEN STEPS.
HEH HEH HEH...
THAT WENT BETTER THAN EXPECTED.
IT'S FINISHED!!
WAH
HA
HA
HA
HA
HA!
THAT'S JUST LIKE YOU, DOLCE-SAN.
HEE HEE HEE!
SAVE THE COMPLIMENTS UNTIL WE'RE SURE IT WORKS...
ZA (SHF)

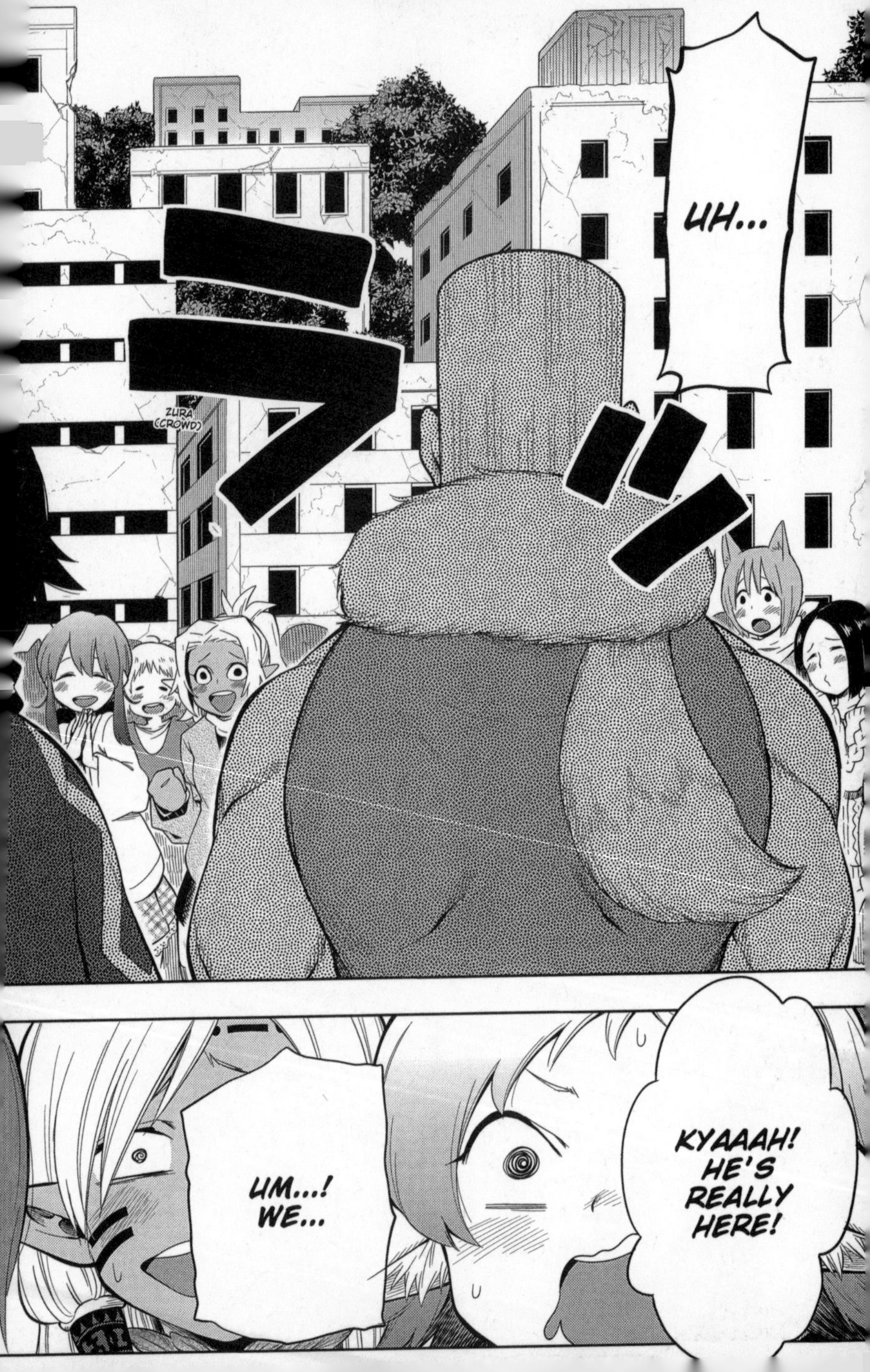
UH...
ZURA
(CROWD)
KYAAAH! HE'S REALLY HERE!
UM...! WE...

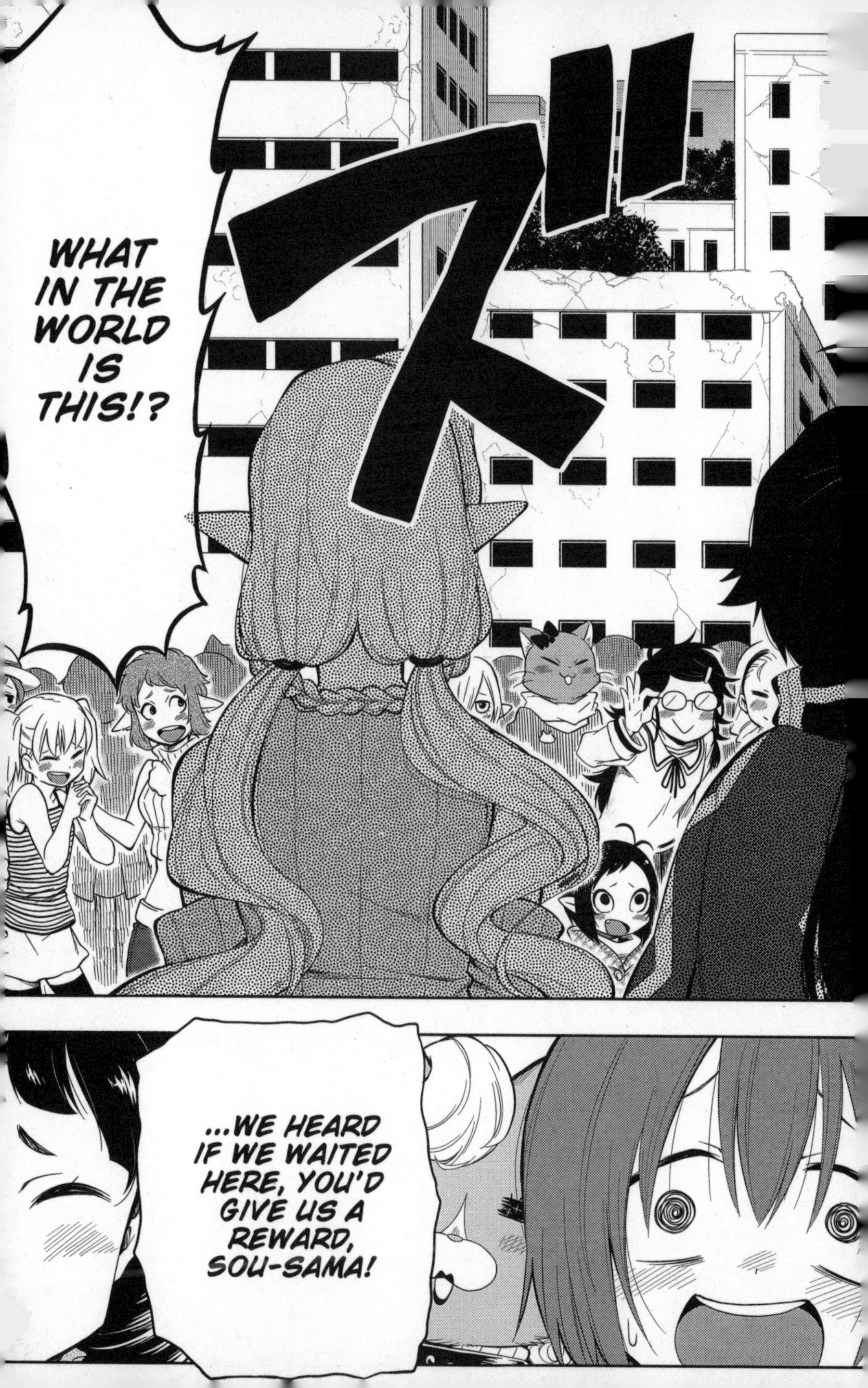
WHAT IN THE WORLD IS THIS!?
...WE HEARD IF WE WAITED HERE, YOU'D GIVE US A REWARD, SOU-SAMA!

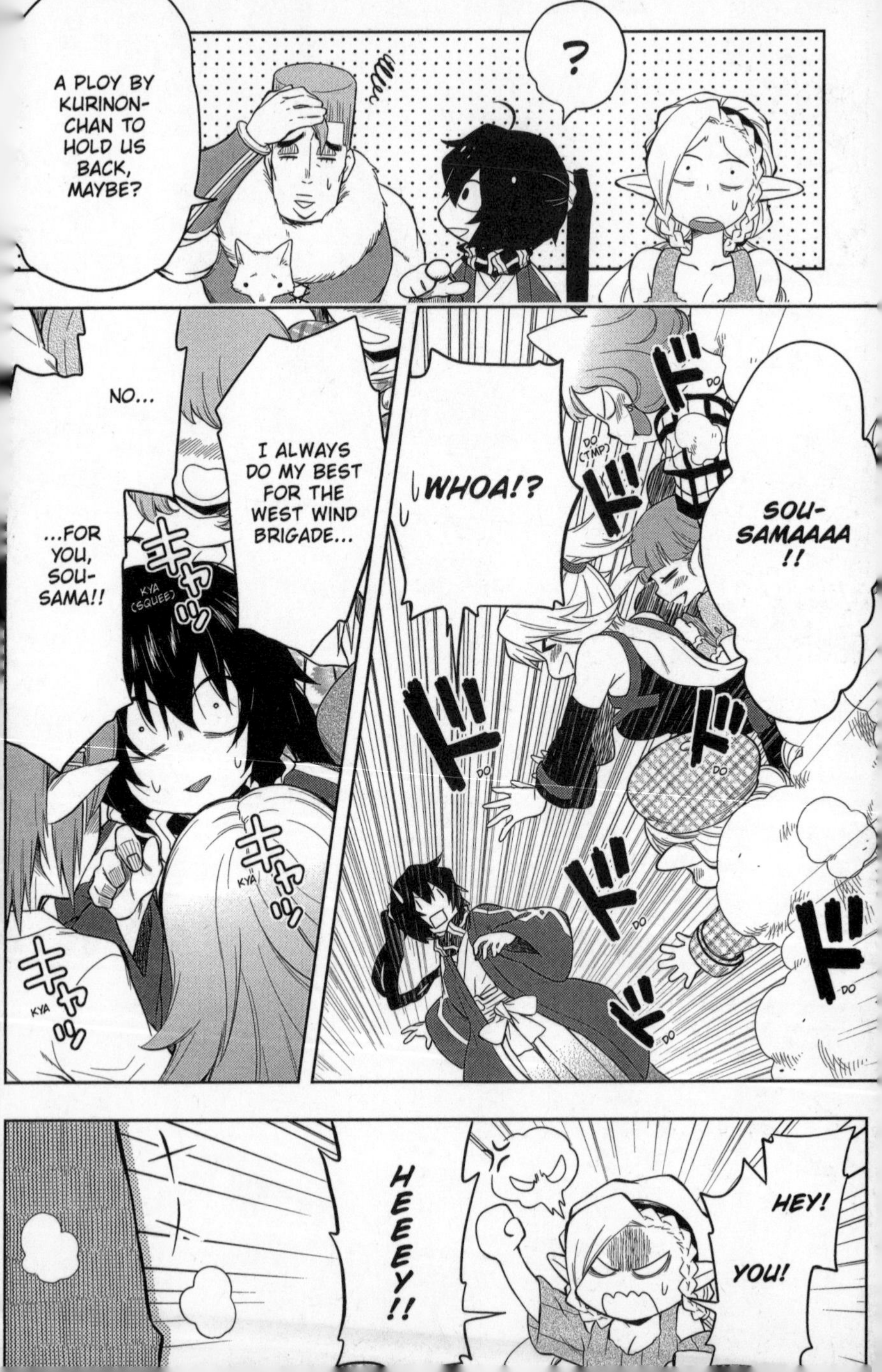
?
A PLOY BY KURINON-CHAN TO HOLD US BACK, MAYBE?
SOU-SAMAAAA!!
DO
DO (TMP)
DO
DO
DO
DO
DO
DO
WHOA!?
I ALWAYS DO MY BEST FOR THE WEST WIND BRIGADE...
NO...
...FOR YOU, SOU-SAMA!!
KYA (SQUEE)
KYA
KYA
HEY!
YOU!
HEEEEY!!

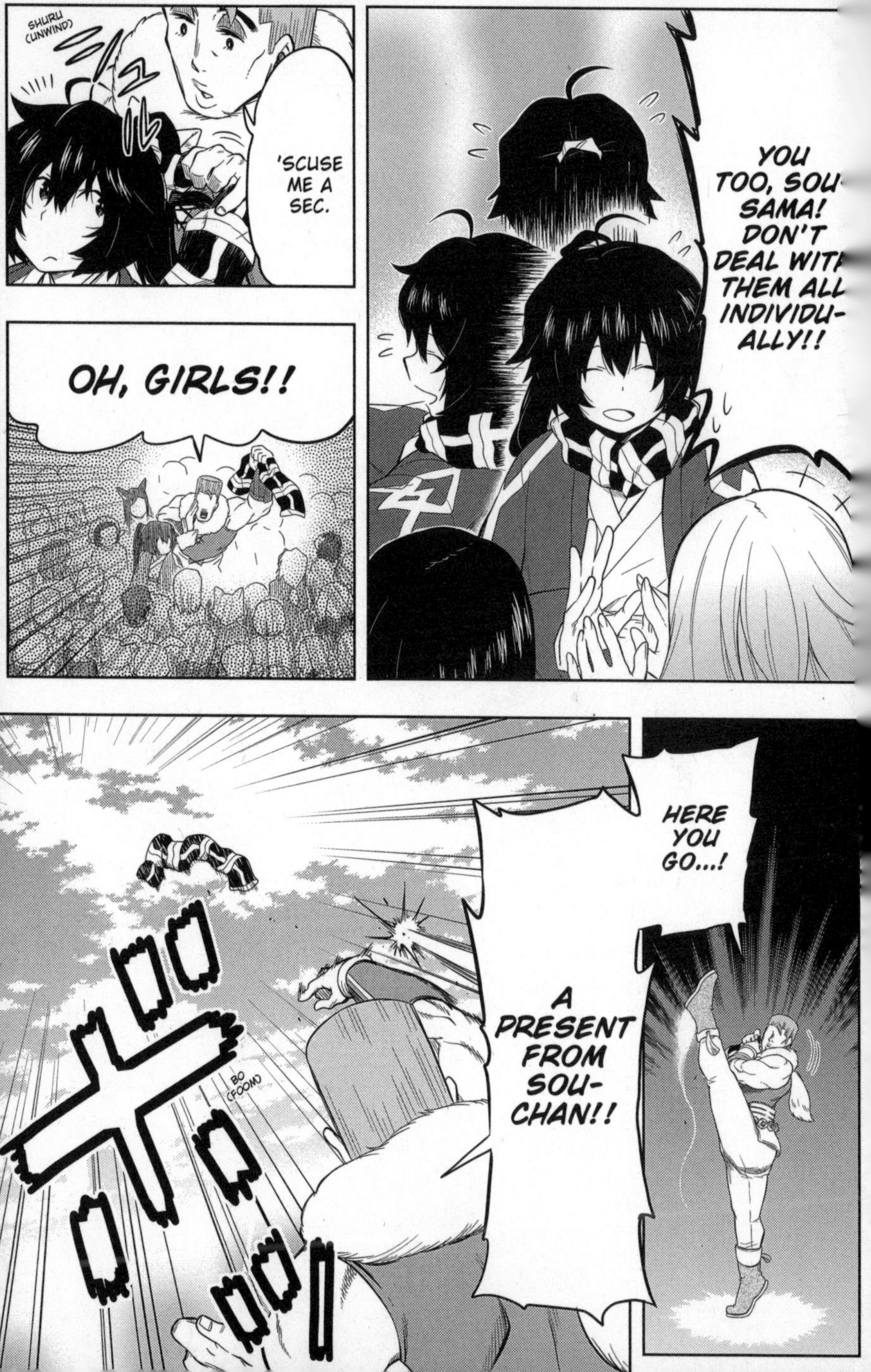
YOU TOO, SOU-SAMA! DON'T DEAL WITH THEM ALL INDIVIDU-ALLY!!
SHURU (UNWIND)
'SCUSE ME A SEC.
OH, GIRLS!!
HERE YOU GO...!
A PRESENT FROM SOU-CHAN!!
BO (FOOM)

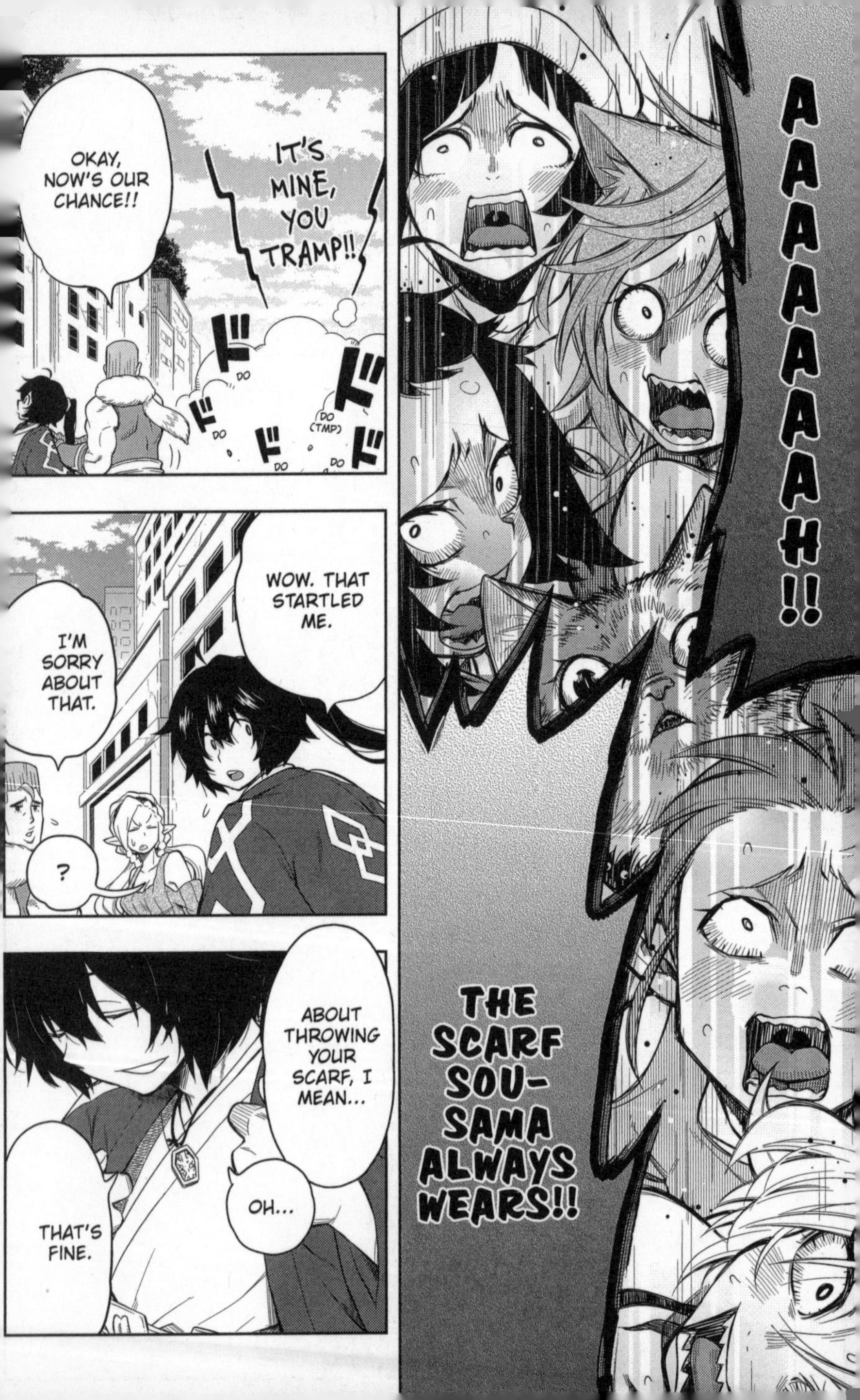
AAAAAAAH!!
THE SCARF SOU-SAMA ALWAYS WEARS!!
IT'S MINE, YOU TRAMP!!
OKAY, NOW'S OUR CHANCE!!
ド DO ド DO ド DO ド DO (TMP) ド DO
WOW. THAT STARTLED ME.
I'M SORRY ABOUT THAT.
?
ABOUT THROWING YOUR SCARF, I MEAN...
OH...
THAT'S FINE.

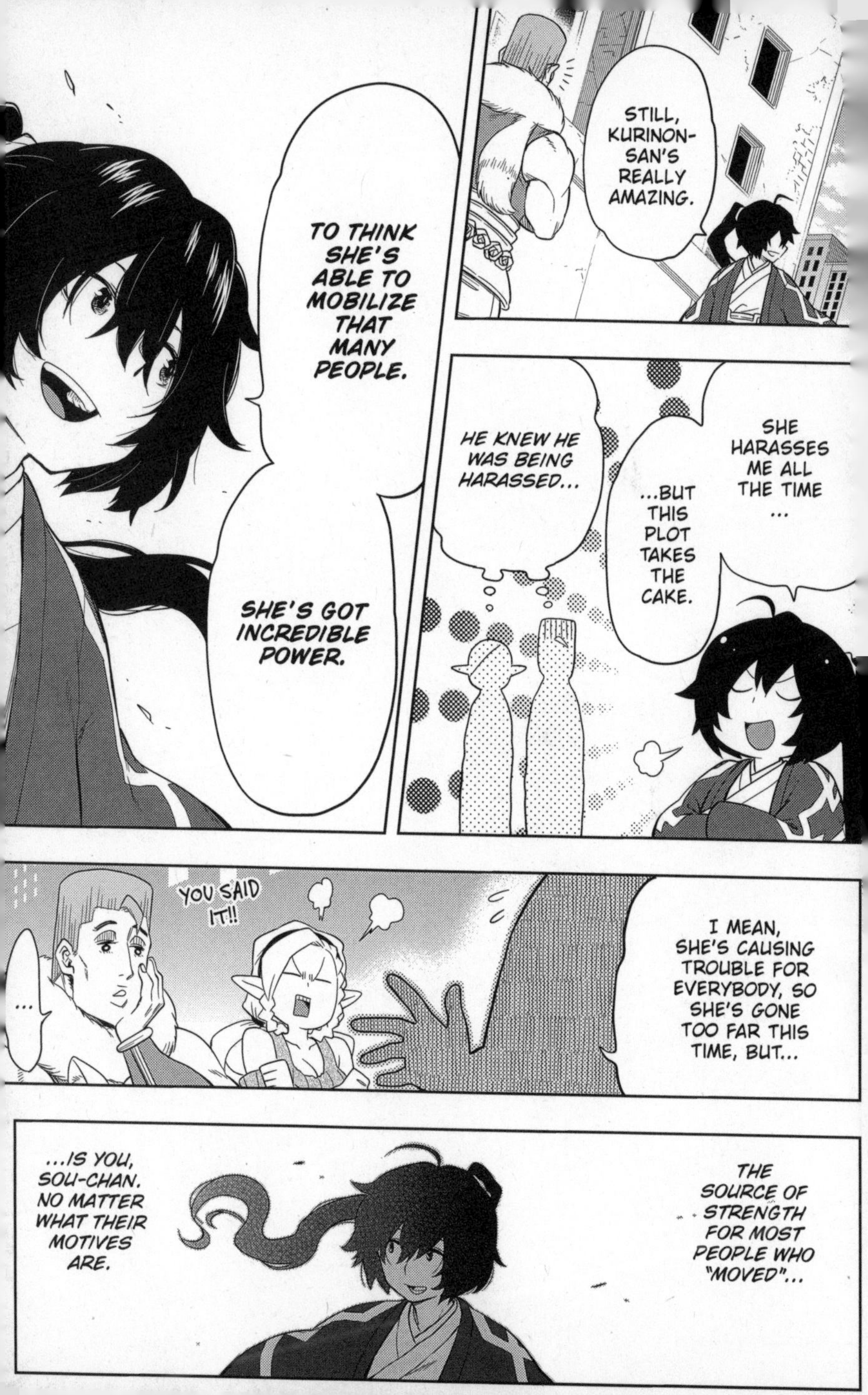
STILL, KURINON-SAN'S REALLY AMAZING.
SHE HARASSES ME ALL THE TIME ...
...BUT THIS PLOT TAKES THE CAKE.
HE KNEW HE WAS BEING HARASSED...
TO THINK SHE'S ABLE TO MOBILIZE THAT MANY PEOPLE.
SHE'S GOT INCREDIBLE POWER.
I MEAN, SHE'S CAUSING TROUBLE FOR EVERYBODY, SO SHE'S GONE TOO FAR THIS TIME, BUT...
YOU SAID IT!!
...
THE SOURCE OF STRENGTH FOR MOST PEOPLE WHO "MOVED"...
...IS YOU, SOU-CHAN. NO MATTER WHAT THEIR MOTIVES ARE.

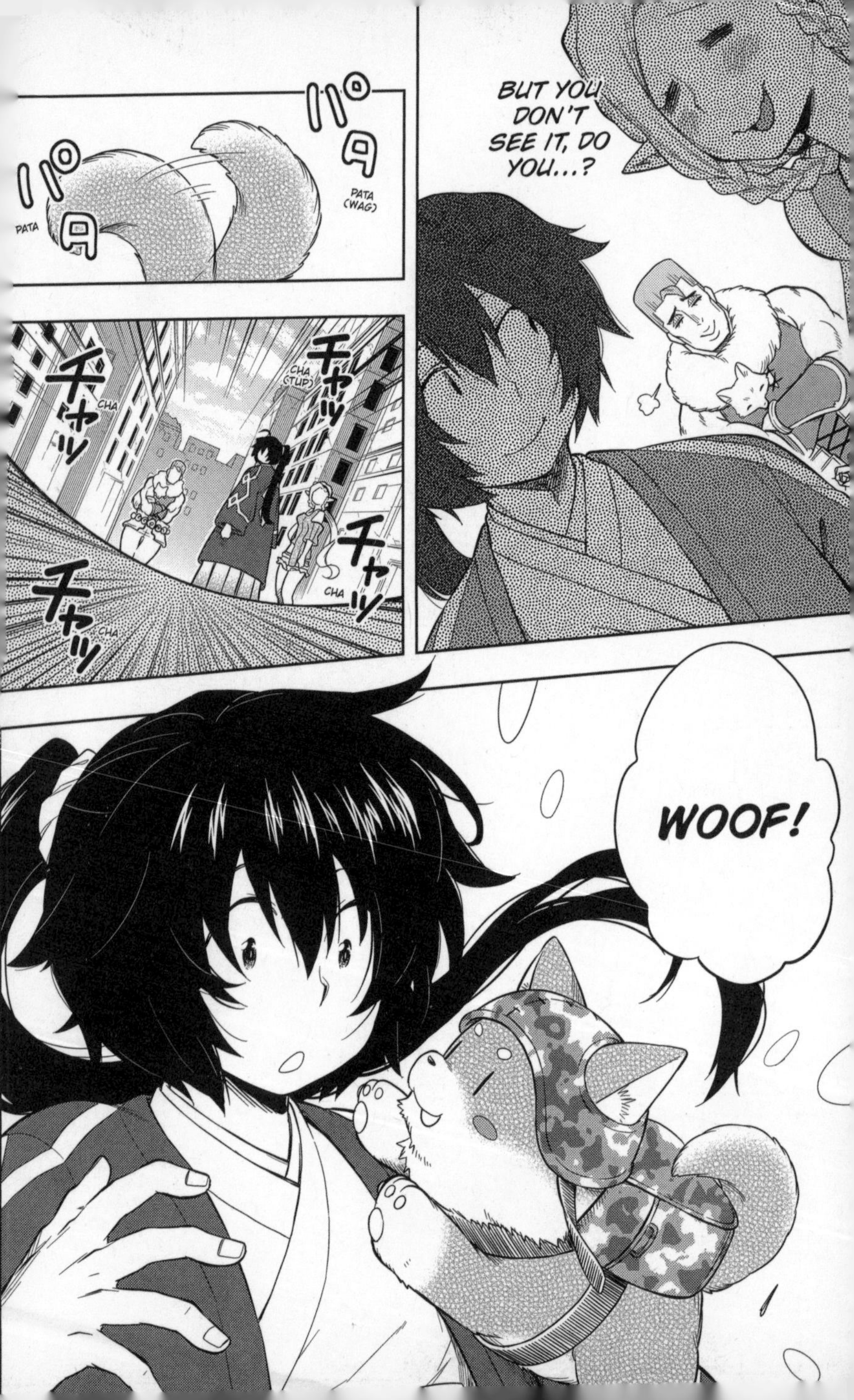
BUT YOU DON'T SEE IT, DO YOU...?
パタ
PATA (WAG)
パタ
PATA
チャッ
CHA (TUP)
チャッ
CHA
チャッ
CHA
チャッ
CHA
WOOF!

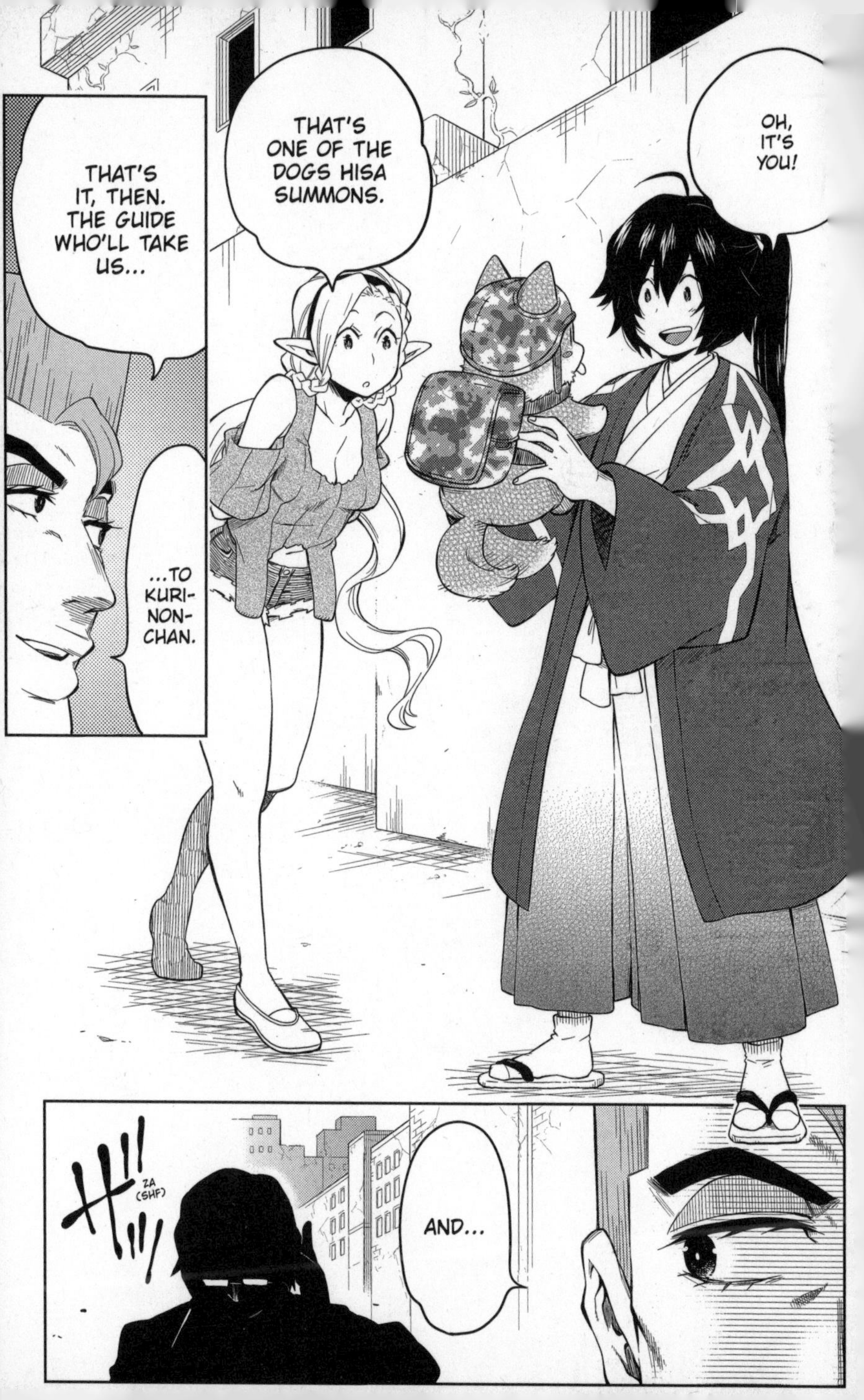
OH, IT'S YOU!
THAT'S ONE OF THE DOGS HISA SUMMONS.
THAT'S IT, THEN. THE GUIDE WHO'LL TAKE US...
...TO KURI-NON-CHAN.
AND...
ZA (SHF)

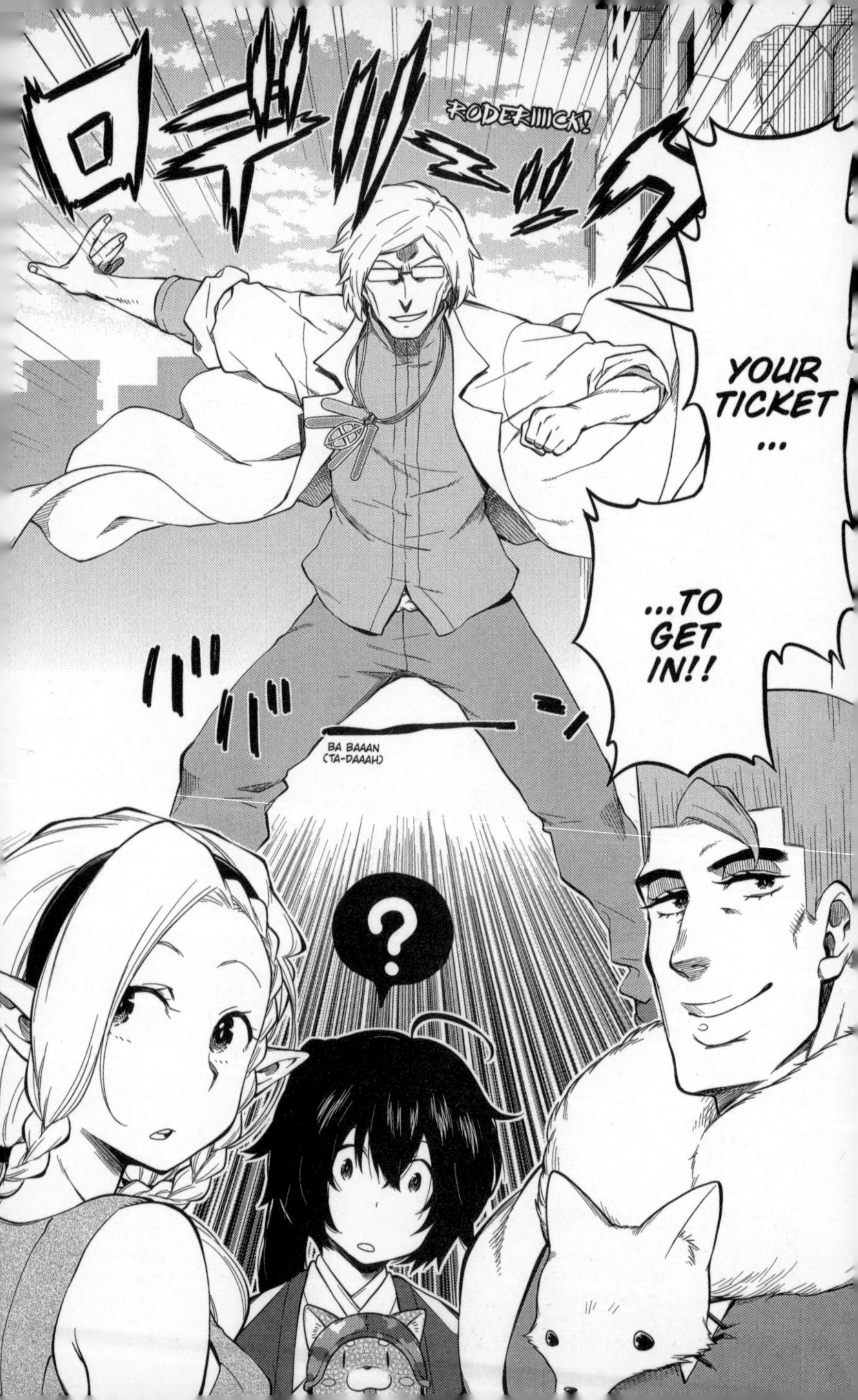
ロデリィーーック
RODERIIIICK!
YOUR TICKET ...
...TO GET IN!!
バ バ ーーン
BA BAAAN (TA-DAAAH)
?

LOG HORIZON

THE WEST WIND BRIGADE

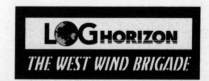

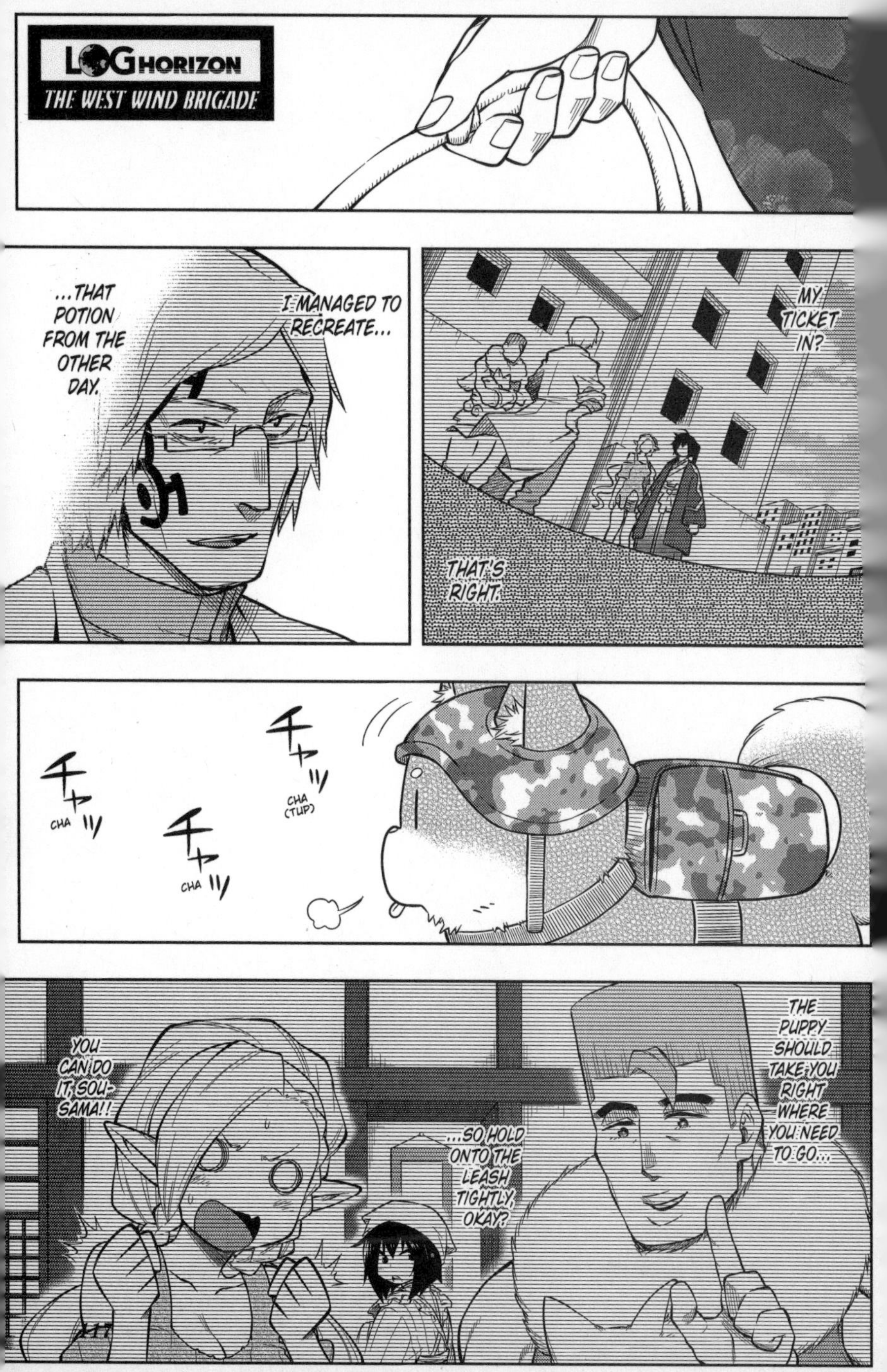
LOG HORIZON
THE WEST WIND BRIGADE
MY TICKET IN?
THAT'S RIGHT.
I MANAGED TO RECREATE...
...THAT POTION FROM THE OTHER DAY.
チャッ
CHA (TUP)
チャッ
CHA
チャッ
CHA
THE PUPPY SHOULD TAKE YOU RIGHT WHERE YOU NEED TO GO...
...SO HOLD ONTO THE LEASH TIGHTLY, OKAY?
YOU CAN DO IT, SOU-SAMA!!

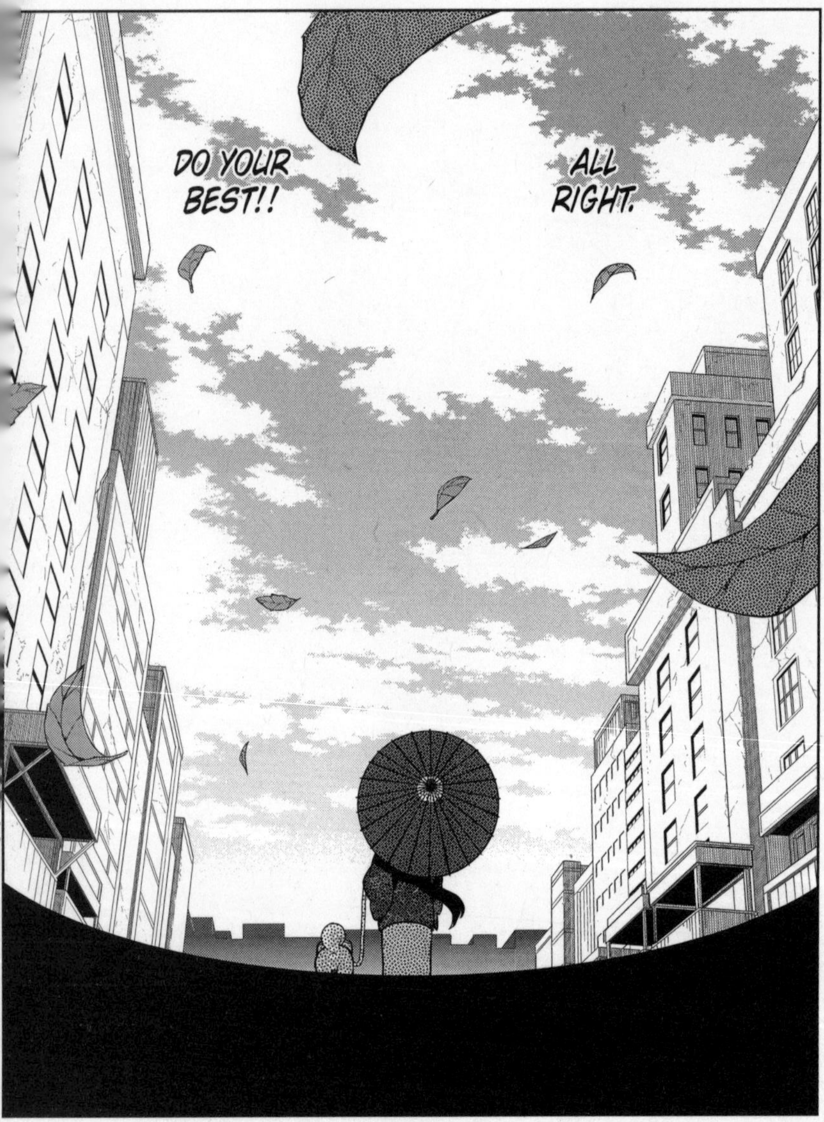
ALL RIGHT.
DO YOUR BEST!!

CHAPTER: 35 **CAPTURE KURINON!** (PART 3)

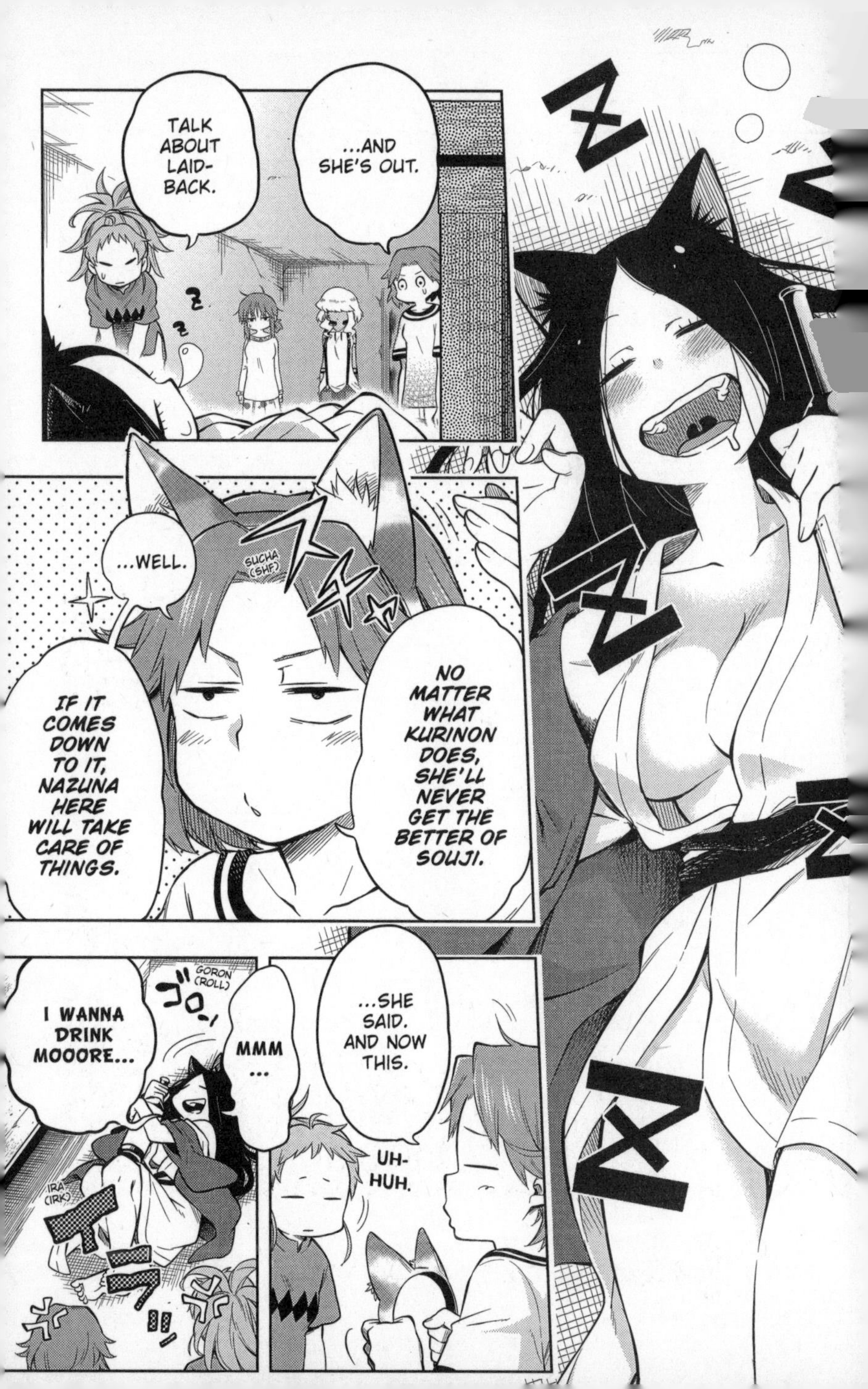
...AND SHE'S OUT.
TALK ABOUT LAID-BACK.
NO MATTER WHAT KURINON DOES, SHE'LL NEVER GET THE BETTER OF SOUJI.
SUCHA (SHF)
...WELL.
IF IT COMES DOWN TO IT, NAZUNA HERE WILL TAKE CARE OF THINGS.
...SHE SAID. AND NOW THIS.
UH-HUH.
GORON (ROLL)
MMM ...
I WANNA DRINK MOOORE...
IRA (IRK)

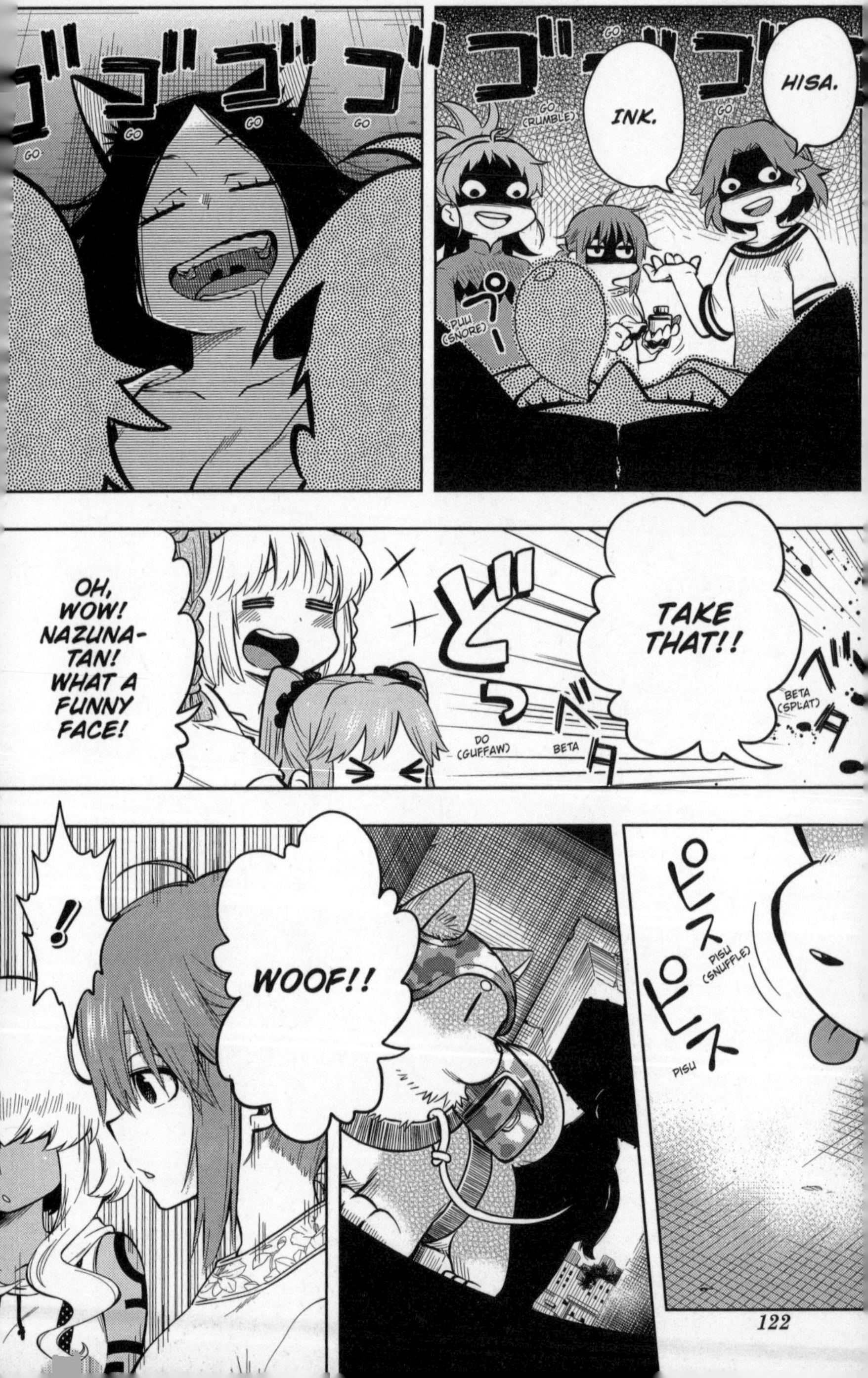
GO
GO (RUMBLE)
GO
HISA.
INK.
PUU (SNORE)
GO
GO
GO
GO
BETA (SPLAT)
TAKE THAT!!
BETA
DO (GUFFAW)
OH, WOW! NAZUNA-TAN! WHAT A FUNNY FACE!
PISU (SNUFFLE)
PISU
WOOF!!
!

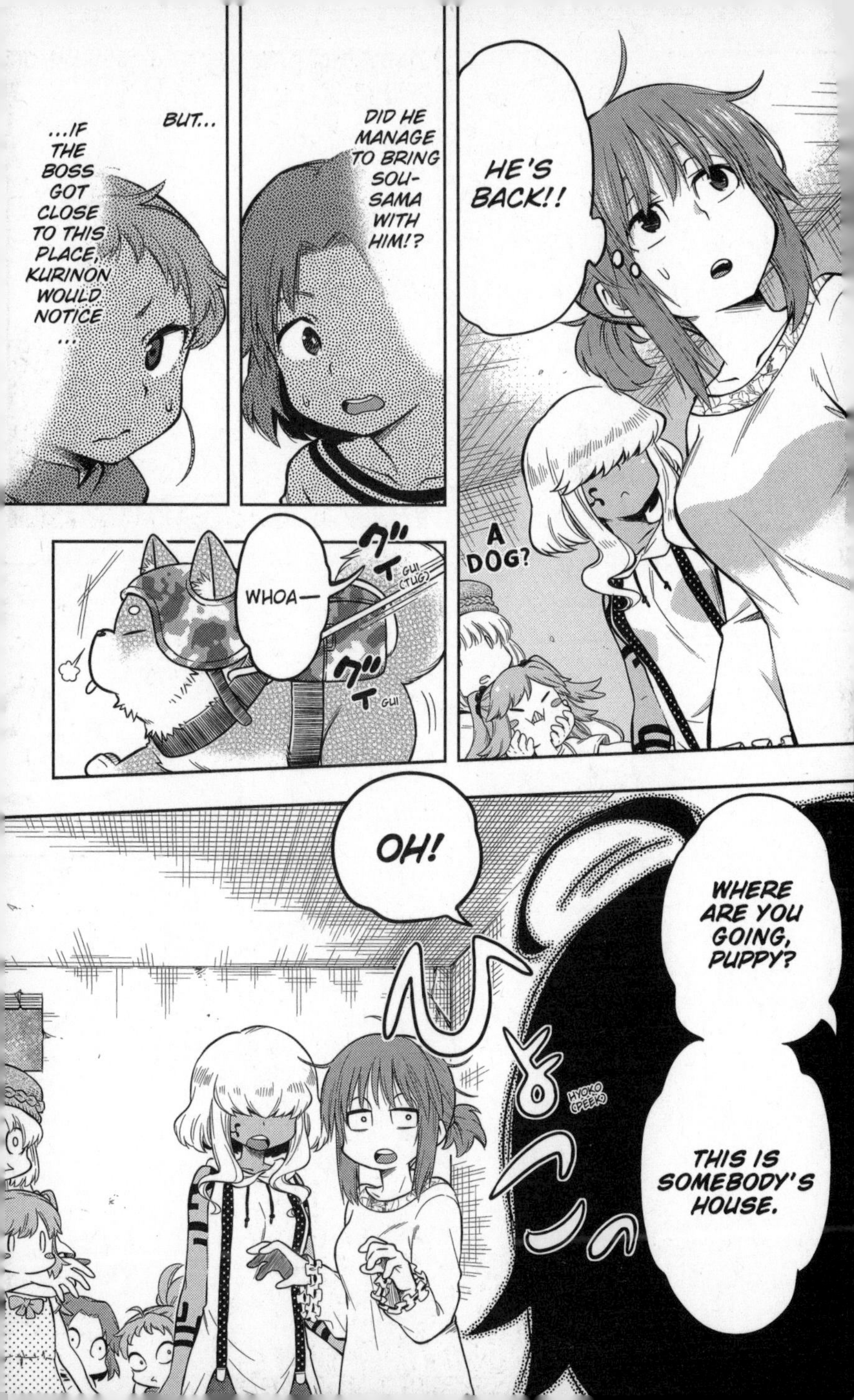
HE'S BACK!!
DID HE MANAGE TO BRING SOU-SAMA WITH HIM!?
BUT...
...IF THE BOSS GOT CLOSE TO THIS PLACE, KURINON WOULD NOTICE...
A DOG?
GUI (TUG)
WHOA—
GUI
WHERE ARE YOU GOING, PUPPY?
THIS IS SOMEBODY'S HOUSE.
HYOKO (PEEK)
OH!

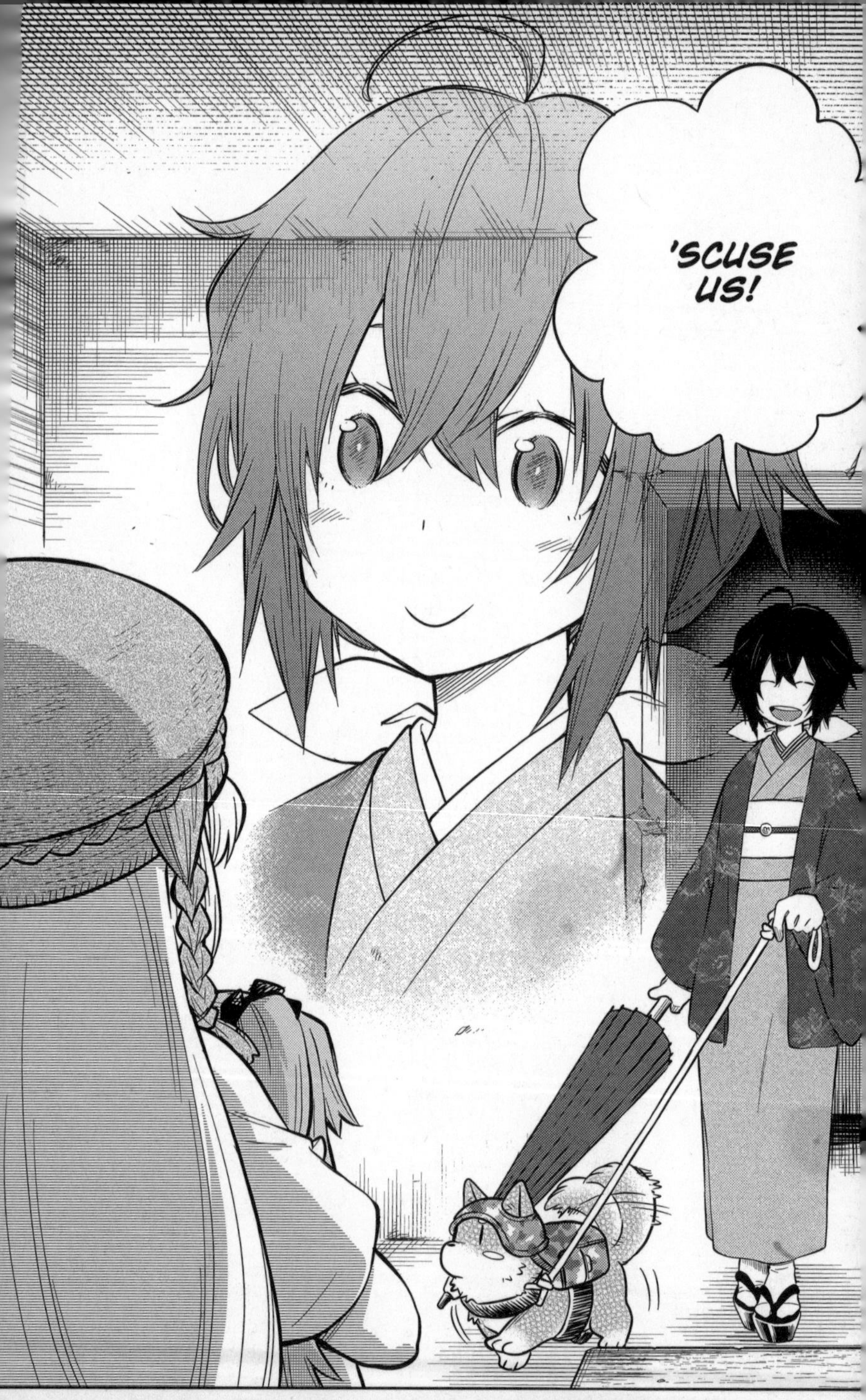
'SCUSE US!

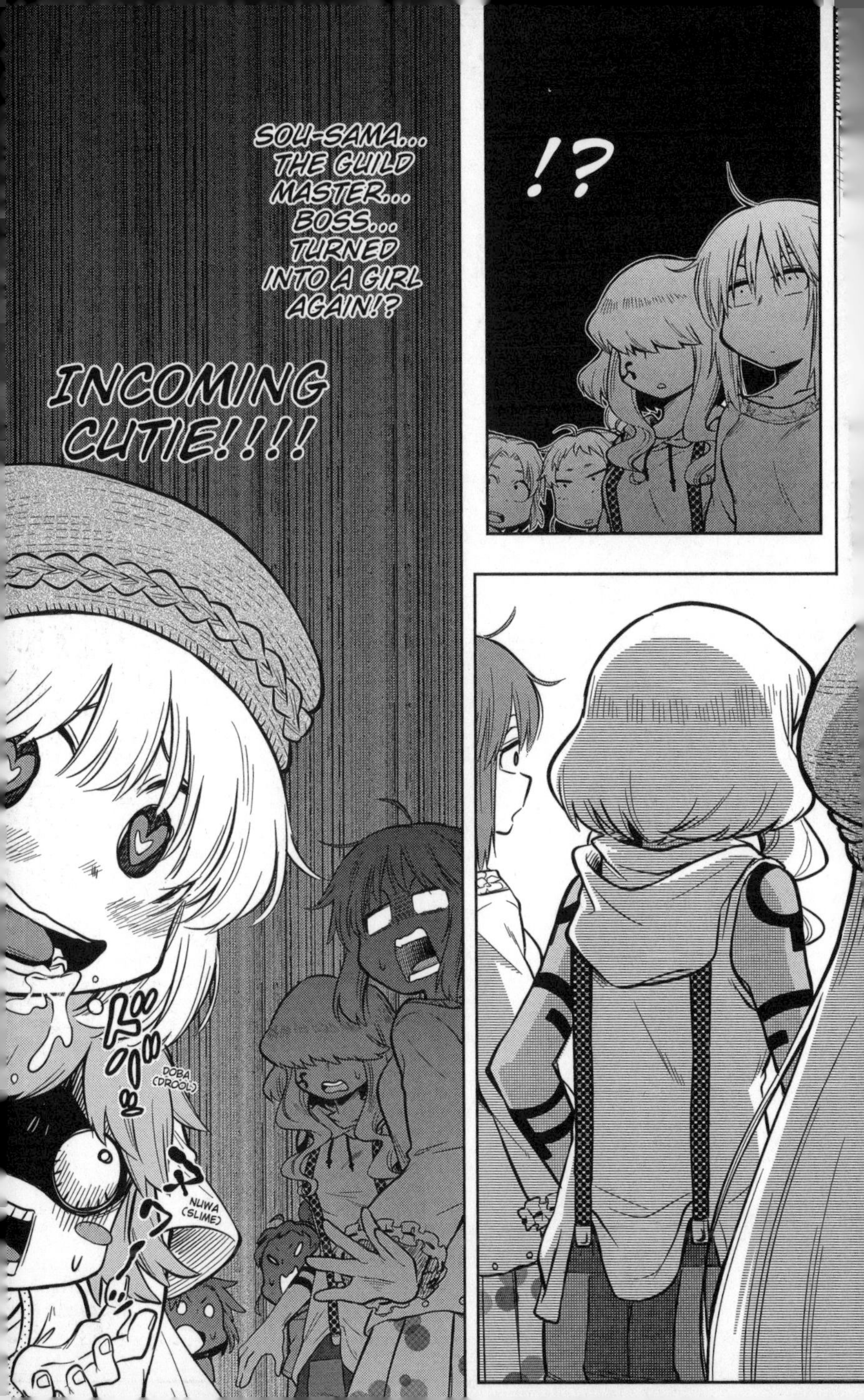
!?
SOU-SAMA... THE GUILD MASTER... BOSS... TURNED INTO A GIRL AGAIN!?
INCOMING CUTIE!!!!
DOBA (DROOL)
NUWA (SLIME)

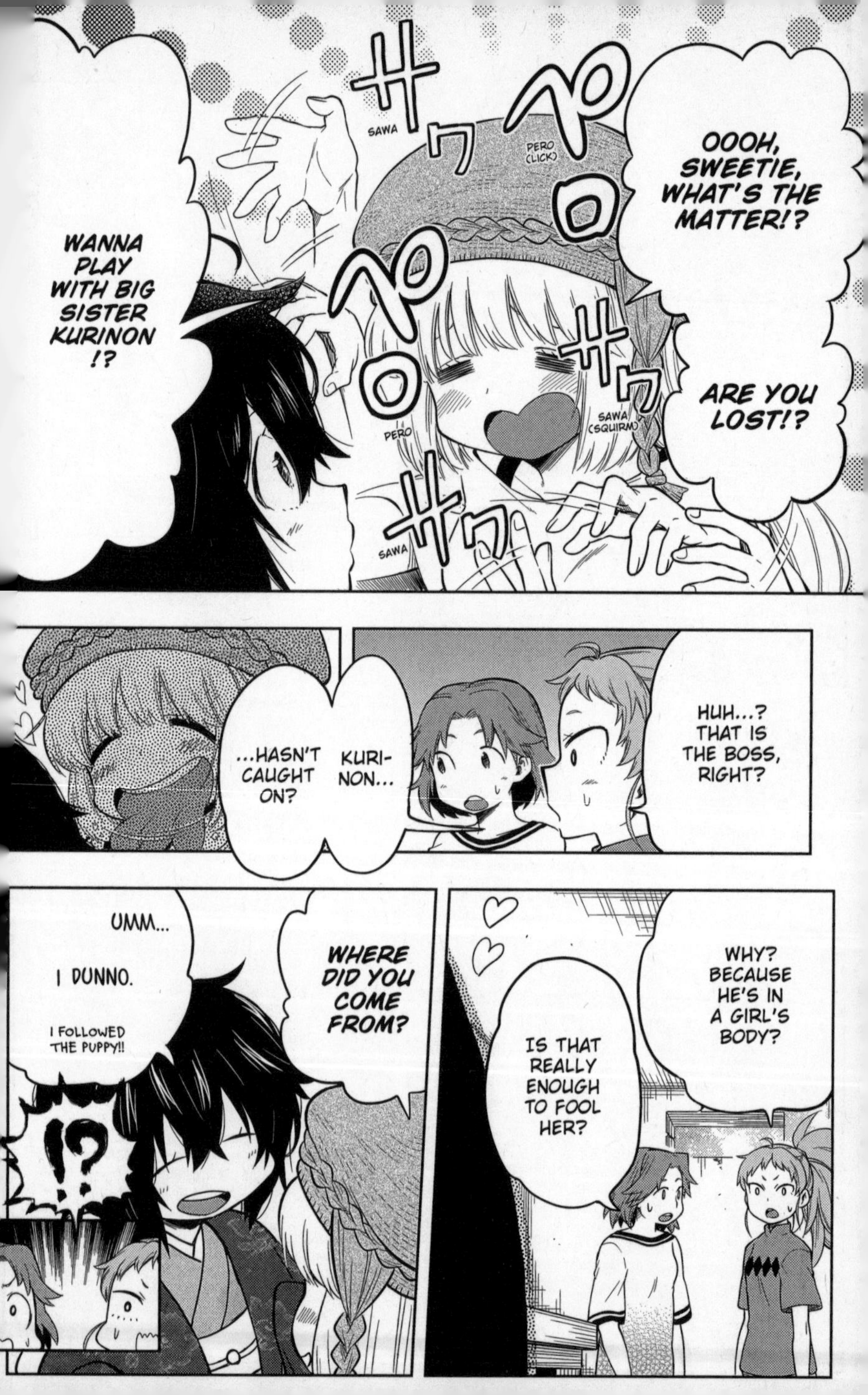
OOOH, SWEETIE, WHAT'S THE MATTER!?
ARE YOU LOST!?
SAWA
PERO (LICK)
SAWA (SQUIRM)
PERO
SAWA
WANNA PLAY WITH BIG SISTER KURINON!?
HUH...? THAT IS THE BOSS, RIGHT?
KURI-NON...
...HASN'T CAUGHT ON?
WHY? BECAUSE HE'S IN A GIRL'S BODY?
IS THAT REALLY ENOUGH TO FOOL HER?
WHERE DID YOU COME FROM?
UMM...
I DUNNO.
I FOLLOWED THE PUPPY!!
!?

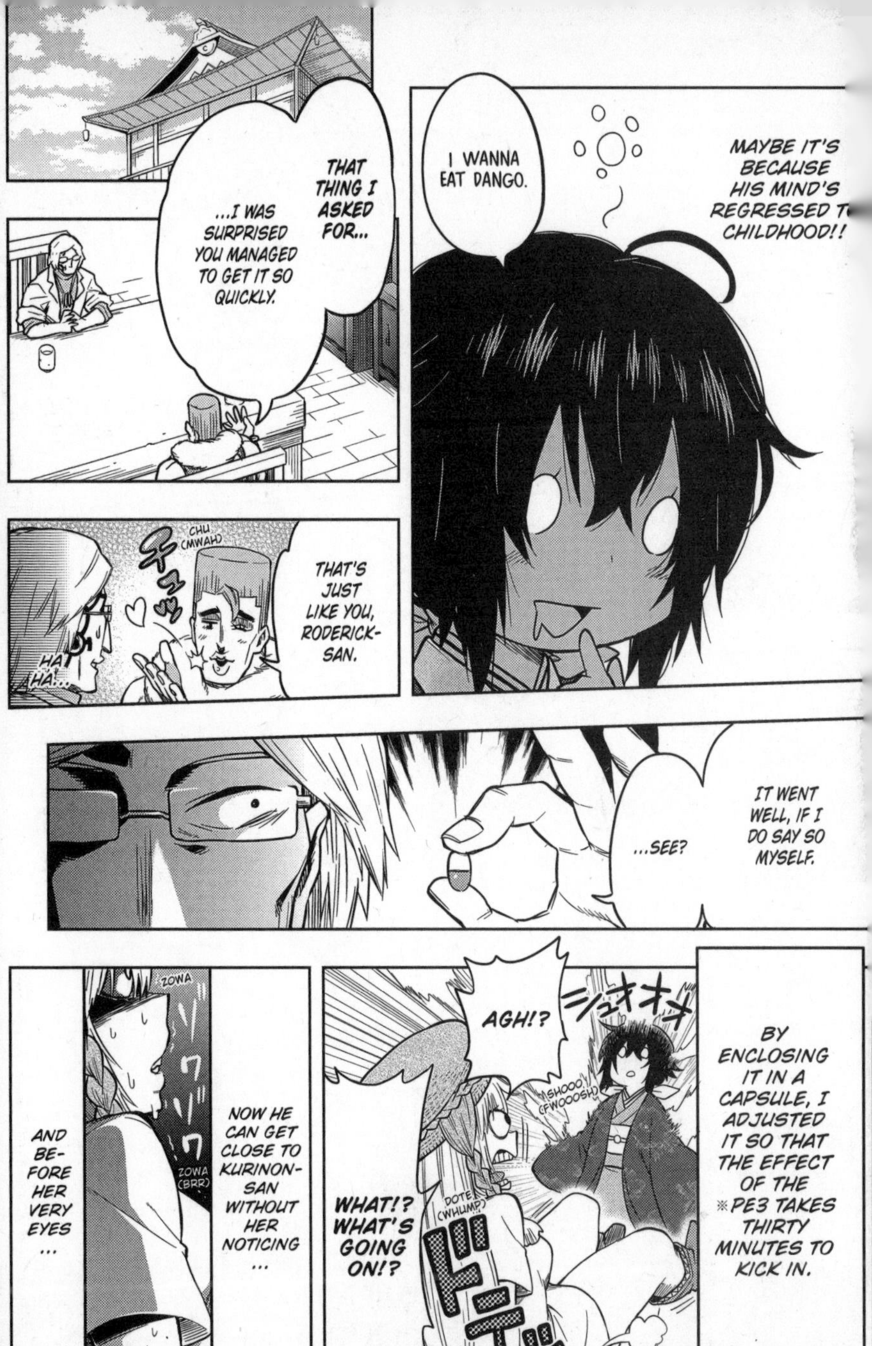
MAYBE IT'S BECAUSE HIS MIND'S REGRESSED T CHILDHOOD!!
I WANNA EAT DANGO.
THAT THING I ASKED FOR...
...I WAS SURPRISED YOU MANAGED TO GET IT SO QUICKLY.
THAT'S JUST LIKE YOU, RODERICK-SAN.
CHU (MWAH)
HA HA...
IT WENT WELL, IF I DO SAY SO MYSELF.
...SEE?
BY ENCLOSING IT IN A CAPSULE, I ADJUSTED IT SO THAT THE EFFECT OF THE ※PE3 TAKES THIRTY MINUTES TO KICK IN.
AGH!?
SHOOO (FWOOOSH)
WHAT!? WHAT'S GOING ON!?
DOTE (WHUMP)
ZOWA
NOW HE CAN GET CLOSE TO KURINON-SAN WITHOUT HER NOTICING...
ZOWA (BRR)
AND BEFORE HER VERY EYES...

※PE3 – PREVIOUS ELIXIR EFFECT ENDS

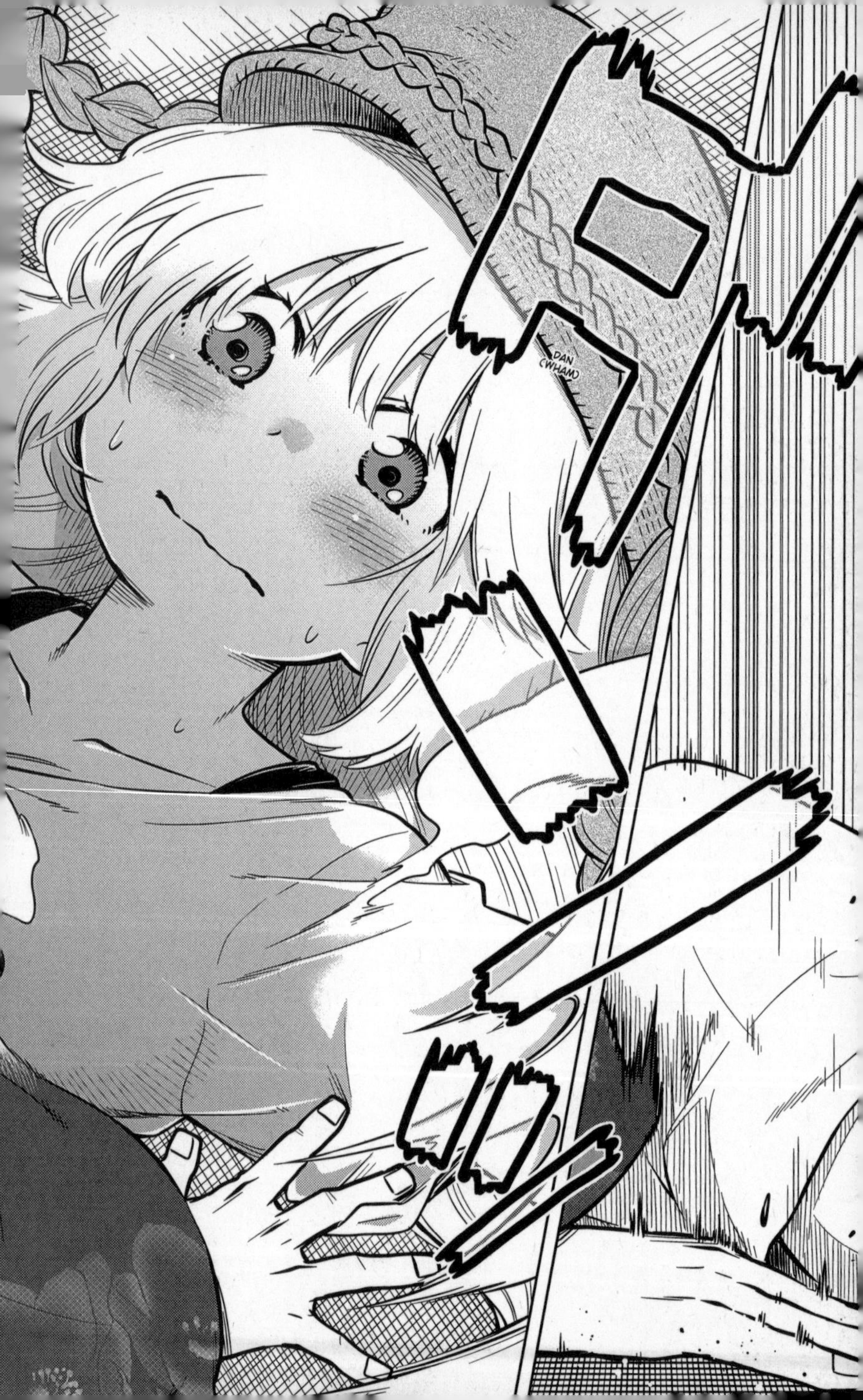
DAN
(WHAM)

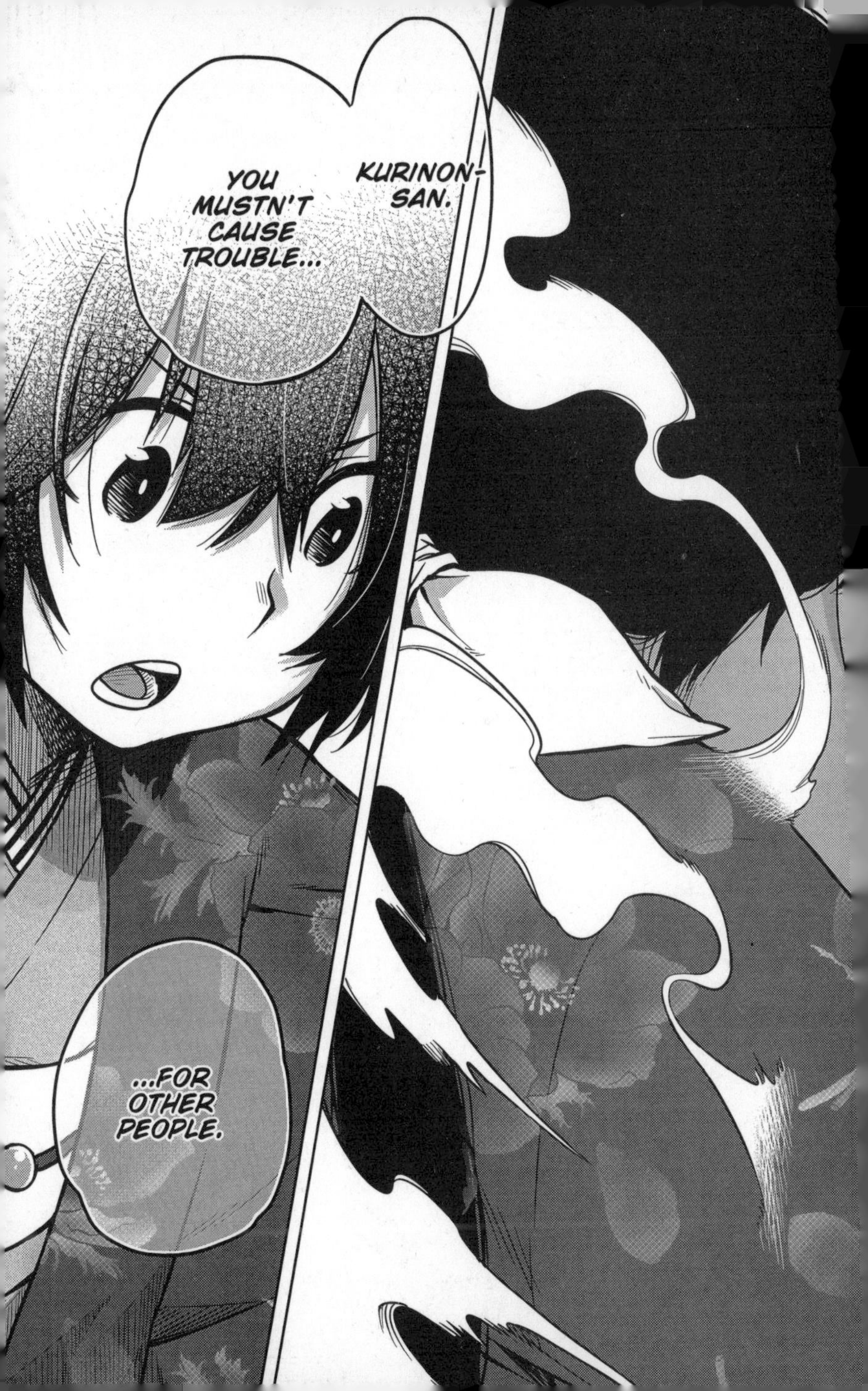
KURINON-SAN.
YOU MUSTN'T CAUSE TROUBLE...
...FOR OTHER PEOPLE.

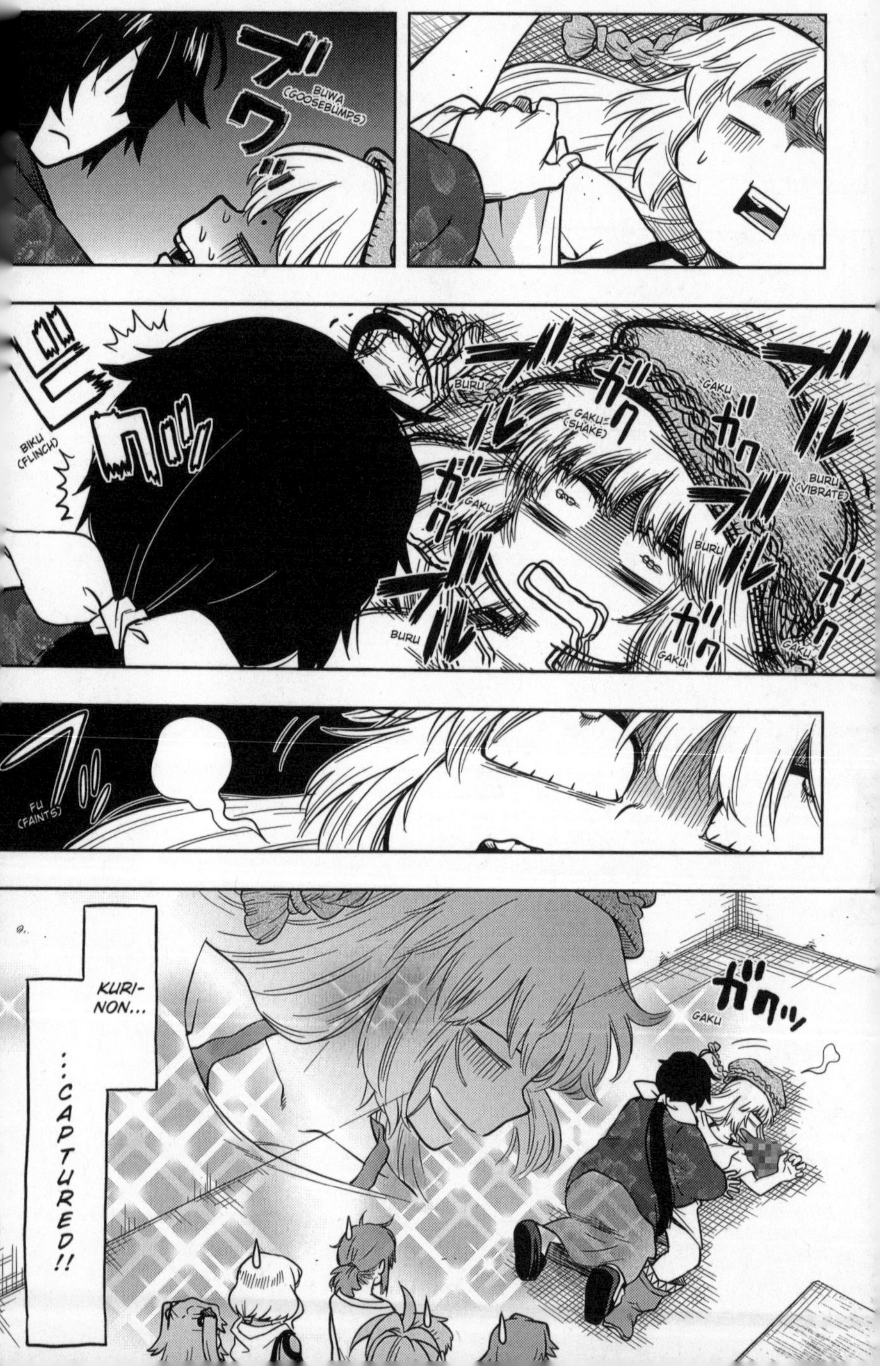

BUWA (GOOSEBUMPS)
BURU (VIBRATE)
GAKU
GAKU (SHAKE)
BURU
BURU
GAKU
GAKU
GAKU
BURU
BIKU (FLINCH)
FU (FAINTS)
GAKU
KURI-NON...
...CAPTURED!!

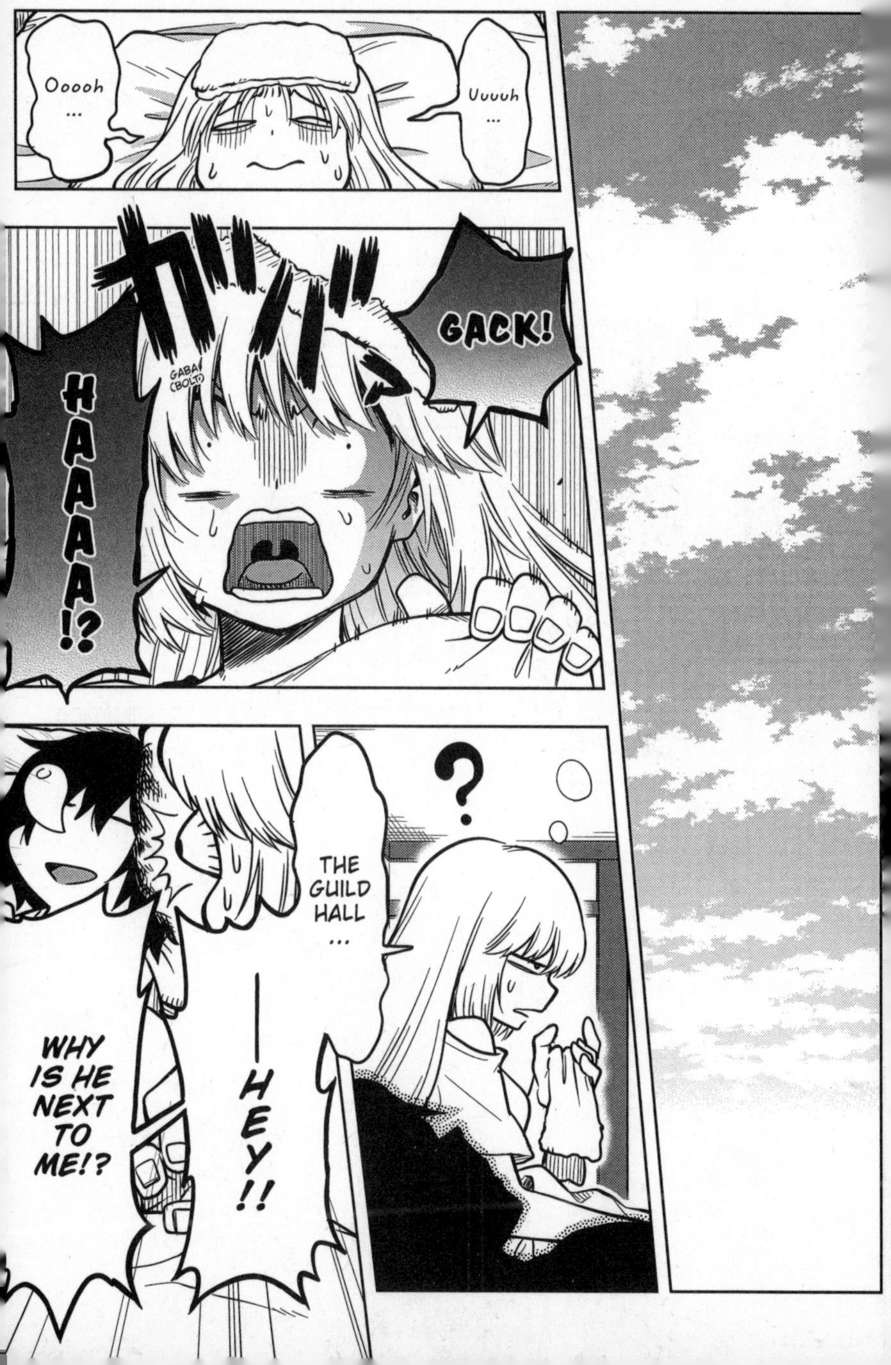
Uuuuh ...
Ooooh ...
GACK!
GABA! (BOLT)
HAAAAA!?
?
THE GUILD HALL ...
—HEY!!
WHY IS HE NEXT TO ME!?

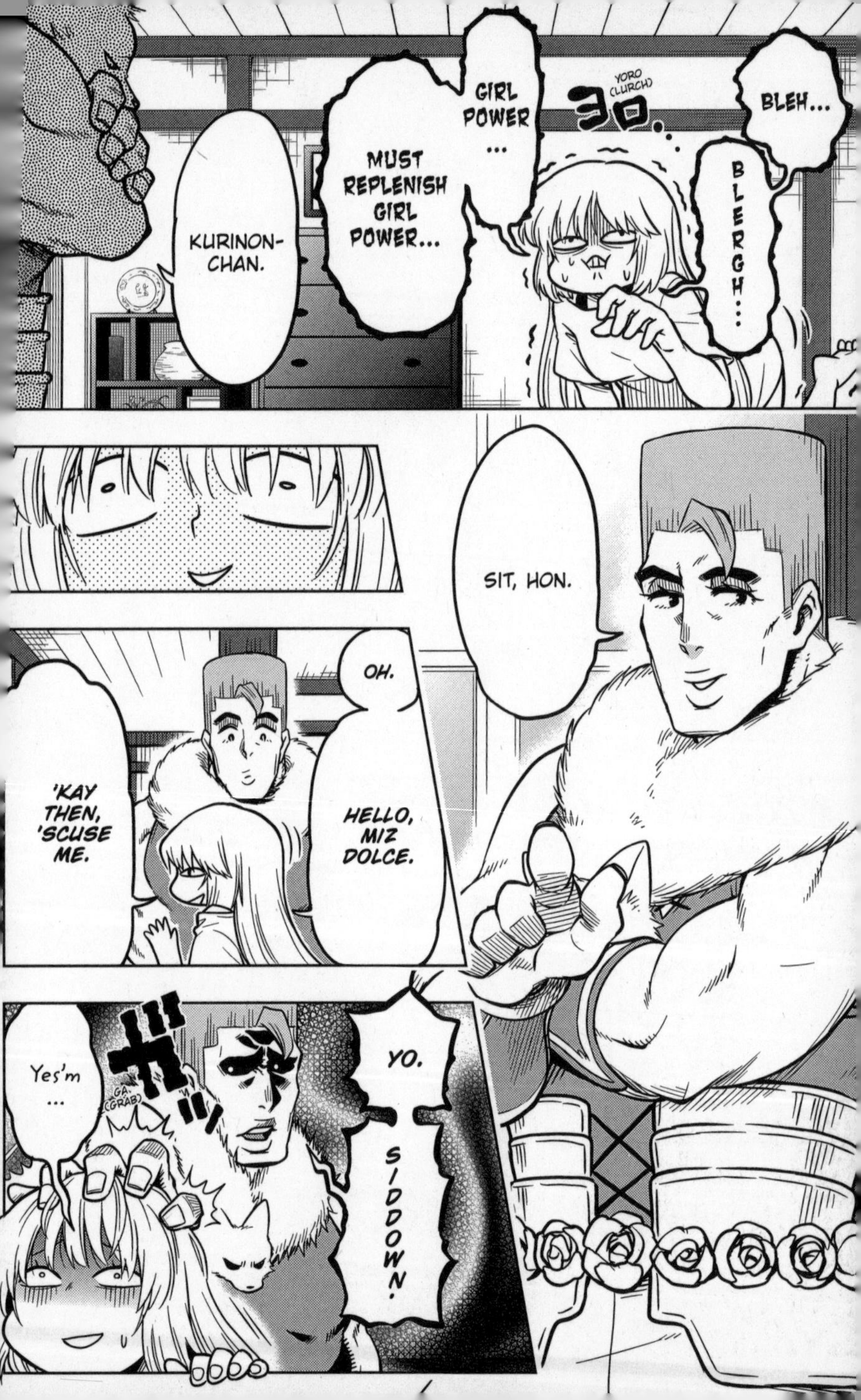
BLEH...
BLERGH...
ヨロ
YORO (LURCH)
GIRL POWER ...
MUST REPLENISH GIRL POWER...
KURINON-CHAN.
SIT, HON.
OH.
HELLO, MIZ DOLCE.
'KAY THEN, 'SCUSE ME.
YO.
SIDDOWN.
ガッ
GA (GRAB)
Yes'm ...

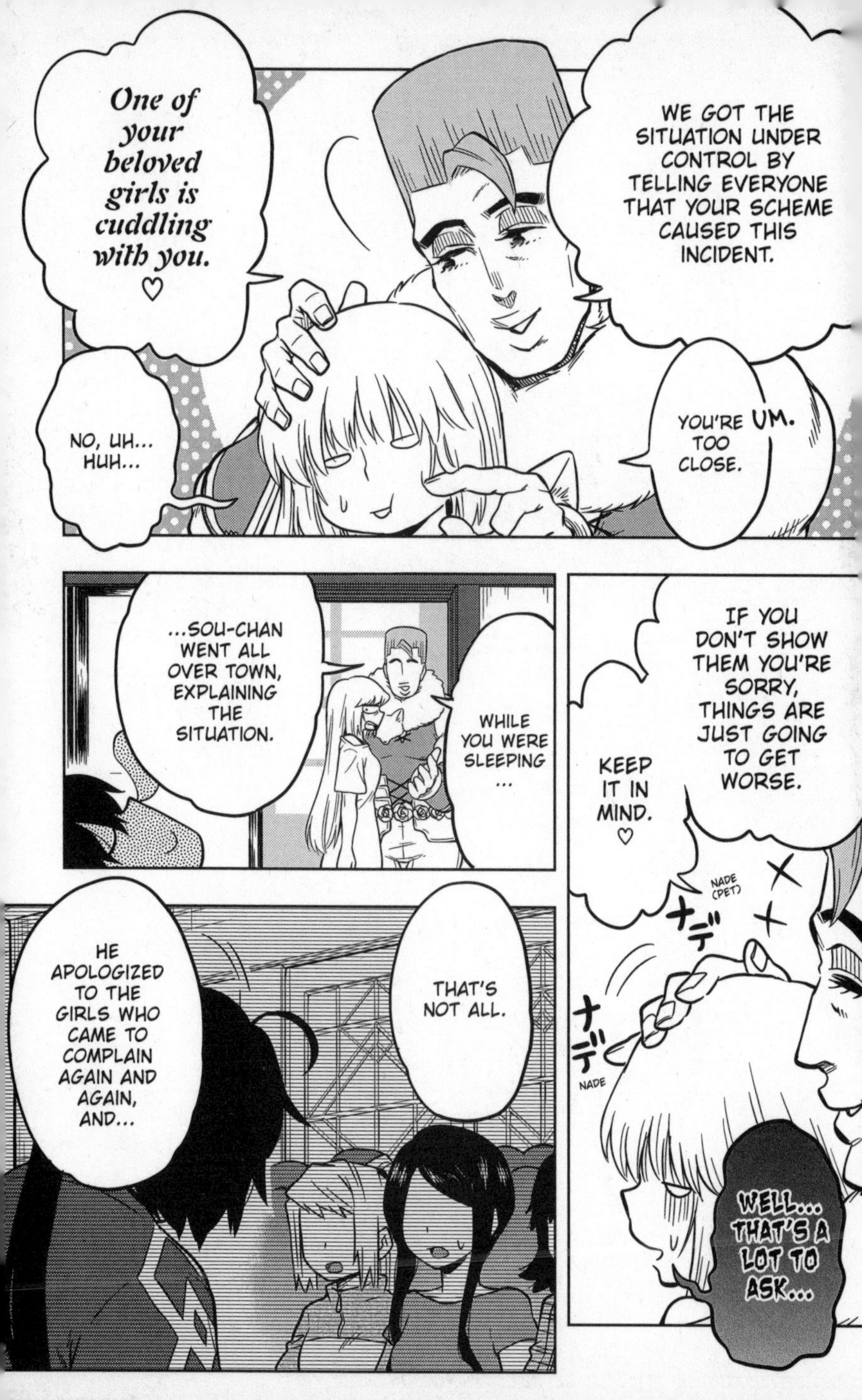
WE GOT THE SITUATION UNDER CONTROL BY TELLING EVERYONE THAT YOUR SCHEME CAUSED THIS INCIDENT.
One of your beloved girls is cuddling with you. ♡
UM.
YOU'RE TOO CLOSE.
NO, UH... HUH...
IF YOU DON'T SHOW THEM YOU'RE SORRY, THINGS ARE JUST GOING TO GET WORSE.
KEEP IT IN MIND. ♡
ナデ
NADE (PET)
ナデ
NADE
WELL... THAT'S A LOT TO ASK...
WHILE YOU WERE SLEEPING...
...SOU-CHAN WENT ALL OVER TOWN, EXPLAINING THE SITUATION.
THAT'S NOT ALL.
HE APOLOGIZED TO THE GIRLS WHO CAME TO COMPLAIN AGAIN AND AGAIN, AND...

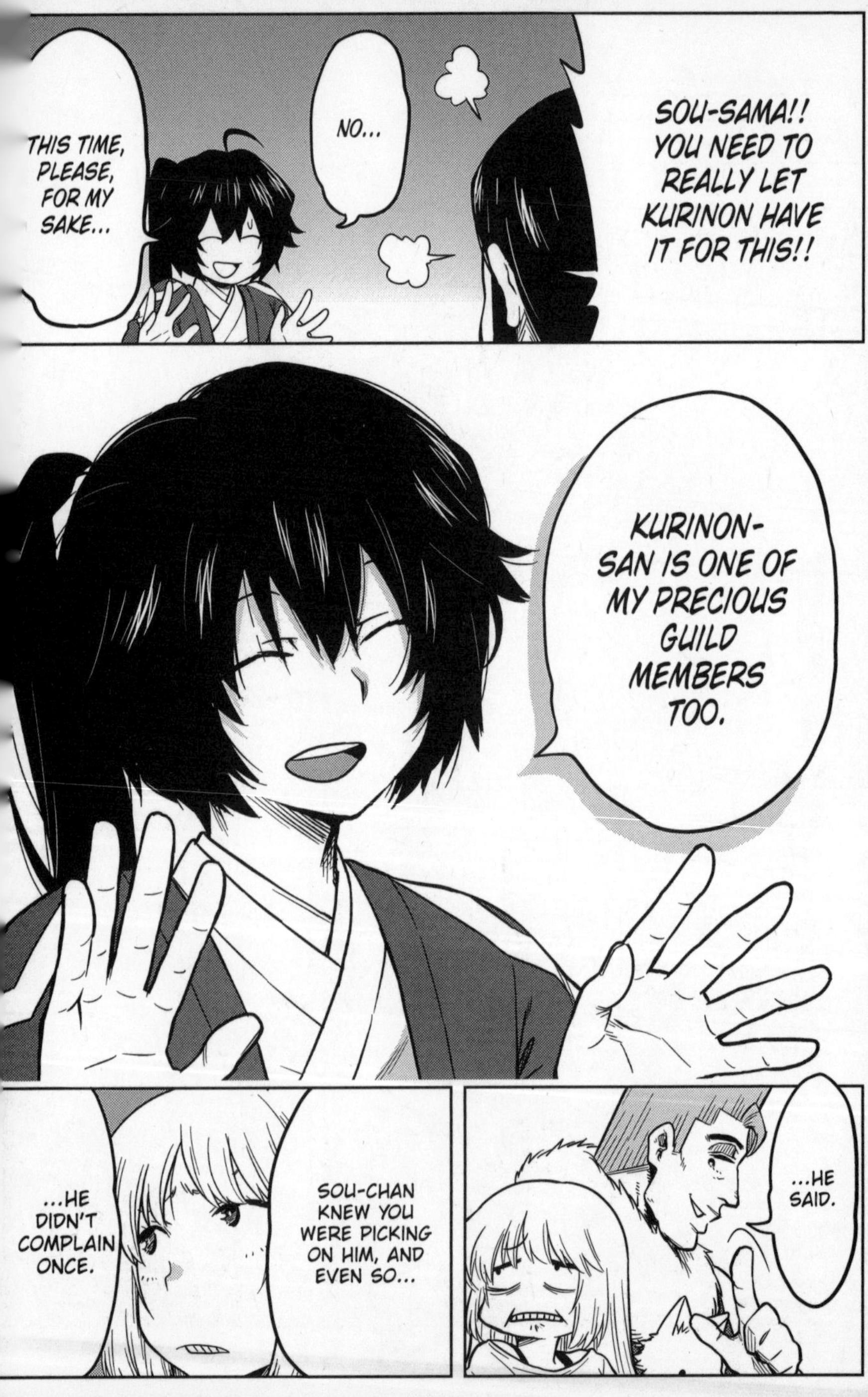
SOU-SAMA!! YOU NEED TO REALLY LET KURINON HAVE IT FOR THIS!!
NO...
THIS TIME, PLEASE, FOR MY SAKE...
KURINON-SAN IS ONE OF MY PRECIOUS GUILD MEMBERS TOO.
...HE SAID.
SOU-CHAN KNEW YOU WERE PICKING ON HIM, AND EVEN SO...
...HE DIDN'T COMPLAIN ONCE.

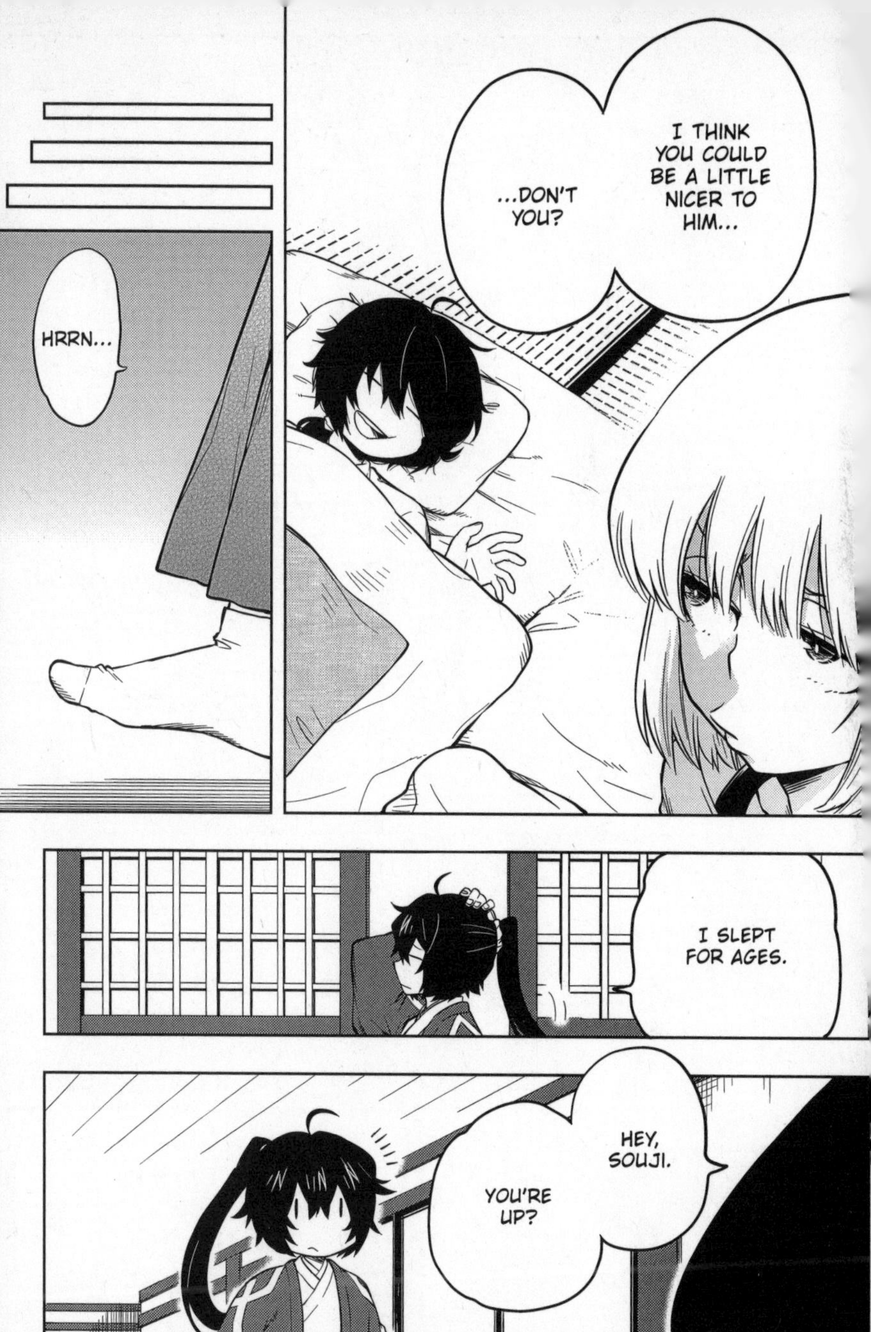
I THINK YOU COULD BE A LITTLE NICER TO HIM...
...DON'T YOU?
HRRN...
I SLEPT FOR AGES.
HEY, SOUJI.
YOU'RE UP?

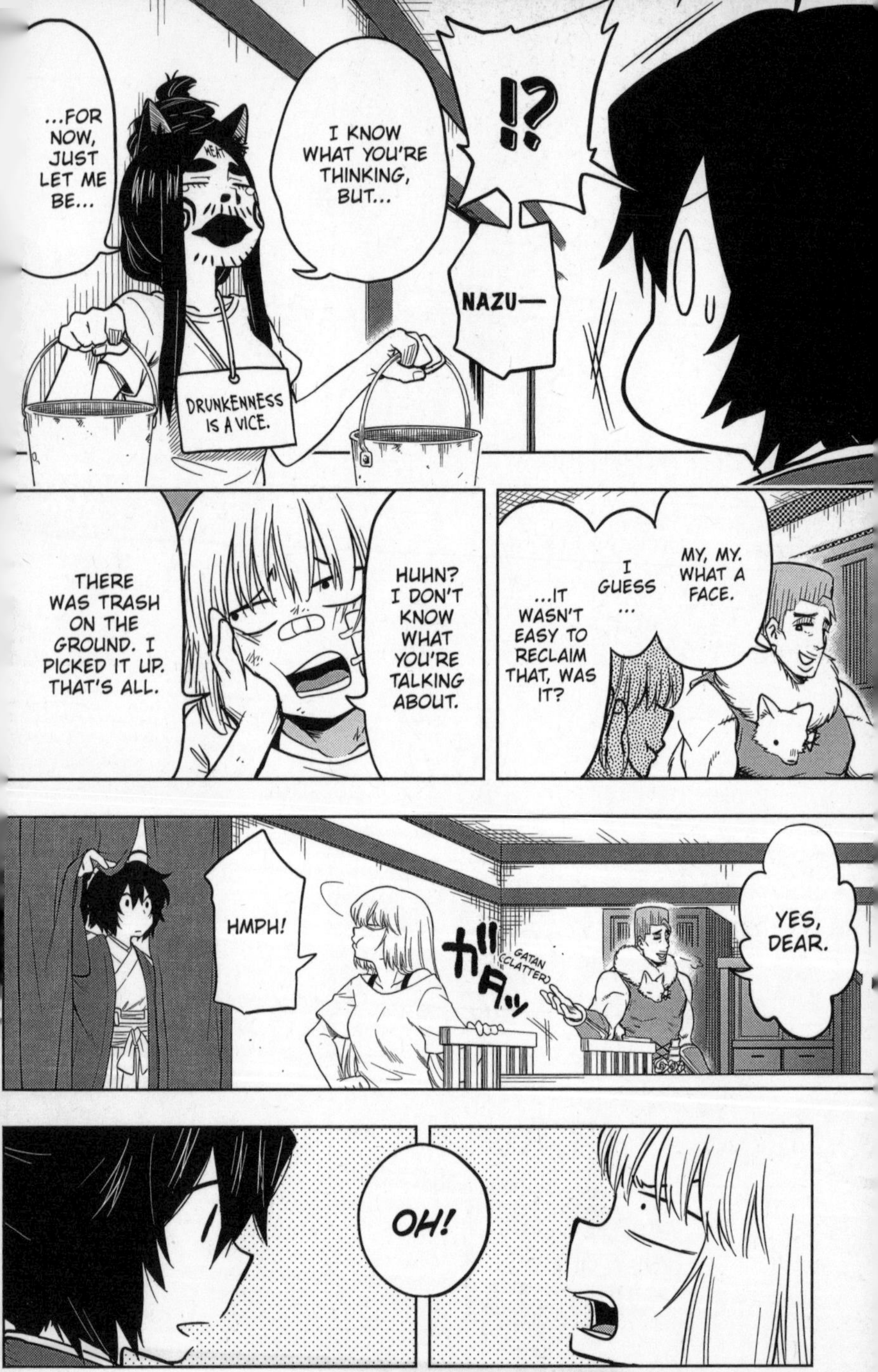
!?
NAZU—
I KNOW WHAT YOU'RE THINKING, BUT...
...FOR NOW, JUST LET ME BE...
DRUNKENNESS IS A VICE.
MY, MY. WHAT A FACE.
I GUESS...
...IT WASN'T EASY TO RECLAIM THAT, WAS IT?
HUHN? I DON'T KNOW WHAT YOU'RE TALKING ABOUT.
THERE WAS TRASH ON THE GROUND. I PICKED IT UP. THAT'S ALL.
YES, DEAR.
ガタッ
GATAN (CLATTER)
HMPH!
OH!

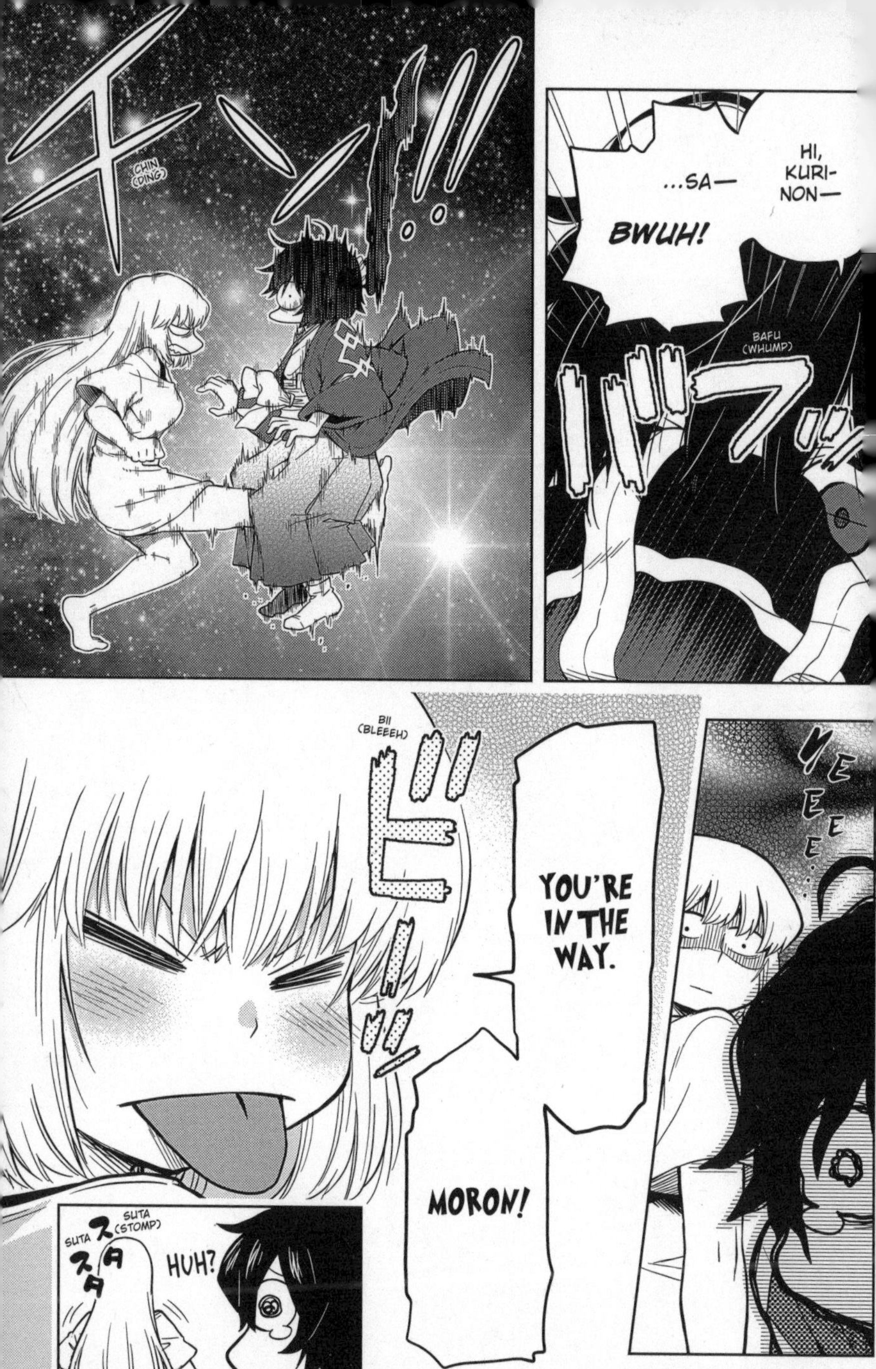
HI, KURI-NON—
...SA—
BWUH!
BAFU (WHUMP)
CHIN (DING)
YEEEE...
BII (BLEEEH)
YOU'RE IN THE WAY.
MORON!
SUTA SUTA (STOMP)
HUH?

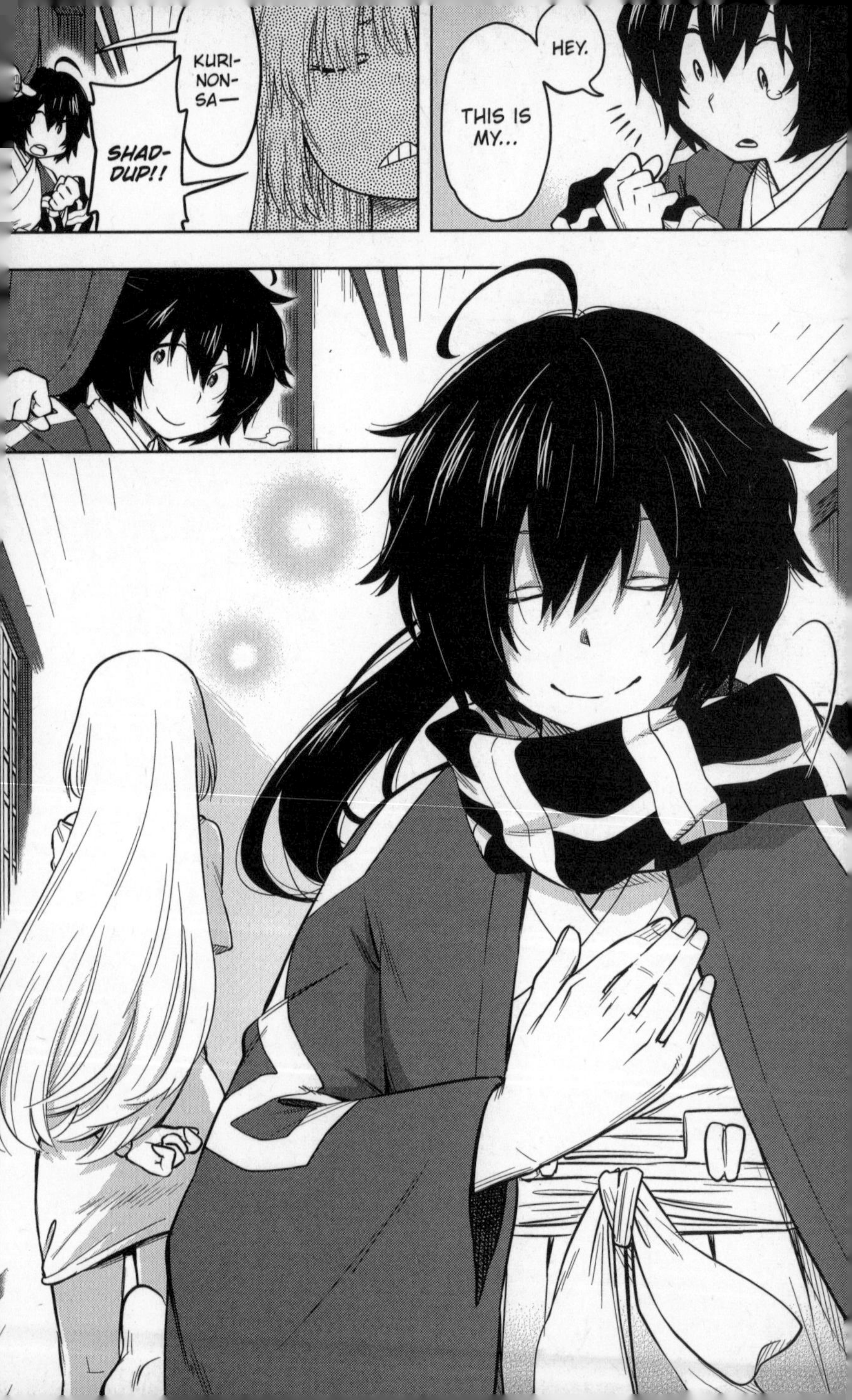
HEY.
THIS IS MY...
KURI-NON-SA—
SHAD-DUP!!

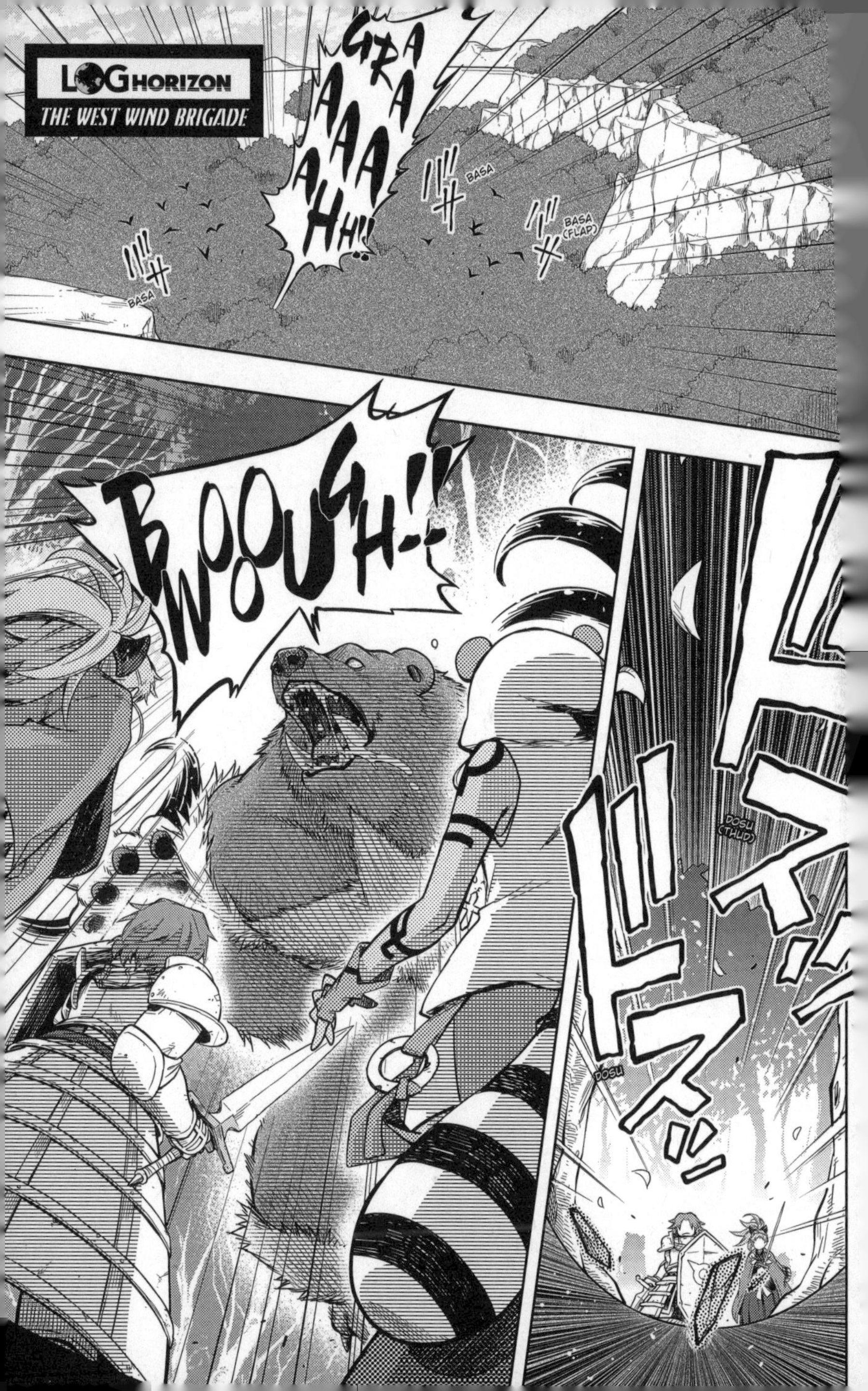
LOG HORIZON
THE WEST WIND BRIGADE
GRAAAAAAHH!!
BASA
BASA (FLAP)
BASA
DOSU (THUD)
DOSU
BWOOOUSH!!

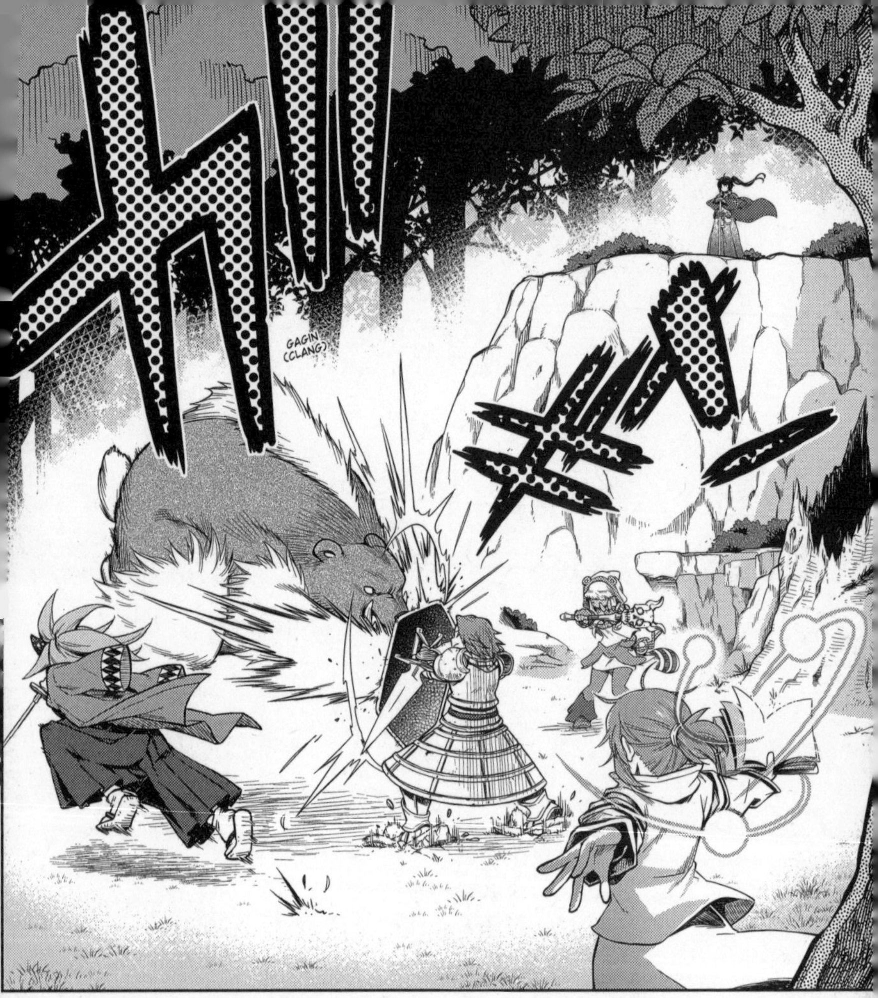
GAGIN (CLANG)

CHAPTER: 36 RISK

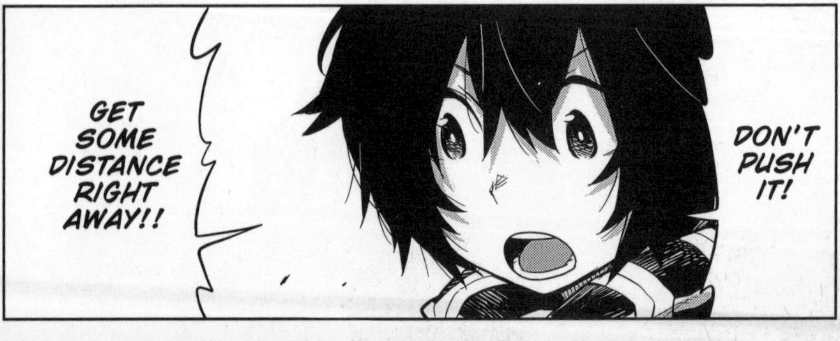
DON'T PUSH IT!
GET SOME DISTANCE RIGHT AWAY!!

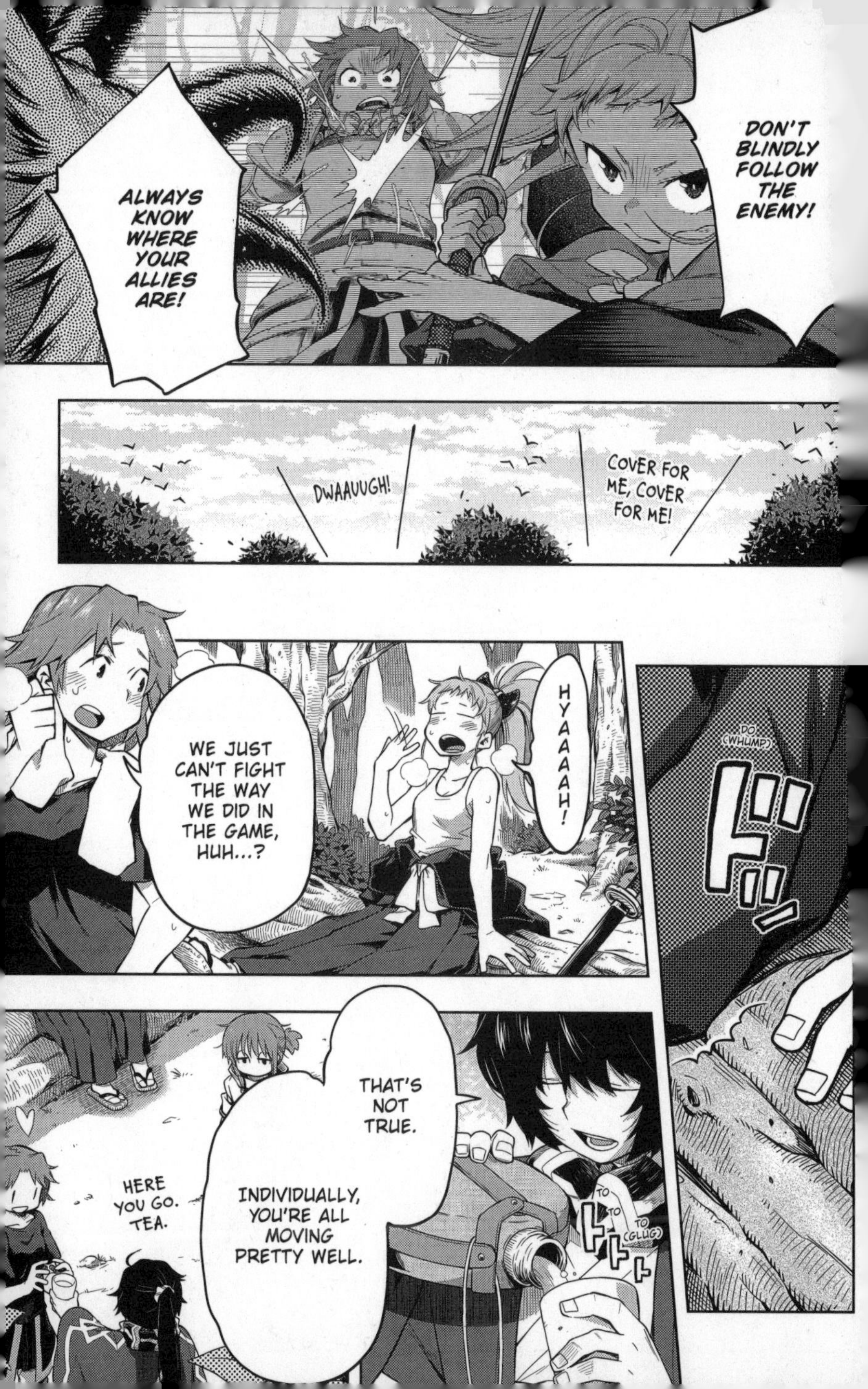
DON'T BLINDLY FOLLOW THE ENEMY!
ALWAYS KNOW WHERE YOUR ALLIES ARE!
COVER FOR ME, COVER FOR ME!
DWAAUUGH!
DO (WHUMP)
HYAAAAAH!
WE JUST CAN'T FIGHT THE WAY WE DID IN THE GAME, HUH...?
THAT'S NOT TRUE.
INDIVIDUALLY, YOU'RE ALL MOVING PRETTY WELL.
TO TO TO (GLUG)
HERE YOU GO. TEA.

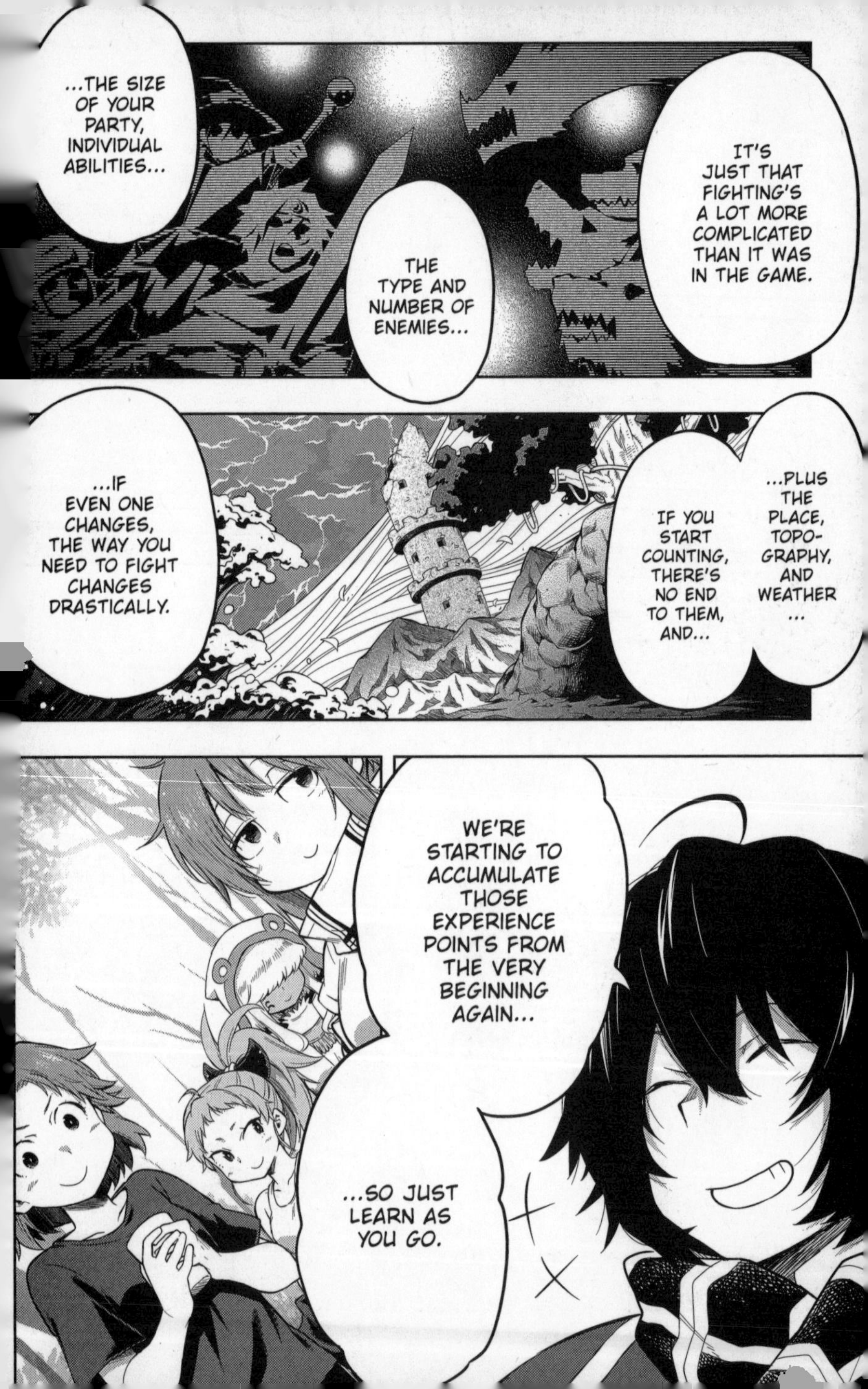
IT'S JUST THAT FIGHTING'S A LOT MORE COMPLICATED THAN IT WAS IN THE GAME.
THE TYPE AND NUMBER OF ENEMIES...
...THE SIZE OF YOUR PARTY, INDIVIDUAL ABILITIES...
...PLUS THE PLACE, TOPOGRAPHY, AND WEATHER...
IF YOU START COUNTING, THERE'S NO END TO THEM, AND...
...IF EVEN ONE CHANGES, THE WAY YOU NEED TO FIGHT CHANGES DRASTICALLY.
WE'RE STARTING TO ACCUMULATE THOSE EXPERIENCE POINTS FROM THE VERY BEGINNING AGAIN...
...SO JUST LEARN AS YOU GO.

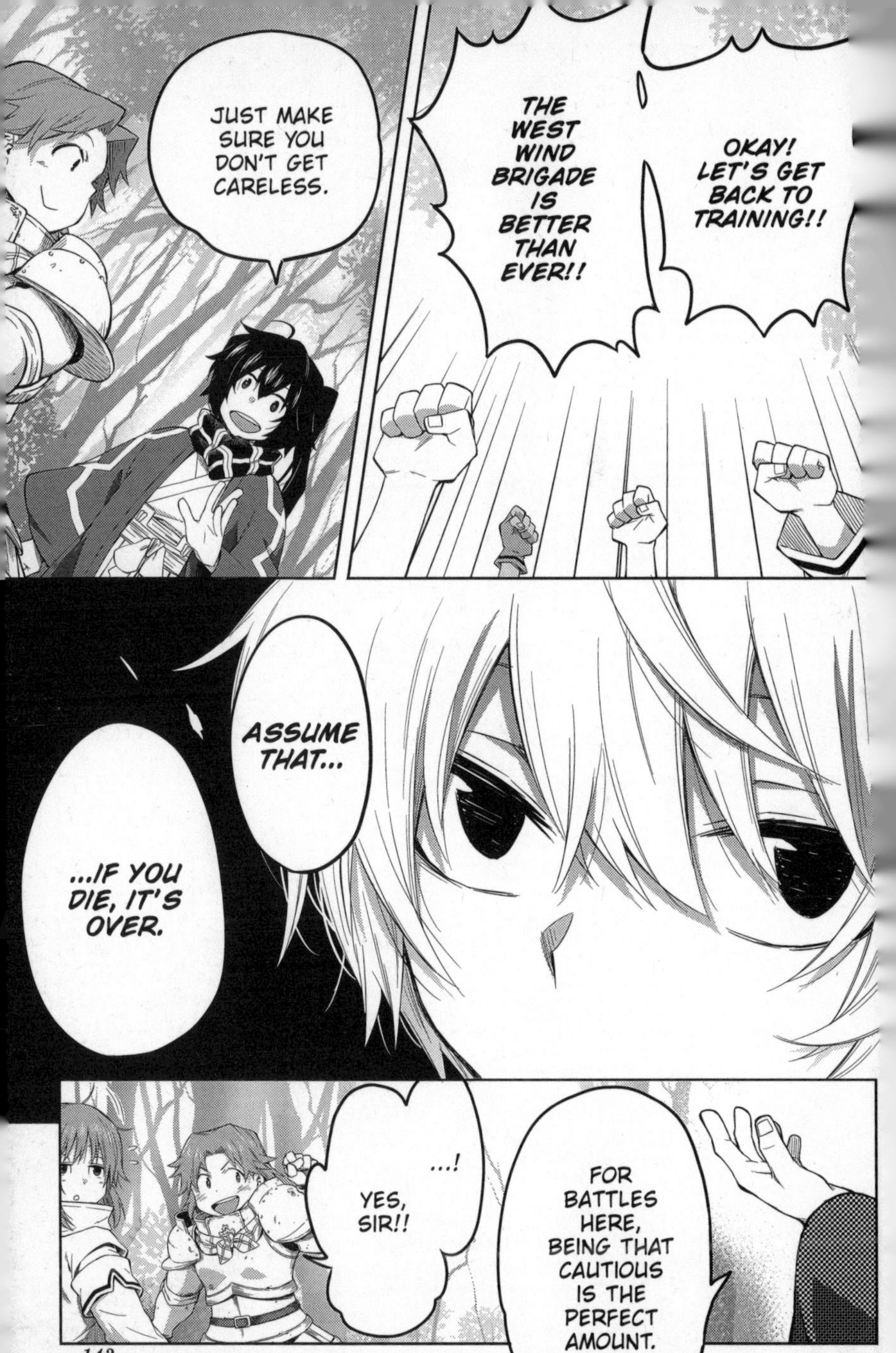
OKAY! LET'S GET BACK TO TRAINING!!
THE WEST WIND BRIGADE IS BETTER THAN EVER!!
JUST MAKE SURE YOU DON'T GET CARELESS.
ASSUME THAT...
...IF YOU DIE, IT'S OVER.
FOR BATTLES HERE, BEING THAT CAUTIOUS IS THE PERFECT AMOUNT.
...!
YES, SIR!!

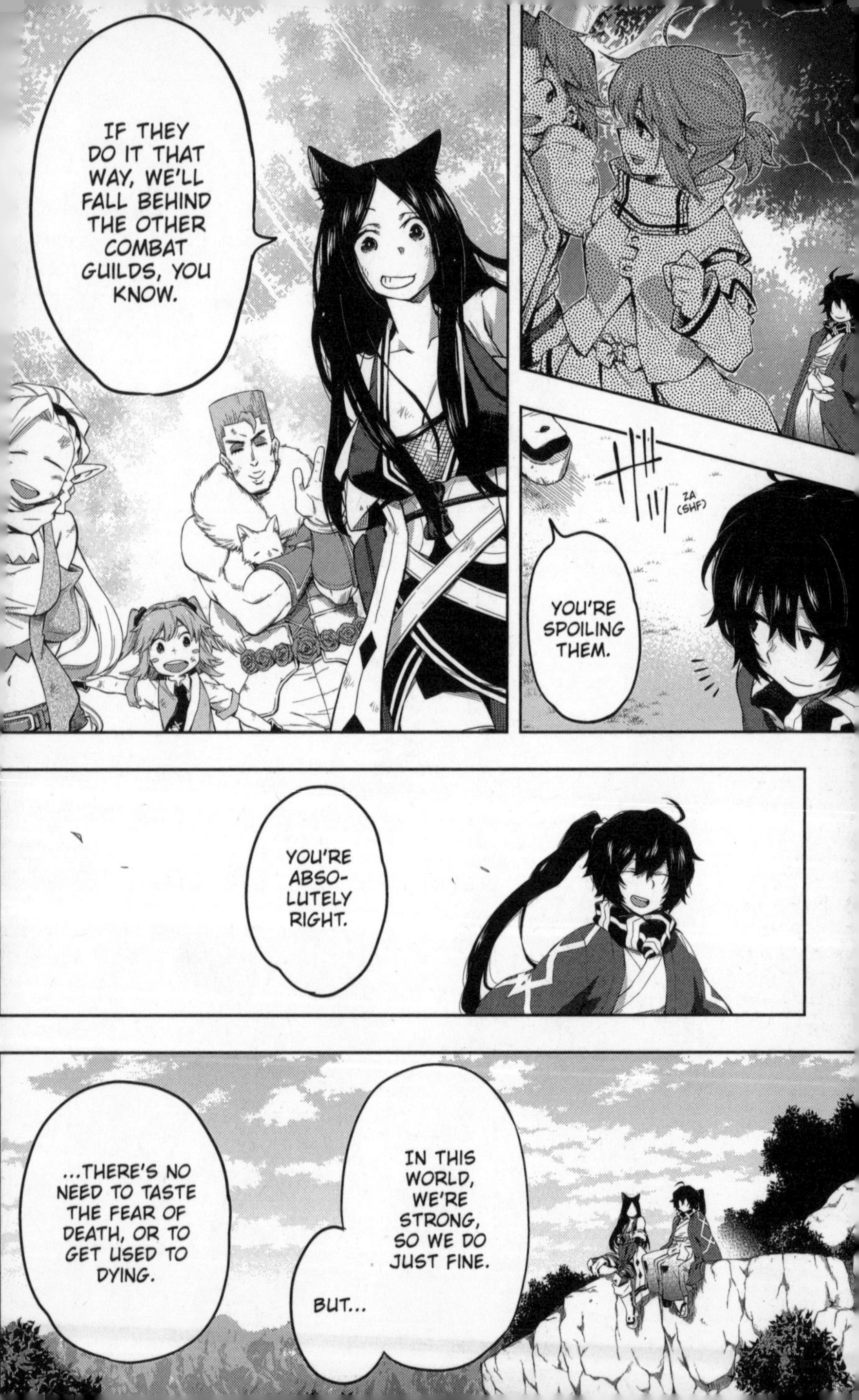
ZA (SHF)
YOU'RE SPOILING THEM.
IF THEY DO IT THAT WAY, WE'LL FALL BEHIND THE OTHER COMBAT GUILDS, YOU KNOW.
YOU'RE ABSOLUTELY RIGHT.
IN THIS WORLD, WE'RE STRONG, SO WE DO JUST FINE.
BUT...
...THERE'S NO NEED TO TASTE THE FEAR OF DEATH, OR TO GET USED TO DYING.

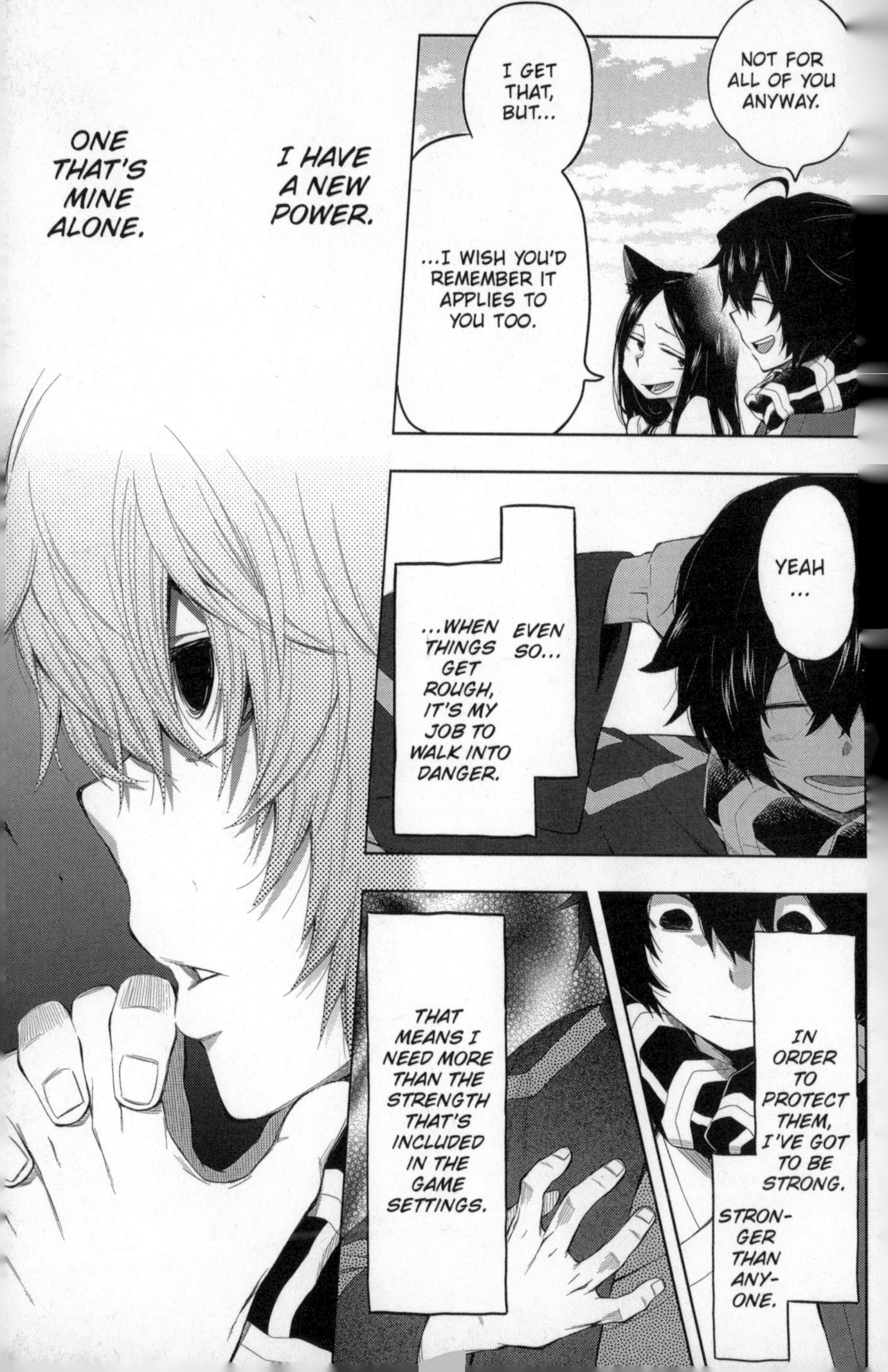
NOT FOR ALL OF YOU ANYWAY.
I GET THAT, BUT...
...I WISH YOU'D REMEMBER IT APPLIES TO YOU TOO.
YEAH...
EVEN SO...
...WHEN THINGS GET ROUGH, IT'S MY JOB TO WALK INTO DANGER.
IN ORDER TO PROTECT THEM, I'VE GOT TO BE STRONG.
STRONGER THAN ANYONE.
THAT MEANS I NEED MORE THAN THE STRENGTH THAT'S INCLUDED IN THE GAME SETTINGS.
I HAVE A NEW POWER.
ONE THAT'S MINE ALONE.

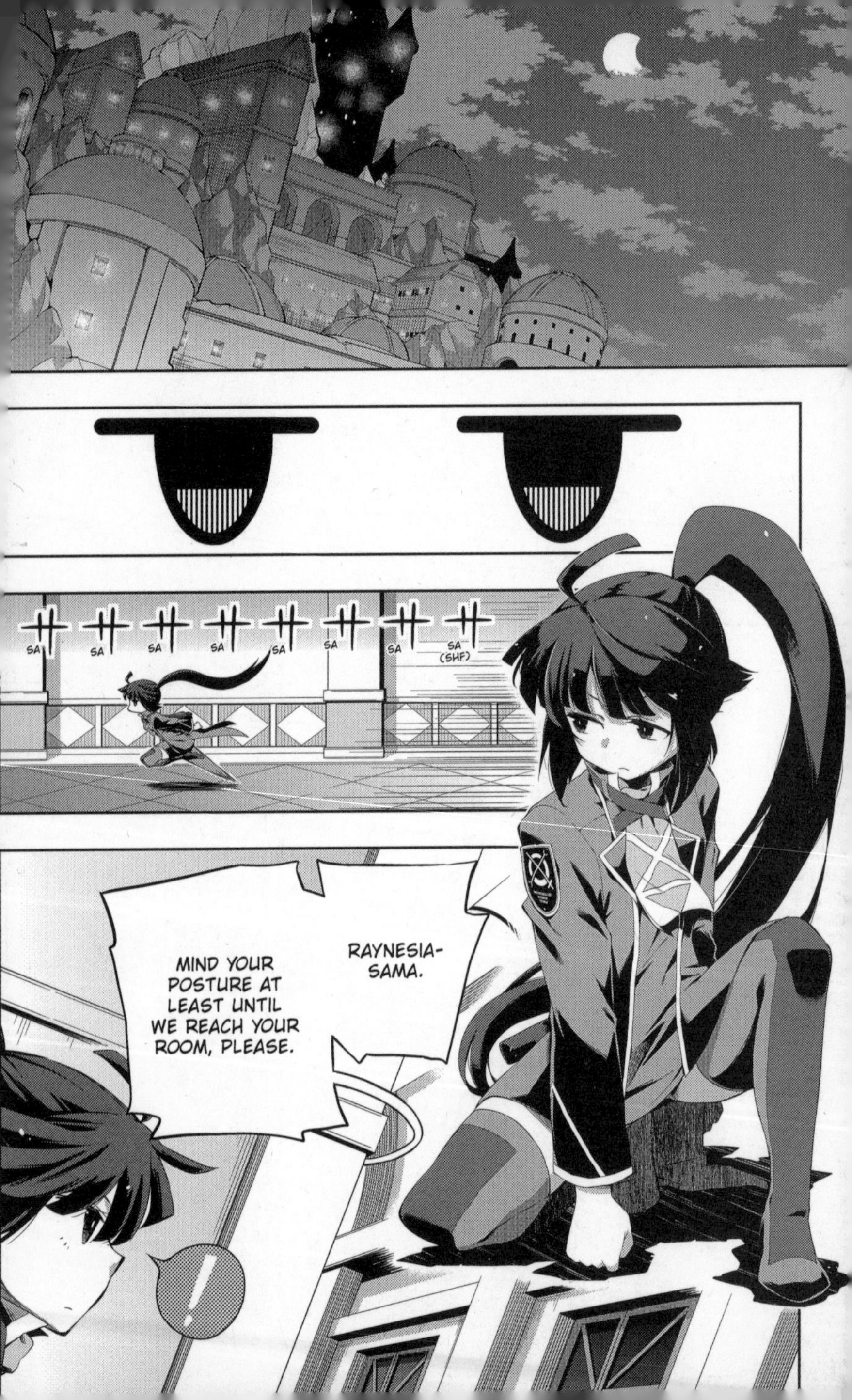
SA (SHF)
SA
SA
SA
SA
SA
SA
SA
RAYNESIA-SAMA.
MIND YOUR POSTURE AT LEAST UNTIL WE REACH YOUR ROOM, PLEASE.
!

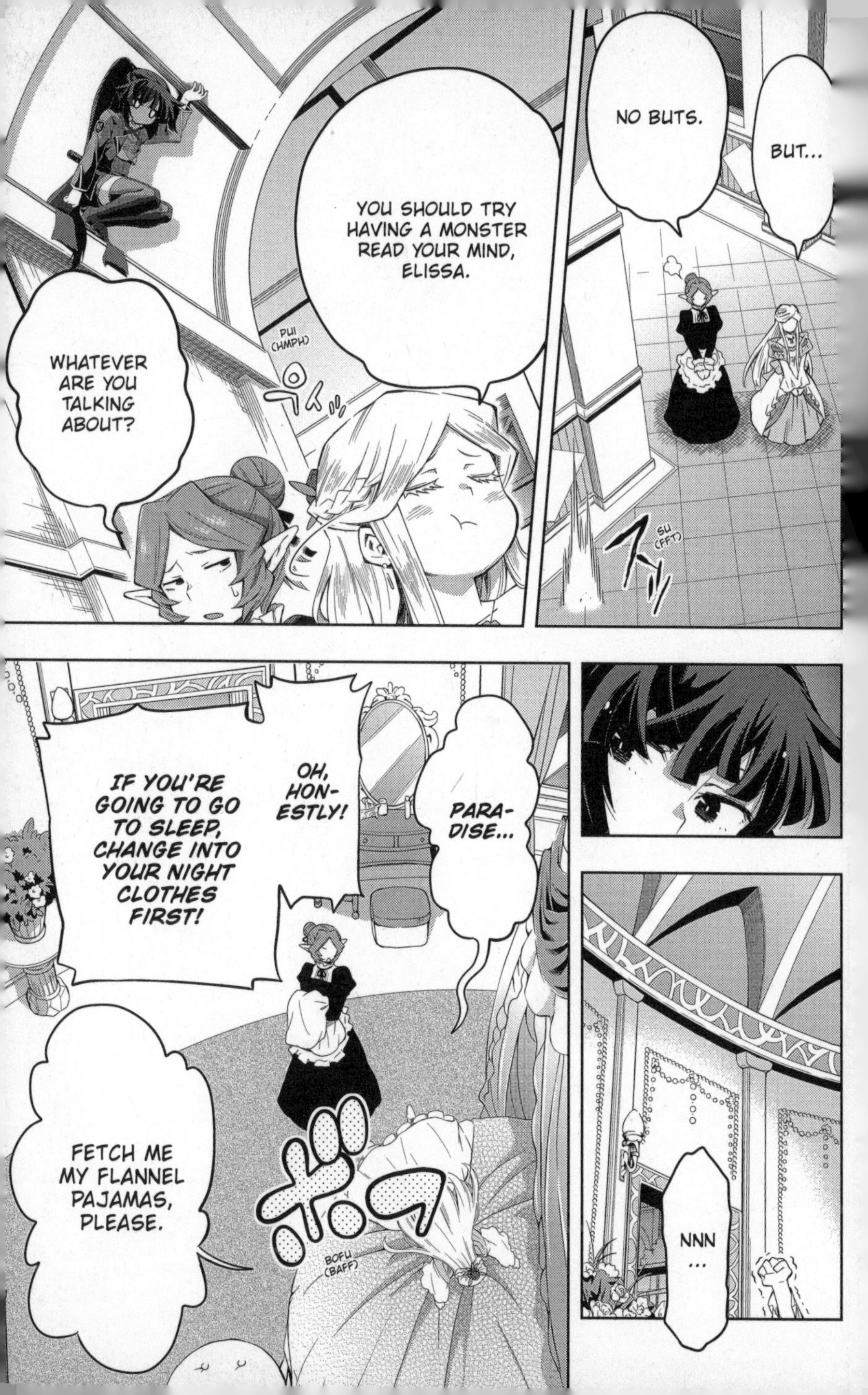
BUT...
NO BUTS.
SU (FFT)
YOU SHOULD TRY HAVING A MONSTER READ YOUR MIND, ELISSA.
PUI (HMPH)
WHATEVER ARE YOU TALKING ABOUT?
NNN ...
PARA-DISE...
OH, HON-ESTLY!
IF YOU'RE GOING TO GO TO SLEEP, CHANGE INTO YOUR NIGHT CLOTHES FIRST!
BOFU (BAFF)
FETCH ME MY FLANNEL PAJAMAS, PLEASE.

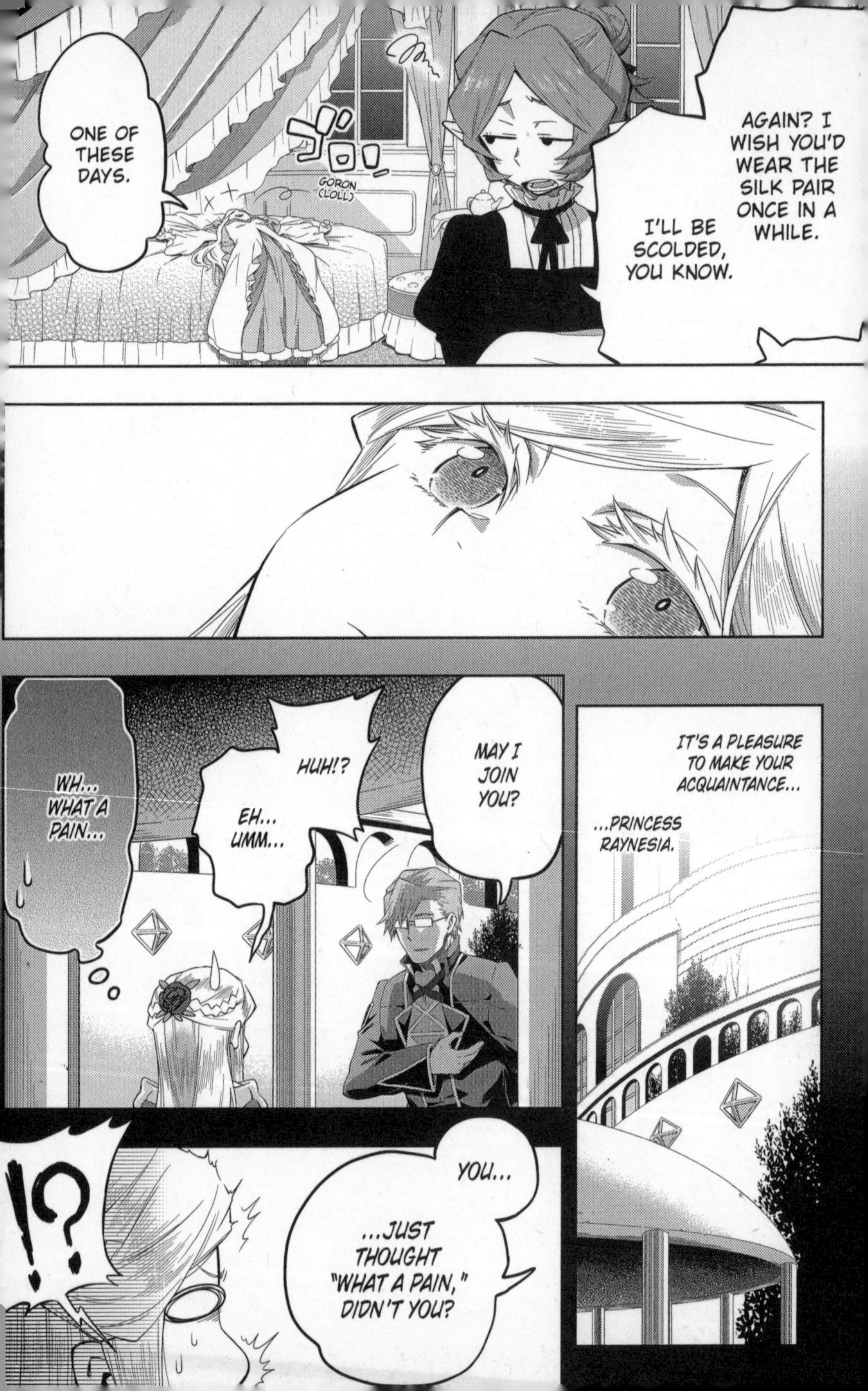
AGAIN? I WISH YOU'D WEAR THE SILK PAIR ONCE IN A WHILE.
I'LL BE SCOLDED, YOU KNOW.
ゴロン
GORON (LOLL)
ONE OF THESE DAYS.
IT'S A PLEASURE TO MAKE YOUR ACQUAINTANCE...
...PRINCESS RAYNESIA.
MAY I JOIN YOU?
HUH!?
EH... UMM...
WH... WHAT A PAIN...
YOU...
...JUST THOUGHT "WHAT A PAIN," DIDN'T YOU?
!?

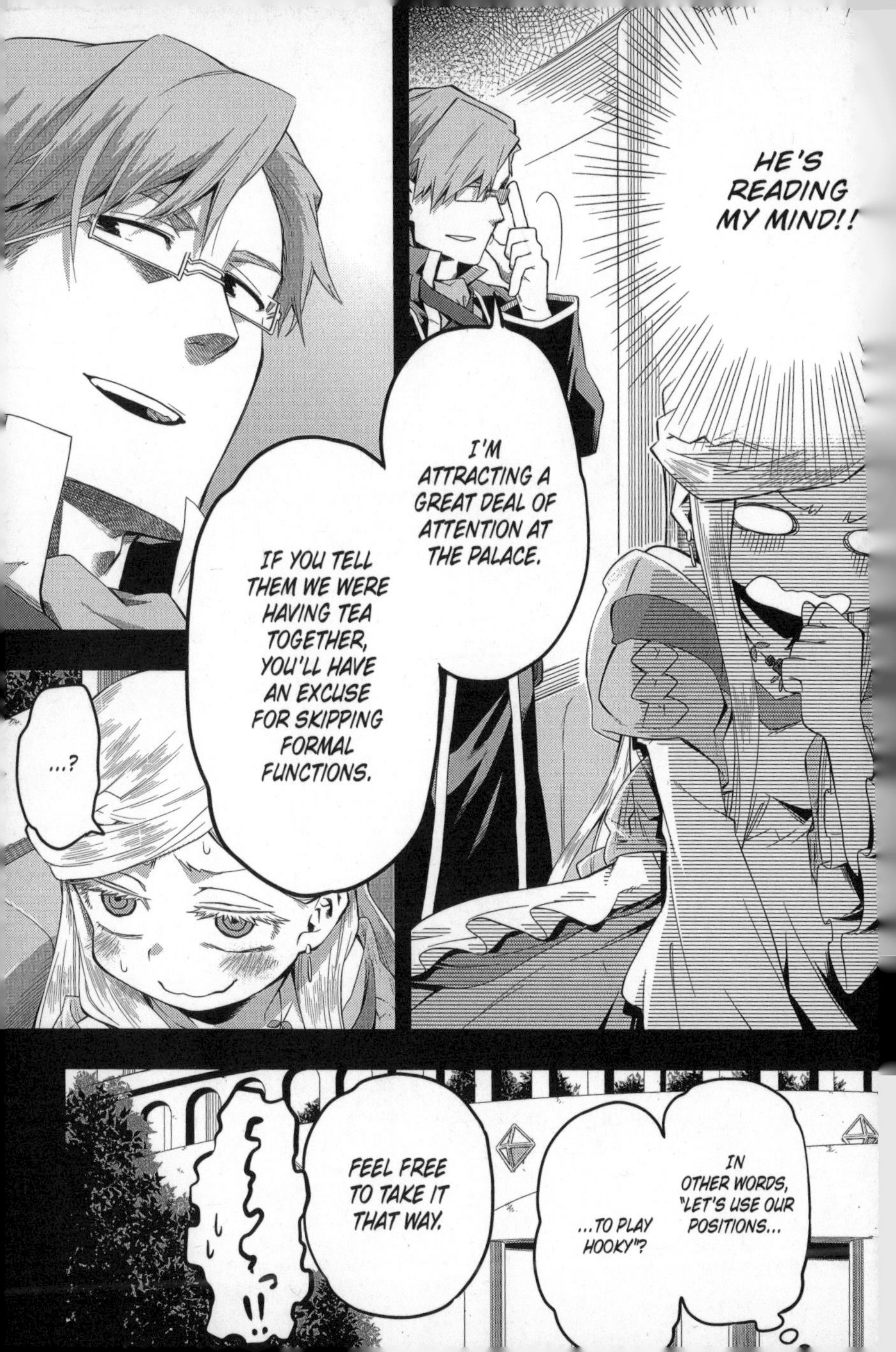
HE'S READING MY MIND!!
I'M ATTRACTING A GREAT DEAL OF ATTENTION AT THE PALACE.
IF YOU TELL THEM WE WERE HAVING TEA TOGETHER, YOU'LL HAVE AN EXCUSE FOR SKIPPING FORMAL FUNCTIONS.
...?
IN OTHER WORDS, "LET'S USE OUR POSITIONS...
...TO PLAY HOOKY"?
FEEL FREE TO TAKE IT THAT WAY.

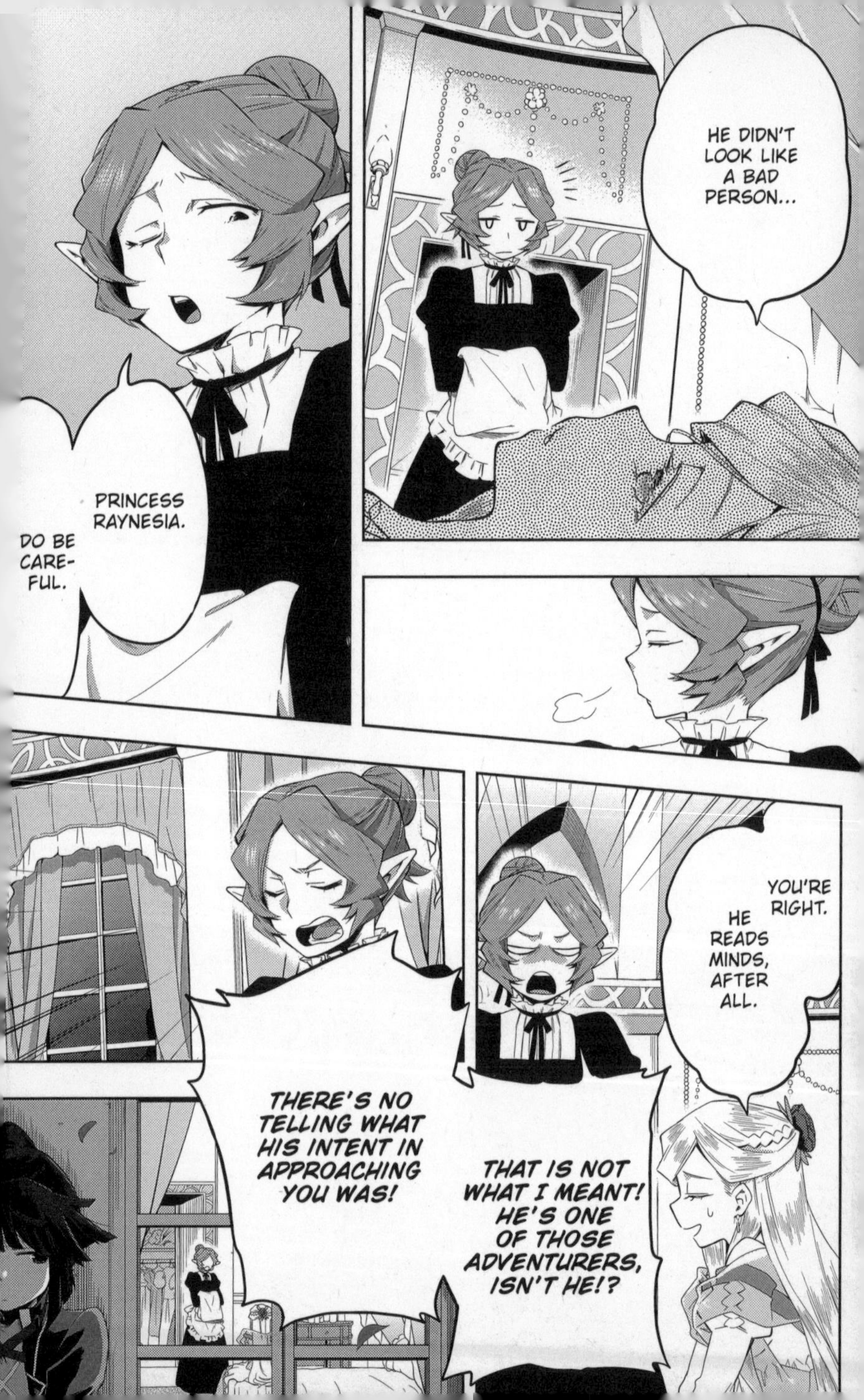
HE DIDN'T LOOK LIKE A BAD PERSON...
PRINCESS RAYNESIA.
DO BE CARE-FUL.
YOU'RE RIGHT.
HE READS MINDS, AFTER ALL.
THAT IS NOT WHAT I MEANT! HE'S ONE OF THOSE ADVENTURERS, ISN'T HE!?
THERE'S NO TELLING WHAT HIS INTENT IN APPROACHING YOU WAS!

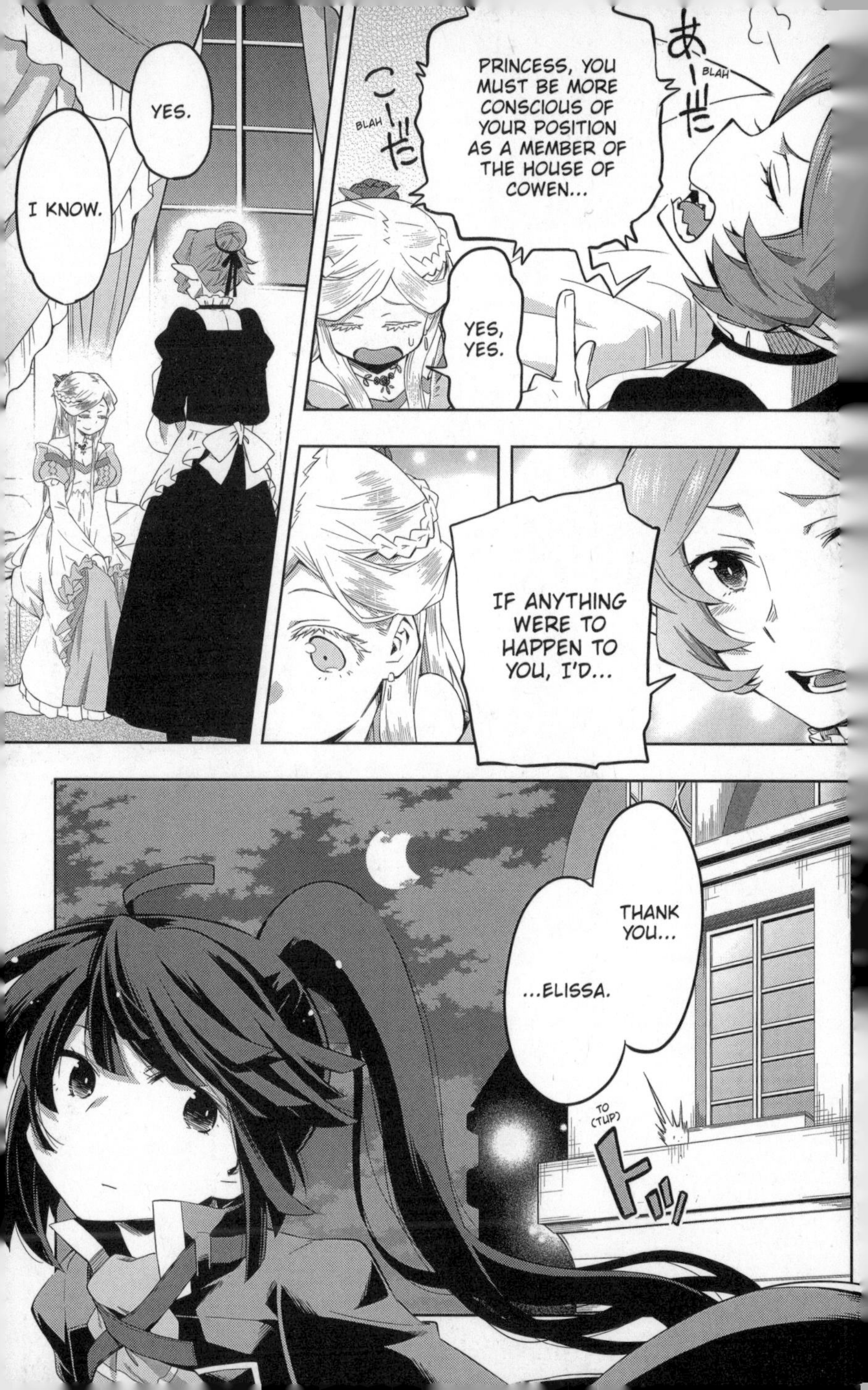
あーだ
BLAH
PRINCESS, YOU MUST BE MORE CONSCIOUS OF YOUR POSITION AS A MEMBER OF THE HOUSE OF COWEN...
こーだ
BLAH
YES, YES.
IF ANYTHING WERE TO HAPPEN TO YOU, I'D...
YES.
I KNOW.
THANK YOU...
...ELISSA.
TO (TUP)
ト

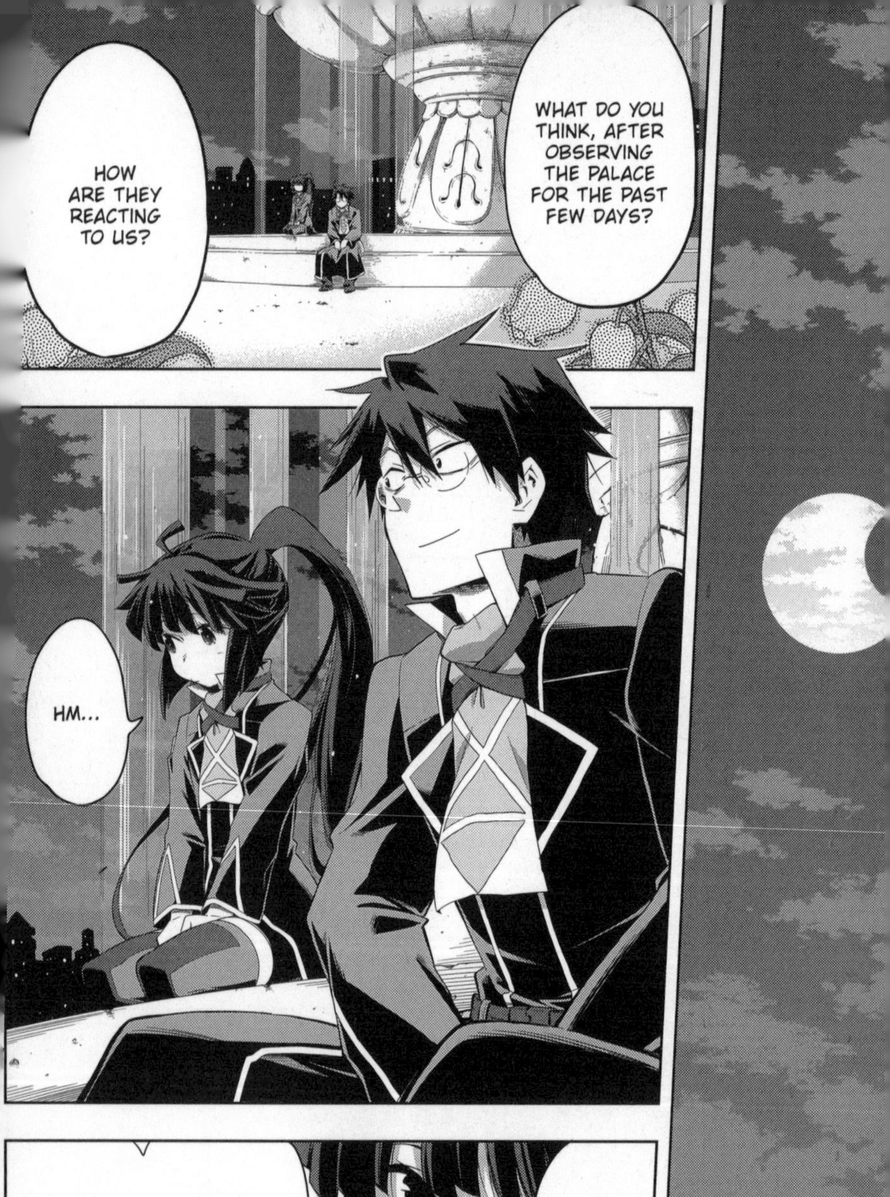
WHAT DO YOU THINK, AFTER OBSERVING THE PALACE FOR THE PAST FEW DAYS?
HOW ARE THEY REACTING TO US?
HM...
INTENSE INTEREST.
GOODWILL AND HOSTILITY...
...ABOUT EQUAL PARTS EACH.

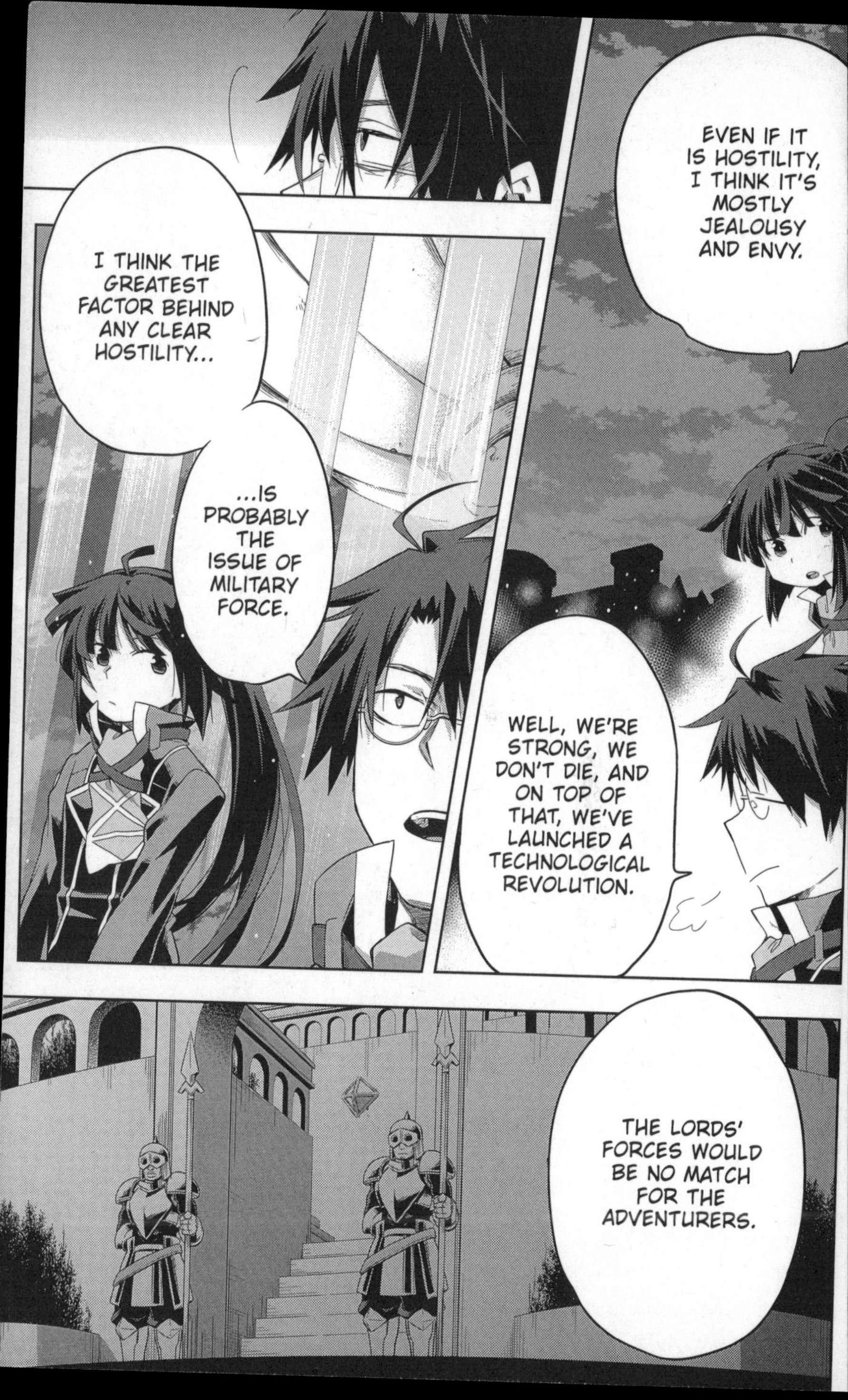
EVEN IF IT IS HOSTILITY, I THINK IT'S MOSTLY JEALOUSY AND ENVY.
WELL, WE'RE STRONG, WE DON'T DIE, AND ON TOP OF THAT, WE'VE LAUNCHED A TECHNOLOGICAL REVOLUTION.
I THINK THE GREATEST FACTOR BEHIND ANY CLEAR HOSTILITY...
...IS PROBABLY THE ISSUE OF MILITARY FORCE.
THE LORDS' FORCES WOULD BE NO MATCH FOR THE ADVENTURERS.

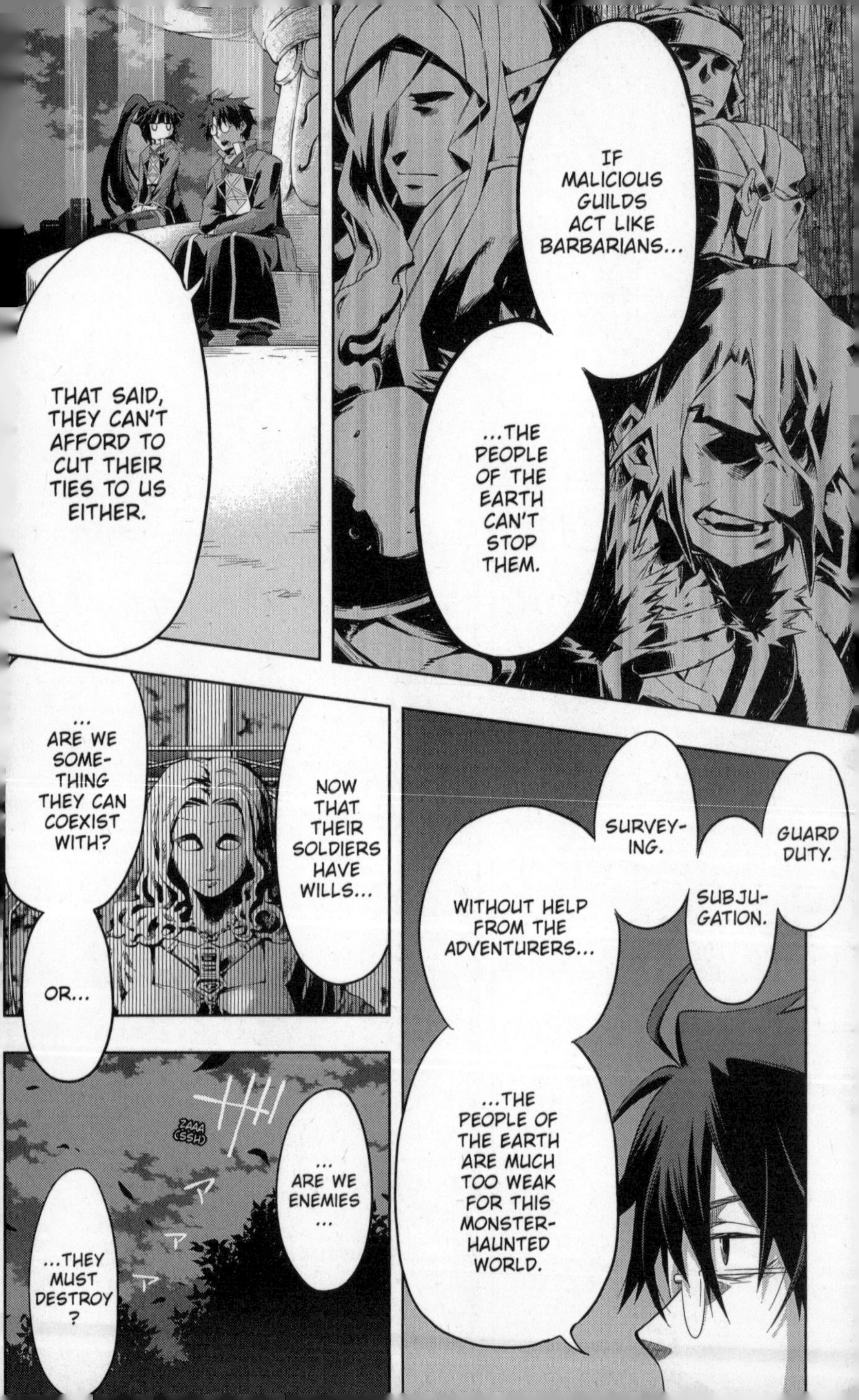
IF MALICIOUS GUILDS ACT LIKE BARBARIANS...
...THE PEOPLE OF THE EARTH CAN'T STOP THEM.
THAT SAID, THEY CAN'T AFFORD TO CUT THEIR TIES TO US EITHER.
GUARD DUTY.
SURVEYING.
SUBJUGATION.
WITHOUT HELP FROM THE ADVENTURERS...
...THE PEOPLE OF THE EARTH ARE MUCH TOO WEAK FOR THIS MONSTER-HAUNTED WORLD.
NOW THAT THEIR SOLDIERS HAVE WILLS...
...ARE WE SOMETHING THEY CAN COEXIST WITH?
OR...
...ARE WE ENEMIES...
ZAAA (SSH)
...THEY MUST DESTROY?

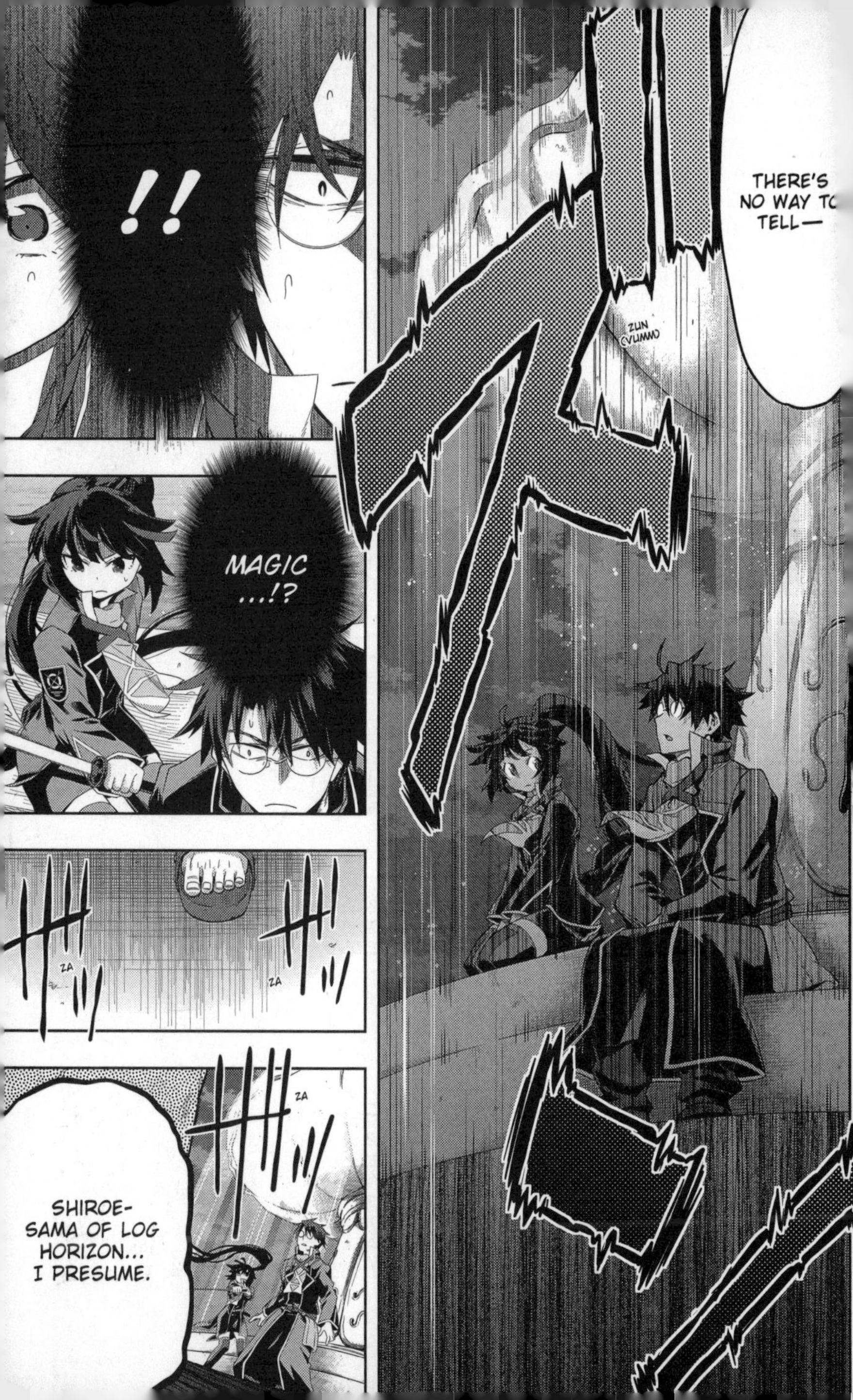
THERE'S NO WAY TO TELL—
ZUN (VUMM)
!!
MAGIC ...!?
ZA
ZA
ZA
SHIROE-SAMA OF LOG HORIZON... I PRESUME.

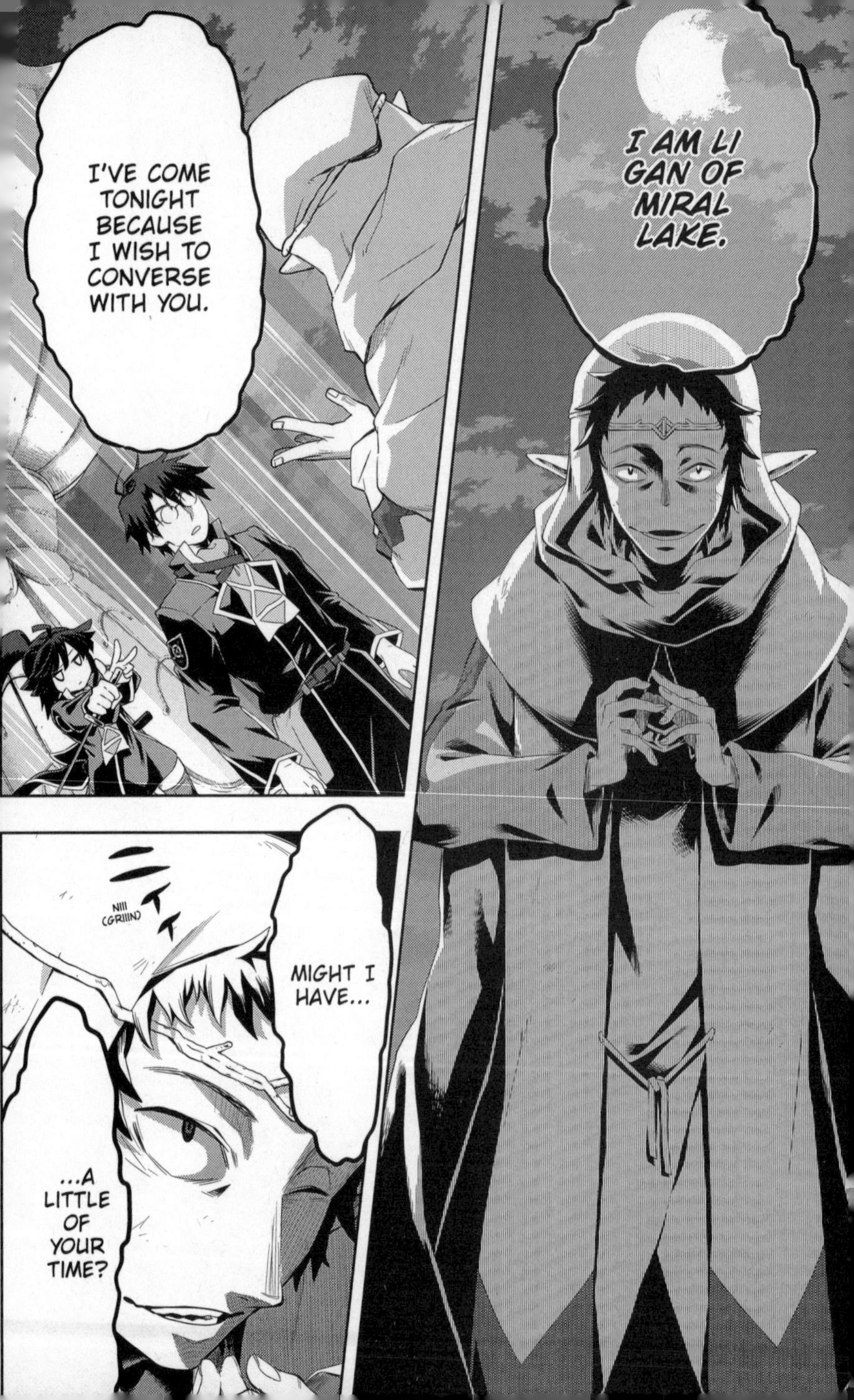
I AM LI GAN OF MIRAL LAKE.
I'VE COME TONIGHT BECAUSE I WISH TO CONVERSE WITH YOU.
NIII (GRIIIN)
MIGHT I HAVE...
...A LITTLE OF YOUR TIME?

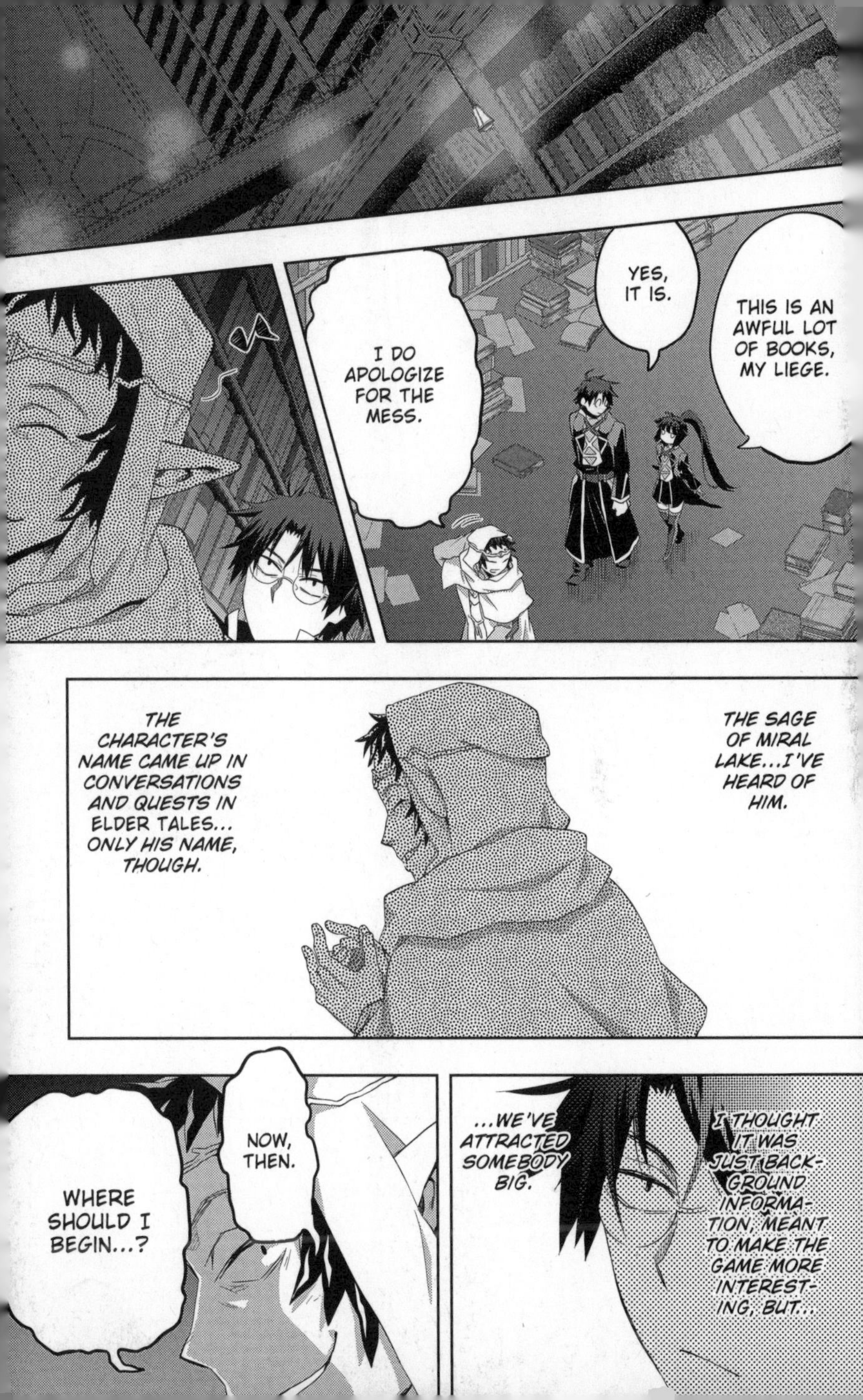
THIS IS AN AWFUL LOT OF BOOKS, MY LIEGE.
YES, IT IS.
I DO APOLOGIZE FOR THE MESS.
THE SAGE OF MIRAL LAKE...I'VE HEARD OF HIM.
THE CHARACTER'S NAME CAME UP IN CONVERSATIONS AND QUESTS IN ELDER TALES... ONLY HIS NAME, THOUGH.
I THOUGHT IT WAS JUST BACK-GROUND INFORMA-TION, MEANT TO MAKE THE GAME MORE INTEREST-ING, BUT...
...WE'VE ATTRACTED SOMEBODY BIG.
NOW, THEN.
WHERE SHOULD I BEGIN...?

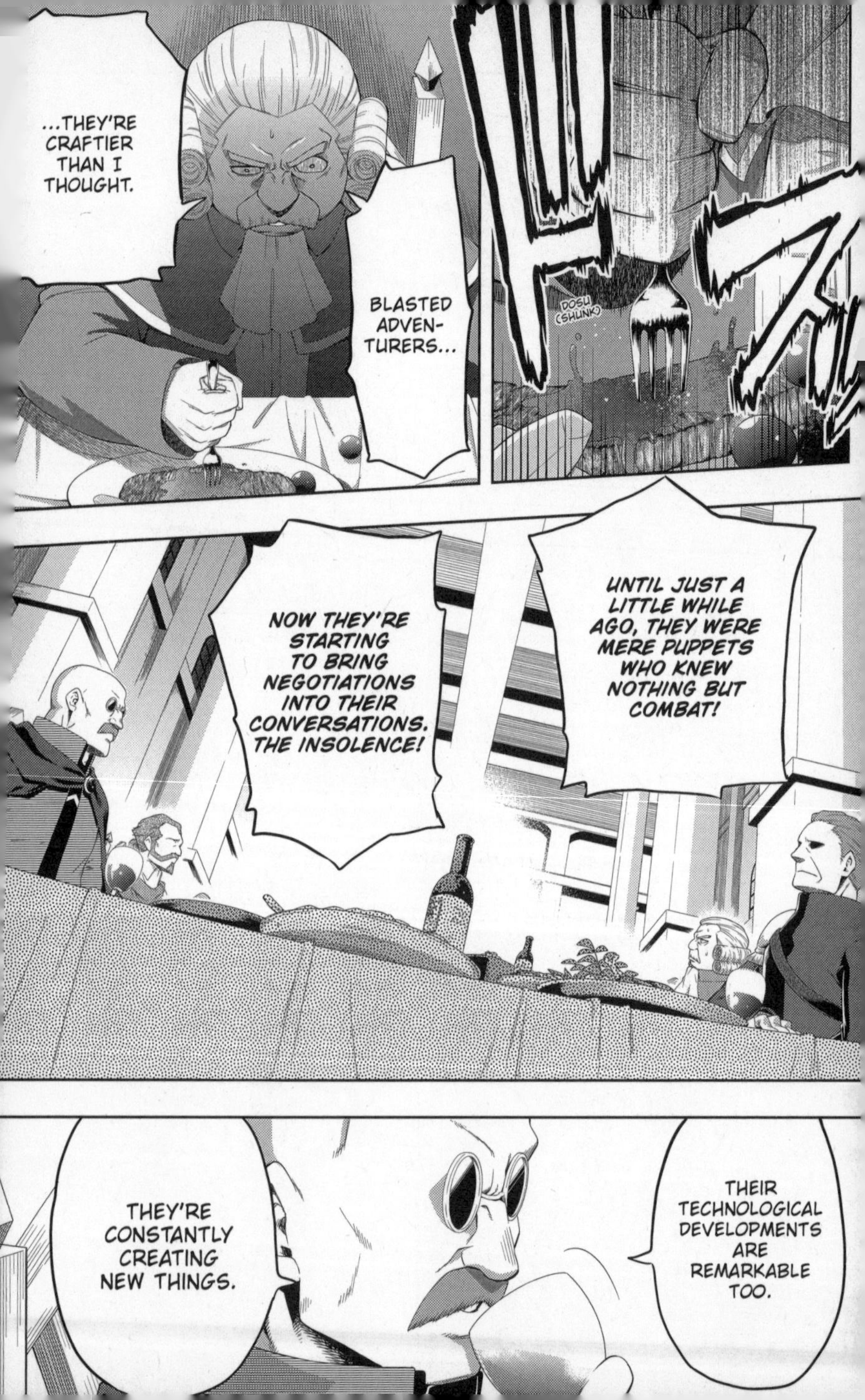
DOSU (SHUNK)
...THEY'RE CRAFTIER THAN I THOUGHT.
BLASTED ADVEN-TURERS...
UNTIL JUST A LITTLE WHILE AGO, THEY WERE MERE PUPPETS WHO KNEW NOTHING BUT COMBAT!
NOW THEY'RE STARTING TO BRING NEGOTIATIONS INTO THEIR CONVERSATIONS. THE INSOLENCE!
THEIR TECHNOLOGICAL DEVELOPMENTS ARE REMARKABLE TOO.
THEY'RE CONSTANTLY CREATING NEW THINGS.

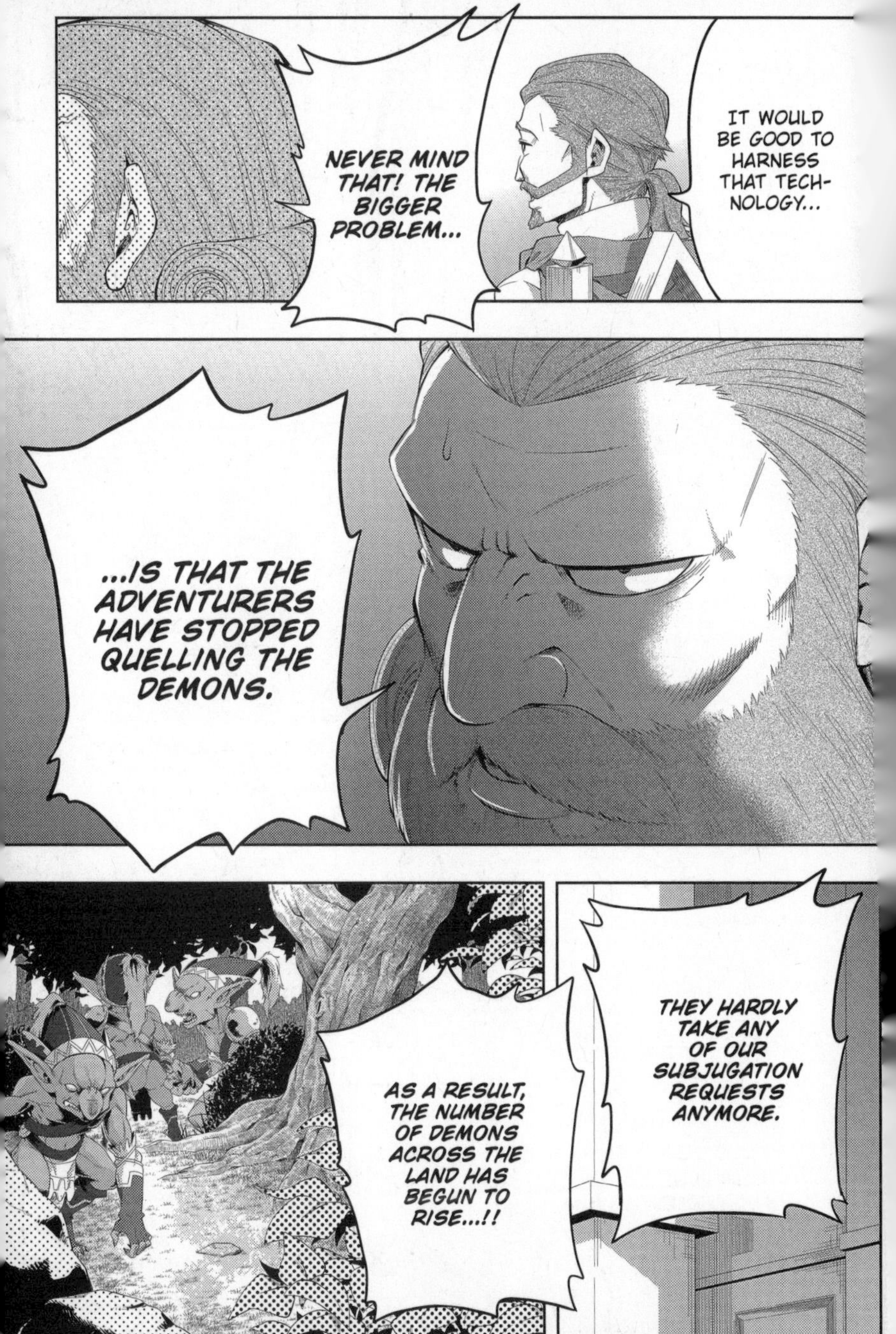
IT WOULD BE GOOD TO HARNESS THAT TECHNOLOGY...
NEVER MIND THAT! THE BIGGER PROBLEM...
...IS THAT THE ADVENTURERS HAVE STOPPED QUELLING THE DEMONS.
THEY HARDLY TAKE ANY OF OUR SUBJUGATION REQUESTS ANYMORE.
AS A RESULT, THE NUMBER OF DEMONS ACROSS THE LAND HAS BEGUN TO RISE...!!

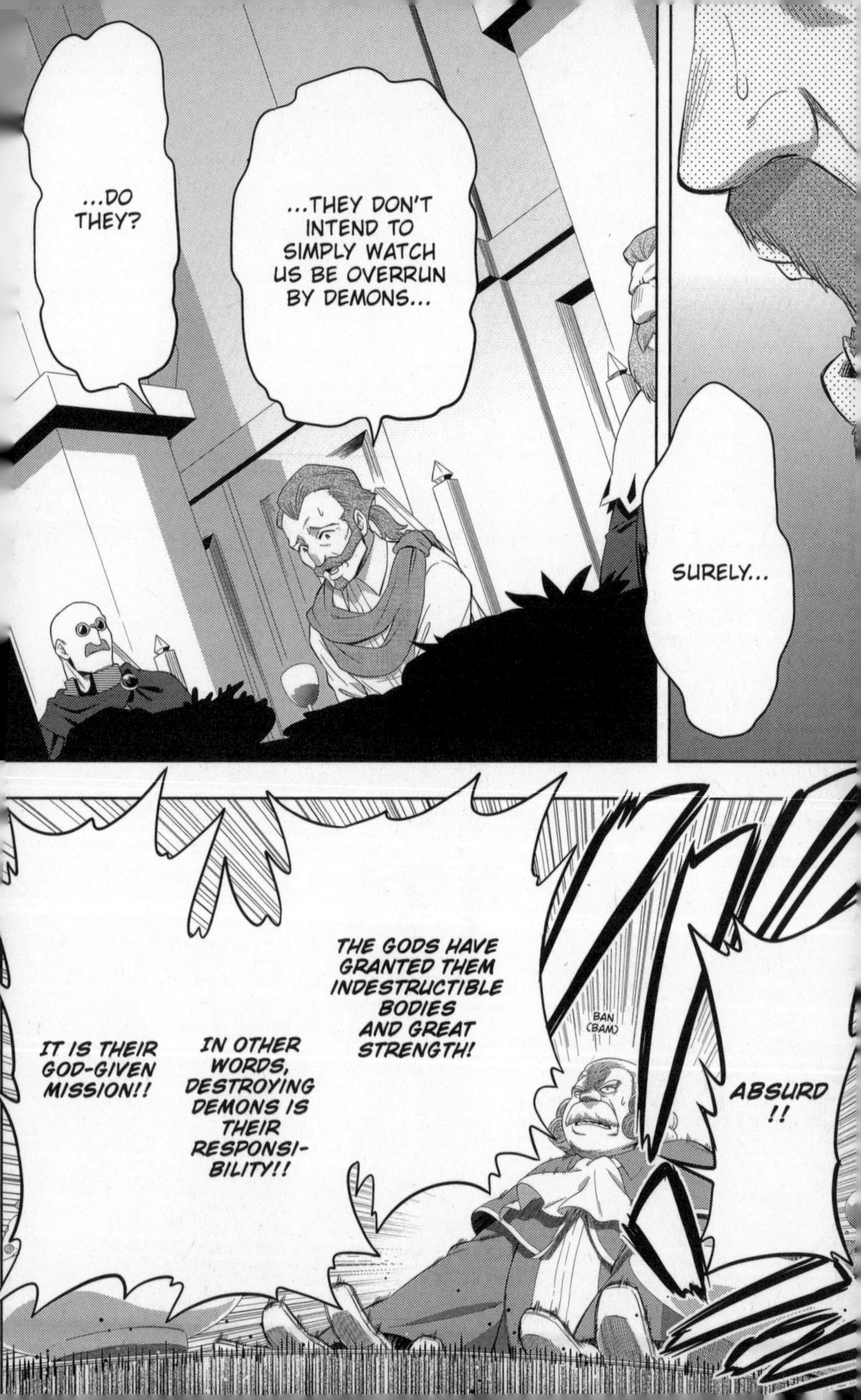
SURELY...
...THEY DON'T INTEND TO SIMPLY WATCH US BE OVERRUN BY DEMONS...
...DO THEY?
ABSURD!!
BAN (BAM)
THE GODS HAVE GRANTED THEM INDESTRUCTIBLE BODIES AND GREAT STRENGTH!
IN OTHER WORDS, DESTROYING DEMONS IS THEIR RESPONSIBILITY!!
IT IS THEIR GOD-GIVEN MISSION!!

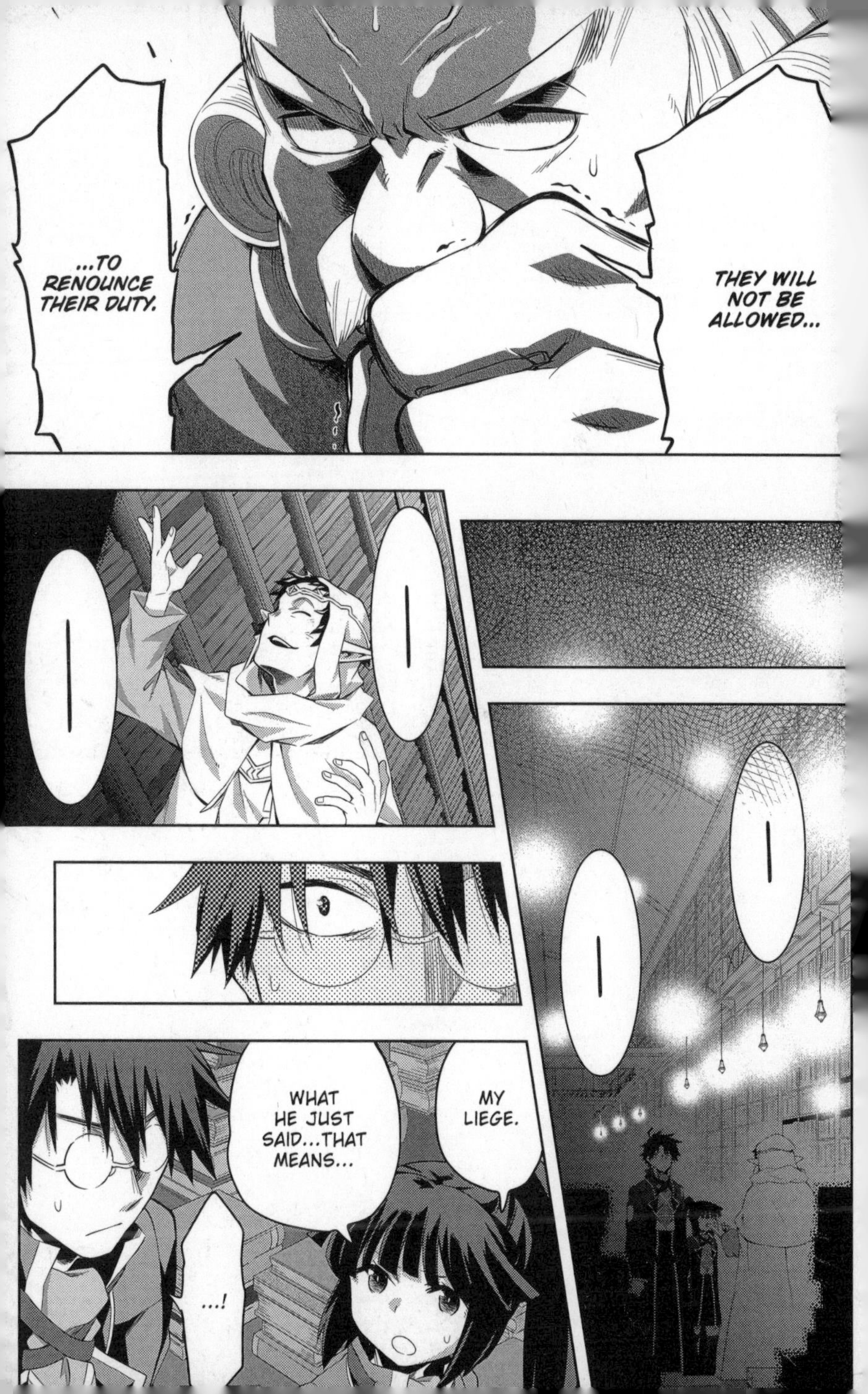
THEY WILL NOT BE ALLOWED...
...TO RENOUNCE THEIR DUTY.
MY LIEGE.
WHAT HE JUST SAID...THAT MEANS...
...!

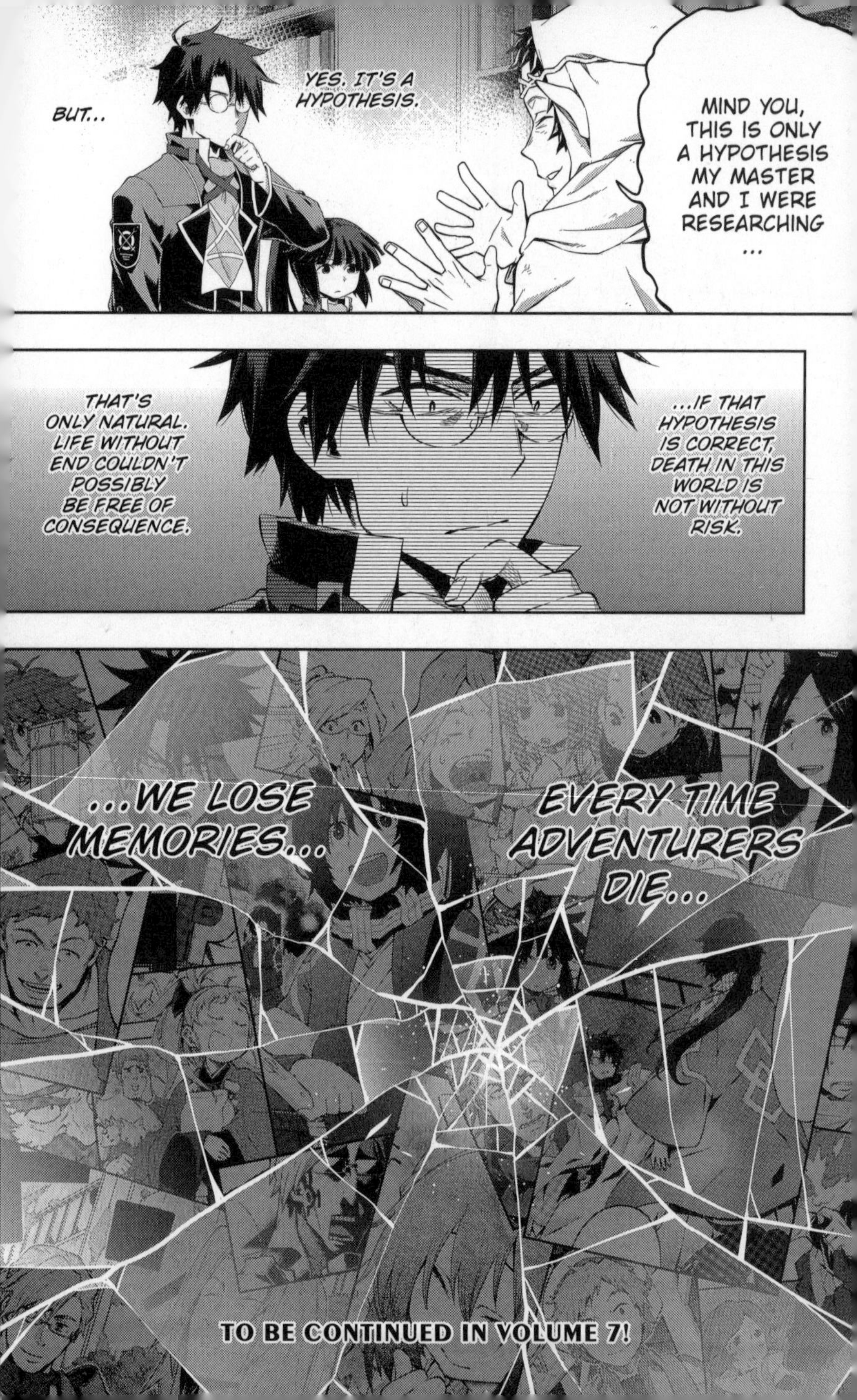
MIND YOU, THIS IS ONLY A HYPOTHESIS MY MASTER AND I WERE RESEARCHING...
YES. IT'S A HYPOTHESIS.
BUT...
...IF THAT HYPOTHESIS IS CORRECT, DEATH IN THIS WORLD IS NOT WITHOUT RISK.
THAT'S ONLY NATURAL. LIFE WITHOUT END COULDN'T POSSIBLY BE FREE OF CONSEQUENCE.
EVERY TIME ADVENTURERS DIE...
...WE LOSE MEMORIES...
TO BE CONTINUED IN VOLUME 7!

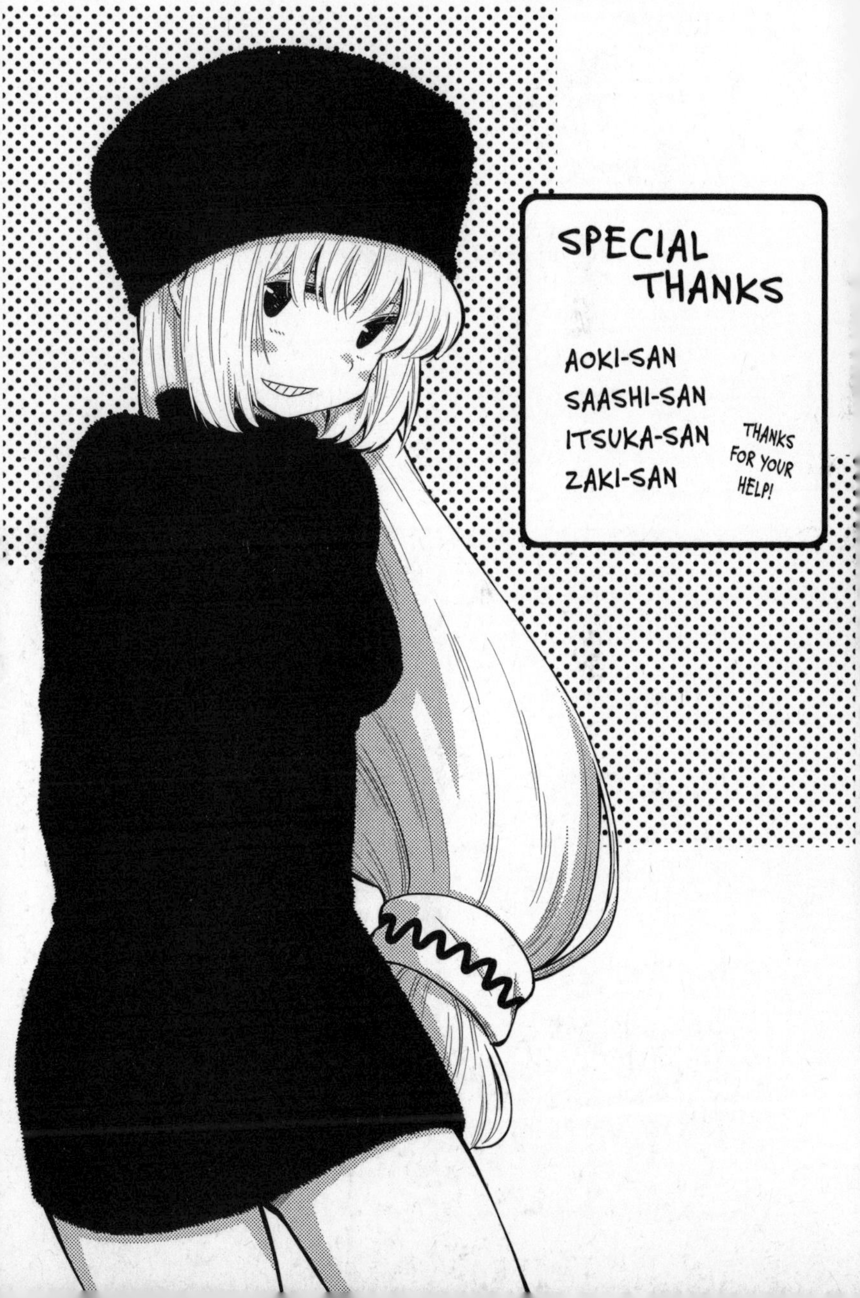
SPECIAL THANKS
AOKI-SAN
SAASHI-SAN
ITSUKA-SAN
ZAKI-SAN
THANKS FOR YOUR HELP!

LOG HORIZON
THE WEST WIND BRIGADE ❻

ART: KOYUKI
ORIGINAL STORY: MAMARE TOUNO
CHARACTER DESIGN: KAZUHIRO HARA

Translation: Taylor Engel
Lettering: Brndn Blakeslee

LOG HORIZON NISHIKAZE NO RYODAN volume 6
© KOYUKI 2015
© TOUNO MAMARE, KAZUHIRO HARA 2015
First published in Japan in 2015 by KADOKAWA CORPORATION, Tokyo.
English translation rights arranged with KADOKAWA CORPORATION,
Tokyo, through Tuttle-Mori Agency, Inc., Tokyo.

English translation © 2017 by Yen Press, LLC

Yen Press
1290 Avenue of the Americas
New York, NY 10104

Visit us at yenpress.com
facebook.com/yenpress
twitter.com/yenpress
yenpress.tumblr.com
instagram.com/yenpress

First Yen Press Edition: August 2017

Yen Press is an imprint of Yen Press, LLC.
The Yen Press name and logo are trademarks of

The publisher is not responsible for websites
owned by the publisher.

Library of Congress Control Number: 2015952586

ISBNs: 978-0-316-55865-5 (paperback)
        978-0-316-51024-0 (ebook)

10 9 8 7 6 5 4 3 2 1

BVG

Printed in the United States of America

BCPL
Baltimore County
Public Library